STEPS TO STARDOM

My Story

To TERRA with my love,

Paul Picerni

Nov. 3, 2007

BY PAUL PICERNI

WITH TOM WEAVER

156
of 200
P.P.

PUBLISHED IN THE USA BY:

**BearManor Media
PO Box 71426
Albany, GA 31708
www.BearManorMedia.com**

LIBRARY OF CONGRESS CATALOGING-IN-PUBLICATION DATA:

Picerni, Paul, 1922-
  Steps to stardom : my story / by Paul Picerni with Tom Weaver.
    p. cm.
  Includes index.
  ISBN 978-1-59393-082-8
  1. Picerni, Paul, 1922- 2. Television actors and actresses--United States--Biography. I. Weaver, Tom, 1958- II. Title.

  PN2287.P49A3 2007
  791.4502'8092--dc22
  [B]
                                          2007008003
Printed in the United States.

Design and Layout by Valerie Thompson.

TABLE OF CONTENTS

To my son, Michael

INTRODUCTION

When I was under contract to Warner Brothers studios in the early 1950s, there were dozens of movie magazines. One magazine, I think it was *Photoplay*, did a story on me around the time of my appearance in Warners' *House of Wax*. It included my wife Marie and the five kids we had at the time. (Marie and I went on to have *eight* children, four boys and four girls.)

The article was titled "5 Steps to Stardom" and head shots of each of the five kids were laid out in the form of a staircase (each head shot was a stair). I had told the *Photoplay* reporter that it seemed that, with the birth of each child, my career took another step up the ladder of success.

Argentina Brunetti, an Italian actress I once worked with, told me, "Ogni bambini che lasce porte un pane sul braccia." Translation: "Each baby arrives with a loaf of bread under his arm." It seemed to be true, because each time Marie and I had a child, my career took another step upward and my salary increased as if to pay for the extra expense of a new baby. I thought it would be a good title for this book, *Steps to Stardom*. It will have a double meaning because in the course of the book I intend to give beginning actors some good pointers on how to become successful in their careers.

In this book I will also tell stories about the many great stars I've worked with . . . what *made* them stars . . . and reveal the things that have helped me in my career, which has lasted 60 years. In the process, I hope I will give readers some laughs, and maybe a few tears, as I describe some of the trials and tribulations of the motion picture and television industries.

1
THE EARLY YEARS

My father was born to a royal family: His father (my grandfather) was an Italian count.

Grandfather's name was Orazio Picerni (1867-1943). Orazio was married to a woman named Eleanora Pascarelli (1868-1917) and they lived in the small mountain town of Abriola, approximately 80 miles south of Naples, in the province of Potenza. Orazio also had a plantation in Brazil, and while he and his family were there in Brazil in December of 1895, tending to the plantation duties, a son—my father—was born. They named him Fabrizio. When he was six months old, the plantation was sold and the family went back to Abriola. For the next 11 or 12 years, Fabrizio was raised in Italy.

Orazio later came to America alone to try and establish a new life, settling in Brooklyn. Around 1907, Orazio sent for the rest of his wife and their children, Fabrizio, Dominic, Clara, Raphael and Cesare—four boys and a girl. Brooklyn at that time being largely Italian, and my grandfather being a well-educated nobleman, he became the leader of the Italian community there. My father, who had attended grammar school in Italy, finished high school in Brooklyn and then went into the service during World War I, becoming an artillery corporal. He was a very athletic young man—about 160 pounds, 5'9", very strong, and had a great, courageous heart. He got into boxing over in Europe and eventually became the middleweight champion of the Third Division. He took part in five of the great WWI battles in France and Germany, including the battle of the Argonne.

When my father boxed in the Army, one of his seconds was a

fellow named Thomas Della Bovi. In Paris on leave, Thomas showed him a picture of his 16-year-old niece, Niccoletta Leone. When my father saw the dark-haired, big-eyed beauty in the photograph, he immediately fell in love with her and vowed that when he came back from the War, he would meet her.

Born in Connecticut, the oldest of 13 children, Niccoletta Leone—or Lena, as everybody called her—was raised in a small town in Queens, New York, called Corona. Corona was perhaps seven miles from Manhattan, but it was all farms and all Italians. When Lena was 13 or 14, her mother died in childbirth at the age of 29, and Lena was charged with raising her siblings. (Out of the 13 children, only six were still alive; the rest, including two sets of twins, had died.) Lena became like a mother to all those little kids.

Thomas Della Bovi brought my father to Corona to meet his family, including Lena. As soon as he met her, it was instant love. He was a good-looking guy with light skin and beautiful black hair. His nose was a little bent from the boxing, but other than that he was flawless. She was an Italian beauty, like a young Anna Magnani. In those days, a fellow couldn't be alone with a young girl; there always had to be a chaperone, an aunt or someone like that. When Fabrizio and Lena went out, they were always chaperoned. Back then, if you got to kiss your girl before you married her, that was really something! In fact, I don't think Fabrizio and Lena kissed until their wedding night.

By that time, Fabrizio had become a professional boxer, and quite a good one. A middleweight, he had 60 fights, and won 54. He even fought "Tiger" Jack Flowers, the black champion, at an arena in Rockaway Beach. In those days, Irish fighters were predominant, so he fought first under the name of Kid Donovan and then later as Young Donovan. When he married my mother, she told him that as soon as their first child was born he'd have to give up fighting. Nine or ten months after their wedding day, I was born in the house where they were living, the house of her father, Armando Leone, on Granger Street in Corona. My birth name was Horace, the English equivalent of Orazio (my grandfather's name). When I was born, my father, true to his word, gave up boxing.

Armando Leone was a great guy. A short, very typical Italian, every morning he took the subway or the trolley car to Brooklyn, and Manhattan sometimes, and all day long he would press new shirts and put them into boxes to be sold. When he wasn't working, he liked to play the piano (we had one in the house) and to drink—Armando loved his wine!

In addition to raising me, my mother still had her sister Nancy and her brothers, Ernest, Michael, Edward and Dominick (also known as Ace), to take care of. One day when I was six months old, my Uncle Edward, who was then about 18, was riding his bicycle with me sitting on the bar in front of the rider's seat. At that time, the streets of Corona were unpaved. He lost control and began to fall, and, in order to protect me, he put his arm under my body. I wasn't hurt at all, but he had a scrape on his left elbow from going into the dirt and gravel. He never told my mother or father about it. He developed lockjaw and, unfortunately, medicine in those days wasn't what it is today. He died at 18 years of age as a result of saving my life. It was a tragic thing for the family. I don't remember my Uncle Edward, but I've always prayed for him.

In those days, the best job you could have, especially if you were in an Italian or Irish family, was for the city or for the government. My father eventually got a job with the Department of Water. Because he spoke English and Italian fluently, he moved up in the ranks until he was a foreman with a weekly paycheck of $60, which was good money in those days. He, too, was a kind of leader in the Italian community. By this time the name Fabrizio had been dropped and everybody knew him as Charlie. Everybody looked up to Charlie for any help they needed, and he supplied them with leadership. He was a good man and well liked.

The first time I fell in love was with Dorothy DePaul. She had long curls and I carried her books home from school. We were six years old and in the first grade. She looked exactly like Shirley Temple.

In the seventh grade at P.S. 14 in Queens, I fell in love with my teacher, Miss McDonald. Hopelessly in love. One day a school bully chased me down the hall and I ran into Miss McDonald's classroom. She held me in her arms, pressing my head to her bosom as she yelled off the bully. A moment I'll always remember.

She would sometimes have lunch with another teacher, Miss McManus, in a coffee shop across the street from the school and

This is me, at about age three, in Corona with a visiting pony. It doesn't look like I was cut out for Westerns!

sit by the window. I'd hide behind a tree and watch her. One day she assigned her students to select a poem, memorize it and recite it to the class. I chose Rudyard Kipling's **Gunga Din**. After my recitation, I got an ovation. For the first time, I felt that great feeling of being as one with an audience. (That's something that actors seldom feel, and when you *do* feel it, boy, you *know* you've *got* it.) The look of amazement and approval on Miss McDonald's face was unforgettable.

Then, one day, I saw our fat, balding math teacher, Mr. LeBow, kissing Miss McDonald in the cloak room. I was shattered!

Growing up, there were several other infatuations, including Rose Renna and Dorothy Darwell. One summer, when I was 12, my family rented a bungalow in Rockaway Beach and I fell in love with the girl next door. Ruth, a German girl, was 16 and a head taller than I was. We walked along the boardwalk on a warm summer night, but she refused to hold my hand—she was embarrassed because she was so much taller, and four years older. She was practically a woman, and I was really still a boy. We fought, we argued, and separated.

It rained for three days. I sat on my porch and she sat on hers, no more than 20 feet apart, watching the rain. Neither of us looked at nor said a word to the other. Suddenly, I started to sing "Stormy Weather," including, of course, the lines, *"Since my girl and I ain't together, Keeps raining all the time . . ."* Suddenly she looked over at me and she giggled. That was all it took. We were back. One day when we were showering in outdoor showers after a day at the beach, she lowered the top of her bathing suit, baring her breasts. I almost keeled over!

Soon the two weeks were over and she went home to the Bronx and I went home to Queens. I begged my folks to drive me to the Bronx to visit her and her grandmother, so they did. But it wasn't the same. The magic was gone. I never saw her again.

Getting back to my father: He raised beagle hounds, and, at one time, we had six of them. He also loved to fish and to hunt—rabbit, pheasant and quail. He started me hunting when I was 12. One day I bagged a crow and then I began bragging about what a great shot I made. My father said, "When you do something good, don't brag about it. If what you did *was* good and worthwhile, let *other* people notice and talk about it. And they *will*. Don't *you* talk about it." That was a piece of advice I never forgot.

I played hooky from school one day and my cousin, Joey Della Bovi (Thomas' son), ratted on me—he told my mother he saw me swimming in the Flushing Meadow Creek. My mother took me in to see our assistant principal, Mr. O'Hagan, who scolded me in a way I never forgot: "How could you *do* such a thing? Your mother is out working in a dress factory to feed and clothe you and send you to school. How could you disappoint your *mother* like that?" I felt so ashamed, I cried. From then on, I never missed another day of school. After that run-in with Mr. O'Hagan, I made a complete turnaround. From that point on, I was just outstanding. I recently ran across a picture of my grammar school's graduating class, and there I was right in the foreground, in the middle, because I was the graduating class's president. I was also the valedictorian, and I made the speech, and I received a proficiency medal. My friendship with Mr. Romuald R. O'Hagan gave me principles that have lasted a lifetime.

A turning point in my life: I had the lead in the graduating play. I played a boy growing up in Sicily, and I remember adlibbing a line: "I pick grapes just like my father did when he was a boy." (My father had told me stories about the fruit in Italy, how big the grapes and cherries were. At an appropriate point in the play, I stuck in that line.) After the play was over, our principal, Mr. Mayer, came up to my mother and father and congratulated them on having "such a fine boy," and he added, "Mr. Picerni, your son is a *born actor*." I was only 14 then, but from that day on, that line just resonated in my head. I wanted to be an actor!

Left to right, my sister Eleanor, my mother, my brother Charlie, my sister Mildred, my father and I at a farm near Kingston, New York.

Mr. O'Hagan was also a scoutmaster, so I joined the Boy Scouts. I moved up through the ranks quickly: I was a tenderfoot, then a Second Class Scout, then a First Class Scout and eventually an Eagle Scout. In fact, I was chosen the Most Outstanding Scout in Queens one year, and I got a trip to Ten Mile River, a place for Scouts up in the Adirondacks. The next year, when I was the Outstanding Scout again, I was sent to the World Jamboree, all expenses paid. I spent about two weeks in Washington, D.C., at the Jamboree.

To qualify to become a First Class Scout, you and another scout had to make a 14-mile hike. (The whole patrol would go, each pair of kids about 200 yards apart.) We would be walking seven miles of dirt roads to Valley Stream Park and then seven miles back. This was a time when Valley Stream Park was all willows and punk bushes, with a winding creek going through it. There were 12 boys paired off into groups of two, and my partner, Peter Fulvio, and I were the last pair.

We were on our way back from Valley Stream Park, near the future site of the 1939 World's Fair, when I looked up ahead and saw that the other five groups had stopped and congregated together, and standing in the middle of these ten boys was a man. We got closer and suddenly realized that the boys were being terrorized by this guy. He was about 20 years old (we were maybe 12) and he had a fiendish look in his eyes, so we were all frightened to death. "All right, give me your money," he said. "Give me your knives; give me everything you've got!" The guy was so wild that we did exactly what he said, dropping our knives and hatchets and whatever money (change) we had onto the ground. Gathering up everything, he told us, "Just start walking and don't look back."

We didn't know what to do so we ran to a nearby two-lane road and began waving at passing cars. Well, who happened to come down the road but my father in his new 1934 Plymouth. With him was his friend Joe and one of our beagle hounds; they were on their way to the local animal shelter to get a dog license. He stopped, of course, and excitedly we all told him what happened. Then I spotted the thief in the distance and shouted, "There he is, he's crossing the road!"

Three or four of us Boy Scouts hopped on the Plymouth's

running board and my father drove in the direction of the thief. But he spotted us and dashed into the tall willows and tried to get away through the meadow. The willows were almost as tall as corn stalks, seven or eight feet high, so it was very difficult to see him. My father stopped the car, got out and said to his friend, "Joe, stand on the roof of the car and direct me on which way to go, left or right, by waving your arms."

My friends, Peter and Willie Esposito, and I followed my father as he took off after the thief in the willows. We kept looking back and getting directions from Joe, who was waving his arms and shouting: "To the left! To the left! Now to the right!" We kept tracking this guy through the deep willows and finally we trapped him at the river's edge. By the time we got to him, all the stuff he stole from us was on the ground in front of him, and he was standing there with one of our little Boy Scout hatchets in one hand and a knife in the other, looking like he was ready to fight. "Don't come any closer!" he screamed.

My father was very quiet when he responded. "Look, my friend, we don't want to hurt you," he said in an understanding voice. "You *keep* the money. Just give the boys back their Boy Scout knives." As he talked slowly and calmly, he moved closer and closer to this maniac. "You didn't really do anything wrong, you must need the money," my father said to the guy, who at this point looked like he was mesmerized. "You *keep* the money, my friend, and the only thing I ask is that . . ." At that point my father had gotten in close and, *boom*, he hit him with a left hook and then with a right! Peter, Willie and I were shocked—my father seemed so sincere, he had even convinced *us* that he was going to let the guy keep the money and get away. When the guy went down, my father pounced on top of him and *continued* belting him. The other boys and I just stood there, flabbergasted by how quickly he put this guy on his back!

With the guy down and pretty close to being out, my father reached for his wallet and showed the guy his badge. What it *was*, was a Water Department badge, but he gave the guy just a flash of it so he'd have the impression it was a police badge. "You're going to jail!" my father announced.

"Don't hit me anymore, don't hit me anymore!" the guy begged. From a raving maniac, he became a sniveling weakling. He got to his feet and my father pushed him ahead of him, back through the willows to the car. My father sat in the backseat with him as Joe drove to the police station, where the guy was placed under arrest. It turned out that the police had been looking for this guy because he had burglarized several homes in the area. We got back our knives, hatchets and all our money—everything that the guy hadn't dropped as he was fleeing through the willows.

I'll always remember my father doing that, and how easily, how casually, he did it. That was the only time I saw my father do something like that. One other time he broke the jaw of Smitty, my Aunt Nancy's boyfriend. After they broke up, Smitty began bothering her, so my father hit him with a left hook that broke his jaw. Aunt Nancy never had any more trouble with Smitty.

Back in the days of the First World War, mustard gas was often used by the Germans on the Allied soldiers. When my father was in either France or Germany, he'd been gassed. I guess this created a weak spot in one of his lungs, and when he was about 43, he contracted tuberculosis. He was taken to Veteran's Hospital in Upstate New York and he was there for about six months; we used to visit him every Sunday. He was very depressed to be there. In those days they didn't have a cure for T.B. They used to collapse one lung until it healed, revive it, and then collapse the *other* lung until *it* healed. It wasn't a very good system. He got tired of being there and insisted on coming home, even though he was very weak. Needless to say, he wasn't able to go back to work.

One day my father and I were supposed to go out hunting to Long Island with my father's hunting friend Willie Festa and Willie's younger brother Eddie. At five o'clock in the morning, I went to my father's bedroom where he was still in bed and said, "Dad? Time to get up. Willie's going to pick us up in about 20 minutes." He looked at me and said, "You go ahead, you guys go and hunt. I don't feel that good this morning. You go without me . . . " So when Willie and Eddie came, it was only me and my father's beagle Miss Nora, a wonderful tracker, who joined them for the trip to Long Island. In those days you only had to go about 25 miles out into the Island to be in hunting territory, with pheasants, rabbits, quail, squirrel and crows.

At 12:00 noon, Miss Nora walked away from us and went back

to the car; Sadie, Willie's dog, followed her. Willie, Eddie and I were mystified. Willie said, "It doesn't look like the dogs want to hunt anymore. We may as well go home." So we packed everything up, got in the car and headed home, arriving back in Corona about two o'clock. A block before we got to my house, we saw my neighbor Nicki Renna, a guy about 18 years old, standing on the corner; he signaled for us to pull over. As we got out, he looked at me and said, "Horace, I've got bad news for you. Your dad died." I dropped to my knees, like somebody hit me with a sledgehammer.

In those days, wakes didn't take place in funeral parlors; families had them right in their own homes. My father's coffin was in the living room. Before they closed the coffin, I kissed him on the forehead, and I remember thinking how cold he was. It was a really weird feeling. Later, as the coffin was moved out the front door of the house, we heard Miss Nora, who was out in the backyard, let out a howl, like she knew he was leaving the house for the last time. It's funny how animals know things like that. Miss Nora quit hunting at noon; he had died at noon. Miss Nora just knew.

By this time I was 17 and about to graduate from high school. I was the oldest boy, so *I* was head of the family now. There were my sisters, Eleanor and Paula, my brother Charles and my little sister Marilyn, who was then just two.

I finished high school and I started attending Queens College. But after six months there I realized I couldn't go to college, I had to get out and work, *do* something to help support the family. My mother, who had started working in a dress factory around the time that my father got sick, was making only $40 a week, and there was rent to pay and food to buy. I quit college and, with the help of Willie Festa, got my first job. It was at the Lion Match Company in Long Island City, where Willie also worked. I made $11 a week. I was in the basement working with the big rolls of thick paper that they made match covers out of. Back then, in 1940, we didn't have the lifting equipment they do today; in those days, it was just me and another guy picking up these two-, three-hundred-pound rolls of paper.

I went to the movies a lot in those days; I'd started when I was about ten years old. We had two theaters in Corona: The Loew's Plaza, which was a big, plush, big theater where the admission was

Outside the dress factory where my mother worked, I posed with her (to my left), the rest of the girls employed there, and the boss.

25 cents, and The Palace, where the admission was just a dime. (It was named The Palace but we called it The Itch because you itched in those old, dusty seats.) Every Saturday at one or the other, my buddies from school and I would see about five cartoons and a double-feature. In those days, Clark Gable was everybody's favorite actor, and Spencer Tracy and Robert Taylor were very big too. In addition to going to the movies, I'd also look at some of the weekly movie magazines—there were dozens of them on the stands, usually with the beautiful women stars like Betty Grable on the covers. It was a glamorous era and the top Hollywood stars were its kings and queens—they were our "American royalty."

The first play I ever saw on Broadway was a revival of *Tobacco*

Road with Will Geer as the old man, Jeeter Lester. In one scene, as a kid was throwing a ball against the wall of a rickety house on stage, Geer said, "Dude Boy, stop chucking that dang ball agin' the house." The kid snapped back, "Shut up, you old son of a bitch!" I thought, "Gee, how do they get away with that kind of language?" How times have changed! I also thought, "Oh, God, that was beautiful . . . what a great play!"

At 17, I met Wilbur Colbert, the head of the Annandale Players, a small theater group in Annandale, New York. Will was only 19 but one of the most talented actors I ever met. He directed me in my first play at Annandale, *Me, Him and I*, a farce which also featured two local girls, Dorothy and Marge Darwell. We had so much fun, the four of us. We became inseparable.

I quit my $11-a-week job with the Lion Match Company and took a $21-a-week job in the filing department at Brewster Aeronautical Corp. in Long Island City. This was early in 1941 and the war was raging in Europe, but the United States wasn't in it yet. At Brewster we made Brewster Bobcat fighter planes which the Royal Canadian Air Force picked up at Newark Airport and ferried to Canada; eventually they'd end up in England. One of my filing department co-workers was a fellow named Kim Blanchard from Dobbs Ferry, New York, a few miles up the Hudson River from Manhattan. He was a high-class kid who played drums with a band at a Dobbs Ferry roadhouse on weekends. Kim got a big kick out of me because I was always horsing around and doing imitations; he was a great audience. One day he said, "Why don't you come up to the tavern in Dobbs Ferry where I'm playing some weekend and I'll introduce you to some of the good-looking chicks up there? You can stay at my place and we'll have a great weekend."

I thought a trip to Dobbs Ferry would be a chance for me to perform some of my "new characters": Will Colbert and I spent hours on end going around playing parts for our own amusement. Once when we were playing detectives, we actually raided a whorehouse on 8th Avenue in Manhattan! Then we felt sorry for the girls and let them all off the hook. We would stage fake fights in the streets off Broadway. People would be horrified by the way he pummeled me with blows to the face. I'd stagger and fall and he would walk away, then a passersby would come and sympathize with me.

With Will Colbert, left, in my first play, *Me, Him and I.*

Sometimes we would drive around all night and stay in character the whole time. Once we were two hoodlums as we rode around and even when we stopped in a railway diner at two or three A.M. With this in mind, I told Kim that Will and I would come up to Dobbs Ferry, and I described the two characters we'd be playing: Will would be Lt. Percy Harry Nelson, an Englishman, and I would be Lt. Henri Duval, a French-Canadian. Lt. Nelson and Lt. Duval were both in the Royal Canadian Air Force and stationed at Newark Airport, from where we ferried the Brewster Bobcat planes to Canada. We had our backgrounds down pat: Henri grew up in Manitoba and his father was a hunting guide who flew a pontoon plane, ferrying hunters up to his hunting lodge. It was Henri's father who taught him how to fly. Percy was born just outside London, went to Oxford and joined the RCAF after he was turned down by the Royal Air Force because of a mysterious personal problem that Percy never wanted to talk about. We got some RCAF wings for our jacket lapels and even found some RCAF magazines,

killing these baboons. During one such hunt, we came upon a field where there were about 20 baboons, but they smelled us or spotted us and they scattered. I took off after one, trying to get a shot at it, with several young native kids running with me. The baboon ran into a nearby village and we followed. As I came around one corner, standing at a well was an Indian girl who looked to be about 16 . . . and absolutely beautiful. I stopped as the boys continued on after the baboon. I was frozen in place . . . and I felt like I was frozen in time . . . and I fell in love with her. And I knew that she fell in love with me. But then the impetus of the chase forced me to go on. The whole thing lasted two seconds, but I've remembered that my whole lifetime because it was a moment of instant, mutual love. I went back to that village looking for her several times and never did see her again, but I've never forgotten her face. It was as if I'd had a beatific vision.

Many of our missions were to bomb individual targets. We would fly to an area in Burma or Thailand in squadron formation and then separate, and each plane would have its own target—a bridge, a railway yard, a train, a port, or any Japanese shipping that we might run into. On one mission, we were assigned to bomb a bridge in Thailand.

The name of the B-24 we flew on that mission was Snafu, and the symbol on it was a skull with a bomb protruding from its mouth.

The usual procedure was for the navigator and pilot to get you to "the i.p."—the initial point. The i.p. was usually a spot on the ground where (say) two rivers crossed, or something like that, usually about three or four miles from the target. At that point, the bombardier (in the glass nose of the plane) would take over. With the plane now on automatic pilot, he would be flying it via the adjustments he made with his Norden bombsite, the amazing "first computer." The bombsite would lock on the target; you would open the bomb bay doors; and with all the proper calculations (air speed, altitude, wind) punched into the bombsite, the bombs would release and the target would be destroyed.

Well, it wasn't always that simple. On this one mission, Karl looked down at the passing landscape, saw what he thought was the i.p. and said to me, "There it is. Take over." I looked down and I said, "*That's* not the i.p., Karl. Look at the photos here. It's *similar,* but that's not it." He insisted, "That's it, that's it. Look ahead—see! There's the bridge!" There *was* a bridge, but it didn't look exactly right. I had to take his word for it, even though I had doubts. He was always one of the best.

I got the bridge in my crosshairs. The eight 1,000-lb. bombs were armed—I had removed the pins on the little propellers on the noses of the bombs a few minutes earlier. On the way down, the little propellers would spin several hundred revolutions, and then drop off. The bombs would then be armed, and would explode on impact.

At our briefing that morning, we had been told that there would be no flak or enemy fighters. Well, when we were halfway to the bridge, all hell broke loose. For a target where there was to be no flak, we were getting a *lot*. The puffs of black smoke were going off all around us. I said, "Bomb bay doors opening!," and Jerry Roach in the waist (the middle) of the plane was supposed to respond, "Bomb bay doors open, sir"—Jerry could see from his position if the four doors were open, to make sure the bombs were clear to leave the plane. I never heard him respond. Because of all the flak bursts, he evidently was laying low, probably behind a bulkhead. But the green light went on in my compartment, indicating that the bomb bay doors were open.

Suddenly, a burst of flak exploded near the pilot's compartment, breaking the window next to Bob. He was hit by flying glass. He yelled, "Salvo the bombs!"—he was afraid that if we continued to the target, we would be shot down.

Over the intercom I responded, "Give me ten more seconds!"

"Salvo the fucking bombs!" he shouted a second time.

I hit the salvo handle. There was a loud noise; the plane shuddered and suddenly dropped about 200 feet. I looked down through the window below my bombsite and I could see the eight bombs on their way to the ground, and our four bomb bay doors floating down *with* them! The doors had never opened—evidently the flak damaged them, and when the bombs went, so did the doors. Bob put the plane into a steep bank to the left and we got the hell out of there. The bombs landed and exploded in the wooded area way off target. Which, we later found out, was the wrong target anyway.

Because of the drag created by the open bomb bay, we never

made it to our base. We landed at a base near Calcutta, 200 miles short of our airfield. When we landed, we were amazed how many flak holes were in our plane. We counted 64 from nose to tail. We were lucky no one was seriously injured. Bob could have applied for a Purple Heart for his cut face, but he never did.

Many of our missions were unbelievably long. We bombed Rangoon, Bangkok, and as far away as Singapore. To get to one particular target in lower Thailand, we needed two bomb bay tanks of extra gasoline in addition to our regular tanks. The target was Kanchanaburi Bridge, the railroad bridge which later became famous because of the movie *The Bridge on the River Kwai*.

We usually bombed this bridge from a high altitude, from 10,000 to 20,000 feet. Many times our bombs damaged it, but then the Allied prisoners from the P.O.W. camp adjacent to the bridge would be forced by the Japanese to repair it. Early one morning we went into the briefing room and the operations officer said, "The target today is the Kanchanaburi Bridge." All the flight crews let out a groan—we were all familiar with that long, tedious flight we'd made three times already. Then he said, "Altitude . . . 200 feet." *What*?? Unheard of in a B-24! The British had done some bombing in heavy bombers from that low altitude but we Americans never had. And we would be using the Sperry Bombsite rather than the high-altitude Norden Bombsite. None of us bombardiers had used the Sperry Bombsite since advance training. But we were given a quick brush-up on the Sperry and soon we were on our way, with two 400-gallon bomb bay tanks of gas and four 1,000-lb. bombs.

The flight down to Kanchanaburi was *long*. On the way down we would double-check our 50-caliber machine-guns (we had ten of them), test-fire them, make sure they were in good working order, and keep our eyes open for enemy Zero fighter planes. We would also have lunch. My mother frequently sent me "care packages" with all kinds of goodies—caponota (canned eggplant), other canned goods, nuts, cookies, candy bars and, one of my favorites, a big, beautiful pepperoni. I was on my way to the waist area of the plane to share my stick of pepperoni with some of my crewmates. On my way through the bomb bay, as I was walking along the very narrow catwalk that went from the pilot's compartment to the waist, the plane hit an air pocket. I lost my balance and the pepperoni flew out of my hand, landing on the far side of the bombs, against the corrugated bomb bay doors. Slowly it rolled down the door, over the corrugations. Brrrrip. Brrrrip. Brrrrip. I stretched to get it, but the bombs were between me and the pepperoni and I couldn't quite reach it. The bomb bay doors were always slightly open at the bottom, so that the incoming wind would clear the bomb bays of any gas fumes. Brrrrip. Brrrrip. The pepperoni continued down the door. I stretched and strained and suddenly . . . it was gone. Out the opening and on its way down to the Indian Ocean for some fish to enjoy! I had experienced one of my worst moments of the war!

Finally we reached the i.p. I was all set with my Sperry Bombsite to start my bomb run at 200 feet. We were low over the river heading for the bridge on the River Kwai, just above the treetops. (I'm sure Bob, our frustrated fighter pilot, enjoyed skimming the trees.) I still remember seeing a small tank in the riverbed with two surprised Jap soldiers on top of it. My nose gunner gave them a short burst from his twin 50-caliber machine-guns. We were flying so low, I could see their faces as we sped by!

My bombs had seven-second delay fuses so that we would be safely away by the time they exploded. The bridge was coming up fast—too fast. I forgot about the Sperry Bombsite. I put the toe of my left shoe to the window below the bombsite and lined it up with the bridge. When my toe hit the bridge, I hit the toggle switch. The bombs were gone.

The first bomb landed in the river—short. The second landed at the base of the center pylon, and the third went through the upper superstructure of the bridge. The fourth bomb landed in the corner of the prison camp.

When we were seven seconds past the bridge, my tail gunner, young Wayne Ferguson, could see the explosions. He screamed in the intercom, "We *got* it, Lieutenant! We *got* it!"—the entire bridge had collapsed into the river. In my mind's ear, I can still to this day hear him shouting, "We *got* it, Lieutenant! We *got* it!" I had destroyed the Bridge on the River Kwai.

Twelve planes from my squadron bombed the Kanchanaburi Bridge that day, but my bomb caused the most serious damage.

When you drop bombs from the air, you never really see all the devastation and loss of life they can cause. In this case, a strange thing happened more than a year and a half later. I'll describe that event in the next chapter.

We flew our 25 missions, which qualified us to return home. Not so easy! By this time, B-29s were being manufactured—bigger, more sophisticated long-range bombers, capable of dropping bombs on more distant targets, including the Japanese mainland. The Japanese wondered, "How can we be bombed from 2,500 miles away? No one has a plane with such a range!" Gen. Doolittle once bombed Japan with B-25s (two-engine medium bombers), taking off from a carrier, dropping the bombs on Tokyo and then crash-landing the planes in China. But *now* B-29s were bombing the Japanese and then safely returning to their bases. What we were doing was this: The B-29s were based in India. They would fly to Luliang, China, which was about halfway between India and Japan, refuel, load bombs, fly to Japan, drop their bombs, fly back

USAAF photo of the destruction of the Kanchanaburi Bridge.

to Luliang, refuel and return to their base in India. The new job of the crews of the old B-24s was now to haul gas for the B-29s over the Himalayas from India to Luliang. My crew, all ten of us, was one that was assigned to this task and told to prepare for a relocation flight, from Pandeveswar, India, to the base at Luliang.

Posing plane-side in India.

We were transferred to Luliang with another crew; they were assigned to fly a B-24 to Luliang, and my crew were merely passengers. The plane, needless to say, was crowded—two crews (20 men) with all their personal gear. As we neared Luliang, flying at an altitude of 20,000 feet, the pilot of the other crew (the captain who was flying the plane) called the tower for landing instructions. He was notified that the runway was being bombed by a single Japanese Betty at about 5,000 feet, and ordered to keep circling at 20,000 feet and to maintain radio silence. Once the raid was over, he would be re-contacted.

We circled for about 60 minutes in the pitch blackness 20,000 feet above Luliang. Finally the tower called: "The runway has been damaged. Proceed to auxiliary field #640." But by now, this captain and his crew were completely lost due to the hour they'd spent circling. The navigator was unable to get a fix, and the radio operator couldn't raise anyone at the auxiliary field—and we were running out of fuel. The captain was tired and beginning to panic. He screamed at his navigator and his radio operator.

Bob Lindquist took matters into his own hands: He quietly told the captain, "Get out of that seat. Our crew will take over the plane." Bob and Ross moved into the pilot and co-pilot's seats; Bob ordered Karl to take over the navigation; he told Bob Morgan to get on the radio and get whoever he could; he told me to get in the waist and stay on the intercom. In effect, it was a mutiny; our crew had taken over the flight. But the captain certainly did not mind; he was so frustrated and out of sorts by this time that he welcomed somebody else taking over in this desperate situation. Karl finally got a fix on our position and Bob Morgan made contact with a small British fighter field in the middle of the Himalayas. But we weren't out of the woods yet.

The waist was crowded with personnel, about 12 of us, and tons of baggage. I was sitting on my chest pack (parachute), wearing my headset, when Bob called me. He said, "We're very low on fuel and we may have to bail out. Make sure everyone has their chest packs on and their harnesses well adjusted." As I stood up in the pitch blackness and started to put on my chute, I shouted over the loud drone of the engines, "Everyone put on your parachutes; we *may* have to bail out."

This old B-24 didn't have a ball turret in its belly, it had a Plexiglas door with crossbars where you could put a 50-caliber machine-gun barrel and shoot at any Japanese fighters that were coming up from underneath. In the sudden spurt of activity as all the men got up to put on their chutes, I was bumped hard, and my foot went right through the Plexiglas in the door on the floor of the plane. I dropped through it, but my arms caught the iron crossbars. There I was, at 20,000 feet, hanging out of the plane with no chute, and only the crossbars of the door holding me from falling into oblivion. I yelled for help, hoping that even in the darkness some of the guys would see what was happening and pull me up before the air flow pulled me out. Fortunately, some of them did hear and see me, and hauled me up by my parachute harness.

By the time we were coming in for a landing, it was almost daybreak. We landed on a small fighter airstrip . . . taxied to the end of the runway . . . and, one by one, our engines quit. We were completely out of fuel.

We evacuated the plane and every one of us, all 20, got on our bellies and kissed the tarmac. Some British soldiers arrived in a truck and we all loaded aboard, babbling like a group of kindergarten kids, so happy to be alive. We were taken to a Quonset hut, which was a small mess hall, and the British soldiers served us some powdered eggs, bread and coffee. We didn't stop talking the whole time. It was so good to still be alive. It was a weird, exhilarated feeling—as if we had miraculously come back from the dead. Chalk up another one for the big Swede Bob Lindquist, with an assist from our co-pilot Ross Noltimier and our navigator Karl Schricker and our wonderful radio operator Bob Morgan.

Once in Luliang, we were assigned to the 14th Air Force of Gen. Claire Chennault of Flying Tigers fame. I met two great officers of the 14th, Dave Nettles, of Oshkosh, Wisconsin, and Nick "Big Nig" Richardson, who was from Port Angeles, Oregon, and in later years became its mayor. We became fast friends. The B-29s softened up the Japanese and soon President Truman ordered that the atom bomb be dropped. The bombing of Pearl Harbor got us into the war and the bombing of Hiroshima and Nagasaki ended it.

Our crew and Richardson's crew were sent to Tezpor, India, to await orders to return home. While we waited, they put me back in Special Services and I headed the unit to entertain the troops. I put on several shows with the help of some of the Red Cross girls, and each night before the movies I would read the news of the day from the Army newspaper *The Stars and Stripes* over the p.a. system.

Big Nig Richardson and Blackie (that was me) would entertain ourselves by hunting jackals by night and vultures by day. One evening we dated two nurses from a nearby ATC (Air Transport Command) base. About two in the morning, we drove the girls back to the huge base where they were billeted, dropped them off and then headed back to *our* base. While we were still on their base, a jackal crossed in front of our Jeep. I fired my .45 and hit it. It ran about 50 yards and died on the porch of one of the many *bashas* (thatched-roofed buildings).

The next day, the nurses came over to see us and they gave us the bad news: The jackal had died at the front door of the base commanding officer, and he was *furious*. It was against the rules to fire a gun on the base, and he wanted the individual responsible for this act. Through the MPs at their gate, the two nurses had been tracked down. When they were interrogated, they'd had to admit that, yes, they were the ones who came through the gate at two A.M. with two officers. They were pressured to reveal our names, but they claimed they only knew us as Big Nig and Blackie. The colonel wasn't buying it, and he was going to continue to put pressure on them. The girls begged us to turn ourselves in.

Being chivalrous, we did. We were ordered to report to the ATC base colonel and explain our actions.

We walked into his office, saluted and said, "Lt. Picerni and Lt. Richardson reporting as ordered, sir." He said, "At ease." So help me, God, it was Jimmy Gleason the actor. But it really *wasn't*: It was a guy who looked *exactly* like him—the small mustache, the balding head, and the skinny frame. But twice as feisty!

When he stood up from his desk, we could see that he was wearing tan Army shorts that revealed his skinny legs. He walked around us and let out with a tirade: "You combat guys think you're hot *shit*, dontcha? You bastards with your bomber crews! You think you're *better* than us here at Air Transport Command, dontcha? Well, we fought the war, too! Without us, you'd have had no supplies, no food, no bombs to drop! *We* brought all that shit over here for you! You get all the glory, but you'd be *nowhere* without us, you cocky *fucks*! Well, you're gonna get your asses court-martialed, that's what you're gonna get!"—he went on and on, really pouring it on. We didn't get a chance to say a word. Finally he said, "*Dismissed*!"

Back at our base, Nig's commanding officer told him, "Forget about it. Fuck him!" *My* commanding officer, Major Bradford, said, "You're confined to quarters, Lieutenant. Consider yourself under house arrest, awaiting court-martial." Firing a gun on the base was a serious matter. A few weeks earlier, right after the Japan surrender, there had been big celebrations on some of the bases; soldiers were firing their guns off in the air, and one poor guy was accidentally shot in the head and died. There was another factor, too: Major

Decades after the war's end, Bob Lindquist and his wife Shirley visited my wife Marie and me at our Tarzana home.

Bradford, the officer who confined me to my quarters, was a little envious of me; he was jealous because in the Officer's Mess Hall I was always surrounded by the nurses and Red Cross girls I was directing in the shows.

For two weeks, Karl Schricker brought me my meals in my quarters. Finally he told me that my name was on a long list on the bulletin board—my orders had come through to go home. But I was still awaiting court-martial. I requested a meeting with Major Bradford and I pleaded with him: "Major, I flew 25 combat missions. I hauled gas over the Hump to China. And now my orders have come to go home. Please, Major. Give me a break. Let me go home."

He paused for a long time, then he said, "Go home, Lieutenant—and good luck." I was off the hook. Major Bradford turned out to be a good guy after all. Either *that* or he figured that, with me gone, he'd have all the nurses and Red Cross girls for himself!

A short time later, First Lt. Horace Picerni was on the *U.S.S. Horace Greeley* headed for New York out of Calcutta.

3
AFTER THE WAR YEARS

It took the **U.S.S. Horace Greeley** about two weeks to get from Calcutta to New York, going west through the Suez Canal, the Mediterranean and the Atlantic Ocean. The 5,000 people aboard included officers, enlisted men and nurses. We were assigned small bunks in the lower decks. It was unbearably hot down there, and we were stacked six high. Almost all of us used our blankets to stake out small spots on the upper deck where it was a lot cooler. They were hard to come by, but I found one.

Using the many comedy sketches I learned at Miami's Pine Tree Bandstand, I began to put together a variety show. With the help of a sergeant, we soon had a band. It included a private whose name you may know—a drummer named Shelly Manne, who later became quite famous. My days aboard ship were directing the show.

One day after rehearsal, I went to "my spot" on deck. My blanket had been cast aside, and a lieutenant had brazenly taken over my place. I said, "Hey! What are you doing? That's my spot." He said with a smirk, "Not anymore." What an unscrupulous bastard. He had no qualms, he felt no guilt about stealing my spot! Besides wanting to beat the shit out of him, what could I do? Technically he was right; "legally," I didn't own that spot. Morally, he was wrong. He was a prick. Later I ran into many unethical people like him in the picture business.

I saw an empty hammock on the balcony of a cabin belonging to one of the ship's officers. I knocked at his door. "Lieutenant, may I use your hammock to sleep in tonight?" He said, "This part of the ship is off limits to passengers . . . but . . . go 'head, lieutenant, you can use it as long as you want." I used it for the rest of the voyage.

I met a few people in Hollywood like *him* too—he was a good guy. The show went on and it was a big hit. It passed the time.

While aboard, I heard that one of the Dead End Kids was in the brig, way below. I went down to visit him. It was Bobby Jordan, an Army private. I talked to him for ten minutes, and he told me a sad story. In an emotional voice he babbled, "You gotta get me *out* of here, Lieutenant! You gotta get me outta here, they're gonna *kill* me!" He obviously had gone bananas—he was nuts. The war was evidently too much for the poor kid to handle. They'd put him in the brig to protect him from his own demons.

As we pulled into New York Harbor, we saw Miss Liberty. What a thrilling sight for returning soldiers! Later, as the ship docked at one of the Manhattan piers, we all stood on deck watching a crowd on the docks assemble to meet us. All I could think of was a nice, juicy cheeseburger and a chocolate malt! I was sent to a base in South Carolina to be separated. Once I received my honorable discharge and all my medals, I was put on terminal leave, which meant that, technically, I was still in the Army, and I would be on salary for the next 90 days . . . but I was free to go home.

For the past three years, the Air Force had done everything for me: Told me what to do, where to go, they fed me, they sheltered me. All I had to do was go in the direction in which they pointed me. They cared for me every step of the way. Suddenly I was on my own. What a strange, empty feeling. I didn't know if I liked it.

When I arrived home in Corona, Long Island, it was late October 1945. After those three years in the service, my crew—the guys I had spent all that time with—were scattered all over the United States. The only one close by was Karl Schricker, my navigator, who lived in the Bronx. There were a lot of "welcome home" parties; I went to one at Karl's house and I met one of his neighbors, Carole Colonelli, a 19-year-old blonde, blue-eyed Italian girl. She was absolutely gorgeous. I was smitten.

When I left India, I was kind of serious with one of the Red Cross girls, Wren Barbe, a Southern belle who was older than me— about 28—and also a beauty. She looked very much like Amelia Earhart, the famous aviatrix. Wren was tall and lean and with a short haircut. She was to arrive in New York a month after me, and we'd talked of continuing our relationship once she got back—even the possibility of marriage.

Carole and I started to see a lot of each other. We got serious. It seemed like a natural match. We were crazy about each other. Suddenly Wren called—she was in Manhattan. I had to see her and show her New York. It was only three months since I had last seen her in Calcutta, but so much had happened. How could things change in such a short time? I was obligated to see her, of course. When I arrived to pick her up at her hotel, there she was in a long gown. I'd never seen her other than in her uniform. I gave her a corsage and took her to the 21 Club for dinner, then dancing at El Morocco. We talked . . . but it wasn't the same. She was so happy to see me, and she talked about a future together, but something was missing. I'm sure she sensed that things had changed. We'd been so close in Tezpor, but now here in New York there was no spark. (For me, there was Carole.)

The next day, Wren left for her home in North Carolina. We never crossed paths again. She was a good woman, and I'm sure she had a happy life. It makes me sad to think about it now. Life takes such strange turns.

Carole and I became closer and closer as we saw each other every night. I'd just turned 24 and I wanted to finish my education and—after that—I wanted desperately to become an actor. I thought of going to Fordham University in the Bronx and majoring in drama. But it was so cold in New York. *Soooo cold!* Evidently, after spending a year in India, my blood had thinned and I just couldn't take the cold New York weather anymore. I began thinking that maybe I should go to school in Miami or California, where the temperatures were more like they were in India.

I saw some of my old buddies, including Al Bonelli, my friend from Brewster Aeronautical and Linden Court Inn. He'd spent the war as a Navy lieutenant and now lived on Long Island. We double-dated a few times with Carole and her girlfriend. Bill Lewis, the Red Ryder from my cadet days, was back working for NBC News in New York, although his wife and baby were by this time with his mother in California. We saw each other frequently and reminisced about our time in Houghton, Michigan, and Santa Ana, California. The Red Ryder and I picked up where we left off. We enjoyed each other so much. We'd meet at a restaurant-bar in Greenwich Village called Asti's, where the waiters were all ex-Metropolitan Opera stars. In rich baritone or tenor voices, they would sing the menu, the list of entrees, and then belt out, *a la* Pavarotti, "What will you have for dinner *toniiiiiiight?*" Even the bartender sang—his specialty was Gay Nineties-type songs. Bill and I loved to sing George M. Cohan tunes like "Yankee Doodle Dandy" and "You're A Grand Old Flag," and also Al Jolson numbers like "California, Here I Come" and "April Showers." The bartender sang one song that Bill and I fell in love with. It was so sad, so nostalgic—so corny!—we *had* to learn it. It was called "Second Hand Store," and 60 years later I still remember the lyrics.

I wrote earlier about how, by a turn of fate, Bill made me become a bombardier when I really wanted to be a pilot. Now, in New York, he again was instrumental in my making a very important, life-changing decision. Despite the cold, I had more or less decided to apply at Fordham and study drama. Going to Fordham had its good points; for one thing, I'd be home with my family, near my new love Carole Colonelli in the Bronx. Plus, Fordham was *also* in the Bronx.

But it was so cold—too cold!—so it was not to be. Ever since India, and right to this day, cold has always gone right through me.

One night, the Ryder called me: "Blackie? Can you meet the Ryder at Asti's? It's important." (We always seemed to talk in the third person!) We met at Asti's and he gave me the bad news: He'd been fired from NBC News. It seems that the Ryder's boss in the news department didn't like him. The Ryder's boss had spent the war years as a 4-F and he was jealous of the Ryder's popularity. You'll run into pricks like this in your lifetime—no-talent fucks who kiss ass, get into positions of authority, and then enjoy pulling rank on the more-talented people under them.

The Ryder had been fired and would be heading back to his home in California, where he was born and raised. We drank, and listened to the singing, and we were sad that we would be separated again. Then he said out of the blue . . . or maybe he had it planned? . . . "Why doesn't Blackie *go* with the Ryder? We could go out to California together. My mom could get you a place right on the water—she manages some apartments in Hermosa Beach. You could go to the Pasadena Playhouse. Lots of famous stars graduated from the Pasadena Playhouse—William Holden and many others. The weather would be nice and warm." Talking faster and faster, he went on and on—and he was very persuasive. I could go to the Playhouse on the G.I. Bill and would be out in only two years rather than four years at Fordham. I was sold. Hollywood! Warm weather! Acting school! A star is born!!

I talked to my mother; I talked to Carole, and she cried. She promised she would write every day, and so did I. I asked Al Bonelli, my good friend, to look after her, and I told her I'd be home in the summer—I planned to come back in June, during the school break.

My friend Al Bonelli said he'd keep an eye on my girl Carole Colonelli while I was in California. He kept an eye on her, all right!

During the war, when I was making $400 a month officer's pay, I had been sending my mother 200 of it, for her to pay bills and help the family. To my surprise, she had put all that money aside—*saved* it for me—almost $3,000. She wanted me to go to college and then to succeed as an actor, and she insisted I take the money. She said, "Buy a car, buy some clothes and go, *go*! Go to California, become an actor. That's what you *want*!" She was such a good mother—she did everything for her five children. She'd raised all of us alone after my father died at 44.

In just three days, on January 11, 1946, we were on our way, me and the Red Ryder in my $300 1939 Oldsmobile, headed for California. While we were driving through the South on a cold wintry night headed for Route 66 (the Ryder was driving), we skidded in the snow. The Olds went out of control and right through a white picket fence. We were okay but from then on, the right front wheel was badly out of line, and every five or six hundred miles we had to change the right front tire. We sang our songs; we acted out parts that we made up (detectives, gangsters, song-and-dance men, movie stars on their way to Hollywood, Al Jolson, etc.). California, here we come! We were young, we were happy, the war was over and we were alive. We were Thelma & Louise!

True to his word, the Ryder's mom, "Gaga," got me a little bachelor apartment with a living room (with a Murphy bed), a small kitchen, a bathroom and big patio overlooking the Pacific Ocean. $25 a month, O.P.A. (Office of Price Administration) ceiling. Bill's wife Etel was French, and a great cook, and so I was a frequent guest for dinner at their house—the Ryder, Etel, their adorable three-year-old daughter Penny and me. They treated me like family. I had it made.

I had my interview with Gilmor Brown, head of the Pasadena Playhouse School for Actors. Gilmor was very . . . shall we say . . . gay. Before I left his office, he said, "If you stop at Harold's Coffee Shop on Colorado Boulevard, you'll meet some of the students who attend the Playhouse. Get a feeling of your future classmates." I stopped at that nearby coffee shop and I saw some of the Pasadena Playhouse students. It was more of the same—gay guys. Not that there's anything *wrong* with that! But I decided the Pasadena Playhouse wasn't for me, Bill Holden or no Bill Holden!

Driving down Sepulveda Boulevard on my way home to Hermosa Beach, I saw a big sign on the side of a hill: **LOYOLA**. Above it was a big white building. Could that be a college? It was. It was in fact a *Catholic* school like Fordham, run by Jesuit priests. I stopped by and talked to Miss Emenaker, the registrar. "Do you have a drama major here?" I asked.

"No," she said, "but we have a theater group, the Del Rey Players. And you could be an *English* major."

It was small, unlike USC or UCLA where you could get lost among 10,000 students. Loyola had only about 1,000 students, and all men. I decided to go to Loyola.

It was a smart move. Most of the students were returning servicemen there on the G.I. Bill. The government paid for all our schooling. It showed the people's gratitude for the men and women who preserved their freedom.

I will never forget what happened in Economics class on the first day of school. Since most of the students were ex-servicemen, the professor said, "Gentlemen, we won't have class today. But please stand up, one at a time, and give your name and tell us what branch of the service you were in and where you served." By this time, I had dropped the name Horace and started using my middle name, Paul, so when it came my turn, I said, "My name is Paul Picerni. I was a bombardier on a B-24, and I served in the C.B.I. Theater of War." It continued to go around the class, and I took special note when one student stood up and said, "My name is John Reilly. I was in the Navy. My ship was torpedoed in the Indian Ocean, and I spent the rest of the war as a prisoner in camps throughout Thailand."

After the class, I caught up with John and I asked, "John, did you happen to be in the Kanchanaburi prison camp?" He said he had. I said, "Were you there the day when the Kanchanaburi Bridge on the River Kwai was destroyed?" He said, "Yes. I was in a foxhole, and as the planes flew over real low, I remember a wrapper from a candy bar floated down into my foxhole. I said to myself, 'Those *bastards* up there are eating Hershey bars and all *we* get is rice and beans!'"

I said more seriously, "John . . . one of my bombs landed in the camp that day. Was anyone hurt?"

He said, slowly, "Fifty-five prisoners were killed that day." I was visibly shocked. He threw his arms around me and he held me tightly a long, long time.

Soon I was "doing my thing" at Loyola: With the help of Samuel James Larsen, a talented writer and fellow student who suffered from multiple sclerosis, I produced and directed my big variety show—basically the same one I did on the *U.S.S. Greeley*. The female parts were played by girls from Mount St. Mary's College and Marymount. (Loyola has since become coed, becoming Loyola Marymount.) Needless to say, the show was a hit. Father Lorenzo Malone, the dean of men, and Father Whelan, the president, were so impressed with the show that, during my second semester, they hired two drama teachers from Catholic University in Washington, D.C. and started a drama department there at the university. I became Loyola's first drama major.

Top With Pat Bigbee in the Loyola Production of A.A. Milne's *Toad of Toad Hall*. Bottom: Another *Toad of Toad Hall* pose, this one with Julie Danton.

Funny thing: I decided not to go to the Pasadena Playhouse because I wasn't sure how well I'd fit in with Gilmor Brown and his students. Now the two teachers who headed our new department, Victor Dial and Charles Steinmetz, were lovers. But did they know their stuff! They were brilliant, especially Victor.

I auditioned for a part in Loyola's first production under the new Drama Department, **Lost Horizon**. Naturally I hoped to get the lead, the part that Ronald Colman had played in the 1930s movie version. Instead, Victor cast *Charles*, one of our teachers! I didn't think that was fair—after all, I was paying to become an actor, and he was being paid to teach me! When I told Father Malone what was going on, he immediately agreed with me. Soon I was playing the lead.

From then on, because of my talent (and perhaps also because I didn't have much competition!), I played the leads in every play done at Loyola during my four years there. Dial and Steinmetz left after two years, and Dale O'Keefe from Yale took over. He too was a great teacher, and a fabulous actor. I often wondered why he didn't become a professional actor; he was really good, and looked like Richard Burton. Later I realized why. He had the talent—an abundance of it—but no drive, no desire to be a professional. You need talent, but you also need that drive.*

Our theater was small (it only held an audience of 100) but the shows we did were *big*: *Ah, Wilderness!, Mary of Scotland, Lost Horizon, Antigone* and many more very good productions. I had the lead in all of them. Today, Loyola Marymount has a theater department, a television department, a cinema department, several beautiful theaters and soundstages. (They invited me back a few years ago to guest star as St. Thomas More in a production of *A Man for All Seasons*.) My granddaughter Katie Moran graduated from LMU with a degree in communications arts. She is currently working on a very successful reality TV show as a story editor and her book, *The On Position*, is in bookstores throughout the country.

In 1946, when I was a freshman at Loyola, I began appearing with the Loyola Band and serving as the master of ceremonies when they performed at Loyola Lions football games. This was usually at Gilmore Field, but we also did some traveling: We made trips to Palm Springs and even to New Mexico and other Western states. In

---

*Some people make it on drive alone. Joel Grey was at Warner Brothers briefly during the time I was there, and that little guy had more drive than anybody I ever saw in my life. Once I went to the preview of a new Gordon MacRae picture in which Joel had a small part. In order to draw attention to himself there, he hired six girls to meet him in the lobby on the way out, after the film, and make a fuss over him in front of the exiting studio brass! He had them acting like the bobbysoxers who used to swarm around Frank Sinatra. The studio executives were no dummies, so they knew he'd put the girls up to it. It was so obvious, it was laughable.

Taking part in a Loyola production of Patrick Hamilton's *Rope* with Bernie Allenberg.

time I became friendly with John T. Boudreau, the capable and innovative band director and head of the Loyola Music Department. That same year, 1946, Dan Reeves bought the Cleveland Rams football team and moved them to Los Angeles, where they would be playing their games at the Los Angeles Coliseum which had been built to host the Olympic Games a few years earlier. Johnny, awarded the job of Entertainment Director for the Rams, had to form a Rams band and produce the pre-game and halftime shows. He needed a master of ceremonies, and naturally I was *it*. I was *it*, in fact, for the next 29 years!

Johnny and I were able to produce some memorable shows down through the years, because we had all of Hollywood at our disposal. Each week we had one or two top stars in our shows—people like Jack Benny, Danny Kaye, Marilyn Monroe, Eddie Fisher, Gordon MacRae and Gisele MacKenzie, to name a few. Top singers like Dionne Warwick stood in line to sing "The National Anthem" before the games. It was great publicity for them—and also for me for those three decades. In fact, a lot of people know me from being the Rams announcer rather than from my television and movie roles. In those days, the Rams used to draw like 90, 100,000 people. Imagine the thrill of speaking to an audience that large!

Johnny and I also originated the Ramettes, a group of 20 beautiful baton-twirlers who performed specialty routines. Today, most or all professional football and basketball teams have squads of girls performing at every timeout during games.

The Rams games were played on Friday nights or on Sunday afternoons, so they didn't interfere with my movie and television work. (And if I did have to go off on location for a movie or TV show, I'd get somebody to pinch-hit for me.) In addition to being paid to emcee each game, I was given seven free tickets for family and friends. Every week, friends like Telly Savalas, Frank Gorshin and Mike Connors, and also my "non-showbiz" friends, like Andy Sorrentino, Lou Enterante and Vic Marasco, would be with me at the games. Also, my brother Charlie and all my kids. (But not all at once—they had to alternate.) I had access to the field and also to the press box, which is where we would watch the games. As I mentioned, I did this for 29 years, and then the Rams moved to Anaheim and eventually to St. Louis. We currently do not have a professional football team in Los Angeles, but we will again one day.

Father Malone saw all my plays and was quite fond of me. One day in 1947 or '48 he called me at home and said, "Paul, I played golf with Louis B. Mayer yesterday. When I play golf with people like that, I think of my friends. You've got an interview with Louis B. Mayer tomorrow afternoon at three o'clock."

I said, "*What?!*" I knew that Mayer was the head of MGM Studios, the biggest in Hollywood.

Father Malone said, "Yep. You be there at three o'clock, and I'll meet you there."

In order to look my best, I got a whole new outfit—I went out to Beverly Hills and spent $100 for a beautiful new suit and a new tie. The next afternoon at three, there I was with Father Malone, in Louis B. Mayer's outer office at MGM Studios, the home of Clark Gable and most of Hollywood's other top stars. And in walked Mayer. Father Malone said, "Mr. Mayer, this is Paul Picerni." Mayer looked at me and immediately said, "The first thing we gotta do is change your name!" This gave me the impression he was going to sign me!

We went into Mayer's office, which was *big*, maybe 40 by 60, with big chairs, like bishop's chairs, along two of the walls. Already *in* the office, occupying all those chairs, were people like Joe Pasternak, Eddie Mannix and many of the other major producers of MGM Studios. Name an important MGM producer of that era and he was probably there—all these giants of the motion picture industry! Father Malone and I sat down and Mayer, now seated behind his desk, said, "All right, Father Malone, give me your sales pitch. Tell me about this young man." Suddenly it all seemed a little ridiculous. Here we were at the home of Gable, Spencer Tracy, Jimmy Stewart, most of Hollywood's superstars—and Father Malone had to "sell" *me*, a guy with no background at all apart from a few plays at the university.

Father Malone told Mayer that I was recently out of the service, and that I'd done this play and that play. "He's just magnificent on stage, and I think he'd be a good property for MGM Studios," Father Malone said.

Louis B. Mayer took the floor: "You know, Father, sometimes these actors come across on the stage a lot different than they do on film. What we'll have to do is make a test of this young man and see if he projects on the screen the way he projects on the stage." That was it. We were there maybe 10, 15 minutes, and we left. And *after* we left, I guess Mayer then had a conference with all his producers and executive producers, to get an idea of what *they* thought, and the final result was that I never heard from Louis B. Mayer again! I guess I was voted down. But I'd gotten to briefly speak to him, to answer a few of his questions, and I had the thrill of being in L.B. Mayer's office!

In October of 1947, I heard that Cathedral Films, a company that made religious movies for Protestant churches around the world, were preparing to shoot a half-hour film called ***The Story of Amos.*** I went over to Nassour Studios on Sunset Boulevard in Hollywood and I met with the producer, Brendon O'Donnell. He asked me if I was a member of Screen Actors Guild, and I said no. "I'd like you for the part of Amos," he said, "but you're not a member of the Guild. If you can get a SAG card, I'll give you the part."

I went across the street to a phone booth and called Father Malone at the University. I knew Father Malone was friendly with actor George Murphy, who was then the president of the Screen Actors Guild. "Father, there's a producer here at Cathedral Films

In makeup as King Creon with Cameron Menzies in the title role of Loyola's *Antigone*.

who says he'll give me a part if I can get a SAG card."

Father Malone asked for the producer's name; I told him it was Brendon O'Donnell. He said, "Give me the number you're calling from. I'll call you back in five minutes."

Soon he called back and said, "Go over to the studio again. You've got the part." I couldn't figure out how he'd done it so fast! Happily, I walked back into O'Donnell's office, and right away he said, "Why didn't you *tell* me you were a friend of Father Malone's?" Soon I was playing the title role in ***The Story of Amos***, and a member of the Screen Actors Guild. Sometimes it helps to know the right people, *but*—you must also be ready for the opportunity.

Carole Colonelli was true to her word: She wrote me every day. Her beautiful letters read like they were right out of ***True Romance***, the popular woman's magazine. She poured out her soul to me, how desperately she missed me. Sadly, I wrote one letter to every 20 of hers. I was always busy rehearsing the next play. My heart was in my work. I was doing what I loved, acting.

Suddenly, it happened: As fast as our romance had started, it ended. I got a Dear John letter letting me know that it was over—she had married my friend Al Bonelli! Al had taken over his father's dress factory in Manhattan, he belonged to the country club, he was rich—Carole knew that Al had it made. Al was "a sure thing," and I was someone who had a dream—a long shot—someone who might *never* make it. Well, I proved her wrong! I sometimes wonder if she regretted nipping our "true romance" in the bud.

The old saying, "All things happen for the best" proved to be true. Soon I met the mother of my eight children, a dear woman who has been by my side for 58 memorable, beautiful years now. The love of my life. I could use every appropriate adjective in the dictionary but it still wouldn't be enough. Let me just say . . . my wife Marie.

In another play during my early career in Hollywood, *Trial by Fire* (1946).

4
MARIE AND ME

PAUL: I first set eyes on my future wife Marie in a dance studio on LaBrea Boulevard in Hollywood, just a block south of Sunset. I walked in the back door of this big hall and I saw three girls in shorts on the stage, singing and dancing. And one girl really caught my eye. That was Marie.

MARIE: I'd started dancing when I was nine years old, in Pennsylvania—I went to a studio with a dance teacher after school every day. And I began thinking, "Yes, this is what I was going to do for a living." My mother was behind me in that, my mom *and* dad. My mother had always talked about moving to California and then, when I was about 19, we finally did. The three of us came out to California by car. It was a great trip; we had a good time.

PAUL: She left Lansdale, Pennsylvania, in a Buick Roadmaster with her mother and father. Now, the strange thing is that she left Lansdale January 11, 1946, and I left New York for California in an old Oldsmobile with my buddy Bill Lewis *the same day*, January 11, 1946. We probably crossed each other on the highway as we were on our way to California.

MARIE: In those days, there weren't many cars on the highways, so that's why we think we had to have passed each other.

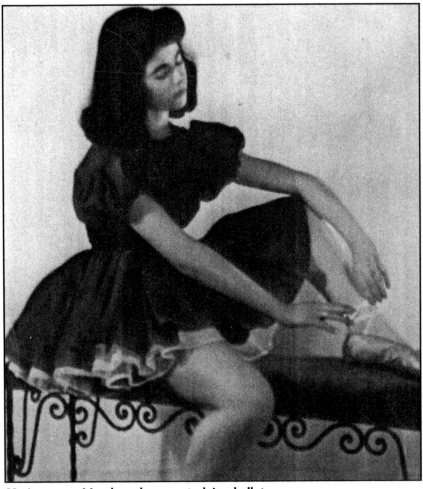

Marie at age 14, when she was studying ballet.

PAUL: We probably crossed each other on Route 66.

MARIE: So I came out to California with my mom and dad. After they bought some property in California, my mom and dad left me here in California with friends, and *they* went back to Pennsylvania to sell *every*thing. They sold their business, which was the world's first supermarket—the first time a market had everything. It had groceries, it had meat, fish, vegetables, fresh fruit. It was the first time ever that anybody combined all those things in one marketplace.

PAUL: In those days, there would be individual stores for all those things. There was a fish market, there was a butcher, there was a grocery store and a vegetable store. But Charlie Mason, Marie's father, was the first one to put 'em all together in what was the first supermarket.

MARIE: So they sold that market, they sold a big beautiful house they had in Lansdale, and they sold their apple orchard. Then they packed up everything that was left and came back with my two younger brothers, Charles and Vincent, and with Miss Mary, our Mennonite housekeeper, who wore a bonnet. We had Miss Mary in Pennsylvania and she promised to come with us for a year. We lived near MGM, in a great big house right on Hughes Avenue in Culver City. My mother and father bought that house, and also a big building on Venice Boulevard with a lot of stores. They were pretty well-to-do!

Fourteen-year-old Marie at New Jersey's Steel Pier.

I was enrolled at a dance studio in Hollywood, and the dance instructor there was helping to cast a movie. Freddie Stewart was a young singer-actor at the time, and our dance instructor was casting the next Freddie Stewart movie.

PAUL: The dance teacher's name was Jack Boyle, and of course most of his students were in these movies—background dancers in these movies with Freddie Stewart and Noel Neill at Monogram. Marie did two of the Freddie Stewart movies, *Freddie Steps Out* and *Junior Prom*.

MARIE: I don't know if I enjoyed them or not. Dancing's hard work, it really, really is, and you need to be very disciplined. *Then* Jack Boyle cast a show for the comedy writer Hal Collins. It was called *At Ease* and it was a live music revue which was going to tour all the Army camps throughout Southern California. It was produced by Harry Revel.

PAUL: *At Ease* was a series of musical numbers and comedy sketches. I was at this time still a student at Loyola University, and a friend of mine, a fella named Bill Griswold,

Marie at 18.

told me, "They're auditioning people for a musical revue at a dance studio on LaBrea." So I went over there with Bill and we walked in and, as I mentioned before, there on stage were three girls in shorts, rehearsing a number with the dance director, Jack Boyle. As I walked in with Bill, I saw them singing and dancing, rehearsing this number called "Cuddle Bunny" that was going to be in the show. "*Cuddle Bunny/What a honey/What a bundle of joy . . .*"

MARIE: ***At Ease*** was all original songs by Hal Collins and Harry Revel. Harry Revel wrote the music and Hal Collins wrote the lyrics, and Hal also wrote the sketches.

PAUL: These three girls were singing and dancing, and the one girl in the middle, with black shorts, was the one who really caught my attention. She had million-dollar "Betty Grable legs," beautiful blue eyes, olive skin—I mean, I felt like I was looking at Hedy Lamarr, *that's* how she struck me. The image has been vivid in my mind ever since.

MARIE: I still have the black shorts [*laughs*]! They don't *fit* anymore, but I still have them!

PAUL: My buddy Bill Griswold and I auditioned for the show. Bill didn't make it, but I was cast because I had a lot of experience from when I was in Special Services in the Army, and from doing plays at the University. And of course, in the first week or so of rehearsal, I kinda cozied up to . . . Marie *Mason* her name was, this cute little 19-year-old girl. I had my eye on her all through rehearsal.

MARIE: Once the show got going, we performed it at different Army camps and Navy bases all over Southern California. And also the government hospitals where they had the wounded soldiers. On weekends we'd all get on a bus and go to a different base and put the show on. If you'd gone to see ***At Ease***, you would have seen all different sketches. There was no story; it was one comedy sketch or one song after another. And different Hollywood stars emceeing every week. Roddy McDowall was in one, and Jackie Cooper did it once. We performed it at different Army camps, Navy bases, all over Southern California, each weekend.

PAUL: Using the Internet, we recently found the program for

one weekend's performance. This performance was January 9, 1947, and it was at McCormick General Hospital in Pasadena. Headlining the cast that day was Roddy McDowall and Jane Withers. The opening number was a big dance number, "Three Cheers for the Audience" with me headlining.

MARIE: Paul sang in the show too.

PAUL: Yeah, I could sing show tunes—I couldn't sing ballads!

MARIE: Paul should have been on stage in a musical, he *loved* singing. Any time he sees a musical, he says, "Oh, I could have done that!" If only he could sing [*laughs*]!

PAUL: Then in the show that weekend in Pasadena there was a comedy sketch about giving a guy a Mickey Finn which featured Phil Arnold, who was a comic. "Hollywood Stand-In" was a big, funny sketch, the classic sketch where the comic—Phil Arnold again—was always getting hit with the powder. In the sketch, a director yells "Makeup!," the leading man steps aside and the stand-in Phil Arnold steps in, and he's hit with a big powder puff that creates a giant cloud of powder all around him!

MARIE: There were other sketches, songs, there were dancers, Roddy McDowall came out and did something, Jane Withers did something, and then we would do our big closing number. Paul was cast in four or five of the sketches, and I was in all the dance numbers and a couple of solo numbers, like "Cuddle Bunny."

This one day, Paul and I were outside the rehearsal hall on Hollywood Boulevard after rehearsals. It was raining, and we were standing in a little alcove, just the two of us, waiting for the bus to come. I was chewing gum as we were waiting and Paul asked me, "Do you have another piece of gum, Marie?"

PAUL: "No," she said, "but you can have some of *this*." And with that, she pushes the gum partway out through her front teeth, offering me the gum between her teeth. I leaned over to get the gum, and I kissed her—that was our first kiss! She had her little suitcase with her dancing shoes and her makeup and all that, and when the bus came I carried it onto the bus. And from that day on, we got closer and closer. One day she invited me home to her parents' house for a spaghetti dinner. That's when I found out for the first time that she came from an Italian family—her mother and father were both from Sicily. I didn't know that, with a name like Marie Mason! Her *real* name was Mussamecci!

MARIE: Later on, *years* later, we went to Italy and lived there for a year, and we went to my father's hometown, San Alfio in Sicily. And the name Mussamecci was all *over* this town; it was a really famous name! Mussamecci sounds like it's a strange name, but over *there* Mussamecci was like Smith is *here*! It was the name of the mayor of the town and everything.

PAUL: But that's how we first met, and that's how Cupid struck us with his arrow. And then we kind of got serious.

MARIE: [*laughs*]"Kind of"??

PAUL: One day we were on the beach at Playa Del Rey, not far from Loyola University where I was going to school. She was wearing this black bathing suit—oh, God, she had such a fabulous figure! We were on the beach, just the two of us, and we were talking about getting married, and I said, "No, I'm not gonna get married, we're not gonna get married until I graduate from college." I was going to stick to that, I wanted to get my degree first, and *then* we could get married. But she had other ideas. She started to cry, and it broke my heart. So that day on the beach I said, "Okay, let's get engaged . . . let's get married."

MARIE: My parents liked Paul right away, but . . . you know . . . my mom kept thinking I should have been a star! You know how moms are!

We met in October of 1946 and it truly was love at first sight. In May of '47 we had an engagement party at my house, and then in August of '47 we were married in St. Augustine's Church, right across the street from MGM Studios. I had just turned 20. I was 18 when I came out here to California and I was just 20 when I got married.

PAUL: She never had to cook or clean before we were married but she learned fast!

MARIE: My parents gave us a Chrysler convertible as a wedding gift and we spent our honeymoon night at Arrowhead Springs Hotel, in the mountains near San Bernadino.

PAUL: Room 602 [*laughs*]!

MARIE: When we walked into the ballroom at that hotel, there was a big band there playing "Mexicali Rose." As I danced with Paul, he said, "Let's make this our song!," and we did. After that, we drove to Niagara Falls, and then to my hometown of Lansdale, where they had a big wedding reception for us. From there we went to New York City, where

The bride cuts the cake.

Paul's mother had a big reception.

PAUL: On the way back to California, we saw Hulda Schauphause. Hulda was of course several years older by the time; she must have been in her seventies. She was very nice to us, and gave us a beautiful gift, a set of dishes that she had kept for years. That was the last time I saw Hulda. Years ago I often daydreamed that someday someone would knock at my door and ask, "Are you Henri Duval?" I would say, "Well, I was at one time." And this visitor would say, "Well, Hulda Schauphause has passed away leaving a large estate, and she left a lot of it to you!" I'm sorry to say, though, that never happened!

MARIE: When we first got married, we lived with my mother and father in the big house, and Paul was still going to college of course. But by the time he graduated, we had two children. Of course by then I had long-ago given up any thought of a movie career and was so happy with my new "career" as a wife and mother. I love being married. We were married in August of '47 and our daughter Nikki was born in November of '48.

The 1942 Chrysler convertible that Marie's parents gave us as a wedding present.

PAUL: The first baby lived in the big house too. Living at Marie's folks' house made things a little easier at first! I had a whole bunch of jobs early on while we were married, and while I was still a student at Loyola. I worked for a real estate company and I had an office right across the street from where we lived on Venice Boulevard. Then I had a part-time job teaching athletics and coaching the teams at St. Augustine's, the school across the street from MGM—I think they were paying me $150 a month. And I also got a job at Mount St. Mary's College, where I taught speech and drama, and directed a show called *Everybody Goes to College* which I co-wrote with my friend Sam Larsen. They paid me 300 a month.

Ingrid Bergman? No. Marie!

MARIE: By the time we had our second child, we were living in a little rented house on Madison Avenue in Culver City. Our son P.V. and our daughter Gemma were both born while we were there.

PAUL: Then we bought a house in Reseda, on Wilbur Avenue, by the time our daughter Maria came along. By this time, I was under contract at Warners.

MARIE: I did work at MGM when Paul and I were first married. That didn't last very long, but it was fun. Not as a dancer, but as a messenger girl—a lot of running around! Peter Lawford, Frank Sinatra, Mickey Rooney, Judy Garland, Janet Leigh, they were all there, and it was fun to see them. The ones getting mail were the producers, the writers, the music department, *all* the departments. But when you're running around delivering mail, to all these offices, you see everybody. And our mailroom was right next to the front gate, so when the stars came in, we could see them and wave to everybody. Clark Gable, I jumped on a tram with him once—I *did* do that [*laughs*]!

PAUL: I'd stand at the gate sometimes in the afternoon, waiting for Marie to finish work, and I'd see the stars come out of the gate. One day I'm standing there and who drives out the gate but Gable. I waved to him and he waved back. My first glimpse of Gable, who was *so* handsome. My God, my heart . . . I was like a teenage fan!

MARIE: The stars were all very nice, they were good to us. Looking back, it was fun.

PAUL: So she was working at MGM, and then she worked as a dental assistant for a while. That helped financially. Of course, her parents were pretty well-to-do and they helped a lot. Her mother Sarah was always a little disappointed that Marie's career was over once the babies started coming. But eventually she was very proud of her daughter's husband. Marie's father Charles didn't care. As long as Marie was happy, *he* was happy. Camilo Charles Mussamecci was a saintly man. We've been through some happy times and some rough times but she's been the strength through it all and still is.

MARIE: We've had a great life. We had eight babies in nine years—we had as many as three in diapers at one time for the first nine years of our marriage. And we raised those eight beautiful children into very productive, happy adults. They love each other, and I love them all very much. Our ten grandchildren are the best. We are very lucky. And best of all, they are all good friends [*laughs*]!

Three generations: My mother, me and my son P.V.

5
THE BEGINNING

Shortly after I arrived in California in January 1946 and got settled in my little apartment in Hermosa Beach, my feature film career started in a most unusual—and inauspicious—way. I was a freshman at Loyola U with no formal training; I had no agent; knew only one person in Hollywood (The Red Ryder, Bill Lewis). And yet a career in motion pictures, one that has so far lasted 60 years, was about to begin.

The Red Ryder's uncle, "Doc" Jose, a first assistant director at Monogram, one day asked the Ryder, "Would you and your buddy Blackie like to work as extras in a movie?" The next thing I knew, the Ryder and I were two of about 50 people on a small gambling casino set at Monogram studios, "background extras" in a scene in a Bowery Boys movie with Leo Gorcey and Huntz Hall. At one point in the scene, Anthony Caruso and his gang came in and Caruso demanded that the Ryder (playing a cashier in a cage) turn over the money. The Ryder's silent bit paid $25. For playing a casino gambler, my extra pay for the day was about $10.

I would appear in very small parts in several other movies of the late 1940s and continue to play much more prominent roles on stage. I also made my first appearance on television. That story begins with *The White-Haired Boy*, an Irish play we did at Loyola in which I played a fat old Irishman and did the whole thing with a brogue. Of all people, the great Irish actress Sara Allgood played my wife. Sara had made a name for herself with the famous Abbey Players in Ireland, acted in films in England, and then came to Hollywood in 1940 and soon received an Academy Award nomination for her performance in John Ford's *How Green Was My Valley*. We

An early head shot.

With the great Irish actress Sara Allgood in *The White-Haired Boy*.

brought her in as a "guest star," so to speak, and it was good having an established actress like her on campus, doing a play with us! We performed *The White-Haired Boy* for two weeks and it was so well done that KTLA decided to have us do it again at a studio for telecasting. (This was like 1947, when television was in its infancy.) We did it on a soundstage in a studio up on top of Mt. Wilson. I believe that it was somewhat of a historic broadcast, one of the very first televised dramatic presentations on the West Coast. Another thing about it that, for me, was memorable: The rest rooms were quite a distance from the stage, and Sara Allgood was always having to pee! There *was*, however, a little room just off the soundstage, and she put a big five-gallon bucket in there so that, when the commercial came on, or when there was a break between acts, she could run in there and relieve herself in the bucket!

When I was playing the leads in all those plays at Loyola, I was seen by several casting directors. One in particular, a woman named Ruth Burch, was very impressed with my work—and also liked me very much. Ruth was the casting director for the Actors Company Playhouse in La Jolla, which was run by Gregory Peck, Dorothy McGuire and Mel Ferrer, and during the summer of 1947 she cast me in several plays there. The plays were staged in the La Jolla High School auditorium (Peck grew up in La Jolla). Because La Jolla was 150 miles from Hollywood, too far to commute back and forth from home, I stayed at the La Jolla Hotel.

In my first play there, *The Front Page* with Michael O'Shea and Pat O'Brien, I played a small part as one of the reporters. One of my favorite memories of that time is of Pat inviting the whole cast (about ten of us) to his La Jolla beach house, and we played touch football on the beach with the same football he used in the movie *Knute Rockne, All American* with Ronald Reagan as George Gipp ("Let's win one for the Gipper!"). At the end of *The Front Page's* two-week run, O'Brien gave me an autographed 8x10 picture. I'll always remember the inscription he wrote above his name: **TO PAUL, MAY YOU ATTAIN THE HEIGHTS. —PAT O'BRIEN** He never told me this, but somehow I knew what he meant: May you attain stardom and, more importantly, may you attain the heights of Heaven. I never asked any other star for an autographed picture since.

The autographed photo I was given by Pat O'Brien.

Marie came down to La Jolla and joined me while I was in *Command Decision*, my second play there, and we had a great time. It was like a vacation sitting on the beach at "The Cove" during the day and doing the play at night. *Command Decision* starred John Lund, Ward Bond and Albert Dekker—a wonderful, professional cast. I played a bombardier. (Typecasting!) Mel Ferrer was our director.

A scene from *Command Decision* with Paul Marion, Albert Dekker, me and John Lund.

On stage in this *Command Decision* scene are John Lund, seated (I'm standing behind him), Albert Dekker, Kenneth Tobey (seated), Ward Bond, Michael Ross, Kent Taylor and Harry Carey, Jr. (seated).

Albert Dekker was a big man, and he loved to horse around during rehearsals; he'd try to break other actors up while they were on stage by standing in the wings making faces and other weird things like that. Ward Bond was also a big man, and he didn't appreciate Dekker's playful antics. Dekker played a visiting Congressman investigating the bomb group because they were losing too many planes and too many crews. In one scene, Dekker had a line directed at Gen. Miles, the group's commanding officer, played by John Lund. The line, delivered as the two men were looking at a big map of Europe hung on a wall, was, "What's our target for tonight, Gen. Miles?" As you know, a line can be delivered in many different ways—sometimes not the way the writer intended. Dekker said, "What's our target for tonight? . . . Gen. *Miles?*"—he purposely made it sound like he was asking if the target was Gen. Miles! Well, he got a big laugh from the opening night audience, but it was a cheap laugh. After the performance, pictures of the cast were being taken on stage and Dekker continued to horse around, holding things up. Ward Bond finally blew his stack. "Stop fuckin' around! I wanna get *home*! I'm tired of all your fuckin' *bullshit*! And besides, that was a cheap way to get a laugh in the show tonight, you dumb fuck!" Well, Dekker fired back, "What's *your* problem, you asshole? It was only a *joke*!," and for a second it looked like these two gorillas were going to go at it. Fortunately, they didn't. About 20 years later, Dekker was found dead in his bathroom, naked, a note written in lipstick on the mirror. He had committed suicide. Bob Stack said to me once, "The picture business is great . . . when you're working. But when you're not, it can be tragic." It was tragic for Albert Dekker.

The reviews I got for my performance in **Command Decision** were excellent. I liked working with Mel Ferrer. Not only was he a good actor, but also a talented director; in fact, he was under contract to Howard Hughes at RKO as a writer-actor-director. Later he cast me in another play at the Coronet Theater in Hollywood, **Eurydice** with Viveca Lindfors, the Swedish actress, Alf Kjellin and John Beal. I played Viveca's lover. Then he gave me a small part as a doctor in a film he directed for Hughes, **The Secret Fury** with Claudette Colbert. I had one scene with her, a nice, long scene with a lot of dialogue, and a strange new word that I had to learn how to pronounce, "electroencephalograph"! Claudette Colbert was a gorgeous woman and it was a thrill just to be on a set with her. Working with her made me feel like Clark Gable in *It Happened One Night*!

I got the role in *The Secret Fury* on a day I'll never forget: January 13, 1950. A *Friday* the 13th! It was the day that Paul Vincent, my first son was born. That was also the day that my agent Wilt Melnick sent me on three interviews. The first one was with director Otto Preminger at 20th Century-Fox for a picture called *Where the Sidewalk Ends* with Dana Andrews. I was so proud of having my first son, I was handing out cigars that day, but as I walked into Preminger's outer office, the secretary said, "Don't let Mr. Preminger see those cigars. He doesn't like people who smoke." I took them all out of my pocket and put them on the secretary's desk and went in to see Preminger. I still remember being so happy and so full of life, because my son had been born. After a brief interview with Preminger, I got the job, a one-day part in a scene with Dana Andrews. I picked up my cigars from the secretary and went over to RKO Studios for my second interview and I saw Mel Ferrer, who knew me from *Eurydice* and liked me and said I would be playing the doctor in *The Secret Fury*. And after that, I went to Columbia to talk to a director about a small part in a picture called *The Killer That Stalked New York*, and I got *that* part. So the day my son was born, I got three parts at three different studios, and as it worked out, they didn't conflict. It helped pay the hospital bills! Remember, "Each baby arrives with a loaf of bread under his arm." I'll always remember that Friday the 13th as one of the luckiest days of my life.

The stork brought Marie and me the first of our eight children on November 15, 1948: Niccoletta Maria, a wonderful daughter with a bubbly personality and the knack of making us all laugh at family gatherings. Nicci graduated from Louisville High School, the Catholic girls' school in Woodland Hills, and then went to Pierce College, where she majored in Dramatics. I thought she was very good in a few plays that I saw her in; not surprisingly, she had a natural flair for comedy. She married Charles Moran, a Loyola graduate who eventually became a very successful film sound editor. Charles won an Emmy for his work on the TV series *Miami*

Vice and an Oscar for the feature film *Meteor*. Nicci and Charles had two children, Katie and Nicholas. In 1984, Charles was returning from a trip to Alaska in his private plane when he ran into severe weather, crashed in Canada and was killed. Nicci has since remarried and had another son, Stephen, who is now an outstanding football player at Notre Dame High School in Sherman Oaks. Today Nicci is a special-education teacher at a Woodland Hills school, working with handicapped children. She

Marie with our first child, Nicci.

has many friends, that same bubbly attitude and loves her family, especially her three kids.

I got to play a bombardier again in the classic World War II film *Twelve O'Clock High* with Gregory Peck, directed by Henry King. I landed the role when Wilt sent me to 20th Century-Fox to meet a fellow named James Reilly, one of the studio's casting directors. He asked me, "Can you operate a Norden bombsight?" and I said, "Yeah, of course. That's what I did in the war; I was a bombardier." And just like that, I got the part as Gregory Peck's bombardier. Very excited, I called my mother in New York and told her I was playing the bombardier in *Twelve O'Clock High*, so of course when it came out several months later she went to see it. And then she called me and said, "Paul, I didn't see you in the movie."

I said, "You *didn't*?? I'm the fellow in the nose of the plane. I've got this big leatherjacket on, and I've got a helmet on, and an oxygen mask—" She said, "Oh, that was *you*??" Even though I had about 14 lines in it ("Bombs away!," "Bombardier to pilot . . . ," lines like that), you couldn't really see me. There was one quick glimpse of me before we put the oxygen masks on—that was the only time you really saw my face. But it was so brief that my mother phoned and said, "I didn't *see* you, Paul!"

After I'd done a number of one-day parts, Wilt took me out to Universal Studios to see about a comparatively *big* part, a part that ran three or four weeks in a Western with Joel McCrea and Wanda Hendrix (Mrs. Audie Murphy), *Saddle Tramp*. Millie Gusse was casting, and at one point in the interview she asked, "Paul, can you *ride?*"

I said, with a note of surprise in my voice, "Millie . . . I was in the *cavalry* in the War!"

Millie said, very satisfied, "Well, if you were in the cavalry, I guess you're a pretty good rider. Okay, Paul, you got the part."

After we walked out of her office, Wilt, who knew me well of course, said with a bit of astonishment, "*Paul* . . . ! You weren't in the cavalry in the War; you were a bombardier. And besides, we didn't even *have* a cavalry in World War II!"

"I know that, Wilt. You know that. But *Millie Gusse* doesn't know that!"

I learned to ride a horse in preparation for my role in Universal's *Saddle Tramp* with Joel McCrea (right) and Peter Leeds (center).

After that, I proceeded to go see Ace Hudkins, an old wrangler who supplied horses for a lot of Western films. At his ranch in the Valley, I took about two weeks of intense riding lessons from him (or perhaps from his son), and by the time we did the picture, I was getting around on a horse just fine. That was my first long-running part in a picture, three weeks on *Saddle Tramp* with Joel McCrea.

I remember riding to work one morning in a limousine with Joel, down Ventura Boulevard in the western San Fernando Valley. There was nothing but orange groves and farmland. When we reached Woodland Hills, even further west, it was all open land. Joel said, "Someday this will be the center of Los Angeles." I laughed to myself. At that time, you could buy 40 acres for about a thousand dollars an acre. If only I had listened to him, I'd now be a *billionaire!* Woodland Hills is today the center of a metropolis: high-rise buildings, shopping centers, apartment complexes. Land here today is literally a million dollars an acre. So, my advice to you is: Invest in land! You can never go wrong . . . *especially* in California.

Needless to say, Joel McCrea bought thousands of acres in the Conejo Valley. He made a fortune, and he and his lovely wife Frances Dee lived a long and happy life. Many other actors also got rich on land investments, notably Bob Hope, Dean Martin and Fred MacMurray. I didn't invest in land mainly because I didn't have any extra money *to* invest. I was investing in a family—the kids just kept coming. As I mentioned, on January 13, 1950, my first son Paul Vincent was born. We called him P.V. so as not to be confused with the old man (me). He's a duplicate of Charlie Mason, Marie's father. Charlie was a saint—he was "St. Francis of Assisi," so to speak, a simple man, but wise and good. Everybody liked Charlie Mason. Everybody *loves* P.V. He graduated the University of California at Northridge as a journalist major. He's a good writer, and has written several screenplays, short stories and a book, *The Old Gaviotta Pier.* But even though he's a fine writer, he (like many writers) makes his living elsewhere. He worked as Paul Michael Glaser's stand-in on *Starsky and Hutch*; he worked on *Happy Days* and *Kojak* as an extra—and he became a property master along the way. One of the TV series on which he worked as a property master (five years) was *Diagnosis Murder* with Dick Van Dyke. At one point, he even wrote a teleplay for *Diagnosis*

P.V. and his dad.

Murder and cast me in the guest star part! An excellent swimmer, P.V. comes to our house several times a week to visit, and does 100 laps in our pool. He also still plays baseball—he's an outstanding left-handed pitcher. He's a good son. It's hard to believe that he's 57. It seems like yesterday when I was handing out all those cigars!

I'm getting ahead of my own story. Soon I would get my big break with the Warner Brothers movie ***Breakthrough***. You must be ready when your chance arrives. I was ready. I was ready to break out in ***Breakthrough***.

6
BREAKTHROUGH

A decade before the all-star World War II epic *The Longest Day,* and a half-century before Oscar-winning director Steven Spielberg's *Saving Private Ryan,* D-Day was depicted in all its sound and fury in the 1950 Warner Brothers production *Breakthrough,* the story of an American infantry company at the Omaha Beach landing. The title refers to the platoon's subsequent cross-country trek, their ongoing battles with the German soldiers entrenched in the French hedgerows, and the historic St. Lo "breakthrough" which opened the way for the rapid Allied advance across France to victory. But the title also had personal meaning for me: It was my work in this film that earned me my contract at Warners. This was a turning point, a very important "breakthrough," in my career as a young actor.

The *Honest John* cast and director William Talman, right.

When I landed the role, I was nearing the end of my final year as a student at Loyola University and I was also doing a play called *Honest John* with Buddy

Ebsen at the Las Palmas Theater in Hollywood. Here's how I got the part in that play: Buddy had also written *Honest John* and Bill Talman, the fellow who later played District Attorney Hamilton Burger on TV's *Perry Mason*, was directing. My agent Wilt told me, "There's a small part in this play you might try out for. The part is, you push the mayor around in his wheelchair. That's all you have to do, just push the mayor's wheelchair. Why don't I take you over to see Bill Talman and maybe you can get that part?" We drove over to the Las Palmas Theater and I met Talman for the first time. I thought he was a "regular guy," a blond, good-looking New York kind of fellow. We chatted in the office a while and finally Talman said, "Do you mind coming on stage and reading some of the scenes?" When he said "scenes," my ears perked up—as I had understood it, the guy pushing the mayor in the wheelchair *had* no scenes. Of course I said, "I wouldn't mind at all." And when he

handed me the script and said, "Read this scene," he was indicating the part of a gangster—an Italian gangster who's got a gun moll and who is holding Buddy Ebsen hostage! It was a great role, the "lead heavy." After I read the scene for Talman, he said, "Oh, you'd be wonderful. I'd like you in the part. Let's work it out." I had walked in to audition for the minor role of the mayor's wheelchair-pusher and I walked *out* with the second lead in the play!

Lynne Carter (wife of director William Talman), Buddy Ebsen and me in *Honest John*.

The play ran for six weeks and I guess I was pretty good in it, because after Solly Biano, the head of talent at Warner Brothers, saw it, he brought me out to the studio to meet Lew Seiler, the director of their upcoming film *Breakthrough*. I was going to be auditioning for the part of a platoon member—just a nondescript soldier in an entire platoon of soldiers. While I was in an outer office waiting to see Seiler, I met a fellow named Joe Breen, Jr., who was the son of Joseph Breen Sr., head of Hollywood's censorship office. Joe gave me a script and said, "Read this scene here, this dialogue of Private Rojeck. That's *not* the part you're up for; you're just up for one of the soldiers in the platoon. But this is the scene we've been using to test actors for Mr. Seiler."

I read the scene, and it was a powerful one. A soldier has been mortally injured and the medics are working on him as he's dying, and other soldiers are watching what's going on. A captain comes along, sees all the soldiers standing around, and he barks, "What are you doing, holding a wake? Come on, move out, move out! Get back to your foxholes!" Everybody moves away with the exception of this one soldier, Private Rojeck. The captain snaps, "You heard me, Rojeck. Move out!" And Rojeck looks up at the captain, and in a weepy voice he says:

Joe Breen, Jr. wrote the original story of *Breakthrough* and was a technical advisor on the show. He was there in real life for all the things you see in the movie: the landing at Normandy, the fighting through the hedgerows of France and so on.

I had two uncles in the last war. All they ever talked about was Paris . . . and dames. *This* is what *I'm* gonna talk about when I get home. *This* is what I'm gonna tell the people. *This* is what I'm gonna tell 'em war is all about . . .

The scene went on from there and, boy, it was strong stuff! Finally, Joe Breen asked me, "You ready?"

I went into the office where Lew Seiler, a stocky, sixty*ish*, gray-haired fellow, was sitting at the desk. Because of all the plays I had done at Loyola, I felt like I was a thoroughbred that had been in training for a long time and now was ready to run—I gave it my all. "I had two uncles in the last war. All they ever talked about was Paris . . . and dames. *This* is what *I'm* gonna talk about . . ." I began, and as I went on I got more intense, and by the time I finished the scene, the tears were streaming down my face. Suddenly, Seiler *pounded* the desk and to my great surprise he exclaimed, "Son of a *bitch!* Why haven't I *seen* this actor before?? I want *him* in that part!"

"Mr. Seiler, we've already cast that part," Joe Breen said. "We gave it to Warren Douglas. He's already been to wardrobe and everything."

Seiler was adamant. "I don't care! Pay Warren Douglas off!" And, pointing a finger at me, he announced again, "I want *this* man!"

It seemed too good to be true, but it had actually happened. A meeting with Bill Talman for a wheelchair-pushing part in **Honest John** led to my getting the second lead; and as a result of that, I'd gotten a chance to audition for a small, nondescript role in **Breakthrough** and ended up with a co-starring part! I believe my **Breakthrough** audition was on a Friday, and two days later, on Sunday, I was aboard a bus with Frank Lovejoy, John Agar and David Brian and the rest of the **Breakthrough** cast, heading up to Fort Ord in Monterey, California, to start filming on Monday. Incidentally, that same day (Sunday, June 11, 1950) was the day of the graduation ceremonies at Loyola University. I didn't even want to mention to Warner Brothers that I would be missing my graduation, because I was afraid that might upset the apple cart and I'd miss out on the part. So as I was on the bus going the 300 miles up to Monterey, Marie and our kids, Nicci and P.V., were at Loyola picking up my diploma.

(Incidentally, 11 has always been a very important number in my life. I went in the service on the 11th; I separated from the service on the 11th; I left for California on the 11th; and, as you read above, I graduated from Loyola and I signed my Warners contract on the 11th. Then, in later life, my first granddaughter was born on the 11th, and I expect that my first great-grandchild will be born on the 11th. And I probably will *die* on the 11th!)

My Warner Brothers career got off to a running start in Breakthrough.

Production on **Breakthrough** began on Monday. David Brian starred as the battle-fatigued captain of the platoon, John Agar played a young second lieutenant fresh out of Officers Training School and Frank Lovejoy was the platoon sergeant. Wearing uniforms that had the name WARREN DOUGLAS sewn into them, I played Private Rojeck. There were maybe 15 actors there, and then all of the rest of the soldiers you see in the picture— American *and* German—were played by the real-life soldiers stationed at Fort Ord. All of the equipment in the movie, the tanks and guns and everything, was also supplied by the Army. We shot at Fort Ord (for instance, the opening sequence with the soldiers standing at attention as David Brian talks to them and, for the Battle of the Hedgerows scenes, in the surrounding countryside). At Monterey Bay we shot the scene where the men climb down a cargo net from the deck of their ship and into the landing craft. We were all wearing rubber life preservers but they weren't workable, they were props. As I climbed down that net, loaded with heavy clothes and boots and knapsacks and guns and bandoleer—and an inoperable life preserver—I was very much aware that if one of us slipped and fell, he'd go right down through 40 feet of water to the bottom of Monterey Bay and that would be *it*!

I didn't complain, however; I knew that ***Breakthrough*** was going to be a very important picture for me, and I was really an eager beaver as a young actor. For the D-Day beach landing, they set up five or six cameras on the beach, and as we came off the landing craft, we were instructed to run up the beach and dive close to one of the cameras. I ran up the beach and did a belly-flop in front of one of the cameras—and I hit my chin on the top of my rifle. It actually cut my chin, and I ended up getting some stitches. From then on, one of the other actors in the picture, Dick Wesson, began ribbing me by telling everybody, "Paul wanted a close-up so bad that he hit his chin on the *camera*."

I watch as muscleman Greg McClure gets a ribbing from Dick Wesson.

Dick Wesson and I became close friends and remained so all through the years. Before ***Breakthrough***, back in the days of nightclubs and vaudeville, he and his brother Gene had a topnotch comedy act. Gene was the straight man and Dick was the comic— Dick had a funny crew haircut and he did impressions, and they did a lot of wonderful routines together. And on one occasion when they were playing at a movie theater in Boston, Jerry Lewis, still a young kid at that time, was the theater usher who carried their bags from the limousine to their dressing room. A few years later, the

Wesson Brothers broke up—Gene had an alcohol problem, he liked to go to the racetrack, he'd miss dates, and finally he and Dick had a falling-out and they dissolved the act. But by this time their manager, Abby Greshler, had a singer under contract, Dean Martin, and he also had a new young comic—Jerry Lewis. Abby came up with the idea of putting them together, giving them simulations of a lot of the Wesson Brothers' routines and having them fill in some of the dates that the Wesson brothers couldn't make anymore. Needless to say, Martin and Lewis were a great act and they "clicked" in a big way. And Jerry Lewis copied Dick Wesson—he even made himself to *look* like Dick. If you were to ask Jerry point-blank about it, he probably wouldn't admit it—but ask him if he knew the Wesson Brothers and he'll tell you that he did. So that's how Martin and Lewis started. And Dick Wesson never resented it. He knew that the imitators of stars frequently become bigger than the stars themselves, and that's just what happened in this case. (If you want to see an impression, watch Paul Newman in his first picture **The Silver Chalice**. He did a terrific impression of Marlon Brando all the way through!)

Breakthrough was my first film with Dick Wesson and also my first with Joe Breen, Jr., who I mentioned earlier. In World War II, Joe was a tank commander—and, unbilled, he *plays* a tank commander in one short scene in **Breakthrough**. He's the one who says to John Agar, "When do you want me to bring up the tanks, Lieutenant?" In a way, he was talking to "himself" there—Joe wrote the story, and the Agar character in that story was based on Joe.

Early on in life, Joe had studied to be a Jesuit priest—but he had a short fuse. He was pitching one day for the Jesuit baseball team in Santa Clara, and the priest who was calling balls and strikes kept saying, "Ball!" Joe would throw it down the heart of the plate and the umpire-priest called every pitch a ball. That priest was evidently trying to teach him a lesson in tolerance and patience—but, when Joe and his Irish temper couldn't take it anymore, he blew up and yelled at the priest and told him off—"That was a *strike*, dammit!!" Joe eventually left the priesthood and joined the service, going in as a private and working his way up to major. He was another Audie Murphy. Joe and I were very friendly from the day I first met him in Lew Seiler's outer office, waiting to audition for **Breakthrough**.

He was a brilliant, wonderful guy.

I always wondered if Bryan "Brynie" Foy, the producer of *Breakthrough*, hired Joe Breen on that picture (and others) because Joe was the son of the head of the censorship office, and Brynie thought he could get scripts past that office by having Joe working for him. I liked Brynie, but he was a real character. A funny story about Brynie: While making *Breakthrough*, we stayed at the Monterey Hotel, and one Saturday night we were having a big party in Brynie's suite. There were all kinds of girls there—including one who kept cozying up to me. Brynie got me off to one side and he said, "ListenPaulPaul . . ."—that was the way he talked, real quick! He took me into the bedroom and he asked, "Paul, are you gonna shack up with that girl?"

I said, "No, no, Brynie. I'm married, and I'm Catholic, and—"

"Look," Brynie interrupted, "tell her I want to go to bed with her."

"Oh, Brynie, *I* can't do that!" I objected.

"Just tell her I want to go to bed with her," he repeated.

I didn't know how to go about doing that—I was a young guy, and pretty straight-laced. But Brynie was my boss, and I figured I'd better do what he wanted. Finally I got up my nerve and I said to the girl, let's call her Lucy, "Can I talk to you a second?" So I took Lucy in the bedroom, away from the crowd in the living room, and I said, "Mr. Foy likes you very much."

She said, "He *does?*"

"Yes, he does." And then I blurted out, "As a matter of fact, Lucy, he wants to go to bed with you."

To which Lucy said, "Will he *pay* me?"—I didn't know she was a hooker!

"W-w-why, yes, of course!" I stammered. Without quite knowing what I was doing, I'd come through for Brynie, and he was my pal from then on!

David Brian, the star of *Breakthrough*, had actually served with the Coast Guard during World War II. He was so good in *Breakthrough*, I think he should have been nominated for an Academy Award. He was married to an actress named Adrian Booth, who was under contract to Republic; their first wedding anniversary rolled around while we were at Fort Ord, and she came up to spend it with him. My one vivid memory of that is that one day while she was there, he came to work with scratches all over his face, and the makeup man had a hell of a time patching him up. The rumor was that he had had a fight with Adrian, and that she had scratched him with a wire coat hanger! Working with him on *Breakthrough* was the first time I ever met David; the *last* time I saw him was a couple of years ago, not long before he died, at the Motion Picture Home, and Adrian was there with him. So they had a long marriage and they were very much in love—but, as lovers frequently do, they had their little fights once in a while. I've had a couple in *my* time!

John Agar had a drinking problem. Later on in life, he joined AA and solved it, but when we were doing *Breakthrough*, he was still quite a drinker. One night we drove out of town some place, just he and I, to have dinner at a restaurant, and he got pretty well bombed. After dinner, not wanting him to drive in that condition, I said, "John, let *me* drive. I haven't had a chance to drive this car . . ." "No, no, no," he insisted, "I'll drive, I'll drive . . . " I tried so hard to get the keys from him but he wouldn't give 'em to me. I have to tell you, it was a hairy drive back to the hotel, through some very dark country roads, but we made it okay. In recent years, I'd frequently see him at autograph shows and we'd reminisce about the wonderful times we had on *Breakthrough*. He passed away in 2002.

As for Frank Lovejoy, he was in the first scene I did for the picture. It involved Frank and me and a couple other actors, and I had some big speeches in the scene. After we went through the rehearsal, Frank looked at me with a straight face and he said, "Is that the way you're gonna play it?" An icy feeling shot through my entire body and I said to myself, "Oh, my God . . . I've *failed*!" And from that moment on, I never liked Frank. What a terrible thing to say to a young actor. To this *day* I don't know if he was serious or if he was kidding—that's like a standard joke with actors, "Is that the way you're gonna play it?" But he said it so convincingly that I believed he really *meant* it. And for years, while we were both under contract to Warner Brothers, I never liked Frank. Later, things changed. More on Frank in another chapter.

Warner Brothers would develop and send us back the rushes for *Breakthrough*, and on Sundays we'd all go to a movie theater in

At the screening of *Breakthrough* rushes, director Lew Seiler, the movie's technical director, John Agar, Frank Lovejoy, David Brian and I mug for the still cameraman.

Monterey to see them. Lew Seiler would be there, practically the whole cast, the Army technical advisors—there'd be maybe 30, 40 people. One Sunday we were coming out of the theater after watching the rushes, and Brynie Foy's close friend Johnny Roselli, the big-time Mafia guy who ran Las Vegas, was there with him. Johnny came over to me and he said, "What's your name?"—he talked very quiet like that. I said, "Paul Picerni."

"You're a very good actor," he said softly. "*Very* good. Let me tell you one thing: Don't ever change your name." And he walked away. That was my first meeting with Johnny Roselli. There would be others in the future.

I remember one of the older crew guys saying that this was perhaps the best location he'd ever been on in his life—and telling me that it would probably be the best location I'd ever be on in *my* life. Well, he may have been right—I've been on a lot of locations, but I'll always remember the six weeks I spent in Monterey with **Breakthrough**. It wasn't that big a hit but it *was* a great picture, and part of what made it great is the actual war footage they cut into it. Amazing footage of the big D-Day assault, and even some war footage that was captured from the Germans. Not only were these stock shots spectacular, but they were integrated into the movie so beautifully that you can't tell where the war scenes shot by Warner

Brothers stop and the real stuff begins. Steven Spielberg, who received the Oscar for *Saving Private Ryan*, is a great filmmaker but, let's face it, he's obviously too young to have experienced World War II. *Breakthrough* is a much more honest depiction of the D-Day invasion than Spielberg's film. Trust me: If you get the chance, find a copy of *Breakthrough* and run it and you'll see what D-Day was *really* like.

There was an ironic twist in store for me where *Breakthrough* was concerned. While we were up at Fort Ord shooting the movie, the Korean War broke out. And later, when Jack L. Warner, the head of the studio, saw the rushes of my big emotional scene ("*This* is what I'm gonna tell 'em war is all about . . ."), he turned to Brynie Foy and ordered that most of it be cut out of the picture! The scene was a powerful condemnation of war—and now, unexpectedly, our country *was* at war, and Warner felt the scene would be bad for the morale of our fighting men in Korea. Also, he was of course aware that the Army had provided all the tanks and soldiers and equipment, and he wanted to stay on good terms with them. So it had to be eliminated. Joe Breen happened to be at the rushes when Warner saw the scene; according to Joe, Warner's exact words to Brynie were, "Cut that scene out of the picture—*and put that guy under contract.*" So, except for the very beginning of it, the scene that got me a contract at Warners was never in the film!

I first found out about the Warners contract offer from my agent Wilt. I was having dinner at The Captain's Table, a fish place on La Cienega Boulevard, with my wife and several of our friends. Suddenly I heard someone paging me—I was wanted on the phone. It was Wilt—he had called my house and talked to our babysitter, who told him where we had gone for dinner. Wilt said, "Warner Brothers wants to put you under contract."

I couldn't believe my ears. "No kidding?!" I stammered.

"No kidding," Wilt said. "And $250 a week"—$250 a week was a great deal of money in 1950. "Fan-*tas*-tic!" I told him. Then I ecstatically hurried back to the table to tell Marie and our friends the good news, and everybody was thrilled. That was how I got the news about being put under contract at Warner Brothers. Along with the time I spent on *The Untouchables*, my years at Warners would be the happiest and most productive of my career.

7
GIVE THE
STAR HIS DUE

Warner Brothers was the studio with the grand history of players like Jimmy Cagney and Edward G. Robinson, Bette Davis, Errol Flynn and Olivia de Havilland, Bogart and Bacall—and now, in 1950, a 27-year-old actor named Paul Picerni with a seven-year contract that began at $250 a week, increasing to $1500 a week in the final year.

Early on, Warners wanted me to legally change my name to Paul Pickford, and the publicity department guys even got Mary Pickford to agree to go to the courthouse with me when I made the

An early Warners publicity photo.

name change. The publicity gimmick was going to be that Mary Pickford would say that she was willing to pass her great theatrical name down to me, because I was such a promising young new-comer. But I remembered what Johnny Roselli said to me outside the Monterey movie theater during the production of **Breakthrough** ("Never change your name"), and the way he said it—so convincingly. With that in mind, I told the publicity guys, "No, I don't want to change my name," and I didn't.

What better way to get my feet wet at Warners than with a submarine picture: **Operation Pacific** with John Wayne, Ward Bond, Patricia Neal and another young actor who would become a good friend, Phil Carey. **Operation Pacific** provided this beginning actor with a lesson in how you have to give the star his due. A World War II romance-action drama, it starred Wayne as Commander Duke Gifford, executive officer on a Navy sub which (as the picture opens) stops at a Japanese-held island to rescue a number of nuns and children. As the submarine sails safely away from the island and the evacuees are brought down into the galley, there is some discussion as to how to feed a newborn, four or five months old. This was the point in the script at which my character, Jonesy, who ran the sub's torpedo room, said, "I got an idea . . . " Jonesy took a rubber glove, filled it with milk, cut a small hole in one of the fingers, held it to the baby's mouth—and the baby sucked on the finger. "What a great touch," I thought when I first read it. "Jonesy" had a *couple* of good scenes in the picture, but *that* one, I felt, was just great. But on the morning of the day that scene was going to be shot, there were "blue pages" (rewritten script pages) waiting for us on the set, and all of a sudden it is not Jonesy who feeds the baby, but Duke Gifford (Wayne).

A few days later, there was a mid-ocean scene in which a young sailor in a rubber raft rows away from the sub in an attempt to rescue a pilot (Phil Carey) who is in the water after his plane has been shot down. Suddenly the raft is riddled with Japanese machine-gun bullets and starts to sink—and Jonesy, watching from the deck of the sub, remembers that the sailor can't swim. Jonesy dives off the sub and swims out and rescues his buddy. Another wonderful scene for me. Well, *again*, the blue pages come through and it is not Jonesy but Duke who dives over the side and rescues the sailor. (Of course, a commander should never leave his vessel for one man, but that's Hollywood moviemaking. The hero has got to be the hero.)

Naturally, I was disappointed on both occasions, *but*—the young actor has to accept these situations. John Wayne had been a star for over 20 years at this point and here *I* was, making my first movie as a contract player. *You must give the star his due.* And I certainly did not dislike John Wayne because of what happened—in fact, I loved Wayne and thought he was a great star. But I must admit that I did get a little kick out of what happened the day of the "raft rescue." We were shooting the scene on Stage 22 at Warners, which has since burned down. There was a big swimming pool in there (that was our "ocean") and a replica of the upper part of the submarine, and George Waggner, the director, was out on the pool in a raft with the camera, facing the submarine. When Waggner called "Action!," Wayne swung down from the top deck of the sub, landed on the lower deck, did a beautiful dive into the pool, came back up to the surface and started stroking toward the raft and the camera. All of a sudden, Waggner called, "Cut!" Wayne, his head sticking up out of the water, must have known he'd done the scene perfectly because he sounded genuinely perplexed when he asked, "Why did you cut, George?" And Waggner said, "Duke, when you hit the water, your beaver flew off!" John didn't have a full toupee at the time, just two little "wings" on the sides—and he had lost them in the dive! It was a little like retribution for me, a little like, "You *see*, Duke? You should've let *me* do it!"

Although I missed out on two good scenes, I enjoyed the picture, I liked working with Wayne and I am sorry that I never had the opportunity to act with him again. He was a great, wonderful loudmouth, a Republican who had opinions and who let his opinions be known to everybody on the set. He and Ward Bond, who played the commander of the sub, were inseparable. They started out together as football players at USC and they were friends all throughout their careers. One story I've never forgotten: At one point in his life, Bond was in an automobile accident and the doctors were thinking of amputating his leg. Wayne went to the hospital and wouldn't let them do it. At Wayne's insistence, the doctors sewed that badly mangled leg back together and, against all odds, they *were* able to save it. Bond had to live the whole rest of his life with a limp, but thanks to John Wayne, he had his leg.

Two nice memories of **Operation Pacific**: One, my first scene in the movie. The submarine crewmen are on the beach of the little island rescuing the nuns and children, and I come out of the jungle carrying a dead Jap soldier on my back. As I drop the body on the beach, John Wayne says to me, "I told you not to get in any *trouble*, Jonesy." And *my* line in response is, "It was no trouble at *all*,

Commander!" My "big moment" in the picture.

The other fond memory: Meeting and working for the first time with Phil Carey, who played Ward Bond's pilot-brother (and Wayne's rival for the affections of Navy nurse Patricia Neal). He also was a new contractee at Warners and this was his very first picture. Phil was a couple years younger than me, fresh out of Miami University, a big, good-looking guy who towered over most of the other people on a set. As a matter of fact, Phil was a quarter of an inch taller than John Wayne, and so when Wayne had scenes with Phil, Wayne would wear lifts in his shoes so that *he* would be taller! Phil was 23, 24 years old at the time, and really green—he had no acting background at all.

Phil and his lovely wife, Maureen, and my wife, Marie, and I were all very close; Phil was the godfather of my second son, Charles Philip. He and I would see each other constantly and we did a lot together—we'd go to Vegas together, played a great deal of golf and so on. We were very competitive on the golf course, the same way Telly Savalas and I were years later. (One day Telly got mad enough to throw a golf ball at me. So I threw my putter at *him*!) When I'd play golf with Phil, we'd fight and argue. But Phil was very good to me. After we left Warners, he went over to Columbia and became a leading man in Westerns and other B pictures, and every time he did a film over there, he would try to get me into it. Phil was very difficult at times, yelling at assistant directors and so on, and a lot of people didn't care for him. But I thought he was a good guy.

Marie and me with our close friends, Philip and Maureen Carey, at a Warners premiere.

One day after playing golf with Phil and Freddie Karger, a well-known composer-musician from Columbia Studios, the three of us were sitting at a table in the clubhouse having drinks. Phil and Freddie were womanizers, the both of 'em. I think Phil had affairs with every one of his leading ladies, and that list included gorgeous women like Anita Ekberg, Joan Crawford, Donna Reed and so on. I said, "You two guys have had a lot of women in your time. I tell you what, let's keep score. We'll throw out names of actresses. If it's a star and you've had her, you get five points; if it's a supporting actress, you get three points; if it's a starlet, you get two points." So the names start flying: "Anita Ekberg?," "Yep," "Okay, five points," and so on and so forth. Finally, Phil threw out the name Jane Wyman, a "five-pointer"—and Freddie flared up: "You son of a bitch! *When*?! When we were *married*, or after we divorced?!" I laughed for two days!

Between pictures at Warners, the studio had me doing a little of everything. Contract players usually worked 40 weeks, and then the other 12 weeks they're on layoff. I *never* was off, in my entire time at Warners. They always had me in the looping room doing voices— Jack Warner called me "The Man of a Thousand Voices"—or on the test stage appearing in screen tests. For various pictures, I was in the screen tests of Jayne Mansfield and Mari Aldon and Mari Blanchard and Vera Miles—a *lot* of actresses. I never did play a love scene in a movie, only in the tests! Never once was I out of work. I worked a lot in screen tests for Michael Curtiz, the great director of *Captain Blood, The Adventures of Robin Hood, The Charge of the Light Brigade, Casablanca* and so many other wonderful pictures of the 1930s and '40s. In these screen tests, I would read one part and the actor or actress who was actually "up" for the picture would read the other. I saw Mike Curtiz on the lot frequently, and always he would say, in that thick Hungarian accent, "Hey, Picerni, my favorite test maker! Picerni, I have great part in my next picture for you, great part. I make you big star!" I never *did* get a great part from him, but I did all his tests while I was at Warners.

One of the movies that Curtiz directed at Warners during my early days there was *Jim Thorpe–All-American*, a biography of the American Indian Olympic medal winner. Burt Lancaster, a former circus acrobat, now one of Hollywood's biggest stars, played Thorpe;

also in the cast was Charles Bickford as "Pop" Warner, Thorpe's coach.

Charles Bickford was like steel and the characters he played were like steel, and even Mike Curtiz, who was a great director but also a bully, knew enough not to get on the bad side of Charlie Bickford. During the shooting of one very simple scene, Bickford came through a door and Curtiz immediately said, "Cut, cut!" Bickford looked at him and, in his usual gruff way, asked, "What the hell was wrong?" Curtiz said, "Something wrong with the timing, Charlie, when you come through the door."

With fire in his eye, Bickford snarled, "Are you trying to tell *me* about timing?"—and Curtiz immediately backed down, stammering out, "No, no, not *you*, Charlie sweetheart! Who the hell is the prop man on the door?? *Fix the door!*" Curtiz would bully 90 percent of the actors, but he knew he couldn't intimidate Bickford. An actor like Bickford wouldn't take any*thing* from any*body*.

But this was nothing compared to the blow-up that Mike had with Burt Lancaster. It was a scene of Jim Thorpe (Burt) at a table in a hotel room, drunk and disheveled. Curtiz had a close-up on Burt as he poured a shot of whiskey, lifted the glass to his lips, took a sip and set the shot glass down. "Good, Burt, sweetheart—very good!" Curtiz called out. "Cut, print."

"Mike, if you don't mind, I'd like to do it again," Burt said.

"No need to do it again, Burt. I see vhat you do, the dribble of the vhiskey come down your chin a little bit. It was very real, I like it, I like it."

Burt stayed in place, looking up at Curtiz. "If you don't *mind*," he repeated, "I'd like to do it again."

"Burt! There's no *need* to do it again. I see vhat you do, eez perfect. Let's move to the next shot."

There was no mistaking the impatience in Burt's voice when he said a third time, "If you don't *mind*, I'd *like* to do it *again* . . . !"

By now, Curtiz was fuming. "Who the hell you think you are, tell me vhat to print and not to print!" he raged. "You lousy circus acrobat turned dramatic actor, who the hell you think you are?!"

Burt turned white. He took the table, flipped it up in the air, the glass and bottle went flying. "You Hungarian cocksucker," he hollered, "I'll *kill* you!"—and with that, he lunged for Curtiz!

Curtiz went running for the exit and Burt was right on his tail when Russ Saunders, the assistant director, and one of the grips grabbed Burt, Russ yelling, "Burt, calm down, calm down!" Burt was like a powerhouse, but they managed to get him into his portable dressing room. And once Burt was inside, you could see the dressing room moving from side to side as Burt smashed his fists against the wall and tossed chairs around. At this point I was near Curtiz by the soundstage door, and I heard him say softly, ". . . Vhat the hell I say to him that make him so mad vith me??"

I wasn't in *Jim Thorpe*, I was just visiting the sets . . . but later, through a fluke, I *did* end up with a small part. A short time after the picture wrapped, there happened to be a big banquet in Oklahoma where, with the state governor in attendance, Jim Thorpe was named the outstanding athlete of the first half of the twentieth century; "Pop" Warner was there, and he made a speech. As a result, Warners decided to put *Jim Thorpe* back in production and add a recreation of this banquet scene to the beginning of the picture. They flew the governor of Oklahoma and his wife out to Hollywood and they gave me the part of the master of ceremonies at this formal affair—all I had to do was introduce "Pop" Warner (Bickford) and the governor to the audience.

There were maybe 100, 150 dress extras on the set, all in tuxedos and gowns, when Curtiz announced, "Ladies and gentlemen, I vant you to meet Governor So-and-So and Mrs. So-and-So of Oklahoma. They come here today to be in this film. Governor," he added, kidding around, "I going to make you a big star!" Curtiz made introductions all around, "Governor, this is Charles Bickford, this is our cameraman," so on and so forth, and the governor was very impressed. He was having just a delightful time—he was in Hollywood, he was going to be in the film, his wife was there and everything was beautiful.

Finally it comes time to shoot the scene. I introduce "Pop" Warner (Bickford), he gets up and, in his inimitable style, he says his piece: "Ladies and gentlemen, I coached this young man, one of the most outstanding athletes I've met in my entire career. Coming from the state of *Oklahomer*, he was brilliant . . ." Charlie goes on to finish the speech, and he says "Oklahomer" three or four times; being from Massachusetts, that was how he pronounced it. When he finishes, Curtiz says, "Cut! Print! Charlie, that was magnificent. Beau-ti-ful!"

Mike Curtiz always had a dialogue director on the set—Curtiz spoke broken English, so he *needed* a dialogue director to check all the dialogue. Let's call him Stan. Stan takes Curtiz aside and he says, "Mr. Curtiz, he said Oklahomer."

"There's something *wrong* with that?"

"It's not right," Stan tells him. "He should say Oklaho*ma*."

So Curtiz calls out, "One minute—don't move, everybody. We're going to shoot it one more time, Charlie."

"What the hell was *wrong*?" Bickford says in that ominous way of his. The governor's ears perk up at this—this is the first time there's any little friction on the set.

Curtiz, nervous now, says to Stan, "*You* go tell him." So Stan, script in hand, goes up on the dais, up to the head table, and he says, "Mr. Bickford, you said Oklahomer instead of Oklahoma."

Bickford snaps, "What the hell is wrong with Oklahomer? Oklahomer's all right." He shoots a look at the governor and says demandingly, "Is Oklahomer all right, governor? *Is it all right for me to say Oklahomer?!*" And the governor, who by now is shaking in his boots, says, "Oh, y-y-yeah, yeah—Oklahomer is fine!"

"Okay! Print! Print!" Curtiz yells. "The governor says it's fine!"

Another memory of Burt Lancaster. We had a great gymnasium at Warner Brothers, and running the place was Mushy Callahan, a great former boxing champion. There were only five or six people who used the gym—me, Burt Lancaster, Burt's friend Nick Cravat, Joe Breen and a few others. This gymnasium had a three-wall handball court—that was the big competition—and the best player on the lot was Burt Lancaster.

One day, Burt and Nick were playing handball, and Mushy Callahan and I were sitting there watching the game because we knew they were both great competitors. Nick *loved* to beat Burt. Burt was six-two and a real athlete, Nick was five-three and *also* a tremendous athlete. But Burt was a *better* one. The two of them had known each other for years: They grew up together on the streets of Harlem and both had an interest in stunt gymnastics. They started in a schoolyard, swinging on bars and so on, and later formed a circus act ("Lang and Cravat") and began touring with circuses and

In real life he was Nick Cuccio; in Burt Lancaster movies like *The Flame and the Arrow* and *The Crimson Pirate* he was Nick Cravat. To my kids, he was "Uncle Nick."

appearing in vaudeville and nightclubs. By this time, the early 1950s, of course, Burt had turned actor and come out to Hollywood and become a top star, and his little friend Nick was playing supporting parts in Burt's movies. Burt and Nick loved each other, but there was that tremendous competitiveness and one-upsmanship.

Nick took off to a tremendous lead in the handball game. The winning game point was 21, and Nick was leading 15-2. He was saying, "I thought you said you were a good handball player!" and things like that, mocking Burt—and every time Burt started to turn his back, Nick grabbed his balls with two hands and went, "Yeeeeah!" Of course, Burt was catching this out of the corner of his eye. Burt was deadly serious and Nick was laughing because he had such a lead.

Pretty soon, however, the game was 15-7. And then it was 15-8. And then 17-14. Nick was still in the lead, but Burt was catching up fast and it was getting to be desperation time. Finally it was 19-18 favor of Nick . . . and then 19-19 . . . and then it was 20 Burt, 19 Nick. And then it was 21 Burt—game over. At which point Burt turned around, he grabbed his balls with two hands, looked at Nick and went, "*Yeeeeeeeeah!*" Nick, in a fury, took his fist and threw it right into the wall—punched the plaster wall, driving his fist right through it! He was *that* upset that he had the game in the bag but then lost to Burt. Burt just calmly laughed with his wonderful laugh and walked into the shower, but Nick was in a fury for the next five minutes. Mushy yelled at him, "What the hell are you doing, wrecking my gym? You crazy bastard!" and Nick hollered back, "Get *away* from me, you son of a bitch! Get away from me or I'll *kill* you!" That was the scene, and I'll never forget it!

Nick Cravat lived in a house that he'd built himself on a grassy hill near the eleventh hole of the Woodland Hills Country Club golf course. One day Burt and I were sitting on the hill, watching Nick playing around with Burt's two boys, Jimmy and Billy. They were rolling down the hill, laughing and having a good time. (Nick was great with kids. *My* kids also loved "Uncle Nick.") As Burt and I sat watching and talking, he said to me, "You know, Paul, you'll never be a big star."

I was crushed. Here I was, newly under contract to Warners, filled with anticipation, doing picture after picture. "Why do you say that, Burt?" I asked.

"You're too *friendly* with everybody. On the set, you say hello to this guy and that guy. You talk to *every*body. *I* never say hello to *any*body, unless they say hello to me first." And that *was* the way Burt behaved on the lot: He'd walk down the street between soundstages looking straight ahead. Only if somebody said, "Hello, Burt!" would he respond—and then only with a curt "Hello." He maintained an air of mystery. I guess he was right, because I never did become a big star. But I sure have had a lot of friends through the years, and I still do. To each his own. Be yourself.

Incidentally, Burt's son Billy, who had a bad leg as a result of polio, became a writer; his credits included the **Bad News Bears** movies. And I remember once when Marie and I were up at Burt's house sitting around the kitchen table, talking, when a nine-year-old Jimmy walked in, opened the refrigerator door, looked for a moment, then turned to us and said, "Goddamn adults drank all the ginger ale!" Burt and Norma, his wife, never said a word. I think Jimmy became a theatrical agent in later life. Strange kid!

There was another location trip, one of the most unusual of my career, for my next picture: Steve Cochran, David Brian, Phil Carey and I found ourselves **Inside the Walls of Folsom Prison**. Written and directed by Crane Wilbur and produced by "my pal" from **Breakthrough**, Bryan Foy, this was a tough film about the brutal conditions at that state prison prior to the reforms that had been

As a convict in *Inside the Walls of Folsom Prison*, which was actually shot inside that Sacramento facility.

enacted just seven years earlier. In addition to the regular cast, Brynie planned to use as many real-life Folsom prisoners as he could in the movie, which he did, "paying" them with packs of cigarettes or with cartons of cigarettes, depending on how much they had to do.

Folsom Prison was exactly the kind of hard-hitting, fast-moving picture Brynie made best. Decades earlier, when Brynie was a child, he was a member of "Eddie Foy and the Seven Little Foys," the famous vaudeville family—Brynie was one of Eddie's children, one of the Seven Little Foys. Talking about his movies, Brynie once said to me, "I always try to cut my pictures real fast. I figure if you cut 'em fast, the audience won't notice any mistakes." And, he went on, he learned to think that way from dancing in his father's burlesque act. "I was a lousy dancer," he told me, "so my father said, 'Move your feet real quick, nobody'll notice you can't dance!'" Well, Brynie kept that "life lesson" in mind years later when he became a B-movie producer: Cut 'em fast and make 'em move, so the audience won't see any flaws in 'em!

We went up to Sacramento, where (per the title) we were going to shoot the entire picture inside the walls of Folsom, a top security-risk prison for hardened criminals. Ted de Corsia played the sadistic warden who metes out severe punishments to convicts for the slightest infractions. In an early scene, several of the men (including my character, Jeff Riordan) attempt a jailbreak, but it fails. In an effort to force some information out of me, de Corsia beats me with his fists and breaks my back.

The day we got to the prison, director Crane Wilbur announced that he wanted everybody to get a short haircut and he sent us to the prison barbershop where Joe the barber, a prisoner himself, proceeded to cut our hair the same way he did all his fellow cons. We soon discovered that Joe, an Italian guy, was in for life—for murder. Joe had cut somebody's throat in a barberchair, back home some place, over some argument, and he was sentenced to life in prison. Well, *we* found him to be a nice, sweet guy!

This situation with Joe gave us an idea. Steve Cochran had an actor friend coming up there to be in the picture, a real funny Southerner named Monty Pittman (later a writer-director). Monty was going to be arriving in a few days to play a small part as one of the prisoners, and of course he was going to have to have *his* hair cut by Joe before he could start in the picture. Steve said, "Let's build up and embellish this story about Joe." We let Joe in on the gag, naturally: We told Joe that we were going to warn Monty, "Don't let Joe use the razor on you, he goes berserk every once in a while. He's in here for killing a guy in a barber chair."

In the meantime, the shooting of the picture began. The first thing in the morning, of course, was makeup. I believe there were three makeup men, and if I'm remembering right, Emile LaVigne and Bill Phillips were two of them. One day Emile said to me, "You know, every day I notice my hair cream is gone. My Vaseline hair cream, and other stuff like that. I put a full tube up there and by the next day it's disappeared." Of course, some of the prisoners who were working in the picture were free to walk around there while we were getting made up, and we figured they had to be the culprits, but still . . . why? Well, it all became clear later on: We discovered that they were stealing Emile's Vaseline, to use for sexual purposes! *That* was what was goin' on!

In one scene, a large number of the actual convicts were all supposed to run across to the back wall of the prison yard as guards fired their rifles in their direction. This one oldtimer got to the middle of the yard, grabbed his leg like he was wounded, took out a white handkerchief and waved it toward the camera! Crane

Wilbur yelled, "Cut, cut! What the hell are you doing?" Well, what he was doing was adding to his part—he thought he'd get an extra carton of cigarettes!

After a few days, Monty Pittman arrived, and our plan went into operation: We all began warning him about Joe the barber. Me, Steve Cochran, Ted de Corsia, Phil Carey, all of us. "Whatever you do, don't let Joe cut your sideburns with the razor. He'll go crazy"— and, believe me, we got Monty built to a high crescendo of fear, worried about Joe pulling out the razor. When Monty went in for his haircut, a whole gang of us stood outside the barbershop, peeking in through the door, watching this whole situation. (Monty didn't know we were there.) It was just the two of them in the barber shop, Joe clipping Monty's hair. Finally it got to the point where Joe was just about done . . . and he started eyeing Monty's sideburns. And he got out the straight razor. And he took out the strap, and he started whacking the straight razor on the strap, sharpening it even more. When he put the razor up to the side of Monty's face, Monty let out a scream, leapt out of the chair and ran out of the room! We just roared with laughter.

Folsom Prison shot in the fall of 1950. Around Christmas, Warners started shooting *Fort Worth*, my first Western there, and the first of three Randolph Scott Westerns in which I would appear. Randy Scott was a true movie star. Standing six-two or six–three, broad shoulders, a waist that was maybe 32 inches, he was an Adonis, an absolutely "beautiful" man. And a sweetheart of a guy, I soon learned. It's funny, the way certain things linger in your memory: We used to have photographers come on the various sets and do publicity shots for magazines or newspapers, and of course this happened on all the Scott Westerns I was in. Randolph said to me one day, "Paul, I'll give you a little tip. Whenever you get in a group shot with other actors, always stand on the right side. Let everyone else stand to your left."

"Okay," I said—then, thinking about it a little more, I had to ask, "But why is that, Randolph?"

"Well," he smiled, "when the picture is published, they always name the actors left-to-right . . . Randolph Scott, Paul Picerni and so on. Stand on the right and you'll always get top billing!" Well, I never forgot that little piece of good advice from Randy. Like most

In *Riding Shotgun*, one of the Westerns I did with the wonderful Randolph Scott (right).

of the oldtimers (John Wayne, Cagney and so on), Randy was one of a kind. Today, guys become stars in 20 minutes and then disappear, but Randy was the *epitome* of a movie star. And a great guy to work with.

It was like Old Home Week on the set of my next picture, *I Was a Communist for the FBI* with Brynie Foy producing, a script by Crane Wilbur, and Frank Lovejoy and Phil Carey starring. The director this time was Gordon Douglas, a wonderful guy I loved working with. Gordon would later direct me in one of my favorite pictures, *Mara Maru* with Errol Flynn.

I Was a Communist was a true story about Matt Cvetic, a rabid Communist Party member in the Pittsburgh area for many years. Frank Lovejoy played Cvetic and I played his younger brother Joe, who, like the rest of the family, has contempt for him because of his loyalty to the Commies. Of course, none of us knows that he is

With Frank Lovejoy in *I Was a Communist for the FBI*.

actually an undercover FBI operator who in the end clears his name of the Red taint and puts the finger on his Commie "comrades" in Congressional testimony. Before the rest of the family learns the truth, though, there are some good, powerful scenes, including one where, at the funeral of our mother, I punch him out, thinking that he's a Communist. It was a good film and a true story, and Lovejoy was good in it.

During the shooting of *I Was a Communist*, my close friend Father Menager, from my Loyola University days, visited me on the set. It turned out that Gordon Douglas' wife was dying of cancer, so Father Menager ended up talking with Gordon about it, and the two of them soon became real close. In fact, Father Menager even went to Gordon's house several times and talked to the wife, and became close to the wife as well. One day several years later, after Gordon's wife did eventually pass away, I was in the car with Marie, driving up Mandeville Canyon on our way to visit our actor friend Tony Caruso. All of a sudden, I noticed that we were about to pass Gordon's house, so I said, "Look, here's Gordon Douglas' house. Let me say hello." I parked in the circular driveway and I went up the long walk to the house and knocked at the door, and after a few seconds, Gordon opened the door—wearing a yarmulke. He was getting married, right at that very moment, in a Jewish ceremony!

I felt so dumb. Because of his close relationship to Father Menager, the way that Gordon *and* his wife turned to Father Menager, I had presumed that Gordon was a Catholic. (Looking back, I guess it was the first wife, the wife who had died, who was the Catholic.) I said, "Gordon, I'm sorry. I was driving through the area, and I thought I'd stop and say hello." Gordon was very nice, of course, and told me I was welcome to stay for the ceremony, but I didn't want to barge in on the man's wedding. And also, I just felt a little embarrassed, because the man and I had been such very good friends all through the years with me thinking the whole time that he was a Catholic. I felt so silly, and that made it a very strange meeting!

I Was a Communist started shooting on January 8, 1951, my first picture of the New Year. And on January 22, just two weeks later, my daughter Gemma was born. Like all her sisters, Gemma graduated from Louisville High School, but then she went to a vocational school and became a medical assistant. For the last 14 years she has worked for a Dr. Houston in Culver City, right across the street from the hospital where she was born. His patients all love her because of her warm, generous, helpful personality. She married late in life: Four years ago, on a blind date, she met Michael Saldana, an ex-Marine who served in Vietnam and who now works for the Veteran's Administration. They seemed to be made for each other. They had a beautiful wedding. Untouchables Bob Stack, Nick Georgiade and Abel Fernandez and their wives came, as did other actor-friends like Jimmy Darren, Tony Caruso and Johnny Seven. Gemma and Michael recently bought a beautiful new home in Crystalaire, right on a golf course. With "her babies" (her two little dogs), they are ideally happy.

8
THE LEARNING
PROCESS

My Warner Brothers contract called for me to be there 40 weeks out of 52, but except for weekends and holidays I was there every single day of the year. It's a way of learning, maybe the *best* way: watching and studying. When I wasn't working in a film, doing looping or assisting on tests, I would visit the different sets and watch the Warners stars work under the direction of Mike Curtiz, "Lucky" Humberstone, "Wild Bill" Wellman—even John Ford, when *he* was over there. I would learn by observing them.

This was my routine when I wasn't in a picture: I would go to the lot every day, work out in the gym, have lunch in the Green Room and then visit the different sets and watch Crawford and Cagney and Bogart and Bette Davis and John Garfield and Virginia Mayo and Doris Day and Gordon MacRae and Randy Scott—they were all on the lot. I met Frank Sinatra one day, when he was introduced to me by Gordon Douglas. Even Ronald Reagan I met—I did a sketch with Reagan once, in a stage show that Jack Warner had us put on at the studio for Henry Cabot Lodge, Jr., the senator from Massachusetts. Anyway, that was my procedure every day I wasn't working—to go to the lot and do those things as part of my personal learning process.

I was back in uniform for my next two Warners films, *Force of Arms* with William Holden, an updated (World War II) version of Ernest Hemingway's WWI romance *A Farewell to Arms*, set in Italy, and *The Tanks Are Coming* with Steve Cochran, a sequel of sorts to my first film at Warners, *Breakthrough*.

On *Force of Arms*, I worked again with Mike Curtiz, whose great gifts as a director compensated somewhat for what he lacked in the way of tact and sensitivity in dealing with his players. (In the '40s and '50s, everyone on the lot feared the directors—everyone including the producers, the stars and even the studio heads. Especially an Academy Award winner like Mike Curtiz.) There are so many stories about Mike. On the first day of shooting, we were all on location, sitting amidst the Chatsworth rocks in a group of director's chairs in a half-circle facing Mike, having an informal discussion. Mike was talking to each actor, buttering them up: "Oh, Bill, you're going to be vonderful in this part," "Nancy Olson, how terrific to have you vorking vith us in this picture," "Oh, Dick Vesson, my favorite!," so forth and so on, talking to everybody. Finally he came to Frank Lovejoy, and he said, "Frank, you are going to be marvelous in the part of Major Bradford."

Then, after a pause, he added, "You know, my first choice for this part was Leslie Howard. But he is dead, so I take *you*!" That was a typical Curtiz line!

Mike always had that heavy Hungarian accent to contend with. I was told that, one time when he was directing a fencing sequence in an Errol Flynn picture, his direction to Errol was, "I want you to lungch [lunge] at him. Now lungch. Lungch. Lungch! *Lungch*! *LUNGch*!" And all of a sudden, all the extras left the set—they thought he was saying "Lunch"!

Force of Arms with William Holden and Ron Hagerthy.

But more memorable are the many foot-in-the-mouth stories people tell about Curtiz. He was the director of *The Will Rogers Story*, a movie where I had tested for the part of famed round-the-world pilot Wiley Post but didn't get it. I used to visit the set as they were shooting. Mike was on a high parallel platform with the camera, preparing to photograph the audience in an arena where Rogers (played by his own real-life son, Will Rogers, Jr.) was performing, doing lariat tricks and working with a horse and so on. In the days when this story took place, the audiences were segregated—the whites sat in one section and the blacks in another. From up on the platform, Mike spoke into a microphone, instructions to the crowd, because they were not quite in position. "All right," he announced, "I vont all you niggers to move over *there . . .*"

The assistant director, Russ Saunders, was instantly scrambling up the platform, babbling under his breath, "Mike, Mike! What are you doing, what are you *saying*?! We don't call these people niggers!"

Mike reacted with surprise. "Oh? What do you say?"

Russ explained, "We call them *colored people*"—at that time, that was the term. "You better apologize."

Mike got back on the microphone. "Ladies and gentlemen, please forgive me vhat I just say because I don't speak English too good, and I mean no offense. I apologize for vhat I say. Okay? Please forgive me, *please,* ladies and gentlemen, please forgive me."

Having cleared the air, he went right back to work. "All right, let's get on vith the shot," he announced. "All you colored niggers, move over there!" That was typical of Mike Curtiz.

Mike was also a bit of a phony. I was assisting in the tests for a Curtiz picture called *Trouble Along the Way*, with John Wayne as a football coach at a small Catholic school. In the tests, I was playing Wayne's part and, over my shoulder, they would film the actor who was under consideration. Mike was considering a lot of people for various parts—the leading lady, a priest, assistant coaches and so on. This was on a Friday, and we'd been going all day long. There was this wonderful old actor there—I can't remember his name, but he was along the lines of a Lewis Stone, so let's call him Lewis Stone even though it wasn't. He was in wardrobe (a priest's cassock and collar) and full makeup, sitting there in a chair all day, perspiring, waiting to be tested. It got to be about six or seven o'clock in the evening and finally Mike went over to this old actor and he said, "Mr. Stone, I'm sorry, but vee don't haff the time to make your test today. But you come back Monday, vee make your test on Monday." And Mr. Stone said, "Don't worry, Mr. Curtiz, I don't mind at all, it was very interesting sitting here, watching you work. Thank you very much, and I'll see you Monday." Mike smiled: "Thank you *so* much, sveetheart. You are so vonderful to be so nice. Thank you . . . good night, good night . . ."

Mr. Stone left. And as soon as he did, Russ Saunders came up to Mike and said, "Mike—we're not making any tests on Monday. We're scouting *locations* on Monday." Mike scoffed, "I know dat, but *he* don't know dat. I don't like him anyhow, he's not right for the part!" Again, *that* was Mike Curtiz!

On **Force of Arms**, as on **Breakthrough**, the Army provided actual combat film but, needless to say, we also had to stage some battle scenes of our own. We were shooting on location in (I believe) Chatsworth, and it was a scene where Bill Holden and all his patrol, myself included, were in a trench. The cameras, five or six of them, were behind us, and we were about to be charged by a battalion of extras playing German soldiers. They'd charge at us, maybe 150 German soldiers, firing their guns, and we'd be in the trench firing back and throwing hand grenades—that was going to be the shot. It took quite a while to set it up, because it involved pots with bombs in 'em and a lot of firepower. We had several rehearsals without the explosions and everything worked fine. The shot was supposed to end with all the German soldiers killed off.

Curtiz said, "All right, roll 'em," they rolled the cameras and Curtiz yelled out, "Action!" The German soldiers started charging our platoon, Bill Holden and I and the rest of the guys blazed away and the Germans were dropping dead in front of us. There were smoke pots and hand grenades going off, stuntmen were doing falls and it was just spectacular. Finally there was only one German left, standing alone, frantically jerking the bolt on his rifle back and forth. It was such a weird sight: Everybody else was dead, the explosions had stopped going off, smoke was still rising from all the smoke pots, silence was starting to settle, and this one extra continued to just stand there, pulling the bolt on his gun! The end of the shot was ruined. Mike yelled, "Cut! Cut!," and with a tear in his voice he yelled, "Vhat the hell you are *doing*?" The extra, still standing there in the midst of all these "dead" soldiers, said, "Mr. Curtiz—my gun jammed!" His voice quivering, Mike said, "Vell, vhen your gun jam . . . vhy don't you haff the sense to *die* vhen your gun jam?!"

I learned a valuable lesson from Mike. One day on **Force of Arms**, he said to Dick Wesson and me, "In this picture, there is no comedy. Vherever you feel you can put some comedy, you write it in and give it to me and vee put it in the picture." So Dick and I wrote several little comedy sequences, including one at an Italian bar. Bill Holden walked into the bar, and as he crossed the room, the camera picked up Dick and me on the dance floor, kidding around by dancing with *each other*. After watching some Italian girls dance, Dick started imitating them, acting like a girl and saying to me stuff like, "Oh, nice soldato, you gonna give-a me cioccolata? You gonna give-a me seelk stockings? You gonna give-a me bubbla gum?" I laughed at Dick's line, the way he delivered it, how funny he was. Well, as soon as I laughed, Mike hollered, "*Cut*! Vhat the hell you laughing for, you stupid bum actor?"

A "stupid bum actor" (me!), dancing with Dick Wesson, is about to get a lesson in screen acting from *Force of Arms* director Michael Curtiz.

I said, "Mike, I thought it was in character, I thought Dick was very funny—"

Mike said, "Don't *you* laugh. Let *audience* laugh." And he was right: In a scene like that, you don't laugh at your own jokes because it spoils the scene. That's what made Mike a great director, the fact that he would pick up stuff like that.

Another favorite memory of **Force of Arms** is of William Holden, a sweetheart of a guy. I loved working with Bill Holden.

He had a wonderful love scene in a Jeep, where he was talking to the WAC (Nancy Olson) from whom he was about to be separated. For this tender and very touching moment, Mike was shooting a close-up on Bill. The scene was so beautifully written, and Bill did it so well, that by the end of the close-up, Mike was crying.

"Cut!" Mike called out, the tears rolling down his cheeks. "Oh, Holdy, sweetheart," he said to Bill, "you are so wonderful, that was so beautiful. Here, take this $20"—and he tried to press a 20 into Bill's hand. It was a custom in Hungary that when an actor did a scene especially well, the director would give him a little bonus, some extra money. Bill said, "No, no, Mike, don't be silly," but Mike persisted: "I *want* you to take this $20." The tears still on his face, Mike kept at it: "Please, take $20 from me, Billy!," and Bill said, "*No!* Come *on*, Mike, will ya?"

And at that point—as usual—Mike's temper got the better of him again. "You Pasadena bum!" he yelled at Bill. (Mike knew that Bill had gone to school at the Pasadena Playhouse.) "Humphrey Bogart take money from me, Bette Davis take money from me. How come *you*, you lousy Pasadena bum, don't take money from me??"

Bill Holden liked to drink, I later learned. (I didn't know this when I worked with him, because he never drank on the set.) In those days, every one of the studio's pictures would premiere at the Warner Brothers Theater on Hollywood Boulevard. And, just like *in* the movies, the sidewalks would be teeming with excited movie fans as the stars stepped out of their limousines to be interviewed by Gordon MacRae, or who*ever* the emcee of the night was. One night my car was in the procession, slowly getting nearer and nearer to the theater, and as I came up, I happened to look over to my right and there on the busy sidewalk, leaning up against a pole, was Bill Holden. He was surrounded by movie fans, but they didn't know who he was—he just looked like one more fan, standing there. And he was bombed! I called out, "Bill!," but he put his finger up to his lips—"Shhh! *Shhhhhh!*" I guess he'd just come out of some local bar and he was "drinking in" what it was like to be a fan, and he didn't want the people around him to know that it was William Holden standing there. It was a funny sight, Bill standing there in the crowd like that, with this movie-crazy mob all around him, totally unaware that he was there!

Someone at Warners must have thought I looked good in fatigues because my next picture was yet another WWII picture, *The Tanks Are Coming*, which was a kind of follow-up to *Breakthrough*. It

With my crew in *The Tanks Are Coming*, shot near Fort Knox in Louisville, Kentucky.

opens where *Breakthrough* left off, with Allied troops in St. Lo, France, planning for the big push of the Third Armored Division into Germany. One tank crew is led by Steve Cochran, and I played Danny, a soldier in Cochran's command who resents his brash attitude. Sam Fuller wrote the original story in collaboration with Joe Breen—who had *lived* it. Like *Breakthrough*, *The Tanks Are Coming* was based on events in his life: Joe had been a tank commander during his Army career. The "California Jane," our tank in the movie, was named after Joe's tank in the war. (A gal named Jane was Joe's girlfriend during World War II, but he didn't marry her—he married a wonderful girl named Patricia.)

After capturing the heroic Normandy invasion in *Breakthrough*, Lew Seiler and Brynie Foy were teamed again for *The Tanks Are Coming*. I vaguely remember hearing that, at one point in his youth, Lew had been a strongman in a circus. (Strangely enough, I'd heard the same thing about Michael Curtiz, that *he* started out as a circus strongman in Hungary.) Lew at the time was about 60 and he was well respected in the business, largely because of his war pictures like *Guadalcanal Diary* and *Breakthrough* and several others.

The Tanks Are Coming was shot in Louisville, Kentucky, because Fort Knox was there. There was a tank division there, so we had all the tanks we wanted, there were the soldiers, there were rivers and great terrain—everything that we needed for the picture, as far as locations went. One day just before we started shooting, or maybe in the first day or two of shooting, we were in a small banquet room at the Seelbach Hotel, being interviewed by members of the press. There might have been seven or eight reporters, and *being* interviewed were Lew, Steve Cochran, myself and I think Phil Carey. And Joe Breen, of course—Joe was also the associate producer. One of these wiseass reporters, an older guy, said to Lew, "How do you explain all this immorality that goes on in Hollywood?" There was a pause, and then Lew looked at him and said, "When it happens in Hollywood, they call it immorality. But when it happens here in the South, they call it 'Southern hospitality.'" I always remembered that, it was such a brilliant line!

Lew had gray hair and he was very Jewish-looking: He had a big nose and he was stocky and short, maybe five-seven or eight. (To make a long story short, he was an absolute double for Ariel Sharon. That's *exactly* the way Lew Seiler looked.) I presume he came from New York, because he had a "New York personality." He wasn't an attractive guy, and so you would never think of him as being artistic, or think that he would have a soft touch and a sensitivity. But he *did*. He did *not* have the looks for it—if you ever see a picture of Lew, you'll know what I mean—and yet he was sensitive and strong, and artistic in a lot of ways. But he did some crazy things, too. While we were in Louisville shooting *The Tanks Are Coming*, there were a couple of incidents that were . . . rather strange.

One Sunday afternoon, I was in the lobby of the Seelbach Hotel and somehow I struck up a conversation with two very attractive girls in their late 20s. Society-type women—they were not tramps, they were really classy women. They were asking me questions about the movie and about Hollywood, and somehow we got around to talking about my director, Lew Seiler. I asked, "Would you like to *meet* him?," and one of the girls said, "Oh my gosh, yes, we would love that!" I got on a lobby phone, called Lew's room and told him I was down in the lobby with these two young society ladies who would like to meet him. He said, "Fine, Paul. Come on up!" I hung up the phone and announced, "Girls, Mr. Seiler would love to have you come up and meet him."

The three of us got in the elevator, we went up to his floor and I knocked at the door. The two girls were standing right there with me when the door opened, and there was Lew Seiler, standing there with the attitude like he was dressed in white tie and tails—but he was totally naked! Standing there with everything hanging out, he said, "Come on in, ladies." I was in shock and the girls had to be, too, and yet they walked into the room, maybe because Lew had the demeanor of a man fully—and elegantly—clothed. He walked over to a table where he had several different selections of vodka and bourbon and Scotch and he said, "What would you like?" They ordered their drinks, he said, "Please sit down," and he mixed the drinks standing there totally naked. Oddly enough, *I* was embarrassed—but not Lew! He served the drinks, and then *finally* he wrapped a towel around his waist and we all sat down and we continued the talk and the drinks. I won't tell all the details of the rest of the story, but suffice it to say that, on that Sunday afternoon at the Seelbach Hotel in Louisville, Kentucky, Lew Seiler and I enjoyed some reeeal Southern hospitality!

The other incident I *heard* about from Joe Breen: Lew was known to drink a little bit at night, after shooting. One Saturday night, about two o'clock in the morning, he was drunk when he came back to the hotel after being out in a bar some place. In Louisville in those days, they had black girls operating the elevators. Lew had to pee so bad that he couldn't wait, and he peed in the elevator, right in front of the poor girl! He was a character. But, like I say, he was a very sensitive guy when he was directing. If it was a tough scene, he could be tough, and if it was a sad scene, he would cry. (Curtiz was like that too. You could bring Curtiz to tears with very little effort!)

Dick Wesson was supposed to be in *The Tanks Are Coming* but he was tied up with another picture, so his brother Gene did it. Gene had this fixation where, funnily enough, he wanted to have a profile like John Barrymore. His nose was perfect (in his own mind!), and he would put his thumb under his chin and push it forward and say, "*Now* look at my chin like *that*. Doesn't it look like Barrymore's now?" In fact, he was so possessed with his profile that he eventually had an operation on his chin, to have a John Barrymore profile! Gene Wesson was a talented guy, like his brother, but he had a lot of hang-ups—he loved to gamble and he loved to drink. Gene was by that time already a member of AA.

There was a stuntman with us named Charlie Horvath—I already knew Charlie from *Folsom Prison*. One Saturday night, I was sitting in the lobby bar and I happened to see Charlie walk through the lobby toward the elevator with an attractive young girl. Then about 30 minutes later, I saw him walk through the lobby again, with *another* girl, going into the elevator. The next day, I asked Charlie, "What was goin' on last night, you going back and forth through the lobby with pretty girls?" He said there was a dance going on in town, some kind of a prom, college or high school—and he said he wanted to break his own "personal record" that night. He went back and forth from the dance to the hotel with seven different girls! *More* Southern hospitality!

Taking a right from *Tanks Are Coming* star Steve Cochran.

For most of the rest of us, though, there wasn't much to do in the evenings in Louisville, so when we had a little time, we went to a track (pacers and trotters) owned by Gen. J. Fred Miles. Miles was a retired General of the Army, and like a bantam cock, full of energy. The little guy "ran" the city of Louisville—he owned the track, he owned this, he owned that. Gene Wesson loved to gamble, so he and I would go to the track every night after shooting. The first night we were there, we met the General, because he had the whole *Tanks Are Coming* company as his guests in his Turf Club for dinner. And every night from that night on, the General would send his black chauffeur "Jamesey" to our hotel to pick Gene and me up in a limousine and drive us to the track, where we'd go up to the General's box. We were the only two who did it every single night, so we became very close to the General, Gene especially. Gene was a great talker and a very entertaining guy, and the General just fell in love with him.

Gene loved to bet on the horses. Unfortunately for him, it got to the point where Gene had lost a *lot* of money, and eventually borrowed money from the General (who didn't mind at all). After three or four weeks, he was "in" to the General for two or three thousand dollars. I remember one night when the General said, "I've got the fifth race fixed for you, Gene," and he told us which horse to bet on. Since it was a small track, when you made a hundred-dollar bet, the odds would change drastically, but it was still pretty good odds, I think nine to two. Anyway, the General gave us the name of the horse, I think it was a pacer, the race started and our horse broke in front. Gene had bet $500 on him to win, and I bet *one* hundred—that was a lot of money for me in those days. The horses came around the far turn and our horse was in the lead. But when he came into the stretch, he broke stride. Not only did he break stride, but he crossed the track and jumped over the rail! Gene reacted like a typical gambler: Disappointed, of course, but ready to bet the next race, he turned to Gen. Miles and said, "General . . . loan me another 500, will ya please?" That was Gene!*

Every night we'd go to the track, Gene and I would give away the trophies. One night the General invited Steve Cochran to come to the track to give away the trophy on the seventh race, to the winning owner and the jockey and horse. This was a big race, and usually the governor or the mayor or somebody like that would give away the trophy for this particular race, but the General invited

---

*A few weeks after we finished the picture and came home, the General somehow contacted Gene's brother, Dick Wesson, at the studio and he tried to recover Gene's loan—four, five thousand dollars. The General never got his money.

Steve to do it this one night. Well, Steve was the original hippie of Hollywood. With his dog Tchaikovsky, he showed up in blue jeans, an open shirt—and no shoes. Totally barefoot. And he had his two little girlfriends with him—Steve always had two girls, 16-, 17-year-olds, usually from Sweden or Switzerland, traveling with him. And just *before* this big race, Tchaikovsky the dog got away from Steve and ran out on the track during a race and spooked the horses, and threw the whole thing out of kilter. The General was totally insulted by Steve's attitude and actions in front of all these important people in Louisville, Kentucky, the home of the Kentucky Derby. And, to make things even worse, the General had a lot of influence with Gen. Barr, who ran Fort Knox, which was where we were shooting the picture, and so he was in a position to throw a *very* big monkey wrench into our production.

Grabbing a bite at the racetrack with director Lew Seiler, a stuntman (standing), track owner Gen. J. Fred Miles and Gene Wesson.

On the track, the General had a trailer, and after the races every night, he and Gene and I would go in the trailer and have a drink and talk about different things that went on that day. The three of us went back to the trailer after the events of that disastrous night and the General was still upset about Steve's actions. "How could he show up like this? How *dare* he show up like this and insult me in front of all my people here?" He was ranting and raving, really furious. Gene and I realized the kind of clout that the General had, we knew that if he got perturbed enough, he could call Gen. Barr and say, "Shut the damn picture down, we're not gonna give 'em *any*thing anymore." It was a very tough situation. Gene and I were trying to placate the General and quiet him when, all of a sudden, two o'clock in the morning, there was a knock at the trailer door. Jamesey, the black chauffeur, opened the door, and there was Steve Cochran. Bombed.

Standing there in the doorway, Steve quietly started to speak. "Gen. Miles . . .," he said.

The General was so *moved* by Steve's appearance at that late hour, so sure that Steve was going to apologize, that he looked up at him with high anticipation. "Yes, Steve . . . ?" the General said, his face brightening for the first time in hours.

And Steve slurred, ". . . Go *fuck* yourself!"

The General jumped up, shouting: "You son of a bitch! You fuck! You get off my land! You get *out* of here! You get the fuck out of here!"—the General went bananas! Well, it took *another* two hours for me and Gene to calm the General down, because he was ready to shut down the picture! I'll never forget that moment, or the look on the General's face when he said, "Yes, Steve . . . ?" "Go *fuck* yourself!"

For all his foibles, I liked Steve. I'd done a little Golden Gloves boxing in my youth (my father was a professional middleweight fighter), and so one day in the gym at Warner Brothers, where Steve was under contract too, he asked, "Can you give me some pointers on boxing?" We got in the ring there and we started to box. He was well-built, and a ballsy guy, but I couldn't help but hit him a few good shots! But he came right back and *tried* to fight, even though he didn't know anything about fighting. I admired his energy and his desire to learn how to fight.

One night Marie and I went to a party at Steve's house. We walked around the grounds, which were on a hillside, and found one part where you could walk down some steep back steps—no railing—to the entrance of a *cave*, 30 or 40 feet long, that Steve had excavated into the mountainside. It was lit by candles, and once you'd walk in a ways, you came into a little "room," with a dirt floor, carved out of the mountain. In the room was a bed, and some more candles, and that's all there was!

Later, back up at the house, Marie and I were sitting at the bar getting a big kick out of watching an Englishman who was on the make for a girl. A stereotypical Englishman, with the handlebar mustache and all, he was loaded, *very* drunk, and telling her about his safaris in Africa—he was painting himself to be a big hero, an African jungle guide. The girl, young and apparently very naive, was eating it all up, and finally she walked out of the bar and went down those hillside steps, headed toward the cave. The Englishman realized, "My chance has arrived!" He followed her out the door, started down the steps—but he was in such a drunken stupor that he walked right over the right side of the steps, where there was no railing and landed 30 feet below. But he didn't get hurt at *all*, because he *was* drunk, and very "loose." It was so funny, after watching him all night making a move on this girl, that finally when his big moment came, he blew it and walked off the cliff! Marie and I couldn't help but laugh.

My next picture for Warners was scheduled to be yet another war movie, **Retreat, Hell!**, with Frank Lovejoy. But before I had shot a single scene, I was taken off the film and put in another—one of the luckiest breaks I got during my years at Warners. Because the new film, **Mara Maru** with Errol Flynn, instantly became one of my top favorites.

9
IN WITH FLYNN

Could I ever have imagined, back when I was a kid watching Errol Flynn in *Captain Blood* and *The Charge of the Light Brigade* and *The Adventures of Robin Hood*, that someday I'd be co-starring in a movie with him? Never. I did dream that maybe someday I'd have my face on the cover of one of the movie magazines—but then I would look in the mirror and say to myself, "Oh, no. No chance." As for appearing with Errol Flynn—never in a million years.

The story of how I finally did get to work with Errol begins on the day that I learned that Gordon Douglas was about to direct a Flynn picture called *Mara Maru* and that there was a great part in it I felt I'd be just right for. I wanted that role *very* badly, and I thought there was a good chance of getting it—I'd already done *I Was a Communist for the FBI* for Gordon, and he loved me. And, sure enough, Gordon screen-tested me for the part along with quite a few other actors, among them Ramon Novarro no less—Novarro, the great romantic leading man of the silent days. But Warners was at that same time preparing yet another service film, *Retreat, Hell!*, this one about the Korean War, and one day I got the word that I had been cast in it. That knocked me out of the running for *Mara Maru*, because the schedules overlapped.

I went down to Camp Pendleton in San Diego with Frank Lovejoy and the rest of the *Retreat, Hell!* cast, very disappointed that I was in that picture rather than *Mara Maru*. I was there for a week or maybe ten days and they were actually shooting but my character, a Marine captain, still hadn't really been "established"—I'd been in the background of shots, but never had any dialogue scenes. There was one funny incident involving Frank Lovejoy: In San Diego, we were very close to Tijuana, the Mexican border city, and one Sunday afternoon Frank said, "Let's take a ride down there and see what it's like." We drove to Tijuana and found the center of town, which was one long street. We walked down maybe half a mile on the right side of this main street, crossed over and walked the half-mile back on the *other* side. We hardly said a word to each other the whole time, and nobody said a word to *us*. We simply strolled down and then back up, looking at all the Mexican people, the vendors, the tourists who were buying stuff and so on. And when we got back to where we had started, Frank turned to me and he said, "You know, Paul . . . it takes a looong time to 'penetrate.'" That's when it dawned on me that he took that walk expecting people to recognize him—and nobody did! I could tell that he was very upset that we had taken that long walk without one person saying, "Oh! Frank Lovejoy! Can I have your autograph?" I'll never forget the look on his face or the tone of his voice when he said to me, "Paul . . . it takes a looong time to 'penetrate'"!

I continued to cool my heels in San Diego waiting to play my first real scene in **Retreat, Hell!**, but then a phone call came that Warners now wanted to switch me to **Mara Maru**—in the part I wanted so badly! After a little back-and-forth dialogue between the **Retreat, Hell!** director and **Mara Maru**'s Gordon Douglas and the studio people, I was able to leave San Diego and come back to Warners and do **Mara Maru**. An actor named Lamont Johnson went

My favorite film role, as detective Steven Ranier, in Errol Flynn's *Mara Maru*.

down there to replace me in *Retreat, Hell!*; in later years Lamont became a director, and one day when I was working in something he was directing, we had a few laughs talking about him getting that break when I was taken off.

Mara Maru is set in Manila with Errol Flynn playing a World War II veteran now in the marine salvage business with an alcoholic partner (Richard Webb). After Webb is murdered, a rich underworld character (Raymond Burr) invites Flynn to enter into an expedition to recover a million dollars worth of diamonds from a sunken PT boat. Flynn is reluctant, but is forced to go in on the deal after his boat is dynamited and his little sidekick, a Filipino boy (Robert Cabal), is killed. Accompanied by Webb's widow Ruth Roman and my character, a native private eye, Flynn and Burr sail on Burr's boat the *Mara Maru* to the spot where the PT boat was lost, and during a typhoon Flynn descends and recovers the treasure (a cross studded with diamonds). This, of course, leads to a series of double- and triple-crosses on land and sea.

My character, detective Steven Ranier, was a great one, one of my favorites in fact, because I was good *and* bad. In the picture, my loyalty constantly shifts back and forth between Flynn and Raymond Burr. If Flynn looks like he's going to be the one to locate the treasure, I buddy up with him . . . but then when it starts to seem that Burr might get to it first, I jump to *his* side. Kind of like the Italians in World War II! It was probably the best part I had up until that time—it was equal to Ray Burr's part, and *almost* as good as Errol's.

Apart from having the fun of sharing shares with Errol, I got to hear many of his great Hollywood stories between takes.

I'm not quite sure why Errol and I gravitated to each other so quickly once we started making **Mara Maru**. We were in a lot of scenes together, and I guess he sensed that I liked him, and I guess that's why *he* started to like *me*. Well, I was just in awe of Errol Flynn, he was an idol to me, and I was thrilled working with him. Of course I knew about his reputation as a drinker, and as a hellraiser—he was a legend by that time. Errol was like Cary Grant and Robert Taylor and Clark Gable—he was a Movie Star. Grant and Taylor and Gable and Errol, these were *beautiful* men. Errol was built, he was six-two or –three, big shoulders and small waist even at the time we shot **Mara Maru**, when he was in his late 40s. Today we have "stars" like Tom Cruise, Tom Hanks—but *these* guys aren't movie stars like *we* had in the old days. You just don't *have* stars today like we had then. Okay, Al Pacino, Robert De Niro, they're good *character stars,* and maybe they're the equal of Robinson and Cagney and Bogart. But our modern "movie stars"—forget it! Maybe some of them are good *actors* and nice guys, but they're not Movie Stars like the ones that I knew.

Errol Flynn used to drive onto the Warners lot every morning in his Jaguar (with the top down). He'd be wearing a John Barrymore-type hat with a feather sticking out of it; a windbreaker (no T-shirt); a pair of tan slacks (no underwear); and a pair of sneakers (no socks). Of course the wardrobe department would have to provide him with T-shirt, underwear and socks every day, and he would still be wearing them when he left the studio after work. One day I asked him, "Errol, what do you do with all those T-shirts and underwear and socks that you wear home every night?" He said, "I throw them in a closet. It's piled *high* with T-shirts!"—I could well imagine that it *would* be; he'd been doing this for weeks. I repeated, "But . . . what do you *do* with them?" He said, "*Nothing*. It just gives me pleasure to steal from Jack Warner!"

His entire wardrobe in **Mara Maru** was the tan slacks, the windbreaker, sneakers and a captain's hat—that's all he wore. But there comes a point in the picture, after Flynn's little Filipino sidekick gets killed, that Flynn and I go to church for his funeral. A couple days before we were due to shoot that scene, Flynn said to Gordon Douglas, "I noticed this scene where I have to attend the funeral of this boy. Do you think that I would go to the funeral in these slacks and windbreaker, and that's *it*? Don't you think that this guy would at least have one blue suit?"

Gordon said, "Errol, it *is* just a short scene. You step up, you kneel down at the coffin and then you walk out. We don't see the need for you to get a blue suit."

Errol said, "Well, *I* do. I think that the fellow should have a blue suit! He should have *one suit* to go to the church with."

Gordon finally gave in and said, "All right. I'll speak to David Weisbart, the producer, and see if I can have them make a suit for you." Well, sure enough, Weisbart okayed it and they made him the nice new blue suit that he said he thought the character should wear at the funeral. Errol wore it in the church. He wore it *out* of the church. He wore it into his car, and he never brought it back!

My character, the devious Ranier, alternates between backing Flynn and Raymond Burr—whichever one Ranier believes at the moment has the better chance of finding the treasure!

These are just two of my many, many fabulous memories of Errol Flynn, a great guy. Perhaps one of my favorites. He was absolutely fantastic to work with. He told me some marvelous stories about his close friend John Barrymore. This one was my favorite: According to Errol, Barrymore went on a bender one rainy night and then showed up at Errol's home in the hills, up in one of the canyons. It was about three in the morning, there was a knock at the door, Errol in his robe opened it and there was Barrymore, in the rain, with the famous fedora, rain dripping down from it. Errol looked at him with a little surprise and Barrymore asked, "Well? Aren't you going to invite me *in*?" Errol said, "Of course! Come on in, Jack . . . ," and he told Barrymore he could stay there for the night, sleep in the den. Barrymore came in—and he stayed for *three weeks*!

Several days later, when Barrymore was out of the house, the maid came to Errol and said, "Mr. Flynn, I want to show you something . . ." She took him into the den, where the window was open, there was a screen in it . . . and the windowsill was covered with urine. Evidently, Barrymore was getting up at night and peeing out the window, which is bad enough, but it was hitting the screen and collecting on the sill! Errol went to Barrymore and he said, "Jack, you're ruining the paint on the windowsill by peeing out the window. You *have* a bathroom right here off the den, why don't you go pee in the bathroom? It's right *there* . . . !" Barrymore said, "All right, dear boy, all right . . ." That, Errol thought, was the end of it. But a few days later, the maid came to Errol and she said, "Mr. Flynn . . . Mr. Barrymore is now peeing in the *fireplace*!" Errol told me, "Jack would *not* be conventional enough to go pee in the bathroom . . . he just *had* to be *un*conventional!" That was just one of the stories Errol told me as we sat around in director's chairs on the set.

Ruth Roman was Errol's leading lady, and for some reason he didn't like Ruth because (*he* said) she thought she was Joan Crawford—Ruth was very dramatic at the time. (When she'd walk on the set, he'd say, "Oh-oh. Here comes Camille.") Errol didn't *dis*like her, but she did nothing *for* him, perhaps partly because she *was* an overly dramatic actress. Ruth came up through the ranks in the 1940s, playing a number of small roles and then getting her big break as the neglected wife of egotistical prizefighter Kirk Douglas in *Champion*. Warners signed her not long after *Champion*, and now Ruth was "feeling her oats." When I worked with her for the first time on *Mara Maru*, Ruth was buxom and very sexy . . . and I liked her. I liked her enough that, one night, I had a dream about her—a very sexual dream. The next day I had to work with her in the looping room, and as I went in I handed her two bucks. She asked, "What the hell is *this* for?" I said, "I had a great dream about you last night, Ruth . . ." And she said, "You *son of a bitch*. Is *that* all I'm worth?!" We kidded about that incident later on when I worked with her in a movie called *The Shanghai Story* with Edmond O'Brien, and then again when she guested on *The Untouchables*.

At the time of *Mara Maru*, Errol was married to Patrice Wymore, a dancer on the Warners lot—she was also under contract there. Patrice didn't do too much in her career, but she was a lovely girl and Errol was devoted to her. When I worked with him, I never saw another woman around. Patrice was pregnant at that time and living in Jamaica, where she and Errol had a house on a small island which was their permanent residence when they were not working. Errol used to call her from the set every day to see how she was. One day while he and I were sitting around on the set, a messenger boy came up to us and said, "Mr. Flynn, I have a message for you from Mr. Warner." Errol took the message from the boy, looked at it and snickered. Then he showed it to me:

DEAR ERROL,
IT'S BEEN BROUGHT TO MY ATTENTION THAT YOUR PHONE BILL HAS EXCEEDED $5000. PLEASE TAKE CARE OF THIS A.S.A.P.
JACK WARNER

Errol took the paper back from me, turned it over and began writing on the back, telling the messenger boy, "I want you to take this back to Mr. Warner, son." What he wrote on it was:

DEAR JACK,
I'M WILLING TO FORGET ABOUT THIS IF YOU ARE.
LOVE, ERROL

Funnily enough, Errol wasn't the only one in that movie who had a streak of larceny: Richard Webb, who was in the early part of the picture playing Errol's partner, said to me one day, "You know, Paul, I furnished my whole house with things that I've stolen from the Warner Brothers sets." He would take lamps, little end tables, whatever he needed, put 'em in his trunk and drive out the gate! Warners had some great stuff in their property department, furniture and books and terrific paintings that they'd dress the sets with—and that Dick dressed his house with! I noticed that Dick only lasted about a year before Warners dropped his contract, but I don't know if his "sticky fingers" had anything to do with that.

One of the places we shot was San Pedro—L.A. Harbor—where they had the *Mara Maru* docked. One day when we were there, Sean Flynn, the son of Errol and his ex-wife Lili Damita, the French actress, was hanging around. In 1951, Sean was not much more than a kid. After shooting that day, Errol said to me, "Come on, dago . . ."—he'd call me dago. "Come on, dago, we'll have a drink," and Errol and Sean and I went back to the place Errol was staying, a fancy motel (very close to the marina) where Errol had a suite. In 1951 when I met him, Sean had none of Errol's physical attributes; he was skinny and he had pimples all over his face. But he had one thing that his father had: the love of women. We were there at the motel having our drinks when Errol turned to Sean and said, "Sean, me boy, while we're down here in San Pedro, I'm going to get you fucked and sucked 'til you get rid of those pimples." And Sean, who had been raised in Paris, responded (with a French accent), "All you do is talk, talk! Where are zee *girls?*"

Other parts of *Mara Maru* were shot at the Warner Brothers ranch, which was in Calabasas. (I still remember, in the old days, driving onto that Warners ranch through a skinny gate on a dirt road and going back into the hills to shoot. Today it's all multi-million dollar homes and an elaborate shopping mall called The Commons with beautiful theaters and restaurants.) Errol never carried any money with him, but when we would stop at a bar to have a drink on the way home from there, inevitably *some*body,

Between takes with Raymond Burr, Errol and Ruth Roman.

some guy standing at the bar would recognize him and would buy drinks. Errol never spent a penny!

Raymond Burr was also delightful. One day on the *Mara Maru* set, he asked me if I knew how to play cribbage. When I told him I didn't, he said, "C'mon, let's go in my dressing room, and I'll teach you." We started playing cribbage and, when he wasn't explaining the game to me, he was telling me about his former wife and his two sons who were in London. On the second or maybe the third day of this, when I took a look up from my cards . . . I saw him *staring* at me. With his big blue eyes. And with this strange expression on his face. For the first time in my life, I felt like a *dame*. Then it hit me: He'd been giving me all this bullshit about his wife and his two kids in London, when in fact he was *gay*, and he was makin' a *move* on me!

I liked Ray, I always did, and we had a lot of fun together all through the years . . . and he always pursued me! I later did three or four episodes of his TV series *Perry Mason* and he'd always say, "Come on back to my place"—when he was working on the series, he lived right there on the lot, in an apartment where he had a young boy looking after things for him. I did a *Perry Mason* during the time that I was a Rams game announcer, and I found that I had a little time to myself between five o'clock and kick-off time at the Coliseum, so on that occasion when he said, "Come on and have a drink with me," I *did* go back to his apartment. And there again he made a move on me and damn near got me drunk! I had two or three Scotches with him and got to the game late—I remember the bandleader saying to me, "Where the hell have you *been*? They're ready for the kick-off!"

Whether it was *Mara Maru* or *Perry Mason* or *Ironside*, Ray and I always had plenty of laughs together. He never caught up to me, though!

The seagoing scenes in *Mara Maru* were shot on the Warners lot, on a soundstage on Stage 22 where they had a big swimming pool and a replica of the *Mara Maru*. Right in that pool, they could make waves, and they could also simulate wind and lightning and all kinds of effects so that the audience would think we were really out on a ship, in a typhoon. Of course, while shooting those scenes, we were wet a lot of the times, and Errol would say to John, his stand-in and Man Friday, "Would you bring me a glass of water, please?" John would bring him a big glass of "water" and Errol would knock it down. Needless to say, it wasn't water, it was vodka. Well, by 4:30 in the afternoon, Errol would be slobbering his words.

One afternoon we were on the soundstage boat and Errol was in his diving suit, and we were shooting the scene where we pull him up from the bottom of the sea and he's recovered the chest with the cross and all the valuable jewels. In this scene are Errol and myself, Raymond Burr, Ruth Roman and the big husky Filipino guy who played Burr's henchman. The dialogue is supposed to go something like this: We pull Errol up, we take off his diving helmet, Raymond and I open the chest and see the treasure, and Raymond says to the big Filipino guy, "Over the side with him!"—Raymond orders the guy to throw Errol overboard, to kill him. At that point, Errol's line is, "Who's gonna navigate the ship?" (He suspected this might happen and so, unbeknownst to Raymond and me, he's destroyed the compass. Now, without Errol's help, we'll be lost in the typhoon.) After Errol's line "Who's gonna navigate the ship?," Raymond's line is, "We'll manage. Ranier and I." And Errol's *next* line is, "Without a *compass?*"—that was his "kicker." That was the scene.

It's now about 4:30 in the afternoon and we're ready to do the scene—and Errol is *bombed*. This is the way the scene went: The crew got everything going (there was rain, wind, lightning and thunder), Gordon Douglas called "Action!," we pulled Errol up, took off the helmet, looked in the chest and Raymond (shouting to be heard over the storm) said to the henchman, "Over the side with him!" And Errol shouted back, "Hooosh gonna naffigate the shhhip?" Raymond cried, "We'll manage. Ranier and I." And Flynn said, "Ah-*haaaaa*! Without a *compash?*!"

Gordon Douglas said, "Cut! Print! That's it, that's a wrap for today, fellas. I'll see you all tomorrow." I was shocked to hear him say that—I knew the take wasn't acceptable. Raymond and I exchanged looks, and even Ruth Roman had an expression on her face like, "What the hell's goin' *on?*"

We all went home; when we got to the set the next day, the cameras were lined up for the same shot. Errol now was sober, and he said, "Gordy . . . I seem to recollect that we shot this last night." And Gordon apologetically said, "Yeah, we did, Errol, but they loused up the film in the lab. We gotta re-shoot it." Only then did I realize how clever Gordon had been when he'd said, "Cut! Print!" and dismissed us. Gordon knew when he heard, "Ah-*haaaaa*! Without a *compash*?!" that it would be futile to say to Errol "Let's do it again," because the second take would have been as bad as the first. So he made up his mind to shoot it again the next morning, with a sober Errol, using that excuse about the lab ruining the film.

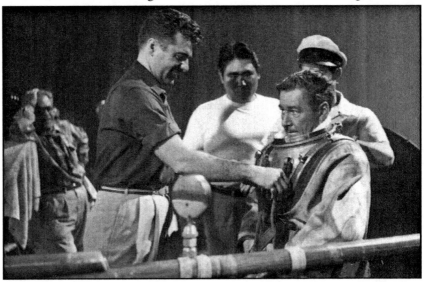

"Without a compash??": Errol suits up to take a dive on Warners' Stage 22.

I never saw Errol Flynn before **Mara Maru** and never saw him after. (I did, however, work on one of his subsequent pictures: He made a buccaneer-type adventure picture called **The Master of Ballantrae** in Spain, and in the looping room at Warners I provided the voices of about ten different characters!) Meeting and working with Errol was a wonderful experience, as well as providing some more on-the-job training for me as a young actor. In the scenes that Errol and I did together, I'd be acting away, being very dramatic . . . and I'd see that *he* was being very matter-of-fact. I didn't say anything, naturally, but I did think to myself, "This guy isn't *doing* anything; he's not acting at *all*." Then I saw it on film and realized that I was a ham, that I was *over*acting, and that Errol was doing it just right.

So spending those six weeks in 1951 working with Errol Flynn was also a real education.

10
When You're Down
There's No Place to Go But Up

Shortly after wrapping up *Mara Maru*, my best movie part to date, Marie and I received yet another gift from the stork: Maria Lucia, born shortly after the New Year (1952). She was our fourth child in four years. As a kid, Maria had great big eyes and such a beautiful face—which she still does. And she was very, very feminine. She was the kind of little girl who loved dolls and dresses; she always *had* to wear dresses. In later years, we owned four horses, but on some of the days that our other kids went horseback riding, Maria preferred to play with her dolls. Today, Maria is married, her three children are Bryan, Mark and Stephanie, and she lives in San Diego, where she has three houses (not to mention a house here in Burbank). She's now into selling real estate, and is *very* good at it! Maria's grown up into a real go-getter.

None of the parts that I played at Warners in the year after *Mara Maru* were as good as Ranier, but they were all good experience and a chance to continue to meet new people. My next picture was *The Miracle of Our Lady of Fatima* with Gilbert Roland, and the way I got my part was almost an instant replay of what happened to me on *Mara Maru*. When *Our Lady of Fatima* came up, I felt it was going to be a very important picture and I wanted so badly to be in it. I think of myself as being a good Catholic; I've fallen along the way a few times, but I go to Mass on Sundays and I'm a graduate of a Jesuit school and I really wanted to be a part of this picture. In fact, I *prayed* to be in the picture.

One day I tested for the part of the villain. So did Frank Lovejoy. But the role ended up going to black actor Frank Silvera. There was

Frank Lovejoy and I tested for a *Lady of Fatima* **role which ultimately went to Frank Silvera. In 1970, Frank died tragically, electrocuted in his home while installing a garbage disposal. I'd worked with him on** *The Untouchables* **and thought he was an excellent actor.**

really nothing else in the picture for me to play, and so I was very disappointed that, after all my prayers, I wasn't going to be a part of this very religious Catholic film. Well, a strange thing happened: After they finished shooting, I got a call from my dear friend Joe Breen, the associate producer on *Our Lady of Fatima*. He knew about my desire to be in it, and he said, "It looks like your prayers have been answered." I said, ". . . *What?!*" Joe said, "They've decided to add an introductory scene to the picture, and the director John Brahm wants you to play a Communist agitator in it. This scene will kind of 'set up' the whole film." Just like with *Mara Maru*, I set my sights on being in the picture, lost out—and then was cast in the picture anyway! So in the end, I did play a part in the film, my prayers in effect were answered—except that I played a Communist who was *against* the Catholic Church!

Later that year, I came in through the back door on yet another picture, the South Seas buccaneer adventure *His Majesty O'Keefe* with Burt Lancaster. Here again, the picture was finished when someone, in this case Burt, decided it needed an extra scene in order to better establish something. So it went back into production and Burt brought me in, to play a sea captain in this new scene in a bar.

When you're under contract, you can be instantly called upon to do *all* these sorts of things—looping, making personal appearances, going on radio to plug movies and so on. It was also compulsory that the contract players attend all the big premieres of the new Warners pictures, which I certainly didn't mind, because it was always fun. I remember one funny story—well, maybe it's not really funny, maybe it's kind of sad—about the premiere of **Goodbye, My Fancy** with Joan Crawford and Frank Lovejoy. Frank had been moving up the ladder there at Warners and now he had been cast in the male lead in this picture. In those days, the studio always had their big premieres at the Warner Brothers Theater on Hollywood Boulevard; at the **Goodbye, My Fancy** premiere, Marie and me and Dick Wesson and his wife Winnie were greeted by Gordon MacRae, who was on a little dais there, introducing all the actors as they arrived. And now, finally, up pulled this limousine, and in the limousine were Joan Crawford, Frank Lovejoy and Frank's wife Joan Banks, a radio actress. The limousine pulled up and Gordon MacRae excitedly announced, "And now, ladies and gentlemen, the stars of the film, Joan Crawford and Frank Lovejoy!" Frank got out of the back door first; he reached in and he said, "Joan—"; and his wife, Joan Banks, put her hand in his. And he *cast* her hand aside and he said, "Joan—," and he pulled out Joan *Crawford!* Frank was basking in the applause, in the limelight of the moment with Joan Crawford his leading lady, and he just left his wife Joan sitting there in the car! Joan Banks climbed out by herself and came over to where Dick Wesson and I were standing with our wives and she growled, "That son of a bitch, I'll *kill* him when we get home!" Frank was so dazzled by the glare of the lights and the excitement of the "big moment" that he totally neglected his wife!

My next film after *Our Lady of Fatima* was *Operation Secret*, a story of the French Underground with Cornel Wilde, Steve Cochran, Phyllis Thaxter and Karl Malden. I had a decent part as a French Underground leader, Cochran's sidekick. The director was, again, Lew Seiler, who not only "discovered" me and gave me my big break in *Breakthrough*, but later used me in three other pictures; it was like I was his protégé.

At the premiere of The Eddie Cantor Story, Phil Carey, George O'Hanlon and I donned Cantor masks for a funny photo op.

Lew, incidentally, had also discovered Richard Jaeckel; Jaeckel was just a messenger boy on the 20th Century-Fox lot in 1943 when Lew found him and cast him in **Guadalcanal Diary.** Lew discovered Jaeckel and me and a few other actors.

My most vivid memory of **Operation Secret** is watching them shoot a scene in which a German staff car, a big limousine-type car, goes off a cliff, hits the side of the mountain on the way down and explodes. That was the shot—there were no actors involved, no stuntmen, just the limousine and the explosion as it went down the mountainside. Lew had three or four cameras set up to photograph the crash, and on the top of the hill, behind the car, were a couple of property men, ready to push it off the cliff. (The property men were out of camera range, naturally, so that all you'd see would be the car rolling, going over the cliff and exploding.)

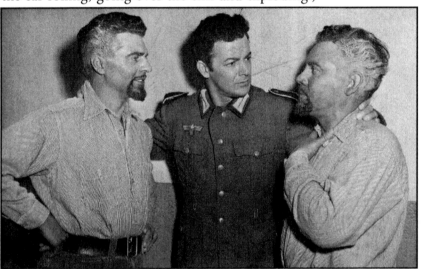

Cornel Wilde and I pose with my *Operation Secret* stunt double, made-up and dressed like me in preparing for a staircase fall.

This is the usual procedure on a shot: The assistant director says, "Roll 'em!" That's the cue for the camera operators to start their cameras. When the film inside the cameras has gotten up to speed, the cameramen yell, "Speed!" Then the director says, "Action!" So it's usually "Roll 'em!," "Speed!" and "Action!," that's the sequence. Lew looked around, he saw that everything was in order, the cameramen were behind their cameras and the prop men on top of the cliff were ready to push the car over. Lew gave the nod to his assistant director to start the shot, and the assistant director yelled, "Roll 'em!" His voice echoed through the entire canyon, so all the cameramen could pick up the cue to start their cameras. But the prop men on top of the hill—*they* took that to be their cue to roll the *car*! So they pushed the car, and it started coming down the hill toward the edge of the cliff! Lew yelled, "No, no, no! *Nooooo!* Hold it, *hold it!*"—but it was too late. The car came over the edge of the cliff and of course automatically all the explosions started going off and it went crashing to the bottom of the canyon in a big ball of fire. And, of course, not a single one of the cameramen had had time to start their cameras to photograph it! It took another three hours to set up all the explosions again!

On *Operation Secret* I learned a valuable acting lesson just by watching Karl Malden. Karl was *so* meticulous in his preparation for a scene: He would go onto the set all by himself, maybe an hour before we were going to shoot a scene there, and he'd go over all the props that were available and he'd work out how he was going to use them. All by himself he would do that. I caught him doing that several times during the shooting of the film and thought to myself, "Boy, *that's* a good idea," and from that time on, I did it myself. So that was a valuable lesson I learned from Karl Malden, who was a wonderful actor and who, one evening while the picture was in production, received a Best Supporting Actor Academy Award for his work in the previous year's *A Streetcar Named Desire*. (At the ceremony, when Claire Trevor announced him the winner, Karl, a recently transplanted New Yorker, seemed confused about what he was expected to do. Once he came up onto the stage, he even went to the wrong podium!) Karl was later nominated again for *On the Waterfront* with Marlon Brando.

I worked with Gordon MacRae for the first and only time in *The Desert Song*, which was based on an old operetta that Warners had already filmed twice (once in the early days of sound with John Boles, the second time during the War, with Dennis Morgan). Getting to know Gordon was the nice part about that picture— Gordon and I became good friends. He was an avid golfer, a *great* golfer, and at that time I was just a beginner. So, while I was on that film, he gave me his set of golf clubs. I started playing golf in earnest from that day on, with Gordon's clubs; as a matter of fact,

I still *have* the four woods he gave me. All through the years since *The Desert Song* I've been a golfer, and I've even played *with* Gordon: He had his own golf tournament, sponsored I believe by Alcoholics Anonymous, and it was usually held at the Tropicana Hotel in Las Vegas. For years I would play in it, along with other actors like Howard Keel, Ernest Borgnine, Fred MacMurray, Robert Stack, Telly Savalas and Phil Carey.

I liked Gordon MacRae but only got to work with him on one occasion, in *The Desert Song.*

Joined by P.V. and Nicci on the Desert Song set.

Directed by "Lucky" Humberstone, *The Desert Song* was set in the deserts of Morocco and the story was basically the same as in the previous versions: A masquerading native leader (Gordon) battling against the cruelty of the governing Arab forces. It was a lot of fun working with Gordon and Kathryn Grayson and of course with Dick Wesson, who provided the comic relief as a New York reporter on the scene trying to get a story. What was *not* fun was watching Gordon's young daughter playing at Chatsworth, where we shot the picture. Chatsworth is all cliffs and mountains, and Meredith MacRae, Gordon's little girl, who was about eight at the time, was playing on the rocks near the edge of a long drop. I have acrophobia, the fear of heights, and so as she was playing on these rocks, I was almost having a heart attack! I gasped, "Gordon! Gordon! *Please*! That girl, she's eight years old—get her off those rocks! I'm afraid she might fall over!" Gordon looked over, watched her for a few seconds, shrugged and said, "Naaah. She'll be okay." It didn't faze him one bit, and I was *dying*! (Meredith passed away at age 56 in 2000. It's hard to believe that that pretty little girl is gone. I worked with her once when I was doing the soap opera *The Young Marrieds*.)

As with most motion pictures, some of the *Desert Song* exteriors were actually photographed on the Warners process stage under the direction of Eddie DuPar, who was brilliant at that sort of shooting. In front of the process screen on a treadmill were two horses, held in place with straps. After Gordon and I climbed up into the saddles, footage of the desert (shot from a moving car) was projected on the screen and the treadmill started moving. Little by little it picked up speed, forcing the horses to walk faster, and faster, and soon they were running at a full gallop. The cameraman, of course, framed the shot so that he could see only Gordon and me and the horses and the projected desert background, so that in the finished film it would appear as though we were racing through the desert. It occurred to me that Gordon and I would have been better off actually *doing* our own riding in the desert: That treadmill was going so fast that, if a strap had broken or if the horses had fallen, we might all have gone flying!

She's Back on Broadway was a romantic musical about a washed-up Hollywood star (Virginia Mayo) who returns to the Broadway stage and conflicts with her stage director (Steve Cochran), a former sweetheart. I loved Virginia Mayo, who I thought was such a beautiful woman. Right to the end, I still saw her off and on; I ran into her on a cruise a couple of years ago and I also saw her at autograph shows, and we always reminisced about the old days. (I also worked with her husband Michael O'Shea; he was one of the stars of *The Front Page* when we did it on stage at La Jolla.) One

Another Warners premiere, this time attending with Phil and Maureen Carey, David Brian and Marie.

day on *She's Back on Broadway*, when there was going to be a big dance number on the stage of the Broadway theater set on the Warners lot, Marie happened to come by to visit me with a couple of our kids, including P.V., who was two and a half at the time. Gordon Douglas, who was directing, picked P.V. up in his arms and he said into a microphone, "All right, ladies and gentlemen, Mr. P.V. Picerni is going to direct this next scene, he'll give you the 'Action' cue. Everybody stand by, get ready . . ." As the cast and crew made their final preparations, Gordon whispered in P.V.'s ear, "When I say to you 'Action!,' *you* say 'Action!' into this microphone." When everyone was ready, Gordon whispered to P.V. "Action!" and P.V. shouted into the microphone, "Action!" When he did, the cameras rolled and the music began playing and everybody started dancing. And when Gordon whispered "Cut!" to P.V., P.V. said into the microphone, "Cut!" So P.V. directed that big dance number in *She's Back on Broadway* when he was two and a half years old!

Dennis Morgan was another great singer (*a la* Gordon MacRae) on the Warners payroll, but my one time working with Dennis was in a Western, *Cattle Town*, his last film at Warners after a dozen or more years there. I played a supporting part in the picture, and I also narrated the opening sequence—*not* as my character, just doing narration. Leonard Maltin, in his *Movie & Video Guide*, called it "a sad echo of a slick Western," and it's true that the picture didn't have much going for it in the action department; in fact, what little action there was was partly stock footage from a great old Errol Flynn Western, *Dodge City*. But, the quality of the picture aside, I had a great time on that show. Dennis was a real nice guy, and I had a million laughs with Rita Moreno, Amanda Blake and George O'Hanlon, who were all in it. The four of us hung out together on the Warners Ranch, which is where we were shooting. Rita Moreno was just delightful. She was maybe 20 at the time and a beautiful kid. There was also a fellow in *Cattle Town* who was under contract at Warner Brothers, but this was one of the few pictures he was in because he was only there about six months. His name was Merv Griffin. Merv, of course, later became a talk show host and one of the richest guys in Hollywood, owning hotels and casinos and producing the great game shows *Jeopardy!* and *Wheel of Fortune*.

George O'Hanlon and I were very friendly. A very inventive guy and a good writer, George was the co-writer and star of the series of Warner Brothers shorts called *Behind the Eight Ball*, in which he played Joe McDoakes, an average guy coping with everyday life's trials and tribulations. They all had titles like *So You Want to Keep Your Hair*, *So You Think You're a Nervous Wreck*, *So You're Going to Be a Father*—dozens of them, and all of them beginning with a shot of George standing behind a giant eight ball. (If you're not old enough to remember George as Joe McDoakes, perhaps you'll remember *The Jetsons*, the Hanna-Barbera cartoon sitcom set in the future; for decades, George was the voice of George Jetson.) George liked to write, and so did I, and at one point we got together and wrote a script which, *I* thought, was brilliant. It was called *Soulmates* and it was written for Martin and Lewis, who at the time were very big at Paramount. In our story, Jerry Lewis was an usher at a movie house and Dean Martin was a singer engaged to be married. Just as Dean is about to say "I do," he has a heart attack and dies. Jerry is a contestant on a game show where they put him in a tank full of water, and he drowns. And by the time they're miraculously revived, their *souls* have risen to Heaven. *They're* alive on Earth, but as soul-less bodies—their souls are in Heaven, where St. Peter says to an angel, "We've had something very unusual happen. These men died, but now they're alive again. We've got to get their souls back into their bodies." So this one angel, kind of a screw-up, is assigned this task, but he gets bollixed up and he puts Dean's soul in Jerry's body and Jerry's soul in Dean's. When Jerry wakes up, now he's a singer, and when Dean wakes up, he starts acting zany like Jerry. Now the bumbling angel is assigned to go back down again and *kill* them and switch their souls! That was the basic script, and I thought it turned out to be quite funny. We gave the script to Hal Wallis, the producer of the Martin and Lewis pictures, and he loved it, but he said, "Unfortunately, the boys are on the verge of a breakup." That turned out to be true, and so we lost the sale. But our script must have stayed at Paramount because, later on, basically the same idea was used for the TV series **Highway to Heaven** with Michael Landon and Victor French as guardian angels! Ours was the same story; as a matter of fact, the first title on our script was **Guardian Angel**.

Meanwhile, back at Warners, I began looking forward to getting another really good part. I had a good long scene in a movie called **The System**, my fourth and final picture for Lew Seiler, where I played a government lawyer conducting hearings in hopes of breaking up a big gambling syndicate. **The System** was a picture that Bogart was originally supposed to do, but Bogie turned it down because it was such a lousy script and Frank Lovejoy ended up doing it. (Frank was like me; he did *every*thing over there at Warners.)

Then along came a movie and a role that I wanted very badly, the same way I'd wanted the roles in **Mara Maru** and **Our Lady of Fatima**. Warners was getting ready to star Keefe Brasselle in a film biography of Eddie Cantor and I had my eye on the part of Eddie's friend Harry Harris, a young Jewish doctor, which was almost a second lead. **The Eddie Cantor Story** was going to be a big picture, in Technicolor, and it was going to be produced and directed by the same producer-director team (Sidney Skolsky and Alfred Green) who'd made **The Jolson Story** a big hit several years earlier. I felt that this was a picture that couldn't miss, and that playing in it would be another step up the ladder for me.

Distraught over losing out on a part in *The Eddie Cantor Story*, I instead found myself cast in one of the most high-visibility roles in my career: One of the leads in the 3-D horror classic *House of Wax*.

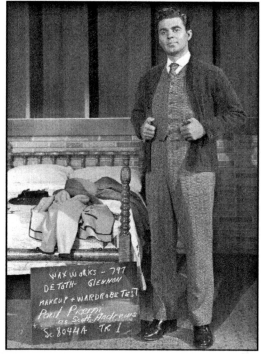

I tested for the part of the doctor, along with about 15 or 20 other actors, and kept my fingers crossed. But one day Sid Skolsky called me into his office and he said, "I've got some bad news for you. We've decided to go with Arthur Franz in the part of the doctor because Arthur has light hair and you have dark hair. Keefe Brasselle has dark hair, and we want a little contrast between Keefe and his best friend the doctor." To say that I was very disappointed would be an understatement—I was *shattered*, because I was really hoping to get that part.

Right across the street from the main entrance to Warner Brothers was a little drugstore; I walked over there with George O'Hanlon and, over a couple of cups of coffee, George was commiserating with me. When Joe Breen walked in and saw what was going on, he asked, "What the hell are you so disconsolate about, Picerni?" I explained to him how I had just lost the part in *The Eddie Cantor Story*.

"Well," Joe said, "when you're down like that, there's only one way to go and that's up. I just found out that you're gonna play the romantic lead in ***House of Wax***."

11
DON'T LOSE
YOUR HEAD . . . !

In the early 1950s, all the major Hollywood studios were trying to figure out what to do about one of the greatest threats in the industry's history: Television. Ever since the introduction of TV, theater attendance had been dwindling. Jack Warner despised television. When TVs first came in, he wouldn't allow the set designers to have a TV on the set of a movie. If you saw a living room in a Warners movie made around that time, there would never be a TV in it!

In an effort to get people away from their sets and back into the movie houses, the studios tried one gimmick after another, including CinemaScope. One short-lived fad was the 3-D movie.

Warners' next picture, *House of Wax*, was going to be in widescreen, WarnerColor, Warnerphonic Stereo Sound—and 3-D. I just *knew* it was going to be big because this would be the first 3-D movie made by a major studio. The other 3-D movies up to that time, including the very first one, *Bwana Devil* with Robert Stack, were low-budget; this was the first time a company like Warners was getting behind the 3-D process. *House of Wax* was a remake of a horror movie from 20 years before, Mike Curtiz's *Mystery of the Wax Museum*, in which Lionel Atwill played a sculptor of wax figures who is horribly burned when his crooked partner torches their Manhattan wax museum for the fire insurance money. Atwill's later return, gnarled and wheelchair-bound, coincides with the appearance of a hideous burn-faced figure who commits murders and steals bodies from the local morgue. It turns out that Atwill and the monster are one and the same: Not really crippled, he wears a wax mask of his old face over his actual fire-scarred face, and is

Fun *House of Wax* publicity poses with some of the heads and figures. All the Chamber of Horrors figures were wax except one: The torturer stretching a girl on a rack was a guy about as muscular as the Hulk! He froze in place like a statue during takes.

re-stocking his museum with the bodies of his victims, lightly coated in wax.

My *Folsom Prison* director Crane Wilbur wrote the *House of Wax* screenplay, making some changes along the way. For one thing, he combined *Mystery of the Wax Museum's* two female leads (played by Glenda Farrell and Fay Wray) into a single character. Brynie Foy got the job of producer, with Joe Breen working as Brynie's associate. For director, they selected 39-year-old Andre de Toth, with whom I had not worked before. Andre, who began his directing career in his native Hungary, had been in Hollywood for a bit over ten years and had directed about a dozen movies here, including two with his then-wife Veronica Lake. (By the time *House of Wax* came around, Andre and Veronica had split.) It struck some people as strange that Jack Warner entrusted the direction of the studio's first 3-D picture to Andre, because the man only had one eye and therefore couldn't even *see* in three dimensions! But this seemed to present no problems—and it was certainly the least of *my* problems with Andre.

At the end of the previous chapter, I told how I learned that I had been selected for **House of Wax**: Joe Breen saw me in the drugstore, moping about having been passed over for a part in *The Eddie Cantor Story*, and said, "When you're down like that, there's only one way to go and that's *up*"—then told me that I had been assigned to **House of Wax**. I retell that anecdote in order to mention that that experience taught me a lesson: When you're really down in the dumps, there's only one way to go and that's *up*! And this was way up for me, getting the romantic lead in a picture like **House of Wax**.

If memory serves, one of the first things I did was work in some tests with Vera Miles, who was up for the female lead. I just *adored* Vera Miles—she was so gorgeous and such a nice girl, and I wanted her to land that part. I didn't know Phyllis Kirk at that time, so I was really rooting for Vera. Phyllis ended up getting it, and she was fine, of course.

Vincent Price played the starring role as the mad sculptor. It's now a cliché in writing or talking about Vince to say that he was nothing at all like any of the villainous characters he played; in real life, Vince was just an angel, one of *the* most delightful people to work with, a very artistic man and very generous. I loved working with Vincent, but, unfortunately, that's the only time I ever had the opportunity.

Second-billed as a New York police lieutenant was Frank Lovejoy (this was my next-to-last feature with Frank); Carolyn Jones had a small part as a golddigger who becomes one of Price's coated-in-wax victims; and playing Price's grotesque deaf-mute henchman Igor was a young actor named Charles Buchinsky.

Crane Wilbur rewrote the old *Mystery of the Wax Museum* script so that **House of Wax** took place back in New York's gaslight era. The film opens at the wax museum of Prof. Henry Jarrod (Price), a humble, gentle artist whose ruthless partner (Roy Roberts) wants to burn the museum for insurance money. There is a fistfight, Jarrod is knocked out and the partner sets the building ablaze. Even though I wasn't in this scene, I stopped by to watch it being filmed. Right there on the soundstage, they burned that elaborate wax museum set and a number of wax statues. I still remember Vincent walking through the flames, and running through a doorway just before some burning beams came crashing down right behind him. Andre de Toth enjoyed watching the actors doing stuff like that; he loved to see people in danger—as I would soon find out!

Years later, Jarrod reappears, confined to a wheelchair but eager to start a new wax museum, this one a Chamber of Horrors. Through his young assistant, Scott Andrews (that was my character), Jarrod meets Scott's girlfriend, Sue Allen (Phyllis Kirk)—who resembles his crowning achievement, a wax figure of Marie Antoinette that burned in the fire. From then on, Sue is stalked by a burn-faced figure who, of course, turns out at the end to be Jarrod. The finale finds my character battling in the museum with Igor while, in the basement workroom, Jarrod has Sue shackled to the bottom of a waxing vat and is preparing to coat her with boiling wax.

Charles Bronson, then acting under the name Charles Buchinsky, got carried away during our fight scene, and I ended up in the hospital getting X-rayed!

Charles Buchinsky was a character. One day he and I were having lunch in the Green Room, a dining room for the actors and directors. On the walls there they had pictures of all the great Warners contract players, Humphrey Bogart, Bette Davis, John Garfield and so on. If you remember John Garfield, you know that he played romantic leads even though he was rather offbeat-looking. Charlie looked up at Garfield's picture and said to me, in a very quiet, serious tone, "Someday I will play romantic leads like John Garfield." And I said to my*self*, "This guy's kidding himself!" Charlie had a crew haircut, sunken cheekbones—he wasn't very attractive at all. For the role of a character like Igor in *House of Wax*, he was perfect, but for romantic leads—forget it! Well, I couldn't have been more wrong. Charlie later changed his last name from Buchinsky to Bronson and, of course, did become a leading man and play romantic leads.

The fight scene between Scott (my character) and Igor was shot on the museum set where there was a real, working guillotine that I assume Warners had borrowed from a French museum. Just prior to starting to shoot the scene, Andre came to Charlie Bronson and me and he said, with his thick Hungarian accent, "The depth of focus of the thrrree-D camerrra is so grrreat that we cannot use stunt doubles. You and Charrrlie must do the fight yourrrselves." We both agreed to do it; I was then a young contract player, Charlie a young, powerfully built guy, and we were both pretty handy. Soon we started the fight, throwing axes and chairs at each other. (Of course, we were really throwing them toward the camera, for the 3-D effect.) Charlie had a tremendous physique that he must have gotten from working in the coal mines in Pennsylvania; for one shot, he lifted me up over his head and slammed me down on the museum floor. I landed on my tailbone, and the pain went through my back like you couldn't believe. I just laid there. Eventually they took me to the hospital and X-rayed me, but it turned out that everything was fine. I did, however, need to take the rest of the day off.

The next day we went back and continued the fight—and Andre proceeded to have Charlie bouncing my head off the floor! I said, "Charlie—y'know—kind of *fake* it a little bit!" Unfortunately for me, though, Charlie was like Jack Palance at the time, he was really living the part, and he was bangin' my head on the floor!

By pounding my head on the floor, Charlie soon rendered me "unconscious." Andre said, "Now, Charrrlie, you pick up Paul, and you carrry him over to the guillotine and you put his head in place." I wasn't sure I liked the sound of that; this was, after all, a working guillotine with a razor-sharp blade. There was even a 35-pound block of wood attached above the blade, to give it impetus as it came down. I went over and checked the guillotine, and I saw that they had two big spikes on each side of the blade to hold it in place so that it wouldn't fall; that eased my mind. I played dead while Charlie lugged me over to the guillotine and placed me on it and positioned the wooden stock over the back of my neck.

Now it was time to shoot the scene of Frank Lovejoy and a squad of policemen rushing in to rescue me. Andre told Frank, "For this next shot, you come in with the other policemen. You see Buchinski! He's got Paul in the guillotine! Charlie's starting to unwind the rope to release the blade! You rrrush over, you grrrab

More frightening on the set than in the movie: My scene on the working guillotine.

Buchinski, you fight, you fight, you subdue Buchinski, the cops take Buchinski. Now you see Paul! You go over! You lift up the block of wood, you pull out Paul and, zoooom!, down come the blade! That's the next shot! Light it!"

Needless to say, his instructions to Frank had caught my ear. "Andre," I said. "Excuse me, but—you *are* gonna shoot this in separate cuts, aren't you?" Andre shook his head: "No, no, no! We do it in one take, one cut! Frrrank pulls you out, zoooom!, down come the blade!"

"Andre, I don't wanna intercede on your job as director," I said, "but how do you propose to do it in one take?" Andre pointed to Red Turner, the prop man. "Red will sit on top of the guillotine," Andre explained. "He will hold the block of wood between his legs. When Frank pull you out, Red will release the blade. And we see it all in one take!"

None of this sat well with me. I asked, "Andre—supposing Red drops the blade prematurely?" Andre said, "Only hurt for a second. Now, don't t'ink about it, it'll make you nervous." And he walked away!

In those days, it took 25 to 30 minutes to light a shot, so I had a *lot* of time to "t'ink about it." I went over to the assistant director, Jimmy McMahon, and I asked him, "Is this a gag?" Jimmy shook his head grimly. "This is no gag. I just called Charlie Greenlaw in the production office and told him about it . . ." I went to Pev Marley, our cameraman, and again I asked, "Pev, is this a gag? Come on, level with me." And Pev said, "No, no. That's the way he plans to shoot it." My heart sank.

Rescued!

Next, I went to Red Turner and asked him if he was *really* going to sit up on top of that thing and hold the blade. "What else can I do?" he said. "If I don't obey the director, I'll get fired. But I just called the head of props, Eric Stacy, and told *him* about it. He's on his way down."

Now convinced that I was actually expected to perform the scene as described, I walked over to Andre and I told him, "Andre, look, this isn't a case of getting hurt. This is a case of being *beheaded* if something goes wrong. Supposing Red Turner has a heart attack. Supposing there's an earthquake. Supposing something happens and he drops the blade prematurely." Again Andre said, "Only hurt you for a second. Don't worry about it, make yourself nervous." More firmly this time, I said, "Andre, we can't *do* it like this," and he said—with a bit of anger—"We *do* it like this! Now, don't talk about it! Go 'way!"

I went to my little portable dressing room on the set, which was 30 or 40 feet away from the guillotine, and I thought some more about it. Stuntman Charlie Horvath was on the set and I realized that he'd be a good person to talk to. When I asked him if he'd do it the way Andre had outlined it, he said, "No way."

"Would you do it at *all?*" I asked him.

"The only way I would do it—and I would think about it 100 times!—is if I had control over the release of the blade. But I wouldn't do it if I were you."

Even Frank Lovejoy told me, "Don't do it, kid."

Finally the set was lit and everybody was ready and Jimmy McMahon was calling out, "Places everybody!" Everybody took their positions, Buchinski by the guillotine, Frank Lovejoy and Dabbs Greer were in their position—and atop the guillotine, Red Turner, a stubby cigar clenched in his teeth, and the blade between his legs. There was a kind of awkward silence on the set, because the people knew that things weren't quite right. I just stood on the steps of my little portable dressing room and I didn't move. I didn't know what the hell to do. I had four kids and one on the way, and so I didn't want to disobey the director and lose my contract.

But I also didn't want to lose my *head.*

"Come on, Paul!" Andre called out from about 60 feet away. "Put your head in the guillotine!"

I just stood there. It was my moment of decision.

And finally I said, "I'm not gonna do it, Andre."

Andre bellowed, "Put your head in the guillotine, you *cowarrrd*!" He *screamed* it out.

I felt the hair stand up on the back of my neck. And I said, very quietly, almost like a Marlon Brando delivery, "If you call me a coward again, Andre—I'll *kill* you." And I meant it! The Corona Italian came out in me! There was a deadly silence on the set. I thought to myself,

Vincent Price and I at LaGuardia, en route to *House of Wax*'s New York premiere.

"Oh-oh. My career is over."

Andre yelled to Jimmy McMahon, the assistant director, "This man is finished in this film! Send him home, McMahon! Send him home! Get rid of him! I don't want to see his face on this set again!" Jimmy told me, "I guess you better go home, Paul," and so I went home.

I sat at home for three days and I couldn't imagine what was going to happen next—I'd been told I was off the picture, but I still had some major scenes left to do. In the meantime, however, Charlie Greenlaw and Eric Stacy went onto the museum set and saw the setup and agreed that it was a dangerous situation. Jack Warner subsequently heard about it and he told Andre, "You go back and shoot that scene and shoot it properly, without endangering anybody's life or limb." And yet this nightmare *still* was not over: Joe Breen came up to my place and he said, "Paul, I'm your friend, but it is my duty to deliver this message to you from Andre de Toth. Andre wants you to come back and he wants you to *request* that he do the scene the way it was staged the first time."

Some of the family greets me at LaGuardia. My mother is center.

"What do *you* think I should do, Joe?"

Joe said, "I think you should say, 'Up your ass, Andre!'"

"Well, that's my answer. Not 'Up your ass, Andre,' but just say no, I won't do it that way."

Fortunately, the next thing that happened was that I got word from Solly Biano, the head of talent, that everything had finally been squared away with Andre and that I was to report back to work the next morning. Well, when I got to there the next day, it was a silent set—a *very* silent set. There was the guillotine, and above it, out of camera range, was a parallel platform where Eric Stacy was standing.

He had drilled a hole in the side of the guillotine, below the blade, and inserted a long iron bar, maybe three feet long, which held the blade up. I was told that, at the crucial moment, when Frank lifted me off of the guillotine, Eric would yank the bar out and the blade would come down. Basically, it was still what Andre wanted, it was still one shot and it was still dangerous, because I had to depend on Eric Stacy pulling the bar out at the proper moment. If his timing was off, my head was off!

I felt that I couldn't renege again, however, because this *was* a considerable change from the original plan of Red Turner sitting atop the guillotine, holding the blade between his legs! So that's the way we did it: Stacy held onto the bar and both hands until I was clear, and then he pulled it to release the blade. When you see the movie, you'll see that it was done in one take. Andre got his way. The man was a devil—the type of individual who liked to put people in spots where they were suffering. Another example: In the scene at the very end where Phyllis Kirk was down in Vincent Price's workshop, bound to the bottom of the waxing vat as Price prepared to coat her with wax, Andre insisted that she be half-naked. Phyllis was *so* embarrassed, she didn't want to do it, but he insisted—he said he wanted it "for the foreign version"! And, once again getting his way, he had her in there with no top on, and just a little bikini bottom. That's the way he was. The waxing vat was up high enough that the people there on the set, on the sidelines, couldn't see her, but, of course, the camera was positioned up high where it could.

At one point, I had to go into the looping room and redo the dialogue in one of my scenes with Vincent Price. P.V., who was about three by then, was with me this one time. When you're looping, you have to wait for your cue to come up before you speak; there's a series of beeps, and then you start talking, trying to match the lip sync. We're doing this one take, beep beep beep—and all of a sudden P.V. says, "Daddy, I gotta go potty!"—right at the moment I was supposed to talk! They played it back, and in this scene between me and Vincent Price, out of my mouth is coming this three-year-old's little voice, "Daddy, I gotta go potty!" We had a few laughs over that!

More pleasant than some of my memories of the making of

At the Paramount Theater with publicity head Mort Blumenstock, Phyllis Kirk and Frank Lovejoy.

House of Wax were my experiences at the premiere at New York's Paramount Theater, the place where Frank Sinatra had first burst onto the scene by becoming a smash hit sensation with the bobbysoxers. The place was packed the night of the *House of Wax* premiere, 5,000 people, and I think 500 of them were my relatives—my mother, my aunts, my uncles, my cousins. Major Warner, who ran Warners' New York office, was there, along with a number of the other studio executives, and Mort Blumenstock, the head of Warners publicity in New York, was backstage.

Singer Eddie Fisher and a big band performed prior to the start of the movie. In his opening remarks, Eddie said, "Ladies and gentlemen, I'd like to dedicate my show tonight to the man who discovered me and helped get me started in show business, Mr. Eddie Cantor." He and the band then did their bit, and after *that* he introduced Vincent Price, and the audience went crazy. Vince said a few words, Frank Lovejoy made an appearance, Phyllis Kirk made an appearance, and finally Eddie said, "Here's the young romantic lead in the picture, Paul Picerni." I came on stage, and the audience just *erupted* in applause, because, as I mentioned, it was all my relatives. They went crazy! I was full of emotion—it was such a big moment in my career.

"Ladies and gentlemen," I said, "at the beginning of the show tonight, Eddie Fisher dedicated his performance to a gentleman who helped him a great deal in his career, Mr. Eddie Cantor. I feel this is quite a step in *my* career, being on stage here at the world-famous Paramount Theater. A lot of people helped me get to this point in my career, but I want to pay tribute to *one* person tonight." And I said, "Ma—take a bow!"

Out in the audience, my mother stood up and they put a spotlight on her. In my mind's eye I can still to this day picture her standing there, a *very* proud mom. I was crying—she was crying—the audience was crying—Eddie Fisher was crying—*every*body was crying. It was just a *great* moment. A great moment. As I came off stage, I ran into Mort Blumenstock, a big, jovial, wonderful guy. He too was crying, he had a handkerchief to his eyes, and in a choked-up voice he said, "Paul—oh, my God, Paul, that was wonderful, that was beautiful . . . Listen, Paul: Can your mother come back for the second show?" I never forgot that!

Publicizing *House of Wax* on the Chicago radio show of Irv Kupcinet (right). Other guests were Gordon and Sheila MacRae and, to my left, the great silent-screen comedian Harold Lloyd.

I was in New York for about ten days, the whole early run of the picture. One night, Vincent Price, his wife Mary and I took a short walk to Sardi's, a famous restaurant in the '40s, right around the corner from the Paramount. We were upstairs having a late supper and there were a lot of familiar faces in the room—all the Broadway actors who'd just come off the stage and come up there for their late snacks. Vincent said, "You know, it's always so embarrassing when you see the familiar faces of these actors and you can't remember their names. But I found a solution to that."

"What is it, Vincent?" I asked.

"As soon as I see an actor approaching me, I stand up, I extend my hand and I say, 'Vincent Price.' And inevitably they will say, 'Joe Blow,' or whatever their name is, and shake hands."

At that moment—at that *precise* moment, like it was written in a script—an actor started walking across the room toward Vincent, and I saw this blank stare come over Vincent's face! But he stood up and he stuck out his hand and he said, "Vincent Price!" And the actor scoffed, "You don't have to tell me your name, Vince! I killed ya in three movies!" We never figured out who he was—I don't know to this day!

After New York, Warners sent me on the road with **House of Wax** for ten weeks. I went to Dayton, I went to Akron, I went to Milwaukee, I went all over. I'd talk about the making of the movie and take questions from the audience, and then everybody would put on their 3-D glasses and the movie would begin. (The movie was filled with great 3-D effects—all the fight scenes, the paddleball man, the chorus girls kicking their legs out and so on.) Every stop I made, the box office went up five, six thousand dollars in that city. At the point when I'd been on the road for eight or nine weeks, Warners had Gordon MacRae, one of the studio's top singing stars, meet me in Chicago—Warners sent him in to help me there, because Chicago was a major city and a good money-making opportunity for the picture. Gordon and I worked out a little comedy routine and did it on the stage of the theater. Gordon and his wife Sheila (who later became an actress and co-starred on **The Jackie Gleason Show**) and I shared a two-bedroom suite at the Ambassador Hotel while in the Windy City.

Chicago was the last stop on my tour and it hadn't come a day too soon: Not only was I really tired, but I hadn't seen my wife or my kids in two months! I was in our Ambassador Hotel suite with Gordon when I got a phone call from the head of publicity at Warner Brothers back in Hollywood. "Paul, instead of coming home after Chicago, we want you to go straight to San Francisco," he told me. "And then up to Seattle, Tacoma and Portland."

My 15-city *House of Wax* tour continues.

"Marvin!" I said. "I haven't seen my wife in eight weeks. I'd like to go *home* now."

Marvin didn't budge. "You can't," he said. "The opening is night after tomorrow; you gotta be in San Francisco. You're doing so well, the picture's doing so great!"

"I guess I *have* to," I sighed, "but I sure don't *want* to . . ."

Gordon could hear the conversation—and at that time, he was a much bigger star at the studio than I was. He said, "Gimme the phone," and I handed him the receiver.

"Marvin," he said, "Paul is not going *any*where after Chicago, he's going straight home. Do you understand this man's been on the road for eight weeks, he hasn't seen his wife and kids . . ." Marvin told Gordon that it was Jack Warner who wanted me to go to San Francisco, and Gordon said, "All right: He'll go to San Francisco if you fly up his wife and kids and meet him at the hotel there." Gordon actually made that demand on my behalf. And Marvin said, "Okay! Agreed!" I'll always love Gordon for that: Warners sent Marie, Niccoletta and P.V. (Gemma and Maria were too little at the time), they met me at the St. Francis Hotel in San Francisco and we had three or four days together there. After that, Marie and the kids flew home and I went on to all the northern cities. I was on the road for a total of ten weeks.

House of Wax was made for about a million dollars, and it grossed like $20,000,000. (I think the cost vs. the gross was bigger than the 1997 blockbuster *Titanic*—percentage-wise, *House of Wax* made a bigger profit.) I came back to Warner Brothers and I was a hero there because every town I was in, the *House of Wax* grosses far exceeded the towns I *wasn't* in. So I returned to the studio feeling pretty good about the whole thing—and I got a call from Solly Biano, the head of talent.

"Paul, I'm sending you a script, a Randy Scott movie, *Riding Shotgun*. There's a part in there for you."

"Oh, great," I said. "Who's directing it?"

"Andre de Toth," Solly said.

"You're kidding!" I gasped.

"Andre requested you," Solly said.

Andre *requested* me—?!

I got the script and began reading. Randolph Scott is riding shotgun on a stagecoach and they come into a way station. Randy gets off the wagon, he comes into the way station and he says, "How are you, Jeff?" Jeff was my character. Randy says, "Jeff, listen, can you do me a favor? Can you take the stage into Dodge City?" Jeff says, "Yeah, I'd be glad to." So Jeff gets on the stage and he rides off; there are a couple of montage shots of the stage going across country; and all of a sudden it's attacked by Indians. And on page three of the script, Jeff is shot dead with an arrow and falls off the stage!

I called Solly back and I said, "Solly, what the hell is this? I just had star billing in the biggest hit of the year, *House of Wax*, and now you put me in a picture like *Riding Shotgun* and I get killed on page three?!"

"You're killed on page *three?*" Solly sputtered. "You're kidding! Jeez, I thought it was a big part!" (He hadn't read the script; all he knew was that Andre requested me.) Then he said, "Paul, I'm sorry. I don't know what to tell you. We have nothing else going on the lot. I guess we'll just have to put you on layoff, because there's nothing else happening unless you wanna do this stupid thing and stay on salary 'til something comes up."

Well, like I did many times in my career, I went along with what they wanted me to do. I did the movie *Riding Shotgun* with Andre de Toth, and I got killed on page three. Then a couple months later, I got a part in another Andre de Toth Western, *The Bounty Hunter*, again with Randy Scott—and again a part so small, you'll miss me if you blink. So I guess Andre got a semblance of revenge. *But*—I'd managed to stay on salary. In all my years at Warners, I was never on layoff. Not one day.

Years later, around 1987 I believe, *House of Wax* was running in 3-D at a theater on Wilshire Boulevard in L.A., and I was invited to appear in person. When I got there, I was happy to see that they had also invited Vincent Price. And suddenly—there was Andre de Toth. "Paul! Sweetheart! So good to see you!" he gushed, as though I were his long-lost brother.

I was so surprised with the warm greeting I received from Andre—but I really should not have been. Like that other Hungarian director Michael Curtiz, Andre was *such* a phony!

12
THE FREELANCE ACTOR

Nothing lasts forever: In September of 1953, I was let go by Warners. I knew it was coming because just about *every*body else, all the other actors, had already been dropped. Television was taking over. Instead of going to the movies, most people were now sitting at home in front of their sets. Soon the studios, most or all of them, were in tough shape. And at Warners, and other studios, actors started being let go as their options came up.

When my option came up, I knew I was going to go, despite the wonderful job I did on the tour with **House of Wax**. What other choice did they have? The lot was dead. Everybody else was gone, including all my buddies—Phil Carey, Dick Wesson, all of 'em. The only people under contract left in September, when I got my walking papers, were me and Doris Day. And after her contract expired, she was gone too.

By this time, fortunately for me, everybody around town knew me because of all the Warner Brothers publicity that I'd had; in the years I was there at Warners, my name had been in **The Hollywood Reporter** and **Variety** constantly. There were a number of producers out there who were anxious to hire me, particularly for television. My first show was with Jack Webb on the popular **Dragnet** series. More on that later.

The first movie I did as a freelancer after leaving Warners was **Drive a Crooked Road** with Mickey Rooney as an auto mechanic duped into driving a getaway car for bank robbers. The director was Richard Quine, who just loved me for some reason and used me in movies two or three times after that. Mickey Rooney was such a great talent—I worked with him on other occasions too, including

Operation Mad Ball, which was also directed by Quine. Right after *Drive a Crooked Road* I played golf with Rooney and he was all over the course, and soon began losing his temper and throwing his clubs—the little man had a big temper on the golf course. Years later I ran into him at the Derby Club, an off-track betting joint in Ventura. He mentioned to me that it was Louis B. Mayer who took him to a track for the first time, years earlier, and he (Mickey) had won six dollars that day. And *since* that day, he said, he'd lost *six million*!

With Yvette Dugay and Philip Ahn in *The Shanghai Story*.

The Shanghai Story was a Republic picture with a wonderful old director named Frank Lloyd, who had directed the original Clark Gable-Charles Laughton *Mutiny on the Bounty*. It was set in a hotel in Communist-controlled Shanghai, where the Commies have interned a group of Americans and Europeans on suspicion of having a spy in their midst. I played an Italian, Mr. De Verno, and the beautiful young actress Yvette Dugay was playing my wife. In one scene, practically the whole cast was all together on the hotel lobby set, being interrogated by a Chinese Communist officer. It took days and days to shoot this sequence, to cover all the different actors who were assembled in the lobby: They would shoot Edmond O'Brien, shoot Ruth Roman, shoot the Chinese officer who had a long speech. My position in the scene was standing behind Yvette with my arms around her. We were in this position for *days*, and between takes Yvette was kind of pressing her beautiful little body against me, and I was pressing back. The perspiration was popping out on her nose; she was getting so hot. Actor James Griffith, who was standing right next to us all this time, was aware of this. At one point after two or three days, I kinda eased back a little bit and Jimmy Griffith slid over and he took my position behind Yvette, without her knowing it. And the pressing resumed, but now it was Jimmy Griffith standing behind her and she thought it was *me*. I slowly walked around the whole group, and then right in front of her. When I appeared in front of her, she gaped up at me with a look of horror and then turned around and saw Jimmy Griffith. She said, "You son of a bitch!"—and she *slapped* him! But playfully. It was a very funny moment.

Right away after *The Shanghai Story* came my second picture for Richard Quine, *Pushover*, with Fred MacMurray as a cop who goes over to the other side of the law because of his infatuation with the moll of a bank robber. Fred is best-remembered by a lot of fans today for the fine job he did as the dad on the TV series *My Three Sons* and for all the Disney movies he made at around that same time, but he was also excellent in *film noir* and crime melodramas like *Pushover* and Billy Wilder's *Double Indemnity*. Fred was one of the richest men in Hollywood, partly because he was also one of the most frugal. He was the only actor I ever knew who used to half-sole his shoes. In the old days, if you had holes in the bottoms of your shoes and couldn't afford new ones, you took them to the shoemaker and he would put on a full sole and a new heel. A cheaper way to do it, instead of putting on an entire new sole all the way from toe to heel, would be a *half*-sole and keep the *old* heel. I heard that that's what Fred did—although I must admit I never checked his shoes to find out!

I do know that one day when we were shooting *Pushover* at Columbia, Fred, Phil Carey, Dorothy Malone and I went to the Naples Restaurant, which was on Gower Street right across from the Columbia studio. As we were finishing up, the waitress brought the check, and (as Hollywood waitresses usually do) she laid it on the table next to the biggest star. She put the check next to Fred, who picked it up. We were all sure he was going to treat, but he looked it over closely and then he said, "Let's see . . . Paul, you owe $4.98 . . . Phil, you're $6.00. Oh, and Dorothy, you had *dessert*, you owe $7.50!" Fred sat there splitting up the check!

On our first day on the set of **Pushover**, Richard Quine, producer Jules Schermer and Phil Carey were talking about the actress who was going to be playing the gangster's moll who leads Fred MacMurray astray. She was new in Hollywood and yet she was playing the lead, and Quine and the producer were asking each other how Max Arnow (the head of talent at Columbia) could put this untrained girl into the leading part in their picture. Neither of them knew much about the actress at that point, but *I* did; in fact, I had been on hand the day that Kim Novak was discovered.

A few months earlier, my agent Wilt Melnick and I were at RKO for an interview, and the casting director happened to suggest that, just for fun, we go over to Stage 13 and get a look at all the beautiful young girls who were there acting in a picture with Vincent Price. When we got to the stage, *I* got the initial impression that it was an outer space picture—it looked like a set representing the Moon— but it turned out to be an Arabian Nights-type adventure called **Son of Sinbad** with Dale Robertson as Sinbad and Price as Omar Khayyam. Sure enough, there in their harem costumes were about 12 beautiful girls, including one who captivated Wilt's attention to the point that he said, "Boy, I want to talk to her." It was Kim Novak—this was the first time that Wilt and I laid eyes on her. We walked up to her and introduced ourselves, and Wilt asked her where she was from. "I'm from Chicago," she told us. "I'm a dancer. This is the first thing I've done."

Wilt told her he wanted to talk to her about possibly representing her. "Come in my office next week," he told her, giving her the address and setting the time. A few days later, I was in Wilt's office on the day she had her appointment, so I got to meet her again then. (Wilt was with the Louis Shurr office, which handled Bob Hope, Debbie Reynolds, Paul Douglas and his wife Jan Sterling, Broderick Crawford, Dan Dailey—a number of big stars of the day.) While Kim was in Wilt's office, which was in the back of this railroad car-type building on Rodeo Drive across the street from Romanoffs, who walks in the front but Max Arnow, arriving for a meeting with Louis Shurr. Wilt came out and said hello to Max, and told him, "I got a girl in my office that I want you to meet her in a couple of weeks. I think she's good contract material."

Max said, "I want to see her *now*."

"No, no," Wilt objected. "I'll let you see her in a couple of weeks"—Kim was just a little bit chubby, and Wilt wanted her to lose a few pounds before he began taking her around.

Again, Max insisted that he wanted to see her immediately, and Wilt finally acquiesced and introduced Max to Kim Novak. And, sure enough, the following week when Wilt brought her in to Columbia, Max signed her up for 150 bucks a week. That was the start of Kim Novak, who in just a few short years would become one of the top stars in Hollywood.

Now, flash-forward again, it's the first day of **Pushover**, Kim's first co-starring picture, and Quine, Schermer and Phil Carey are discussing the leading lady, making comments like "How the hell could Max stick this dame on us?" Finally Kim walks out of her dressing room for the first scene. She's wearing a white silk blouse and that's *it*. Nothing underneath. You could see the outlines of her breasts, her nipples—it was just breathtaking. She had the most beautiful breasts you could imagine, and this was *long* before the days of implants. Hers were natural beauties. She comes out and does her scene, physically she's a sensation, all eyes are upon her— and the guys who were complaining that she was in the picture shut up *quick*!

Kim would stay in her dressing room, come out to do the scenes and then return to her dressing room, every time. I found out later (from Wilt) that Max Arnow had instructed her, "You just go do the scenes. Otherwise, stay in your dressing room. Don't associate with anybody. Don't talk to anybody in the crew. *Not a soul.* After each scene, go back to your dressing room and stay there." And that's what she did. This created an air of mystery about her; it made her seem inaccessible. Once a star *attains* that air of mystery, if they just give you a hello, you feel *honored*: "My God, Kim Novak said hello to *me*!" It actually works!

With her good looks and her beautiful breasts, Kim became a big sensation in **Pushover** and soon she was starring in some of Columbia's bigger pictures, including three more directed by Richard

Quine. I believe that Quine fell in love with her, but I don't know whatever became of that romance. They later did **Bell Book and Candle**, **The Notorious Landlady** and **Strangers When We Meet**; I was in **Strangers When We Meet**, and also in Quine's **Operation Mad Ball**. He would put me in pictures, sometimes a minor role, just to have me there, like a good luck charm. Also, he liked the fact that I could be kind of inventive. In **Mad Ball**, a service comedy set in France, there was a scene in a tent where Private Jack Lemmon is talking to a bunch of fellow enlisted men about his plan to throw a secret party—a "mad ball"—in order to fraternize with the unit's nurses. "We're gonna do *this* and we're gonna do *that* and we'll get whiskey and then we'll pick up the girls"—he's coordinating the whole thing, and getting more and more excited. During the rehearsal, as he was talking, as he was building up in this powerful speech, I started humming "La Marseillaise," the French national anthem, and the other guys in the scene picked it up. Dick Quine *loved* that and he said, "Oh, boy, leave that *in*," and we did—in the finished picture, I start humming, the other guys do too, and then on the soundtrack a big 100-piece *orchestra* comes in playing "La Marseillaise" as background music! I'd dream up little things like that, and Dick Quine appreciated that. In **Strangers When We Meet**, in a garden party scene at Kirk Douglas' house, I had a very small part as a guest. In the rehearsal, my character was supposed to be in the back of the yard, and while I was back there I began looking down at the grass, bending down, *examining* it. Quine asked, "What are you *doing?*" I told him, "I'm checking for crabgrass." (I knew that I had a speech later on in the picture where I asked Kirk Douglas, "How do you have a yard with no crabgrass in it?") That ended up in the picture too.

* * * * * * *

My son Charles Philip ("C.P.") has the distinction of having Maureen and Phil Carey as his godparents. As handsome as all my sons, C.P. went to Crespi Carmelite High School and then to the University of California at San Luis Obispo. C.P. and his lovely wife Angela live in a home on the beach in Carpenteria, one of my favorite places. He has a riding academy in the Santa Barbara area and teaches young people how to jump horses. He and his students compete quite successfully in equestrian events. Every once in a while

C.P. will send me a "pilot script" he's written for a TV series. Like his brother P.V., he's quite a good writer. He has two sons, Rick and Mason.

* * * * * * *

I did quite a few more TV shows between *Pushover* and my next movie, *The Adventures of Hajji Baba*, a color-CinemaScope desert adventure with John Derek in the title role. John played a poor Persian barber who tries to help the caliph's spoiled daughter (Elaine Stewart) avoid being forced into marriage with Nur-El-Din, a ruthless prince of the desert. Along the way they are captured by a band of wild women led by Amanda Blake, and then *all* are captured by the evil prince.

Prince Nur-El-Din, the lead villain, was my part—a magnificent part, my first really good one, post-Warner Brothers. It included a great entrance, some scenes with a harem of beautiful girls and a climactic swordfight with John Derek. I was selected for the role after being interviewed by Don Weis, a young, up-and-coming director at the time.

Don got *his* job on the picture as part of a sort of "package deal." Walter Wanger, the producer of *Hajji Baba*, wanted for the role of the caliph's daughter Elaine Stewart, an actress who was hot at the time after her spectacular staircase entrance in MGM's *The Bad and the Beautiful*. But in order to get Elaine, an MGM contractee, Walter was told by MGM, "We'll give you Elaine Stewart if you take one of our young contract directors with her." Walter didn't *want* to do that but he was forced to do it, and the director he got was Don Weis. Don interviewed me; I was cast as the heavy and taken by Walter to Western Costume, where a beautiful outfit was made for me. They even had boots made for me that were built-up about three inches, to give me more stature. I was five-foot-ten, but with the boots I stood over six feet.

To shoot *Hajji Baba*, we went up to Lone Pine, not far from Mount Whitney, where they are rocky mountains and some wonderful cliffs and, of course, the big sand dunes essential for a desert film. They utilized all of that beautiful terrain in the picture. Also in the cast were 12 lovely models that Walter brought out from New York. They had *very* little acting experience, but they were gorgeous and *that* was the important thing. And, to make

Making love to Rosemarie Bowe in *Hajji Baba*.

things even better, they played Prince Nur-El-Din's harem—and I was the prince! I *told* you it was a great part!

The hero, John Derek, was probably only about five-nine, but he was a well-built, handsome guy along the lines of Tyrone Power. He was *so* handsome, almost "beautiful," that it was as though he had the face of a woman. But he was a masculine, very athletic guy who was good at *every*thing. He was good with the sword, he was a marksman with the bow and arrow, and he was *very* good with horses. In fact, he had his own, beautiful horses up there at that Lone Pine location. John also loved the girls, and in later years he had some knock-out wives like Ursula Andress, Linda Evans and Bo Derek, all very sexy, gorgeous women. I don't remember if he was married at the time we did **Hajji Baba**, but that was when I found out how much he liked girls—no matter what age! He had this "thing" about young girls.

The whole cast stayed at the Lone Pine Inn, where Thomas Gomez (who played a merchant in the picture) was my "next-door neighbor." He was a lot of fun. Tommy loved to eat—he was a gourmet chef and he loved good food. One night he and I and a couple of the harem girls were having dinner at a steak house in Lone Pine, and Tommy ordered a steak rare. The waitress brought it over, he looked at it and he said, "I ordered this steak *rare*. This is well done. Would you please get me another steak?" The waitress left and after a little while she came back with another steak, but it was *still* not quite what Tommy wanted. (In the meantime, the rest of us at the table are already eating.) Tommy told the waitress, "Look, I ordered the steak rare, and this is still well done. Too cooked. I want rare. *Rare!*"—he seemed to be getting a little upset now, and, of course, hungrier and hungrier. The waitress came back and put a third steak in front of Tommy and he cut it open and his face fell. "I said *rare*, not *raw!*"—she'd brought him a raw steak! He never *did* eat that night!

One of my harem girls was played by a young actress named Rosemarie Bowe, who eventually married Robert Stack. One day after we'd been shooting a week or so, Walter Wanger came out to the set and he didn't like the way Don Weis was directing an exterior that involved Rosemarie. When Walter stepped in and tried to give Rosemarie a few pointers on how she should play the scene, there was a big blow-up. "You get the hell off my set," Don told Walter. "I'll not shoot another foot of film until you get off the set! And don't show your damn face on this set *again!*" Don was a feisty, strong-willed little guy, and he kicked Walter Wanger off the set of his own picture! And Walter couldn't do anything *but* walk off the set, because otherwise the shooting would *end* right there. Walter did come back and visit once in a while, but he would always stay 100 yards from where the camera was, so that Don Weis wouldn't see him.

Elaine Stewart was the female lead but I didn't get to know her at all. But I do remember that she had quite an ugly boyfriend! He was a doctor, about five-foot-four, no personality at all, really unattractive, and he was with her *constantly* up there in Lone Pine. She never associated with anybody else but him, and I never saw her off the set: After work, she would go to her room at the hotel and nobody would see her, because she was with this funny-looking little guy. I've noticed in my life that there have been several beautiful women who have had nondescript (translation: ugly!) boyfriends. Myrna Hansen, a Universal starlet of the day, was so

With *Hajji Baba* co-stars Elaine Stewart and John Derek. In 1956, when John and I did *Omar Khayyam* at Paramount, his wife Ursula Andress would visit the set—like Kim Novak, wearing a silk blouse with no bra underneath.

beautiful, and her boyfriend was Chubby Johnson, a fat old Western character actor! He had a "Svengali influence" over her or *some*thing, and she wouldn't go any place without Chubby Johnson. Wilt Melnick represented Myrna, and at one point when Howard Hughes wanted to sign her up, Chubby went with her to the meeting! I guess Hughes didn't give her the contract because of that.

In *Hajji Baba*, Prince Nur-El-Din has to do a lot of the things audiences expect from this sort of character in this sort of costume adventure: fancy horse mounts, swordfighting and so on. I was already good on a horse, having done quite a few Westerns, and the swordfighting wasn't that difficult; for the most part, it was just a few slashes. (At Warner Brothers, Nick Cravat had taught me a bit of swordfighting.) Paul Stader, who later did a lot of big pictures for producer Irwin Allen, was my stunt double, and Paul Baxley was John's. Baxley was also my roommate at the Lone Pine Inn. In those days, the studios were allowed to put two SAG members in a room together.

In the final sequence of *Hajji Baba*, I have a big swordfight on horseback with John Derek, and naturally John subdues and kills me. John and I did a lot of the swordfight ourselves, but Stader and Baxley were involved too. I don't remember now exactly what my bright idea *was*, but I dreamed up *some* touch that I thought would work great in that final fight sequence. I thought it was *so* good, I couldn't hold it in. I saw Walter Wanger sitting in the sand on a dune a couple of hundreds yards from the set, and I went up to him and I said, "Mr. Wanger, I've got a wonderful idea for the finish of this sequence." He asked me what it was, I told him and he said he liked it—in fact, I remember he said, "That's *very* good."

Full of hope, I asked, "Do you think you might talk to Don and see if we can include it in the film?"

Walter paused, and then he said, "Why don't *you* talk to him?" Here was a guy who, in 1951, found out that his actress-wife Joan Bennett was having an affair with an agent, confronted the agent in a parking lot and shot him in the balls. But he was afraid of Don Weis!

I was on *Hajji* about three weeks, working at Lone Pine and then also doing a couple of scenes at the studio, Monogram-Allied Artists. Nat "King" Cole was hot at the time so he was asked to sing the title song, "Hajji Baba." According to *Variety*'s review of *Hajji Baba*, the song became a source of hilarity to the preview audience because it was repeated with almost every appearance by John Derek. Outside of the picture, however, it became a hit. I'll bet the song made more money than the movie.

For me, *Hajji Baba* was a terrific part and a lot of fun and a great location—a good experience all around. So in 2002 it was fun to attend a Lone Pine Film Festival on the strength of my appearance in a film (*Hajji Baba*) that had been made there. A beautiful print of *Hajji Baba* was shown in a nice theater with maybe three or four hundred people in the audience. It was interesting to see it again with an audience and find that it got a good reaction. We even visited some of the locations where it was shot: The festival provides guided tours of the surrounding area, and you're shown the exact spots where Errol Flynn made *this* movie, where Randolph Scott made *that* movie—there are even signposts in the ground with the titles of the movies that were shot in the different places. Marie and

I and our friend John Gloske were among the people who went on one of the tours which included a few of the *Hajji Baba* locations. Some of the Lone Pine restaurants that were there in 1954 were *still* there. And at the inn, Marie and I stayed just a few doors away from the room where I stayed when I was up there for the making of the film!

It was nice to be in Lone Pine, the organizers *and* the fans are marvelous up there, and it was a wonderful film festival.

* * * * * * *

On August 13, 1954, our third son and sixth child, Michael Louis, was born. I had heard that if couples expecting their sixth child went to St. John's, a Catholic hospital in Santa Monica, they would not get a bill; they'd get the sixth child free. Marie and I had had all of our children at the Culver City Hospital, right across the street from where we lived. I went to the Culver City Hospital administrator and I said, "Sir, St. Johns gives you the sixth child free. I was wondering if you could do the same thing for me, this being our sixth child." He said, "Oh, no. No, no, we don't *do* that." I said, "Well, I just wanted you to know that St. Johns *did* that." He paused and then said, "Well, all right, I'll tell you what I'll do: I'll give the sixth child half-price!" True story!

Michael was a lovable little boy. I'd hate to say that I had a favorite, but Michael *was* kind of my favorite. He did everything with tremendous energy. All the kids played Little League baseball and basketball and Mike got the nickname "The Hurricane"—they called him "The Hurk." But he was also very sensitive. I'll never forget the day that I brought home a box of a dozen doughnuts and Michael and all the other kids came in the kitchen to get some. One of the doughnuts was squashed and nobody ate *that* doughnut— pretty soon, it was the only one left. Michael, perturbed, asked in a serious, weepy voice, "How come nobody will eat that poor little, ugly doughnut? How do you think its *mother* feels?"—and he proceeded to pick up the doughnut and eat it! He was always doing cute things like that.

One New Year's Day we were having dinner in the dining room and everybody was gathered around the table, and I said, "I want you all to make a New Year's resolution and tell me what it is." It went around the table, one kid saying, "I'm gonna do better in my

My son Mike.

studies," another saying, "I'm gonna watch my diet and try to lose weight" and so on. It got to Michael and he promised, "I'm gonna do better in school *and* . . . I'm gonna try to improve my table manners." At that point, just as soon as he got out the words "improve my table manners," he let out a big belch. Totally inadvertent! It was so funny, the kids laughed for five minutes.

Marie and I had a merit and demerit system. When a kid got ten merits, he or she would get a special treat—ten bucks or something like that. But if they got ten *de*merits, they would have to go to the barn and get ten spanks with a big fat cowboy belt. I would make sure it didn't really hurt, but it would be a good semblance of discipline. When Mike was six or seven, one day sure enough he got his tenth demerit—he was the only one who *ever* reached ten demerits! I said, "You meet me out at the barn at three-thirty, after school today." He said okay. At three-thirty I went out to the barn and waited and after a minute or two he reported out there, and I put him over my knee. I noticed that the seat of his pants was bulging. Sure enough, under his pants he had ten pairs of underwear—a great big wad of them, to pad the spanking! *His* underwear, and all his brothers' underwear! I couldn't help but laugh, and that was the end of my demerit system.

Another time, when Michael was 10 or 11, one of the girls spotted him and C.P. smoking and reported them to me. I don't know where I got *this* particular bit of discipline, but I probably got it from my youth: My brother Charlie and I took Michael and C.P. out to the barn and we gave them a little lecture about smoking, and then we said, "If you wanna smoke, okay, we'll smoke." I put a pack of cigarettes on the table and the four of us each lit up a cigarette. But it didn't seem to faze Mike. After a few cigarettes, C.P. had had enough, so we dismissed him. But Mike still wasn't fazed by the cigarettes, so Charlie and I went to the cigars—little Italian ginny stinkers. They're short twisted cigars and, oh, boy, they're really rough! All the girls were peeking in the windows giggling and the barn started to fill up with smoke as Charlie and I kept puffing away and blowing the smoke into Michael's face. Well, it ended up that Charlie and I were the ones who got sick from it but Mike continued to smoke the cigar, looking like Eddie G. Robinson!

When Michael was in his early twenties, I went to Kawaii, one of the big Hawaiian islands, to do a two-part *Starsky and Hutch* called "Playboy Island" for producer Joe Naar—I would be playing a gangster who had 12 Playboy bunnies with me on this island. Michael was doing stunts and extra work at the time, so I brought him along to be my stand-in. This was during the big "disco" era, and Michael was a tremendous dancer—a *wild* dancer. He could spin the girls around and pick them up and flip 'em around his head and so on, and the girls all loved to dance with him because he *was* so exciting to be on the dance floor with. The first night we were there, we went to a club and Mike started doing this crazy dance with Joe Naar's secretary. She was having a wild time. He picked her up and spun her around—and when she hit the floor, she broke her wrist! I always remember the night that Mike broke the producer's secretary's wrist!

Michael later got away from the stuntwork and, after a stint in the Air Force, began working as an X-ray technician at the Motion Picture Hospital out in Calabasas. Later he became a radiologist, and then finally he was the head of a radiology school, the Modern Technology College in North Hollywood.

We lost Michael November 5, 1999, when he died of pneumonia at the age of 45. He had gone to Venice, Italy, on vacation, and got caught in a rainstorm, and didn't take care of himself. He came back to the U.S. and went back to work, and after a couple of weeks the pneumonia got very bad. One night my daughter Gemma, who lived in Mike's house, called me and told me that Michael was in the hospital. Of course, Marie and I wanted to go directly over there, but Gemma told me not to come right away, that he was sleeping.

The next morning we got word that he passed away during the night. It was a tremendous shock to the family.

After he passed away, Marie, Gemma and Gina went over to the school to clean out his office and found in his desk several letters from students' parents thanking him for helping their sons and daughters who were on the verge of flunking out; Mike helped them make it through to graduation. He had stayed with his students every step of the way . . . encouraged them . . . made sure they didn't miss any assignments or classes, or lose faith in themselves.

They have since named the school's X-ray lab for him: The Michael Picerni X-Ray Lab. We still miss Michael, every day.

13
A Tribute to
Mike Picerni
by P.V. Picerni

When we were little kids, we'd beg our dad to tell us a bedtime story. Of course with such a big family, it had to be in a group. The stories that were the best were the ones where the main character was an adventurous little hero named Mickey Mikey. My brother Mike, who must have been three or four then, would proudly sit on Dad's lap while all the kids would listen to each extraordinary adventure.

Mike would remind Dad that Mickey Mikey could fly. I could still picture Mike, with his cocky little smile, as Mickey Mikey would always prevail over evil.

All us kids, all eight of us, went to school at Our Lady of Grace. When I was in the seventh grade and Mike was in the fourth, The Duncan Yo-Yo company sponsored a contest at our school, and promised that every participant would get a free yo-yo. (Yo-yos were a big thing back then.) Banners were hanging all over the school announcing the contest. For weeks I practiced tricks like "around the world," "walk the dog," "rock the cradle" and "the whip," and I gave Mike one of my old yo-yos so he could practice with me.

It seemed as though everyone in the school was planning to participate in the contest just to get a free yo-yo, and there were at least 800 students. Every day at lunch and recess all the kids were walking around with yo-yos in hand, trying to impress each other with our moves. I became quite good, and thought I had a good chance of winning this thing. Once in a while, I'd see Mike with his classmates practicing. I thought it was cute.

Then the big day arrived, and representatives from Duncan Yo-Yo passed out the free yo-yos. They divided the kids into groups and prepared to act as judges. I think even they were overwhelmed by the turnout.

The first few rounds went pretty quickly because a lot of the kids still had no idea what they were doing. After each round, the disqualified kids would go back to their classrooms. I lasted 'til the fourth round. I tried to get too fancy on my grand finish and the string got tangled up.

When I got back to my class, there were still about eight empty seats. As other disqualified kids came in, the seats filled up until there was only one left, Steve Meyers'. When Steve came back, he said that they were on the final round. Only three kids were left— two eighth graders and one fourth grader, my brother Mike. I couldn't believe Mike was in the finals. He was just a little kid, and I gave him a yo-yo only a couple of weeks before.

Then over the loudspeaker the principal Sister Enda announced the results of the contest: First place went to Mike Picerni of the fourth grade. I don't think my parents or even Mike understood what a big deal that was. But I did.

Mike with Gina, Gemma and Maria.

When I was in the eighth grade, I had a paper route for the now-defunct afternoon paper *Citizen News*. I think I was getting $9 a month. After about six months, I grew tired of riding my bike all over town after school—there were a lot of hills to climb. I gave my route to Mike, who decided it was easier to deliver the papers on horseback. The paper got wind of this little guy's Pony Express method of delivery and decided to run a story on him. A picture of Mike on his horse ended up on the front page of the paper.

I'll tell you, my brother Mike had already proven to me that his storybook character Mickey Mikey was no bigger hero than the real Michael Lewis Picerni. I could go on and on about my wonderful adventurous brother. I love him very much. I'm so proud of him and so glad he left behind a wonderful son, Bryan, who he loved more than anything.

14
AUDIE MURPHY:
A TRUE AMERICAN HERO

If you were a freelance actor in the 1950s, this is how you'd get most of your parts: You started with an interview with the casting people; if you passed that, you got to meet the director; and if *he* liked you, you got to do a screen test. At that point, you'd be in contention with the 10 or 15 other actors who had also gotten that far. Then you would wait two or three weeks until they made a decision. That was the usual procedure.

But on *To Hell and Back*, it didn't happen like that. Wilt Melnick told me that Universal was about to make this movie on the life of World War II hero Audie Murphy, that Audie was playing himself, and that they were looking for an actor to play Valentino, an Italian-American member of Audie's platoon. Wilt and I walked into an office at Universal, and there was Audie Murphy, sitting behind a desk, and Jesse Hibbs, the director, in the chair next to him. Also in the room was Aaron Rosenberg, the producer. Like John Wayne, Aaron and Jesse had at one time been football players at the University of Southern California—in fact, I think Aaron, an All-American, might have *played* football with Wayne. Wilt and I met the three of them and we sat down, and Audie asked me a couple of questions. (He had seen me in *Breakthrough*.) After no more than two or three minutes, Audie turned to Jesse and Aaron and said, "Paul will be fine for Valentino."

It was as simple as that—"Paul will be fine for Valentino." No reading, no screen test. When Audie made up his mind, that was it. Quick; no quibbling. That's how I was cast as Valentino in *To Hell and Back*.

Born to a desperately poor family of Texas sharecroppers, Audie

The story of the most decorated soldier in American history: Audie Leon Murphy.

Murphy rose from these humble beginnings to become World War II's most decorated G.I.—in fact, the most-decorated soldier in American history. He joined the Army as a baby-faced teenager and fought in Sicily, Anzio, Rome, through France and finally into Germany. They say that by V-E Day he had killed at least 240 Nazis and single-handedly destroyed two machine-gun nests and a German tank in one battle, and held off six tanks in another. He received 24 decorations (every medal the U.S. offers), including the Congressional Medal of Honor and the Croix de Guerre, France's top award. When I was with the Air Force overseas during the war in C.B.I. (China-Burma-India), we used to get *The Stars and Stripes*, the Army-Navy newspaper which gave reports on different armed forces actions around the world, and many stories about Audie Murphy were featured in there. I read them all. After the war, Audie turned his combat experiences into a best-selling autobiography, *To Hell and Back*, co-written by a friend and fellow veteran David "Spec" McClure.

By the time that book was published, he had moved to Hollywood, signed to an acting contract by James Cagney, who had seen his picture on the cover of *Life* magazine. He made his film debut in a small part in a 1948 picture called **Beyond Glory** which, coincidentally, was *my* first picture as well (after I'd done a bit of work as an extra). Cagney loaned Audie to Paramount to do this picture, which starred Alan Ladd as a West Point cadet on trial, accused of cowardice. I was then a student at Loyola University in Los Angeles, and one of my professors was a wonderful priest named Father Gabriel Pierre Menager, a Frenchman. One of Father Menager's former students at Santa Clara University was a fellow named Joe Egli, who now was head of casting at Paramount. Every so often, Father Menager would bring me into Joe's office and he would say, "This boy's a wonderful actor. He's in all our plays at the university. You must give him a part." We made about seven or eight trips there before Burton McKay, Joe's assistant, cast me in **Beyond Glory**.

The director was John Farrow, who was from the old school—jodhpurs, riding crop, the whole bit. I only had one scene: Another actor and I played private detectives who follow Alan Ladd. In this one scene of ours, we hid in the shadows at the bottom of a staircase, and we each had one line of dialogue. The other actor, indicating Ladd, was supposed to say, "Are you sure that's him?," and then I would say, "I certainly am." But when we did the take, after I said, "I certainly am," I adlibbed, "Let's go." John Farrow didn't say anything about it and it ended up in the picture, so I had *two* lines instead of one! I was paid $35, the Screen Actors Guild minimum at the time, for one day's work. Audie played a West Point cadet in the picture but, unfortunately, we didn't work together.

Audie later went under contract to Universal and became one of their most popular Western heroes. Of course, now that he was a star, I began hearing stories about him, including one (told to me by actor Ben Cooper) that I remember to this day. Back in those days when Westerns were very popular, there were a lot of actors who prided themselves on their fast draw. Audie was very good at it. So was another actor on the Universal lot, Tony Curtis. Tony Curtis—real name, Bernie Schwartz—was kind of a loudmouth Brooklyn boy, and one day on the lot, he said to Audie, "Hey, Audie, I challenge you to a fast-draw contest. Let's see who's faster, me or you." Audie ignored him. So after that, every time Tony would run across Audie, he would say, "Hey, Audie, how 'bout that fast-draw contest? You ready for me?," and, every time, Audie would ignore him. One day in the commissary, in front of a lot of people, Tony tried it again: "Hey, Audie, I think you're *afraid* to fast-draw with me."

This time, Audie said, "All right, Tony . . . I'll fast-draw with you. Under one condition."

"Yeah, sure, what's that?"

Audie said, "Under the one condition that we use live ammunition." Tony never said another word!

Obviously Tony Curtis wasn't about to get into a fast-draw contest using live ammo with *any* actor, but especially not with Audie. When Audie was a kid living with his poverty-stricken family in Texas, he used to be the one to go out rabbit hunting, to bring home food for the table. Each time he'd go out, his mother would just give him *one bullet*, because they were so poor they couldn't afford to *waste* a single bullet. As a kid Audie was taught to make every bullet count, and that's why he was such a good shot when he got into the service later on.

In my first picture at Warners, **Breakthrough**, a lot of the guys who played soldiers (American *and* German) and a lot of the military materiel were supplied by the Army. The same thing happened again on **To Hell and Back**: We shot it in a place called Yakima, Washington, because the countryside up there was right for the picture and because there was a nearby Army base that had soldiers and tanks and equipment we could use in the film. The town itself, Yakima, was a

At Yakima, Washington's Camp Lewis for **To Hell and Back**.

strange little town. Back when that town was just beginning to grow, all of the women were German, and I guess they didn't have enough men. So they imported a shipload of Filipino men. In Yakima, Washington, all the women were big, buxom German girls and all the husbands were little tiny Filipino men—a very odd mixture! We were there for about six weeks, and there wasn't much to do in the town itself. They had one golf course, and that was about all that Yakima had to offer. A prizefighter named Art Aragon was up there with us, playing a small part in the picture, and one day he asked me, "Paul, if someone were to say to you, 'I'll give you a million dollars, with the stipulation that you have to spend the rest of your life in Yakima, Washington' . . . would you take it?" Without hesitation, I said, "*No!*"

Audie, Marshall Thompson, Jack Kelly and I were four of the soldiers seen throughout the film's action.

Audie portrayed himself in the movie, of course, except in the early scenes of childhood where a kid actor played the part. The movie opens with Audie as a 12-year-old Texas boy working odd jobs to help keep the struggling family together. Following the death of his mother, Audie, 16, joins the Army (after being turned down by the Marines and the Navy) and is sent to North Africa.

Proving himself in battle alongside the rest of the Third Platoon of Company B in the 15th regiment of the 3rd Division there, he wins the respect of his fellow GIs. Over a 30-month period he rises from private to company commander, at one point forcing an entire company of Jerries to retreat by commandeering a blazing tank's machine gun and conducting a one-man action. The film ends with a recreation of the Medal of Honor presentation.

My character, Valentino, one of Audie's fellow foot soldiers, was always talking about looking up his family in Naples and making Audie a spaghetti dinner. Marshall Thompson, Charles Drake and Jack Kelly were the other stars of the picture, but the characters played by Marshall and Charles were killed and Kelly's character was wounded; I was all the way through the picture. Marshall and Charles were both nice guys, and Jack Kelly was a little bit of a lovable nut. Jack liked to drink and he had a comic flair to him. He later starred in the TV series *Maverick*, playing Bret Maverick's (James Garner) brother Bart.

As for Audie, I was impressed with him even before I knew him, because of the fact that he was the most-decorated soldier in the history of America. I always admired him for that. On the

Jesse Hibbs (left) directs us on the Universal back lot. The Army division depicted in *To Hell and Back* recently swept through Iraq into Baghdad. My father served in the 3rd Division in World War I, and my grandson Mark Atkinson recently served two terms in Iraq!

movie, Audie was a man of few words. The best way I can describe Audie is to ask you to remember the character played by Gary Cooper in *High Noon*. That was Audie Murphy. He didn't say much. Silent, serious . . . a man of his word . . . and you knew that when he said something, he *meant* it. He was a powerful man personality-wise. Despite his size, you wouldn't want to get into a fight with Audie, because you would *lose*. In short, he was a *Texan*—that's the kind of a person he was. But we got him to laugh now and then, and I could tell he had a good sense of humor. You couldn't get close to Audie, but I sensed that he liked me, and I certainly liked him.

As I mentioned, there wasn't much to do in Yakima; at night, a bunch of us would get together in Audie's suite at our hotel and play a little poker. Audie loved to play poker—most Texans do. And you never could tell what Audie had in his hand, whether he had a pair of deuces or three aces, because you couldn't "read" him. Inevitably, Audie always won at the poker games.

And he was a good actor. There's a scene in the picture where Charles Drake stands up during a battle and is shot and dies, and afterwards Audie leans over the body and says, his voice full of emotion, "I told you not to stand up, I *told* you not to stand up . . . " As he spoke, the tears welled up in Audie's eyes. As I watched this, I said to myself, "This guy's a *good actor* . . ." He was reliving a moment he had actually lived during the war, when a buddy of his (the one played by Drake) got killed.

Some of the picture, including all the interiors and the river-crossing scene, were shot at Universal, but all the battle sequences were done in Yakima. (The things Audie did in battle in real life during WWII were so spectacular, they had to be toned down for the movie.) Finally we came up to the scene near the end of the picture where Audie himself is wounded and the medics are getting ready to take him away. My character, Valentino, now the last of the original group, is preparing to continue on with the outfit. As I come by Audie in the field, lying on the ground, waiting for the medics, we talk for a few moments, and then as I'm leaving he shouts after me, "Don't forget, Valentino: You still owe me a spaghetti dinner!" It's funny how lines like that stick in people's minds: To this day, when I attend various events and autograph shows, people like Feller Goff,

Audie's stunt double, still come up to me and they say, "You still owe me a spaghetti dinner, Valentino!"

To Hell and Back became one of Universal's biggest-grossing releases of 1955—in fact, it stayed their biggest grosser until *Jaws* topped it. Audie tragically died in the 1971 crash of a small plane on which he was a passenger, at the age of 46. But the memory of the man and what he did for his country lives on. He is buried at Arlington Cemetery.

Recently, after a long campaign by veterans groups and people like Clyde Easter, who served with Audie, he was honored by the U.S. Postal Service with a postage stamp bearing his image. It was one of a block of four honoring "Distinguished Soldiers" in our nation's history: Audie, Sgt. Alvin York, Gen. John Hines and Gen. Omar Bradley. Announcing the issuance of the Audie Murphy stamp, Vito Fossella, the New York Congressman who fought long and hard for it, said,

AFTER A LONG BATTLE THAT EMBODIED THE VERY CHARACTERISTICS OF AUDIE MURPHY HIMSELF—PERSEVERANCE, RESOLVE AND DETERMINATION—A POSTAGE STAMP WILL BE ISSUED IN HIS MEMORY. I CONSIDER IT AN HONOR TO HAVE PLAYED EVEN A SMALL ROLE IN THIS VICTORY, BUT IT IS A TRIUMPH I WILL CHERISH FOREVER. THIS STAMP WILL REMIND ALL AMERICANS, BUT ESPECIALLY OUR YOUNG PEOPLE, THAT HEROES ARE NOT ALWAYS FOUND ON THE SPORTS FIELDS AND IN ROCK BANDS. TRUE HEROES ARE MEN AND WOMEN LIKE AUDIE MURPHY WHO RISK LIFE AND LIMB TO DEFEND AND UPHOLD OUR MOST FUNDAMENTAL PRINCIPLES. I JOINED THIS BATTLE TO KEEP AUDIE MURPHY'S MEMORY ALIVE AND TO HELP REMIND ALL OF US WHAT IT MEANS TO BE AN AMERICAN. . . . AUDIE MURPHY WOULD PROBABLY BE EMBARRASSED KNOWING HIS IMAGE WILL BE ENSHRINED ON A POSTAGE STAMP BECAUSE HE NEVER SOUGHT THE LIMELIGHT. RATHER, IT WAS HIS BRAVERY AND PATRIOTISM THAT THRUST FAME UPON HIM. IT IS FOR THAT VERY REASON WE HONOR HIM.

A few years ago, Marie and I were at the Williamsburg (Virginia) Film Festival along with Audie Murphy's biographer Sue Gossett and Audie's younger sister Billie Murphy. Our first night there, Marie, Sue, Billie and I went out to dinner, and I picked up the check. The next night, the four of us went out to dinner again, and

I'm standing at the foot of Audie's statue in front of the Audie Murphy Museum in Greenville, Texas.

Another look at Audie's statue.

after the meal I asked the waiter for the check. Billie Murphy said, "I'll take the check tonight, Paul."

I said, "Don't be silly, Billie. I'm the only man here; this check is mine."

She paused, then said, more firmly, "*I'll* take the check, Paul."

"Billie, don't be ridiculous," I said. "I'm paying this check."

Billie said, "Paul . . . this check is *mine*"—and as I looked across the table at her face, all of a sudden it wasn't Billie Murphy sitting there . . . it was *Audie* Murphy. And I said, ". . . Okay!!" I knew I couldn't win. She was very much like Audie: She was a woman of few words, and when she said something, she *meant* it! She was a lot of fun to be around. She calls me every once in a while and I call her, and Marie's become friendly with her. We fell in love with Billie Murphy, a real sweetheart, and she fell in love with us.

I've also met Nadene, Audie's other sister, and his brother Gene at a two-day event called Audie Murphy Days, a celebration of Audie's life, that's held every June 21, on his birthday, in his hometown of Greenville, Texas, 50 or 60 miles northeast of Dallas. They invited me down there to be the guest speaker in 2001 and I met Nadene and Gene—who, like Billie, were both living versions of Audie Murphy. Wonderful people. (Gene, I'm sorry to say, has since passed away.) I had a great time there in Greenville with Judge Joe Bobbitt, the man who runs the whole show, our host Roy McGee, Adrien Witkofsky, the curator of the Audie Murphy Museum, and Feller Goff and his lovely wife Jossie.

At the Williamsburg Film Festival, the other veteran actors and I got to meet Audie's sister Billie (seated in front of me).

I've been part of Audie Murphy Days five times now and always have a marvelous time. In 2002, we dedicated a beautiful new bronze statue of Audie, sculpted by local artist Gordon Thomas. It stands right outside the museum. Audie is dressed in his Army outfit and holds a German submachine-gun, and there are flags all around it. At night, they put a spotlight on it so people can see it from the highway—it's a 12-foot statue on a ten-foot pedestal. It's a thrilling sight.

I'll always cherish the memory of knowing and working with Audie Murphy, a true American hero.

* * * * * * *

As a postscript to Audie Murphy, I want to tell a story about another of the actors in *To Hell and Back*, the wonderful knockout prizefighter Art Aragon. Art, who was Mexican, was a welterweight boxer known as "The *Original* Golden Boy" (named after Bill Holden's "Golden Boy" in the 1939 movie of the same name). Since then, they have named another kid "The Golden Boy": Oscar de la Hoya. But "The Original Golden Boy" was Art Aragon.

Early in his fight career, when Art was just a young up-and-comer, he defeated Enrique Bolanus, a Mexican idol. When they announced the decision, the Mexican crowd booed—which broke young Art Aragon's heart. After the fight, when he was interviewed by newspaper reporters, Art was practically in tears because his own people had booed him, and he lied to the reporters, "And I'm not even Mexican, so I don't *care* that they booed me." Art had renounced his Mexican nationality! They put that in the papers the next day, and the Mexicans booed him from then on, *every* time he walked into the ring. They came hoping to see him lose because he'd said he wasn't a Mexican.

When we got back from *To Hell and Back*, Art and I became very good friends—I found him to be a very bright, very clever guy. He didn't have a manager at the time, and to my surprise he asked *me* to become his manager. "I don't know anything about managing," I told him, turning the job down, "but I'll go with you to the fights and I'll help you any way I can."

From that point on, I would go with Art to all his fights and he would always *win*—about five in a row. I guess I'd become his lucky charm. At that time, Frank Sinatra owned an undefeated fighter named Cisco Andrade, who at that point looked like he was on his way to becoming the lightweight champion of the world. (He eventually *did* become the champ.) Art managed to sign to fight Andrade at Wrigley Field in Los Angeles, the then-Los Angeles Angels' baseball stadium.

Before every fight, the managers and fighters meet with the commissioners and make some arrangements and come to agreements about the fight itself: how much tape they put on their hands,

During the Yakima shooting of *To Hell and Back*, I posed with assistant director Tom Shaw and Art Aragon.

what size gloves they're going to wear and so on. When Art would get hit, he would often cut over his eyes and bleed profusely. To prevent this, before each fight he would put collodion on his eyebrows—layers and layers of it. For this upcoming fight with Andrade, Art insisted that he be allowed to coat his eyebrows with collodion. But Andrade's manager was Ralph Gambina, an oldtimer who was worldly-wise as far as the fight game went, and Gambina said he wouldn't permit it. Finally they compromised and Gambina said that if Art put just two layers of collodion on his eyes, he would let *that* go.

This was going to be an important fight, and the attendance at Wrigley Field that night bore that out: The place was sold out. There must have been 40,000 people, including Sinatra and all his cronies, there waiting to see this big open-air fight. Even Audie Murphy was there at ringside. I was in Art's dressing room as Art began to apply the collodion to his eyebrows. Well, Art didn't put on *two* layers of collodion—he put on about *nine*! I had a feeling this wasn't going to go over too well with Ralph Gambina and, sure enough, when he and the boxing commissioner came in to inspect Art (managers always get to inspect their fighter's opponent just before the start of the fight), he took one look at his eyes, saw all this collodion and said to the commissioner, "No way! No fight tonight unless he removes all that collodion! He's disobeyed the conditions that we agreed to!"

The commissioner told Art he was going to have to take off the collodion, and Art got stubborn: "I'm not takin' off the collodion. This is the way I'm goin' in." They reached a stalemate—with Sinatra, a big Hollywood contingent, and 40,000 *other* people sitting outside waiting to see the fight! The fight was supposed to start at (let's say) eight o'clock and now it was eight-thirty, and the fans were getting impatient. The fighters went to their respective dressing rooms, each waiting for the other to give in. The crowd grew to a screaming frenzy but nothing changed: Art wouldn't take off the collodion and Gambina wouldn't budge.

This was where I came in—Paul "the lucky charm" with his brilliant strategy! I said, "Art, look. You're not gonna take off the collodion. And *he's* not gonna fight *unless* you take off the collodion. So we're at an impasse—ergo, no fight. But all those fans out there in the audience—they don't know a *thing* about what's happening here in the dressing rooms. Here's what you do, Art: You go down the tunnel . . . get in the ring. Once you get in that ring, if Andrade doesn't show up, that means *he's* 'the heavy,' not you." Art said, "That's *great!*"

We started walking down the dark tunnel to the ring, Art with all the layers of collodion on his eyes—and who's coming *up* the tunnel but Frank Sinatra. It was dark and I knew he wouldn't be able to see me too well, so as we passed I said, "Hey, Frank—get your fighter in the ring! Get your fighter in the *ring*, Frank! What *is* he, *chicken*?!" Frank stopped—briefly—and said, "Don't worry, he'll get there, he'll be in the ring!," and he continued up the tunnel as we went down. (Sinatra and I crossed paths several times after that, but he never knew I was the guy in the tunnel shouting, "Get your fighter in the ring, Frank!")

When we got into the arena and Art stepped into the ring, for the first time—for the first time in his *life*—Art was cheered by the crowd. It went *wild*. It was the first time anybody had ever cheered Art Aragon, the Golden Boy! Ten or fifteen minutes went by and now from the crowd you could hear shouts of "Andrade, you chicken!,"

"Andrade! Booooo!" and so on. Ralph Gambina was licked and he knew it, so finally Andrade came into the ring. I turned to Art and I said, "Psychologically, Art . . . we've *won*. You've got the collodion on your eyes and the fight is on. *Psychologically, we've won.*"

Cisco Andrade was an exceptionally good boxer: He was jabbing and throwing left hooks and right hooks, and Art was kind of holding back and doing mostly counter-punching. After six rounds, Andrade was just ripping him to shreds. All the Mexicans in the audience loved it because they were all Andrade fans and they hated the Golden Boy. I was in Art's corner between rounds.

Joey Barnum, a good friend of Art's and an ex-fighter, was on the outs with Art at this time—they'd had an argument because Joey thought Art had a thing for his (Joey's) wife. But Joey still must have felt a loyalty to Art—*or*, Joey had a big bet on him in this fight!—because Joey came to me on the steps in Art's corner and said, "Paul. Tell Art to beat him to the punch. Don't *counter*-punch, *beat* him to the punch." Between rounds I stepped up into the ring and I said, "Joey Barnum said, 'Beat him to the punch.'" That's all I said.

Now in the seventh round, instead of laying back and counter-punching, Art started *leading, boom, boom, boom*. He hit Andrade a shot, and Andrade went down. The crowd went crazy. Art was devastating, especially when he had a guy in trouble. Andrade got up, Art hit him again, boom, and Andrade was on the canvas again. Andrade got up, Art knocked him down a *third* time—and the referee stopped the fight and declared Art the winner.

But that was the end of my being Art's good luck charm. After that, he was beaten by Chuck Davey . . . Vince Martinez . . . Joe Miceli . . . and ex-champ Carmine Bazilio, "The Onion Farmer," who finished Art off in a sold-out Wrigley Field, to the delight of all the Mexican fight fans. Today, Art is a very successful bail bondsman, and does a big business with the Mexican population in L.A.

Art and I share one other great memory: Working with Audie Murphy, a true American hero, in **To Hell and Back**.

15
MY BIG MOVE TO
THE SMALL SCREEN

As I mentioned in an earlier chapter, after my departure from Warners, I began looking for whatever work I could find, including television. I knew that if I could keep busy in TV, I'd be able to support myself and my family. TV salaries weren't great in those days: For the half-hour shows that were done in about three days, the salary was between $300-500. If you did an hour show, then it was more like $600-750.

Dragnet was a half-hour show and, in 1953, the first TV I did after leaving Warners. With Jack Webb as Los Angeles Police Department Sgt. Joe Friday and Ben Alexander as his partner Officer Frank Smith, *Dragnet* was big in the ratings and a good start for me in this new medium (I would eventually do two or three of them). At that time, the series was shot at Disney Studios; in addition to starring, Webb was also the director, producer and owner of the show. Back in the late '40s, Jack had done a Brynie Foy movie at Eagle-Lion called *He Walked by Night*, which was about the L.A.P.D. While shooting parts of that movie downtown at the police department, Jack noticed that they had all these case files there and I think that's where he got the idea for *Dragnet*, which dramatized actual police investigations.

It's been over 50 years but I still remember Jack telling me, the first time I did a *Dragnet*, that he didn't want me memorizing my lines and then coming in and doing the scenes the conventional way; he wanted me to come in cold and just read them off a teleprompter. He had teleprompters on the set and as Jack was talking to me, or me to him, we'd actually be looking over the other's shoulder at the teleprompters and reading aloud the lines.

With Ben Alexander, Tyler McVey and Jack Webb on TV's *Dragnet*.

That's why everybody had that strange, flat, robotic delivery for which the show was famous. Or infamous!

One day on my first *Dragnet*, I stepped outside the soundstage to have a cigarette with Jack and Ben Alexander. As we were standing there, we heard a commotion and looked toward the front gate of the Disney lot, and through a chain-link fence we could see a couple of studio guards chasing a tall guy in our direction. The guy came flying over the fence and landed on our side of it and grabbed a-hold of Jack's lapels and pushed him up against the wall, babbling, "You *gotta* use me on the show! You *gotta* use me on the show!" It was frightening! Turns out it was a madman of an actor named Timothy Carey. With a crazy look on his face, he demanded that Webb let him appear on *Dragnet* and Webb, obviously hoping to calm him down and get him to let go, said, "Yeah, sure, *you're* in the show, when do ya want to start??" Jack assured Carey that he would be in a *Dragnet*, and that quieted him down; the guards arrived at that point and took him away.

Timothy Carey might have been a great *Dragnet* villain but he scared the shit out of us. He was nuts! Carey was an actor who would do *any*thing to get a role; I once heard that he went into the Columbia Studios office of the producer of the motion picture *The Caine Mutiny*, pulled a gun on him and said, "You gonna give me a part in this show?" When you have that burning desire to be an actor and be on the screen, some people will do whatever it takes. I remember once at MGM I was standing on a corner, having a hot dog, and I saw this big agent come out of the casting office. I went up to him and I said, "Do you want to make a lot of money? Give me an agency contract, because I'm gonna be a big star." The *tremendous desire* to act can be almost 90 percent of the success of an actor, and maybe ten-percent is talent. In fact, some guys get by on no talent at all, just that desire.

So *Dragnet* and Jack Webb—and Timothy Carey—were my transition from Warner Brothers to the world of television, where a lot of the shows in those days were live. *Climax!, Playhouse 90, Lux Video Theatre, Philco Playhouse, Matinee Theater*, a show called *Goodyear TV Playhouse* out of New York—I did all of 'em. Today nothing is live, all the weekly dramas and sitcoms are shot weeks or months in advance, but in those early days, live shows were common. And they were all interesting to do for that reason— it was like you were doing a Broadway play and you were not allowed any mistakes! *As* you were doing it, it was going out on the air to 40 or 50 million people across the country, and if you screwed up, that was *it*—40 or 50 million people saw you screw up. I had a couple of goofs, which I'll describe, but in the main, live TV didn't bother me. Having done a lot of stage work really helped a lot— and, too, when you're as young as I was then, you don't have to worry about it too much, because your mind is so sharp and your talent is at its peak. The behind-the-scenes people also had to be on their toes at all times. When you did live shows, the cameras moved on cue according to the dialogue. The director sat in the booth giving orders to the cameramen, who could hear him through their earphones: "All right, Camera 2 get ready to move . . . Camera 3, stand by . . . Camera 2, move . . . " It was all very carefully choreographed on both sides of the cameras.

I had a fun experience preparing to do a live *Climax!* with Shelley

Winters. *Climax!* was an hour show which we shot at CBS on Fairfax Avenue in Hollywood, in a studio that was fairly new at that time. In this episode, "Sorry, Wrong Number," Shelley was going to play a bedridden invalid woman terrorized by a phone caller threatening to kill her, and I would be playing the killer. Throughout the show, I called her on the phone, whispering, low and ominous, things like, "I'm gonna come and kill you. Wait for me there. You can't move out of that bed, and I'm gonna get you." At that time, 1954, she was going through her divorce from the Italian actor Vittorio Gassman—and it was *not* a friendly divorce. I remember the rehearsal of one of the phone scenes: I was speaking into a phone in a phone booth on the set and she was speaking into her bedside phone; we couldn't see each other but we could hear each other because it was a real hookup. I was doing my "menacing" bit and she kept demanding, "Who *is* this? Who *is* this? Who *are* you??" I said, again in a very threatening manner, "I'm not gonna tell you who I am . . . I'm gonna get you . . ."

"*Who is this? Who is this?*"—now she was screaming into the phone. Suddenly I said, cheerfully, and with the Italian accent, "It's Vittorrrio!"

"You son of a bitch!" Shelley hollered out at me!

Another thing I did for fun: There were magazines by her bed, and among them were a couple of movie magazines. I began looking through them and saw that one happened to have a layout of photos of her and Vittorio in their happy days, five or six pictures. Well, I put it on the top of the pile and folded the page so that, when she opened it up, it would open up right to her and Vittorio. Again she called me a son of a bitch, but I could tell she got a kick out of it!

Not everybody could take the pressure of live TV, I learned when doing a *Playhouse 90*. Usually on the *Playhouse 90*s, a 90-minute show, we'd rehearse for ten days and then shoot it live. For this episode, a Navy story, we rehearsed for like six days with Robert Young in the lead as a Naval officer—and then one day Young didn't show up for rehearsal, and we were notified that Brian Donlevy would be replacing him. The director told us, "Mr. Young is very sick. He's in the hospital. He's being replaced by Mr. Brian Donlevy." That afternoon after rehearsal, I happened to be driving

Ida Lupino played my wife on a *Four Star Playhouse*.

down Sunset Boulevard over by the Beverly Hills Hotel, on my way home, and I pulled up to a red light and there in a car next to me was Young! "Bob! What's goin' on? I thought you were in the hospital!" He said, "No, no, I'm okay, I'm okay!"—and I knew right away that what had actually happened was that he simply realized that he couldn't do it and had dropped out of the show. Because it was live and it was too hard.

One of my two live TV gaffes was on *Goodyear TV Playhouse*. I had just finished playing a supporting part in the movie *Miracle in the Rain* with Jane Wyman at St. Patrick's Cathedral in New York (more on this later), and Lester Shurr of the Louis Shurr Office in New York, my agents, said, "While you're here in New York, why don't we see if we can get you a *Goodyear Playhouse*?" There was a starring part as an American Army captain in an upcoming episode about the German occupation and the French Underground, and it got down to where it was between me and John Forsythe. (John hadn't yet made much of a splash in Hollywood but he was pretty well known in New York.) Maybe because I was from Hollywood, I ended up getting the part—the *lead*. I was in every single scene and had dialogue from beginning to end. We rehearsed for ten days and then one Sunday night in June, we were on the air, doing it live.

At one point in the script, I had a line that was something like, "When we go down to the cellar, be sure that you" . . . do this and do that, I forget now what the rest of the line was. But the first part was, "When we go down to the cellar . . . " I was in the middle of that little speech when all of a sudden the various cameras started moving around like crazy, one guy backing up, another camera bumping into tables and chairs and so on. "What the hell's going *on?*" I asked myself as the camera crew began rearranging themselves very hurriedly and in the process banging into each other and the furniture. I kept going with the dialogue, wondering what was amiss and hoping that the audience hadn't been able to tell that, for a minute there, something had apparently gone very wrong. Well, after we finished, I found out from the director, Jack Smight, what the problem was: me! On page 22 of the script, I had that speech that started off with "When we go down to the cellar . . ."—and then on page 24, I had another speech that began with an almost identical line. Both speeches had the same lead-in, and I had gone from that lead-in line on page 22 to the speech that was on page 24—leaving two pages out! The audience didn't know I had skipped two pages but Jack and the crew sure did, and they had to scramble to catch up with where I now was in the script! "You had us goin' nuts in the booth!" said Smight, who I could tell was very relieved that we got through it okay. It was a terrible experience—but worse for Jack and the crew than for me!*

Then there was my worst live TV experience.

Red Skelton, star of *The Red Skelton Show*, was the funniest man you ever saw on TV, as good or better than Jackie Gleason or Bob Hope or any of those great comedians. On an upcoming episode of his live CBS show, there was going to be a sketch with guest star Anna Maria Alberghetti as a Mexican senorita and Red as a matador. Jack Donohue, a wonderful comedy director who liked my work, hired me to play a Mexican announcer who stands in the middle of the bullring set and reads a scroll and introduces the great matador Red Skelton.

I memorized my part and we rehearsed it for a week and everything went fine and then, on the night of the broadcast, it came to

---

*It was fun to be reminded of that *Goodyear TV Playhouse* years later by, of all people, John Astin, who (I didn't know it at the time) had been an extra in it—he appeared as a soldier with no lines. I was in Hollywood playing a supporting role in a show starring John and his wife Patty Duke, and out of the blue he told me that he'd been an extra on that *Goodyear Playhouse* and that he'd been thrilled to meet me. "I'll never forget how wonderful you were to all of us on the set, how you talked to us and told us all about Hollywood," John told me. I was flabbergasted!

air time and we began doing the sketch. (In addition to the 40 or 50 million people watching it live in their homes, there was also a big studio audience in the CBS Theater on Fairfax and Melrose.) There was Red dressed as the matador and Anna as this beautiful girl, and I (also in costume) unrolled this big scroll and I began reading, in my Mexican accent, "Ladies and gentlemen, eet eez my pleasure to introduce at theez time the great matador" and so forth and so on—I began describing what a formidable matador he was, how many bulls he had fought and so on. There was nothing written on the scroll—whoever made up that scroll, a property man probably, just scribbled something that looked like writing. All of a sudden, I couldn't remember my next line. I just went up—I couldn't remember the rest of it for the life of me. I paused for what seemed like 30 minutes—it was probably three seconds, but it seemed like forever. And then I heard myself saying, "Son of a *bitch*!"

Then came the silence.

Red Skelton stepped in front of the live camera that was on me, looked right in the lens and said, "Ladies and gentlemen, we'll be off the air for a few minutes, but we'll be right back." Well, as soon as he said that, the next line came to me and I went into the speech again and got through the rest of it and we finished the sketch.

In those days, when you finished a show, there was a little cast-and-crew party with a lot of eating and drinking. Well, I didn't go to the party—I just went to my dressing room, took the costume off, put my clothes on, got in my car and came home. "Marie . . . I'll never work again," I told my wife. "You won't believe what happened to me . . ." I was so upset.

About a half-hour later, the doorbell rang and I went to the door and it was a telegram delivery boy. He handed me a telegram which I saw was from Jack Donohue, the director, and it read,

PAUL, I WANT TO THANK YOU FOR A GREAT MOMENT ON THE SHOW. IT'S ONE OF THE BEST THINGS THAT EVER HAPPENED AT CBS. THANK YOU, AND GOD LOVE YOU.

Such a nice telegram! He really didn't *mean* it; he just wanted to make me feel better because he knew I was devastated. Of course, that goof did *not* spell the end of my career, but for a few hours there, I was certain that it would.

Any young actors and actresses who may be reading this: Don't get too upset when you go up like that. Dick Powell once played a character that got shot on a live show and he was lying "dead" on the floor and the camera was still on him—but *he* thought the camera was off him, and he got up and walked out of the scene. Millions of people saw that on the air, but that didn't hurt his career, and my slip of the lip on Red Skelton's show didn't hurt mine.

Struggling with TV series *Sugarfoot* star Will Hutchins.

Frequently actors are called upon to do dangerous things. You must be very careful. There's often pressure on the sets of TV series—the director's fighting for time, he's being rushed, and sometimes, to save a few minutes, you'll be asked to do something that really ought to be a stuntman's job. If you don't feel secure about doing something, *don't do it*. I've already described how Andre de Toth tried to cut off my head with a guillotine on *House of Wax*—I've had several experiences like that. Once I was doing a small television Western, Ray Nazarro was the director, and he wanted me to do a fight scene with Leo Gordon, a very physical actor. The fight would entail us rolling around on the ground and under a couple of horses that would be stamping all around us. Not only that, Leo would have a Bowie knife in his hand and I'd be holding his wrist—the old routine. I asked the property master, "Don't you have a rubber knife?," and he said no. Low-budget shows like that didn't have a rubber knife to replace this real knife. I told Ray Nazarro, "*I* can't do this fight with a real knife! And with Leo Gordon"—Leo was one of these actors who believed in realism! "Ray, this is dangerous. I could get cut, *he* could get cut, the horses could trample on us . . ." But Ray talked me into doing it, and I did it, and fortunately nobody got hurt. So sometimes you'll be called upon to do stuff like that, and my advice is, *Be very careful and very cautious.* We've had actors get hurt—you all know the story of poor Vic Morrow, what happened to him and those kids in the helicopter scene in **Twilight Zone–The Movie.** So, as an actor, I'm advising you . . . be careful. Be brave, but be smart.

Ray Nazarro was directing again when I did a small television show called **Fury** with Peter Graves, a kid actor named Roger Mobley and a horse named Fury. The episode was called "Packy, the Lion Tamer" and I played an Italian lion tamer with a circus—I had the beautiful shiny boots, the white pants, an Italian accent, the whole outfit.

The first day, while doing a scene where I had to walk by the lion's cage, the lion suddenly reached out and took a swipe at me with his paw. I'd been told that the lion on the show would be Jackie, the famous lion you see roaring in the MGM logo at the beginning of every MGM movie. "This *is* Jackie, isn't it?" I asked the *actual* lion tamer, a young guy who was there along with a couple of lion handlers.

"No, no—Jackie died," he told me. "This is a new lion we're training, Pasha. Be very careful when you walk by the lion's cage; *don't* turn your back on Pasha, because he *will* take a swipe at you. Look him in the eye and *keep* looking at him as you walk by and deliver your dialogue." I did the scene and did my dialogue— "Pasha, you hungry, eh? I going to *feed* you now, sweetheart!"—and everything went fine.

As the story progressed, the lion escaped from this little circus and went off into the woods (actually Iverson's Ranch), where Roger Mobley, the little boy, was riding around on Fury. The lion spooked Fury and the boy fell off; Fury went back to the stable, now rider-less, and everybody knew that something was wrong. We formed a posse and went into the woods searching for him.

Now it came to the scene where we found the lion: He was hiding in this cave-type place covered with brush, and the scene called for me to stand at the entrance and call "Pasha!" and crack my whip until Pasha came out of the cave and stopped in front of me. For this shot, they were going to put up a big glass plate between me and Pasha—they had to wait for a certain time of day when the lighting would be just right and there would be no reflection on the glass whatsoever. It was going to look like it was just me and Pasha and nothing between us. Pasha was in a cage in the cave as things were being set up.

"When you release the lion from that cage back there, and he comes at me," I said to Ray Nazarro, ". . . isn't he liable to go right through that thing?"

"Nah, nah, don't worry about it," Ray scoffed. "That's Plexiglas, one and a half inches thick. It's the Unbreakable Shield." There was a toothpaste commercial out at the time where a guy threw a baseball and it bounced off an "Unbreakable Shield," and then the commercial explained how their toothpaste puts an unbreakable shield on your teeth. I guess I gave Ray the idea that I wasn't too impressed with this safety precaution because he reassured me again, "The lion *can't* get through there, it's the Unbreakable Shield."

"Unbreakable" or not, I figured I needed to have an escape route. Just to the right of where I'd be standing in the shot, there was a big rock, and above the rock a tree branch hanging down. I figured that if anything went wrong, I could jump on the rock and grab the branch and pull myself up.

It came time for the shot and there I was standing on my side of the Unbreakable Shield, as ready as I was ever going to be. There were a lot of tourists on the set out there at Iverson's ("Oh, look, there's Peter Graves," "There's the camera" and so on), the boy Roger Mobley was nearby and there was a feeling of anticipation in the air. Ray Nazarro ordered, "Release the lion!" and Pasha came out of the cage and saw me—but, of course, didn't see the Unbreakable Shield. He started coming toward me at a pretty good pace and I cracked my whip and said, "*Pasha!*" He kept coming at me and he *hit* the Unbreakable Shield—and in an instant, he was right *through* it. He broke right through the Unbreakable Shield and now he was two feet away from me, his nose bleeding!

He stopped for a second and looked at me and I looked at him, and I remembered my escape route. I jumped up on the rock and grabbed on the branch, the kid sprinted away, the camera crew ran, all the tourists from Oklahoma and Kansas scurried down the hillside—and there was Pasha, loose at Iverson's Ranch!

Pasha scrambled up a hill and sat down looking kind of befuddled, watching everybody running and yelling and screaming. The lion wranglers had a cage on the back of a flatbed pickup truck and they backed that truck up as close as they could to Pasha. As soon as they opened the door to Pasha's cage, he ran down the hill, jumped on the back of the truck and went into his cage. He felt safer in the cage than he did sitting on the side of the hill—and we *also* felt safer with him in the cage! So, fortunately, no one was hurt, and Pasha was rounded up quickly and easily. That was the saga of "Packy, the Lion Tamer," another example of the sort of weird thing that happens frequently on shows. You young actors have to be ready for them.

On another occasion, I got myself into a dangerous situation of my own making. I had the starring part in a **Navy Log**, an episode about the Blue Angels, the Navy's flight demonstration team that performs their maneuvers at air shows. We were down at Los Alamitos Air Base and I was dressed in a Navy lieutenant's uniform as we were shooting by the hangars. Between takes, a real Marine sergeant said, "Hi, Lieutenant," and I didn't admit who I really was, I didn't tell him I was an actor; I just said, "How are *you*, Sergeant?" We started talking, and I asked him, "What do you do, Sergeant?" He said, "I fly the helicopters here. That's my helicopter right there. You ever been up in one?" I told him I never had. He said, "Would you *like* to take a ride, Lieutenant?" He thought I was a real officer.

I looked around and I could tell that I had quite a bit of time before the next take, so I said, "Yeah, sure. I'd love to."

I got in the helicopter and the sergeant got behind the controls and we took off. And, now that it was too late, I began to realize that this guy had had a few beers! The sergeant said, "Watch *this*, Lieutenant," and with that, he flew underneath some telephone wires and then right over the top of a barn. And scared the shit out of me!

"You know, Lieutenant," he said, "I can do a *loop* with this thing!" That did it. "Sergeant, look," I said frantically, "I'm *not* a lieutenant,

Two shots from a *Westinghouse Desilu Playhouse,* "Come Back to Sorrento." In the first is Virginia Vincent and Frank London; the second is a behind-the-scenes shot with co-stars Marisa Pavan and Robert Loggia. Marisa was as pretty as her adorable sister Pier Angeli.

I'm an actor—and you better get me back to the base, I'm in the next shot!" I babbled all that out before he could do the loop! I wanted to get the hell out of there. That was my first helicopter ride.

Earlier in this chapter, I wrote that young actors should always think twice before agreeing to do something (like a fight involving a real knife) that they don't feel comfortable about. But in non-dangerous situations, *always* say yes, never say no. When you have a chance to land a role and somebody asks you, "Can you ride a horse?," "Can you shoot a gun?," "Can you do this?" or "Can you do that?," say yes. Then go out and learn how to *do* it! In a two-hour episode of **Desilu Playhouse** called "Come Back to Sorrento," I had to fake playing a flute. For two weeks prior to filming I studied with John Rotella, an expert flutist who played in Frank Sinatra's band, but I have to admit, I could not quite master the finger movements. I don't think the audience noticed. Flute players probably did.

Charles Marquis Warren, the director of the TV Western
Rawhide with Eric Fleming and Clint Eastwood, was about to go
to Tucumcari, New Mexico, to do an episode involving a traveling
circus, and he offered me the heavy role. But then he asked, "Can
you juggle?"

"Oh, yeah, yeah, I can juggle," I lied.

"All right," Charles said, "you've got the part of the juggler. He's
going to be one of the suspects in a murder."

At that point, I got in touch with my close friend Nick Cravat,
Burt Lancaster's circus partner: "Nick, I know you can juggle.
Teach me how." We picked three oranges off of trees in the front
of my house and he was trying to teach me how to do it . . . and
I found that I couldn't juggle at *all*. I tried and tried, until Nick
finally started getting frustrated. And the next day I was supposed
to go in and meet Charles Marquis Warren for my wardrobe
fitting on *Rawhide*.

Fortunately, I had a brainstorm. When I went in to meet with
Warren again the next day, I said, "You know, Mr. Warren, I'm the
heavy in this *Rawhide* and it seems to me . . . a juggler, he's not
too menacing. Why don't you make me the sharpshooter in the
show? Or maybe the knife thrower . . . ?" And to my great relief
Warren said, "Good idea, Paul! You'll be the sharpshooter. Forget
the juggling!," just like I'd hoped he would, and I played the part!

Kipp Hamilton, a pretty girl who was also in that *Rawhide*
episode, must have given them the impression she was capable of
throwing a knife. At one point in the story, out in the Tucumcari
desert, Eric Fleming and Clint Eastwood line up all the suspects
from the circus—me, Tony Caruso and a few other people. Then
they give Kipp a Bowie knife and they say to her, "Throw it at the
feet of the man you saw the night of the murder." She walks down
the line slowly and looks at each one of us and she finally stops in
front of Tony Caruso, and then she takes this knife—a real Bowie
knife—and she flings it down at the sand at Tony's feet. But she
gave it a little extra spin and it went *right into her own toe*. The poor
girl screamed as the blood spurted out. We were all horrified. Eric
Fleming, like the big leading man he was, swept her up and carried
her over to the limousine, and Kipp was taken away to the hospital.
So, when it comes to knives or guns or weapons of *any* kind, always

have your wits about you as you're acting in a scene.

By the way, as a result of Kipp's accident, we were in Tucumcari an extra five days waiting for her to get out of the hospital and come back to work. The extra week's pay came in handy: Tony used the money to make a down payment on an apartment building in Santa Monica that increased in value many times over.

Another time, it was a brainstorm on my agent Wilt Melnick's part that helped me land a role. Louis Hayward was doing a detective show called *The Lone Wolf* and Lynn Stalmaster was the casting director. I went in with Wilt for an interview wearing a pair of built-up shoes (originally made for Dane Clark) that I'd "liberated" from Warner Brothers. These elevator shoes gave me an inch or two of added height. As we came to the outer office and met Lynn Stalmaster, he looked at me and asked, "How tall are you, Paul?"

"I'm five-ten."

"Gee, you look so much bigger than Louis Hayward," Lynn frowned. "And he doesn't like anybody taller than him to be in the same scene."

"Oh," I said. "That's unfortunate . . ."

"Well, stand by," Lynn said, and off he went. So now we were waiting in this office, Wilt and I, and out of the blue Wilt asked, "What size shoe do you wear?" I told him I was a nine and a half. He said, "So am I. Let's switch shoes!" So we switched shoes—he put the elevators on and I put *his* shoes on. We then went in to meet Louis Hayward and the director, Hayward and I were now about the same height, and I got the job. When Wilt and I came out, we started cracking up, with Wilt saying through his laughter, "It really pays to have an agent who wears the same size shoe!" Then he added, "I *like* these—can I *keep* them?" Wilt was about five-two, and I guess he enjoyed that little bit of extra altitude!

Needless to say, making yourself taller is a good bit easier than making yourself shorter, which I was fortunate enough to be able to do that day thanks to Wilt Melnick. I landed a wonderful part on an episode of *The Loretta Young Show* where she would be playing a widow visiting Rome and I was an Italian who takes her out to dinner and woos her and has love scenes with her—a Rossano Brazzi-type part, very romantic. The first day of rehearsal, Loretta said to me, "Paul, do you have any lifts? Elevated shoes?" I said, no, but I can get them. She said, "I wish you would. I like to look up at my leading men." She was about five-eight and I'm only five-ten, so without lifts we were almost eye-to-eye.

Wanting very much to please her, I had a pair of boots made real quick by the famous Emedio Spezza, a Melrose Boulevard shoemaker who made shoes and boots for Frank Sinatra, Dean Martin, Gene Kelly, *all* the small leading men. He made me boots that got me up to about six-two and Loretta Young loved that. And as a result, I did two subsequent *Loretta Young Show*s. That's another example of how being able to work fast and react to any situation can help you land roles and help you make sure you don't *lose* a role. I used those boots for years; as a matter of fact, I still have them.

And finally, speaking of short and tall actors, I got one of the tallest actors in the business, Chuck Connors (6'6"), started in Hollywood. When I was at Warners, Chuck was first baseman for the Los Angeles Angels baseball team, and one day I saw him reciting "Casey at the Bat" on a television talk show. I was quite impressed with his delivery—it was a very dramatic thing and I could tell he had a lot of personality. At Warners, they were about to do a picture called *Alexander the Great*, the story of a left-handed baseball pitcher. Chuck was left-handed, and I said to Wilt Melnick, "Why don't you get a-hold of him?" He did, and signed him to an agency contract, and brought him out to Warners to test for *Alexander the Great*. Chuck didn't get the part in the picture (released as *The Winning Team*), Ronald Reagan did, but Chuck had gotten a contract with Wilt out of it. A short time later, when Warners was getting ready to make *South Seas Woman* with Burt Lancaster and Virginia Mayo, I told Wilt, "They need a big guy from Brooklyn to play a Marine." Again he brought Chuck out, and *I* was assigned to do the screen test with him! This was the first time I really met Chuck, and I don't think he even knew that I was the one who got him signed with Wilt. Chuck didn't know what he was doing; he didn't know what to do with his hands and so on, so I helped him quite a bit. He did the test and he got the part in *South Seas Woman* and that was his beginning in the acting business.

That's not the end of my Chuck Connors story. One day he came to visit me at my home on Wilbur Avenue (he had a house not far

Chuck Connors, his wife and young son, visiting me at my home. "Buy a horse and do Westerns!" I told him.

from me) and I said, "Chuck, you're a good type for Westerns. Why don't you get yourself a couple of horses, learn to ride and really concentrate on doing Westerns?" A few weeks went by, and one day here he came riding up by my house on horseback with one of his sons. "I'm taking your advice, Paul, I'm learning to ride," he told me, and lo and behold he ended up playing *The Rifleman* on TV, one of the top Western series, and that was the beginning of a great career.

But, strangely enough, I never worked with Chuck Connors in *The Rifleman*, or any of his other shows. To his dying day (we lost Chuck too soon, in 1992), I don't think he ever knew I was the one who "discovered" him.

16
MY STEPS TO STARDOM

Marie and I were married in August of 1947, and by March of 1957, less than ten years later, we had eight kids. Marie was barely 20 when we married, and by 29 she was the mother of eight. "The rhythm system" that the Catholic Church pushed didn't work—every time I touched Marie, there'd be another little one on the way! In the 100 months after the stork brought

Nicci, we had seven more—that's an average of one every 14 months. And that's a lot of kids! We nicknamed the last one (Gina, born in March 1957) "The Caboose" because we somehow knew she'd *be* the last now that we had four girls and four boys.

People would ask us, "How do you *do* it?" as far as handling that many children. For a long stretch there, we had three kids in diapers at all times, and we didn't have every-day help.

My first five steps to stardom, at our little house on Wilbur Avenue.

We need a bigger pool!

Marie's mother and father lived close by and, of course, they pitched in, and *my* mother would fly in from New York and spend a few weeks helping out when each baby was first born. But by the time "The Caboose" came along, it was working out very nicely: Nicci (the oldest) was then about eight, and she could occasionally take care of the younger kids. Gemma and P.V., who were six and seven by then, could also entertain the younger ones and look after them. The bigger kids really helped with the little ones quite a bit. When they all got a bit older, we had one kid in every grade at Our Lady of Grace School, from first grade to eighth.

As an actor, you don't work every single day, especially if you're a freelancer—and I was freelancing a great deal of the time after I left Warners. Now that I was working a lot in television, I had plenty of days off, so I also would feed the kids and dress them and play with 'em and take 'em to the park to feed the ducks and so on.

It was kind of fun to go places with a family of eight. When we went to church, the ten of us (me and Marie and the kids) would take up a whole pew, and people would gape at us like they'd gape at movie stars. And Marie and I looked like Pied Pipers whenever we took them to Disneyland! We'd go to the market shopping and sometimes the kids would all come along, and other shoppers

Sunday dinner. Gina watches as the boys make the meatballs; Marie and the girls stir the sauce.

All the Picernis play, and enjoy, bocci, an ancient Italian game akin to bowling.

would ask, "Are they all *yours?*" It was kind of nice, because we had a lot of fun with it. We had fun, that is, until we got to the cash register! At our local Safeway, we had the one-day marketing record, $165. Of course, *today* $165 is nothing—today we go to Costco and we spend $300. But $165 in one day at a Safeway in the 1950s was a *lot* of money. At that time, bread was ten cents a loaf, milk was 12 cents and so on. To spend $165, you had to buy a *lot* of groceries, so we had the Safeway record for a *long* time.

The kids all took various lessons. The girls had dancing lessons, and the girls *and* the boys had piano lessons, horseback riding lessons, sailing lessons, swimming lessons, etc.— we gave them the full spectrum! As you might imagine, it was very expensive having eight

Playing baseball with Michael, Gina and Philip.

kids, and money got tight *many* times. Apart from the various lessons and the grocery shopping, there was also, of course, the diaper service, babysitter, doctors, clothes, shoes, Catholic school tuition and so on. There was less stress when I was at Warners and had that steady check coming in every single week. Now that I was on my own, I found that an appearance on a TV show paid maybe three, four, five hundred dollars . . . but you may not do *another* one for four weeks. I'd have to do about three TV shows a month to make the salary I was making at Warners. In those days I was doing maybe 12 to 15 TV shows a year, with a picture thrown in here or there, but it was still tough to make the amount of money I made when I was under contract 52 weeks a year. It helped that I was still announcing the pre-game and halftime shows for the Los Angeles Rams—that was another source of income.

* * * * * *

My fourth son, Philip, born a few days before Christmas 1955, was always more interested in our garden than in playing sports with the other kids. He is responsible for most of the beautiful landscaping we still enjoy at our home today. After graduating from Our Lady of Grace and Crespi Carmelite High School, he decided he wanted to become a Catholic priest. He attended Queen of Angels Seminary in San Fernando and then Divine Word College in Iowa. While at Divine Word, he starred in a dance production and was outstanding. The taste of greasepaint and applause was intoxicating and the church lost a budding priest! He left the seminary and decided to go into the motion picture business.

Philip had a brief career in pictures as a dancer, on the film *Grease* and a few others, but eventually he tired of the inactivity between jobs and returned to his first love, landscaping. Today, he is the president of his own landscaping company, Nature's Plan, and is very successful. He lives in Crystalaire, near Gemma and her husband Michael, and he is becoming a wealthy man buying and selling land in the rapidly growing Antelope Valley.

* * * * * * *

We were living in the house on Wilbur that I had bought while I was at Warners, a three-bedroom house that we got brand new for $10,750 (our house payments were $58 a month). The Ford Country Squire was a very popular station wagon at the time, so we had that for Marie and the kids, and I usually drove a Chevy convertible. At one time I had a Cadillac convertible that was custom-built for Al Jolson, and I got that car as an indirect result of making an Allied Artists picture called *Dial Red O*. (To "dial red O" in the 1950s means the same as dialing 911 today.) Bill Elliott starred as a police detective on the trail of an escaped psychiatric patient (Keith Larsen) suspected of killing his wife. I played the wife's lover, an ex-Marine judo expert who is the real murderer (I killed her with judo cuts to the neck when she revealed that she was pregnant and insisted that I marry her).

Dial Red O was a little like the popular TV show *Dragnet* with Elliott playing a just-the-facts-ma'am police lieutenant and actor Robert Bice playing his partner. It was a change-of-pace role for Elliott, who was a cowboy star; the B Western was beginning to fade out, so Allied Artists made him a police detective. My murder victim was a lovely girl named Helene Stanley.

One thing happened on that set which I'll pass along as a warning to young actors. In one scene set in Helene's apartment, she said she was going to get into something more comfortable and so I went to her bar, poured a shot of "whiskey" into a glass and drank it down. We must have done seven or eight takes, and every take I drank a shot of whatever was in the bottle. All of a sudden, I got deathly ill—too ill to go on. The prop man suddenly realized what had happened: Usually when you're drinking liquor in a movie, you're actually drinking from a liquor bottle full of either tea or Coca-Cola. The other bottles in the scene, the row of liquor bottles you'll see on a nearby shelf, are filled with water that's been mixed with a couple of drops of iodine, which gives the water the color of whiskey. But today the prop man had fouled up and put the bottle with the water and iodine on the bar—here I'd been drinking iodine, seven or eight shots! Needless to say, I didn't drink enough to kill me; I went to the hospital and explained what had happened, and they told me to drink a lot of boiled rice water, which did settle my stomach. So there's a valuable tip: When you're drinking "booze" in a movie or TV show, make sure it's not iodine!

Anyway, back to Al Jolson's custom-built convertible: Helene Stanley invited Marie and me to her home in Bel-Air for dinner one night, and introduced us to her husband. Well, it was Johnny Stompanato, a gangster working for Mickey Cohn, the Al Capone of the West Coast at that time. (Johnny had once taken a bullet for Cohn: The two of them were coming out of Frascati's, a restaurant on Sunset Boulevard, when somebody tried to kill Mickey. Johnny, who was then Mickey's bodyguard, took the shot in the belly.) Helene's mother and father were also there at the house, and I got the impression that they weren't too thrilled with having Johnny Stompanato as their son-in-law.

Johnny was a con man who had a few little deals going here and there, including an involvement of some sort with Beverly Hills Hillcrest Motors, a Cadillac dealership. He knew I was looking for a convertible, and one night not long afterwards he called me and said, "Listen, Al Jolson just turned in his '49 Cadillac convertible. We gave him $1800 for it on the trade-in. If you want it, come on over and grab it right away, otherwise somebody else will get it." So I drove over and I bought this beautiful blue convertible. Under the hood, on a silver plaque on the top of the radiator, it said **CUSTOM-BUILT FOR AL JOLSON.** I had that Cadillac for several years, until one day during a terrific rainstorm I filled it up at a gas station near Paramount. Rainwater had seeped into the gas station's main tank, and as I was pumping the gas in, a lot of water went in with it and ruined the engine.

Johnny and Helene later divorced, and soon Johnny started going with Lana Turner. Johnny was a handsome devil, so all the girls, even a star like Lana Turner, fell for him. One day he called me and said, "I'm living at Lana's house now, she's in Europe. Why don't you come over and bring your wife and a couple friends? We'll have a poker game." I knew a kid who was starting out to be an actor, Frankie Bella, kind of a wise guy from back in Corona, New York, so I brought him with us and we played poker over there. (Frankie was trying to get into the business through me—I once used him in a play that I produced, Henri Gheon's *The Comedian*.) Frank and Johnny hit it off that night and started associating on their own, and some time later on, Johnny told Frankie, "Two Greeks are coming into town and they love to play poker. Can you get a friend and get about $5,000 apiece? I'll put in 5,000 too and we'll fix the game and we'll take these guys for all their money." Frankie said, "Great!"—he was a con man like Johnny was. Frankie and a friend from back East got five-grand apiece and went to the Beverly Wilshire and they started a big poker game in a suite up there. By two o'clock in the morning, Frankie was broke, his friend was broke and Johnny Stompanato was broke, and the two Greeks had all the money. Afterwards, when Frankie told me about it, I said, "You dumb fuck, don't you know what happened? Johnny was in cahoots with the Greeks and they *took* you two pigeons! He double-crossed you and split your ten-grand with the two Greeks!"*

I had a good-sized part in *Dial Red O*, an okay movie, certainly better than some of the other movies I did around that time. With so many kids to support, I would take *any*thing. *Lord of the Jungle* was an Allied Artists movie starring Johnny Sheffield, who was once Boy in the Tarzan series; now he was a teenager and starring in his own series as Bomba the Jungle Boy. Ford Beebe, the writer-director, was a typical oldtime director *a la* Cecil B. DeMille, with the boots and the jodhpurs (the pants that flared out), and even a pith helmet! But he was a sweet man. Also in the picture was Wayne Morris, the big, blond-haired veteran of dozens of Warner Brothers pictures of the '30s and '40s. Wayne was a wonderful, lovable guy, now in the

---

*Johnny died not too many years later, when during a fight with Lana he was stabbed by Lana's teenage daughter. I think the bullet wound he received during his days as Mickey Cohn's bodyguard was still a vulnerable spot, and she must have made contact with it, which really ripped him apart. That's my theory, because people don't die from a stab wound that easy.

twilight of his career—and he liked to drink.

Wayne, William Phipps and I were playing hunters hired by the government to exterminate a herd of rogue elephants, and Johnny's Bomba the Jungle Boy, friend of the elephants, thinks we should kill only the rogue leader, not the others. The script was as corny as you could possibly imagine. We shot jungle sequences at the Arboretum in Pasadena, where there was a little lake where I believe I was told some of the old Tarzan films had been shot. We also shot some of it at Allied Artists, which was located

Wayne Morris kept things light during the making of Lord of the Jungle, a Bomba the Jungle Boy movie with Nancy Hale.

on Prospect and Sunset Boulevard. Every lunch-time while we were shooting at Allied Artists, Wayne and I would go across the street to a bar-restaurant and have lunch, and he would have about six martinis. As I said, he loved his drinks. By the time we'd get back to work, he was feeling pretty good—he had a big, wonderful grin anyhow! We came back from lunch one day and sat down in a couple of director's chairs with scripts, rehearsing the next scene with Ford Beebe. Wayne said to him, "Ford, you were telling me the other day that you don't drink."

Beebe said, "I haven't had a drink in my life. I've *never* had a drink."

Wayne looked at him for a long moment, serious and straight-faced. Then, holding up the script, he asked, "How the hell can you write this *shit* and not *drink?*" I can still picture in my mind the shocked look on Ford Beebe's face when Wayne said that!

Some of the movies may not have been anything special, but I was still getting some good roles on television. I did an episode of Ann Sothern's series **Private Secretary** just about the time that Marlon Brando hit Hollywood in a big way and became the hottest thing in the business. Everybody thought he was really something—and he *was*, when he first hit. In fact, a lot of actors started imitating him. On this series, **Private Secretary**, Ann was the girl Friday of a New York talent agent (Don Porter), and in this particular episode I was their client, a Marlon Brando-type actor. It was a wonderful part—I wore jeans and a leather jacket and I did crazy, unorthodox things, like walking on the railing of the office balcony. But what made it even more memorable for me was that when I got on the set and we started shooting it, the director Christian Nyby said to me, "Paul, do you know who you beat out for this part? Jack Lemmon." And, right after that, Jack Lemmon got the Academy Award for **Mister Roberts**. I just wanted to mention that once I beat Jack Lemmon out for a part!

Ann Sothern was a delight, just lovely, and Gale Storm was the same way. On Gale's series, **The Gale Storm Show**, she starred as the social director on a luxury liner and ZaSu Pitts, the oldtime comedienne, played her sidekick. This was the era when Rossano Brazzi was popular in movies like **The Barefoot Contessa** and **Summertime**, and again (after **The Loretta Young Show**) I was playing a Brazzi-like lover, with the Italian accent and everything else that goes with it. I guess I was the poor man's Rossano Brazzi! Only *this* time I didn't make love to Gale Storm, as you'd expect— I made love to ZaSu Pitts! I had fun working with Gale, and when I saw her again recently at one of the autograph shows, she was just as sweet and warm as I remembered her.

TV also gave me a last chance to play opposite Frank Lovejoy, with whom I had worked numerous times at Warners. As I mentioned in the chapter on **Breakthrough**, one day on that film, he looked at me in the midst of a rehearsal and he asked, "Is that the way you're gonna play it?" I thought—and still think—that's a terrible thing to say to a beginning actor, and from that day on, I really didn't much care for Frank. But now, seven or eight years later, he was doing a tough-guy TV series called **Meet McGraw** and I was cast in a guest part. On the set one day, between takes, he made a face and he sat down and, sounding very out-of-breath, he said, "Paul—do me a favor, will you? In my dressing room . . . on top of my dresser . . . you'll find a little bottle of nitroglycerin pills. Go get 'em for me . . . will ya?" Looking at his face, I could see that he was in pain from angina, the chest pain that can precede a heart attack. I rushed and got the bottle and brought it back to him. He put a couple of tablets under his tongue and, still gasping a little, said, "Thanks a lot . . . thanks . . . " At that moment, I suddenly finally liked Frank, I said to myself, "He's okay," because he trusted me enough to have me go get them, not the assistant director or somebody like that. A few years later, Frank was back East appearing in a play when he suffered a fatal heart attack in his New York hotel suite. He was only 50.

With so many mouths to feed, it was nice when a part would come up unexpectedly. Early one morning the phone rang and it was Bert Leonard, the producer of Phil Carey's TV series *Tales of the 77th Bengal Lancers*. "We have an actor here who can't remember his name," he said. "Can you get out here right away? We'll make it up to you, Paul!" I hurried out to Vasquez Rocks, learned about two pages of dialogue (I was playing an Arab character), and we did the scene with no problems. I had rushed in and "saved the day," but now that the scene was in the can, Bert Leonard began singing a different tune: "Paul, I can only give you $300 for this day's work, but the next show I'm gonna triple your salary and I'll make it up to you." Naturally, I never heard from him again!

In later years, I was a last-minute replacement for Forrest Tucker not once but *two* times, on episodes of *Love, American Style* and Angie Dickinson's *Police Woman*. The way it happened on *Love, American Style* was that I got a call about three o'clock in the morning from Billy D'Angelo, the show's producer. "Paul, you gotta do me a big favor. Forrest Tucker is sick, he can't come to work tomorrow." (He was probably on a bender!) Billy said he wanted me to step in and play the lead in the episode.

I knew it had to be the starring part and a lot of lines, so I was very hesitant.

Billy said, "I'll give you a thousand dollars for the day's work—"

"What time do I report??!"

Not knowing how this was going to play out, I got to Paramount early the next morning and went over the lines with Billy; it was an episode called "Love and Murphy's Bed," in which I would be playing a salesman who shows up at Jo Ann Pflug's apartment, where she finally puts me in her Murphy bed (and it goes up into the wall!).

My eight steps to stardom.

Les Martinson was a crazy director, always very nervous, but he was a *prince* on this particular day. He handled me so well, because he knew of all the pressure I was under—I'd had to learn the entire half-hour script while sitting in the makeup chair, being cued by Billy D'Angelo. Unlike Bert Leonard, Billy really appreciated what I did, and through the years used me in almost every show that he produced—***Batman, Alice, Sledge Hammer!*** and a TV movie called ***Papa and Me***. We became real good friends.

When you've got the proper acting background, you will be able to step in like that, at a moment's notice, and do the job. You never got much rehearsal time on shows like that anyway. Normally we would simply come in and the director would give us our positions and our instructions: "You move here, then move there, then there . . ." Then we would demonstrate it for the cameraman and the technical crew, so that they could light the positions. In those days we would shoot a master shot (the whole scene in its entirety), and then break it up into singles, two-shots, three-shots, whatever. The only "rehearsal" you got was in doing it over and over again, in different angles. You tried to save your best performance for the closeups—I learned that from watching Joan Crawford at Warners. She would just breeze through the master shot, not doing much of *any*thing acting-wise, but then when it came time to shoot her closeups, boy, she would really turn it on. Later on, when the footage was being edited, this didn't give the editor much choice but to use the closeups! That was a lesson I learned from Crawford.

Sometimes the grind of TV can get a little tiresome. Once I was doing a **Colt .45**, a Western TV show, with Margaret Whiting guest-starring. I was bored with the part, so I decided to play it with my Cary Grant impression. I read all the lines as Cary Grant and, guess what? Nobody ever noticed! I did that frequently, I'd read a line like Cary Grant would read it, or Clark Gable, just for my own enjoyment.

I learned what I felt was an important "life lesson" as a result of a visit to Tucson, where I did two episodes of the Western series **Boots and Saddles**. A friend had once told me, "When you travel, in Europe or *any* place, if you see something you want, *buy* it. You may say to yourself, 'It's too much, I don't really need it . . . ,' but— always buy it. Because you'll never see it again." Well, that happened to me on **Boots and Saddles**, and I've regretted it all these years. I was there several weeks and an artist there, a very good one who did Western-type oil paintings, came around and saw me and said he wanted to paint me sitting on a horse. He did a beautiful painting of me in my Western outfit, posing on the horse, and when he was finished, he wanted to sell it to me $100. Well, a hundred bucks was a lot of money in those days, and I didn't buy it. Then, for years afterwards, I wished I had. And if anybody out there *has* that painting, I'll give you *five* hundred for it!

So if you ever see something that you really like, *buy* it, and don't worry about the price. I learned my lesson: Later on, when I was in Mexico City doing a nightclub act, Marie and I were walking past a jewelry store and in the window I saw a gold charm bracelet, very beautifully hand-crafted. It was $200 but, over Marie's objections, I bought it for her. "Oh, why did you *do* that?" she asked. "It's so expensive. We don't have *that* much money that we can spend $200 on a gold bracelet."

I said, "You know something, honey? Forty years from now, we'll *still* be broke—but you'll have the gold bracelet." And now that it's exactly 40 years later, I know that it's true. We still don't have the money, but, she's got the gold bracelet.

17
ABOUT ACTORS & DIRECTORS—THE GOOD THE BAD AND THE UGLY

In 1955 I was cast as a young priest by Warner Brothers in the romantic drama *Miracle in the Rain* with Jane Wyman and Van Johnson, my first job for the studio since my contract there ended. I enjoyed working once again for Warners and I, of course, didn't have any hard feelings about the fact that they had let me go. The only reason they did was because of television—they let *every*body go. Jack Warner, Steve Trilling, Solly Biano, Bill Orr, all the guys there at the studio still knew me and liked me, and, because they were aware that I was a Catholic and a graduate of Loyola, a Catholic university, they felt that the part of the priest in *Miracle in the Rain* was a natural for me.

Another thing in my favor: Parts of the film would be shot in New York, in the world-famous St. Patrick's Cathedral, and Warners wanted the actor playing the priest to be somebody who would make a good impression on Cardinal Spellman, who could say yea or nay to Warners' request to shoot in the Cathedral. If the Cardinal *was* going to let a movie be shot in there, he wouldn't want the priest being played by an actor who was a roustabout. He would want an actor who was a family man and a Catholic.

I was going to have several scenes in the movie and was scheduled to be in New York for two weeks, so Marie and I decided we would make a nice vacation out of it. Warners, of course, paid my way to New York, and *I* paid Marie's airfare so that she could come along with me. Mrs. Asher, who was our number one babysitter for quite a few years, took care of the kids while we were gone.

Warners put us up at the St. Moritz right on Central Park. The first day we were there, the director, a wonderful Hungarian named

Rudy Maté, told me that he wanted me to come with him the next morning to pay a call on Cardinal Spellman. One of the conditions that the Cardinal had laid down was that the cast, crew and all the equipment be out of the Cathedral every night before four A.M. so that we didn't interfere with their regular six o'clock mass. (This was the first time anyone was allowed to shoot inside St. Patrick's.) Rudy was very anxious to make a good impression on Cardinal Spellman, to give him confidence that we'd be in and out of there on time each night and that everything was gonna be correct, so he said to me (in his Hungarian accent), "Paul, since you're playing the priest, I want you to see Cardinal Spellman with me tomorrow morning. Be in the lobby nine o'clock and we go." I told him I would.

Karl Malden visits with me, Jane Wyman and Eileen Heckart at St. Patrick's Cathedral.

The next morning Marie and I went down to the lobby where we met Rudy and Jimmy, the production manager. Rudy was all prepared. Under his arm, he had the script, breakdowns, artists' drawings of all the shots—a big book packed with material he was going to show the Cardinal. When Rudy saw Marie, he got a little panicky. "Marie can't go *with* us," he said. I couldn't understand why not and I told Rudy I *wanted* her to come, but Rudy was firm: "No! The appointment is only for you and me and Jimmy." I told him not to worry and promised that Marie would wait in an outer office or somewhere like that while the rest of us met with Cardinal Spellman. We then went in a company limo over to St. Patrick's, where a monsignor greeted us in the rectory. Rudy was still worried because Marie was with us, so when the monsignor said, "Let's go in and see the Cardinal," Rudy said, "Paul's wife will wait here." And to Rudy's dismay, the monsignor said, "No, no, I'm sure his eminence would love to meet her too!"

We went in and met the Cardinal, a saintly man. He was a cute little guy who reminded me of Santa Claus without the hair. Back then, everybody knew of Cardinal Spellman—he had been the archbishop of New York and vicar of the United States Armed Forces, and then in 1946 was elevated by the Pope to the College of Cardinals. He was the first American cardinal. Introductions were made, we all sat down, and right away Cardinal Spellman turned to my wife and he asked, "Marie, what parish are you in?"

"We're in Our Lady of Grace Parish in Encino, California, your eminence."

He asked, "Do you have children? How many children do you have?"

"Yes, we have five children, and one on the way," Marie said, and then she proceeded to talk about them. Well, the Cardinal spent the next 20 minutes talking to Marie. He never said a *word* to Rudy Maté, who was sitting there shifting in his chair, or to anybody else! And at the end of the 20 minutes, he said, "Everything is fine, you can shoot your movie. You can go in at midnight, but you have to be out of there along with all your equipment by four o'clock because we have the six o'clock mass to get ready for." He then gave a prayer book to me and another one to Marie, autographed with a beautiful inscription. But he didn't give prayer books to Rudy or the production manager! Rudy was so disappointed that he didn't have a chance to show the Cardinal the production sketches or any of the rest of the material he'd brought along—the Cardinal spent the whole time talking with Marie! To this day, Marie and I still have those beautiful little leather-bound prayer books.

Miracle in the Rain was based on a novel by the great Ben Hecht, who also wrote the screenplay. It was a wonderful, heart-warming story with Jane Wyman as a young, rather plain New York

Between scenes with Van Johnson and Jane in St. Pat's vestibule.

stenographer who meets a soldier, Van Johnson, while waiting for a rainstorm to let up. Their feelings for each other develop into love, but soon Johnson's outfit is shipped overseas into World War II action. Some time later, Jane receives a letter from an Army chaplain notifying her that Johnson was killed. She comes to St. Patrick's Cathedral looking for some solace and advice, and I have a nice scene with her. Then one rainy night some time later, very ill, Jane gets up out of her sickbed and comes back to the Cathedral, and in her delirium she sees in front of the church Johnson, professing his love for her. Now Johnson tells her he has to go back, but before he does he gives her a memento, a gold Roman coin.

After he leaves, Jane collapses on the church steps in the pouring rain. I come out to close the Cathedral doors and see her lying there, so I pick her up, carry her into the Cathedral and tell an altar boy to fetch a blanket and call an ambulance. Jane's best friend, Eileen Heckart (in her first film), shows up as Jane expires in my arms inside the church. As she lies there, I open up her hand, and there is the gold Roman coin. That was the Miracle in the Rain.

It was summer when we started shooting the interiors of the cathedral, and with the high arc lights and the New York humidity, it made for a very hot set. I took a break between shots to go outside and get some fresh air. On the patio on the side of the Cathedral they had some director's chairs for the actors and for anybody in the crew who didn't happen to be working at the moment. Across the street from St. Patrick's this balmy June night were hundreds of people standing around looking in our direction, hoping to get a glimpse of Jane Wyman or Van Johnson. For my role as the priest I was of course wearing the traditional wardrobe, including a black cassock and white collar, and I came out onto the patio between takes and found Marie sitting in my chair. I told her she didn't have to get up but she did, insisting, "No, *you* sit, you're tired." So I sat down and she sat on my lap and I put my arms around her. Right away the monsignor (who was acting as technical adviser on the picture) came over. "*Paul . . .?!*" he said with a note of urgency. "*I* know you're an actor, *you* know you're an actor, *Marie* knows you're an actor. But those people across the street, *they* think you're a priest. Get *up*, Marie!"

Mom visits me at St. Pat's.

The Cathedral interior was all lit up, filled with big arcs and cables and parallels and equipment to the point that it looked exactly like a soundstage. One night Arthur Franz, an actor friend, came by to see me. When he spotted me in the Cathedral, he greeted me with, "Well, you son of a bitch, you beat me out of *another* one!"—he was forgetting that we were in St. Pat's because it looked so much like a soundstage. "Arthur, Arthur!" I shushed him. "Remember where we *are*!"

There was another funny moment when we shot that death scene. Jane Wyman and I rehearsed it several times for Rudy Maté (as I described earlier, a very nervous man, and with no sense of humor), and then Jane and I chatted while the crew put the finishing touches on the lighting and so on. (St. Patrick's Cathedral was going to be beautifully lit behind us, right up to the altar.) When we finally did the first take and it got to the point in the scene where she expired, as a gag I leaned over and kissed her flush on the lips. Rudy Maté was so naive; *he* thought that I was doing it for *real*! "Vot the hell are you *doing*?? What are you, crrra-zee? You *prrriest*, you can't kiss the girl!" Jane and I busted out laughing when we realized he thought I meant it seriously!

Needless to say, while in New York I saw a lot of my mother, my brother Charlie and my sisters, all my cousins and uncles and aunts—the whole family. In fact, they came and watched some of the shooting of **Miracle in the Rain**. Charlie was just out of his teens at the time and he was doing construction work on new high-rise buildings, walking around on steel girders 20, 30 stories carrying two-by-fours and so on. At the same time, he was with the Corona Dukes, his gang, picking up numbers and horse bets for Joey Narro, the boss of Corona. (Gangs in those days weren't the gangs that we have today; they were more like clubs. The Corona Dukes were a bunch of young guys that hung out together and caroused and played pool and stuff like that.) Charlie at that time was very shy— he was always in the background, he never said much. Even in his younger days, when I was under contract at Warners, he came out to visit me a couple of summers and he would come on sets with me, and other actors would ask, "Who *is* that kid?" Somehow silence gives the impression of strength and mystery, and Charlie had that certain something about him, almost like a Marlon Brando type. A lot of actors use that quality, but with Charlie it was real.

It was on **Miracle in the Rain** that Charlie first met Bobby Hoy, a stuntman who sometimes also played small parts. Bobby had doubled me in a couple of movies and he was a good friend, and while visiting New York he came by the Cathedral to see me. Charlie was there that same day and I introduced them—Charlie was very interested in meeting Bobby. Then a few years later, when I brought Charlie out to work on *The Untouchables*, Charlie got reacquainted with Bobby, who eventually sponsored him into the Stuntmen's Association. Charlie went on to become a tremendously successful stuntman and stunt coordinator, and it all dated back to that meeting with Bobby Hoy during the making of *Miracle in the Rain*.

And speaking of the director Rudy Maté, I worked for him a second time a few years later in a World War II story called *The Deep Six*, a Warner Brothers picture with Alan Ladd. What stands out in my mind about that one is that part of it was shot on location on San Clemente Island. There isn't much to do between takes when you're on an island, so there were a lot of poker games. One day after a run of bad luck, I lost all the cash I had brought. But it didn't really matter; I was finished in the film, and I was about to be flown to Burbank Airport and from there taken to Warners, where Marie was going to pick me up. Joey Bishop was one of the players in the game and knew I'd lost all my pocket money, so he

With college buddies Len McLean and Sam Larsen, seated. Sam, who was disabled, was a writer who typed with a pencil held in his mouth.

offered me the loan of two dollars. I said I didn't need it but he insisted; "Suppose you and Marie miss each other and you need money to make a phone call? You better take the two dollars." So I took it. Well, to this day, every time I run into Joey he always says, "Hey! Where's my two dollars?"—it's become a running gag. I've paid him back at least five times, but I know if I run into him again he'll still be asking for the money!

Movies like *Miracle in the Rain*, stories with a message of faith, were common back in the 1950s, as were Biblical epics. I came close to landing a good role in one of the first big Biblical movies of the 1950s, MGM's *The Prodigal* with Lana Turner. The idea for the movie started with my old friend Joe Breen. Joe had been Brynie Foy's associate producer at Warners—the brains *behind* Brynie Foy, I sometimes thought—but by this time he had left Warners and was living near me in Woodland Hills. Joe knew that my college buddy Samuel James Larsen was a brilliant writer, so one day Joe said to me, "You know what'd make a great story? The Biblical story of the Prodigal Son. Why don't you have Sam write the Prodigal Son?" That story (less than 300 words), found in St. Luke's gospels, tells of two sons, one of whom asks his father for his inheritance. While the other son remains with the father and works hard, the Prodigal Son moves away and squanders the money on courtesans, drink and "riotous living." Later, destitute and starving, he decides to come home. The father, jubilant, calls for his servants to kill and serve up the fatted calf, to celebrate the son's return. The other son is angry and jealous that the father has had the fatted calf killed for the Prodigal Son, but the father explains, "Son, thou art ever with me, and all that I have is thine. It was meet that we should make merry, and be glad: for this thy brother was dead and is alive again; was lost and is found again."

Sam Larsen, who lived at St. John of God Hospital and typed with a pencil in his mouth, wrote the outline for a movie version of the story—of course embellishing the parts where the Prodigal Son is out with the courtesans and sowing his wild oats. This was soon after Burt Lancaster and Nick Cravat had starred in hit movies like *The Flame and the Arrow* and *The Crimson Pirate*, so Sam wrote it with them in mind, Burt as the Prodigal Son and Nick as his mute sidekick. It was a damn good story that Joe took to MGM

(Dore Schary was then running the lot) and, lo and behold, MGM bought it, paying Sam $2500.

MGM hired Joe and a couple of other producers to develop it, they put some other writers on it, and pretty soon Joe lost control. When it came time to cast it, MGM didn't cast Burt Lancaster, they cast Edmund Purdom. Then I was brought in for an interview with the director, Richard Thorpe—who has *me* in mind to play the sidekick! I said, "Mr. Thorpe, this part was written for Nick Cravat. This is *his* part," and Thorpe said, "That character has a love interest in this story, Lana Turner's maid. The public doesn't like to see unattractive people as lovers on the screen. That's why we want somebody like *you*." (Nick wasn't exactly unattractive, but he *was* only about five-foot-two and was not a romantic figure.) I thought about it and finally said, "I can't do it. This was written for Nick, and he's a close friend. I'd feel hypocritical if I did it."

By casting Lana Turner as the courtesan, they ruined it by making it a Turner vehicle rather than focusing on the story of the Prodigal Son. I never saw the film, but I know it was a bomb. Sam was heart-broken because he really wanted it to be a good story.

As for Joe Breen, he left MGM and went to Spain and did a picture called **The Life of Christ**. He produced and directed it, and it was beautiful. (I looped about six of the Spanish actors for Joe on that film.) 20th Century-Fox bought Joe's movie saying that they were going to cut it and fix it up and release it—but as it turned out, what they were *really* doing was buying it just to get it off the market, so it wouldn't compete with a similar picture *they* were going to do. Of course they didn't tell Joe that, they kept him working on the picture: "You gotta cut *this* out," "You gotta change *this*," "You gotta do *that*," anything they could think of, to stall him. Joe would do what they requested each time, and Fox would keep on with new demands. After several months of this, finally Joe had a meeting with six executives in New York and at last he realized what they had done—bought his picture just to keep it from being seen by the public. They also felt it was anti-Semitic. At the close of the meeting, Joe said, "Gentlemen, in the last war, Adolf Hitler killed six million Jews. I regret that he didn't kill six million . . . *and six*." And with that, he walked out. Needless to say, that was the end of Joe Breen in this town! His career was over—he was blacklisted and couldn't get a job. So Johnny Roselli, who was running Vegas and had control over many different places, offered to give him a gift shop at the New Frontier Hotel. Joe and his wife and kids moved to Vegas and he lived out his life there. His picture, *The Life of Christ*, has seldom if ever been seen.

Speaking of Samuel James Larsen, he also wrote an adaptation of Henri Gheon's French play *The Comedian* which I produced as a play at the Immaculate Heart College Theater in Hollywood. It was the story of the Roman actor and Christian martyr Genesius, the patron saint of actors. I played Genesius, I had a wonderful professional cast and an English Shakespearean actor named Abraham Sofaer directing it. Also in the cast were Bob Denver and his twin brother, carrying spears!

One night during its two-week run, Edmond O'Brien came to see me in it; he and I were doing the movie *The Shanghai Story* together at the time. After the performance he came backstage with his brother Liam, a writer . . . and they just tore my performance apart! Edmond, who was so great in MGM's *Julius Caesar,* said, "You're *acting* too much because it's a classical-type play. Just speak the lines. Don't perform them!" Well, it *is* true that you're never too old to learn: Eddie was *so* right. My next performances were much better, because he gave me some constructive criticism. The play was a critical success but financially I lost a lot of money. As it turned out, I didn't do another play for many years, until I played St. Thomas More in *A Man for All Seasons.*

Phil Karlson was one of my favorite directors. I first worked for Phil in 1955, when Wilt Melnick brought me over to Paramount to do a picture with John Payne that Phil was directing. In *Hell's Island* I played a flyer who is now a convict in an island prison colony and Mary Murphy is my wife, who asks her former lover John Payne to help me escape. Payne arrives by boat and finds me in my hospital cell and explains that my wife sent him—and I tell him (using the same accent I did in *Mara Maru*), "No, I refuse to escape. You don't know that woman. She has tricks up her sleeve!" I had a great scene where Payne is trying to help me to escape and I don't want to leave the prison, because I feel safer there than I would on the boat with Mary, who wants to kill me (it turns out she is the heavy). Phil liked what I did in that, so later on, when

Richard Conte, me and Jimmy Darren as
The Brothers Rico.

Columbia was preparing to do a film called *The Brothers Rico*, about three Italian brothers involved with the Mob, I did something that I've only done twice in my life (and both times it worked). I sent Phil a telegram saying something like, "Dear Phil, I just read the book *The Brothers Rico* and I feel that I would be very right to play the middle brother, Gino. I hope we can renew our friendship" and so forth and so on. Sure enough, Phil brought me in and cast me opposite Richard Conte and James Darren in *The Brothers Rico*. (The other time I sent a telegram was a year or two later, when I was very gung ho about landing a part in *The Young Philadelphians*, and again it paid off.)

Richard Conte being Italian and me being Italian, I was a big fan of his. The very first time I saw Conte, it was 1947 or '48 (I was still in college) and I was the doorman at Hollywood's Las Palmas Theater, the same theater where I later starred with Buddy Ebsen in *Honest John*. I was at the door in tuxedo opening night for a show called *Lend an Ear* with William Eythe, Carol Channing, Gene Nelson and Marge and Gower Champion, a wonderful musical that eventually went to Broadway. (It was the show in which Channing, Nelson and the Champions were discovered. They all took off from there.) There were a lot of celebrities that opening night and Richard Conte was one of them; I took his ticket stub when he came in and I was just so excited seeing him for the first time. When the show started, I was still in the lobby waiting for a few stragglers to come in. But soon I was drawn into the theater by the music and the laughter, and I left my post and went into the theater and began watching the show from the back door. The manager of the theater saw me and said, "Hey, hey! Get back on the door!"

"There's nobody else coming in now," I told him. "And if anybody *does* come in, I'll catch 'em here."

"No, no," he said. "Get back on the door." So I went back on the door, but I could hear music and laughter and finally I just couldn't stand it anymore. I went back into the theater and the manager saw me and said, "I *told* you to get back on the door!" Well, I told him, "I *quit!*," and I stayed right there and enjoyed the opening performance of a great show.

That was my first exposure to Richard Conte, and then about ten years later came **The Brothers Rico**. He was not what I expected. He was like Frank Lovejoy in a way—not that friendly. Kind of distant, in fact. I have a feeling that Lovejoy and Conte were the type who always looked at young up-and-coming actors as threats to them, and therefore didn't want to help 'em or do *any*thing for 'em. But I always liked Conte's acting. Charlie later doubled Conte in an episode of **The Untouchables**.

Another actor who looked out for himself—although I liked him a lot—was Ernest Borgnine. In 1958 I worked at MGM in a picture called **Torpedo Run** with Glenn Ford and Borgnine, and after a few weeks I became very close to Ford and with Dean Jones, who was also in the film. The three of us hung out together and had lunches together; we even went to a few ballgames together. Although I'd worked with Ernie Borgnine before, I never really hung out with him even though he's Italian. One day there was a commotion on the set: Ernie began screaming at Joe Pevney, the director. "How come Glenn Ford's always giving the orders? He says 'Up periscope,' he says 'Down periscope,' he looks in the periscope, and I don't say a damn word! After all, I'm supposed to be the co-star of this film, and I never give an order!" Pevney explained, "Well, look, Ernie, he's the commander and you're the executive officer. He's the one who's *supposed* to say 'Up periscope' and 'Down periscope.'"

But that didn't satisfy Ernie; Ernie was acting like a ten-year-old kid who wasn't getting (what he felt was) the proper treatment. It turned into a big thing: Glenn went to his dressing room and Dean Jones and I went with him, and we waited. Finally Ernie's agent

L.Q. Jones, Glenn Ford and me in Torpedo Run.

came on the set, and the executive producer, and I don't know *how* many other people, and they had a big powwow. After about six hours of delay, we finally got back to shooting and Ernie wasn't pouting anymore. I think they let him say "Up periscope" a couple of times, just to make him happy!

Another part that felt almost like it was written for me (like the priest in **Miracle in the Rain** and Gino in **The Brothers Rico**) was Louis Donetti in **The Young Philadelphians** (1959), a big, deluxe Warner Brothers drama based on a best-selling novel. Paul Newman was set to star as an ambitious law student who uses unprincipled methods in his relations with others to carve out a successful law career for himself and to become part of the city's high social set. He steals a great summer job with a famous attorney from a character named Louis Donetti, a law student from the other side

As the D.A. opposite Paul Newman in *The Young Philadelphians*.

of the tracks. While Newman's character climbs the social ladder and becomes a high-priced attorney, Donetti goes into politics, works hard and ends up the district attorney. Finally they oppose each other in a murder trial.

It was a great part, and I don't think there was an actor in Hollywood at the time that was better suited for it than I was. They tested 10 or 15 actors for it—I was one of them, and so was Nick Georgiade, who later played Rico on *The Untouchables*. At that time, Nick was doing *A View from the Bridge* on stage in Hollywood, and if I'm remembering right Newman saw him in that play and liked him. I think Newman may have wanted Nick for the part. I *know* he didn't want *me*.

After I did my test, about six weeks went by and Wilt Melnick hadn't heard anything. But we also didn't hear that anybody *else* had been cast in it. I still knew Steve Trilling (Jack Warner's top executive when I was under contract at Warners) quite well, so I wrote Steve a telegram:

I THINK I'D BE RIGHT FOR THE PART OF LOUIS DONETTI IN "THE YOUNG PHILADELPHIANS." I TESTED FOR IT SEVERAL WEEKS AGO BUT I STILL HAVEN'T HEARD. I'D LIKE YOU TO TAKE A LOOK AT MY TEST AND SEE IF YOU AGREE.

Well, the next day Trilling got in touch with the right people and they called me in and set me for the part!

I loved getting that role and I loved Vince Sherman, the director. I did not love Paul Newman, who used to walk on the set like he was King Tut. He'd done *Somebody Up There Likes Me*, the Rocky Graziano story, and *The Long Hot Summer* and *Cat on a Hot Tin Roof* (for which he was Oscar-nominated), all big moneymakers; he was hot, he knew he was hot and he was feeling his oats. In 1954 he'd come to Warners from a New York soap opera to make his first film, *The Silver Chalice*, in which he was awful. His performance was an imitation of Marlon Brando if you ever saw one—a *bad* imitation! But here it was a few years later and now he was the star of *The Young Philadelphians* after getting nominated, and he was pretty full of himself. He was trying to tell Vince Sherman how to direct, he was trying to tell actors how to act and he had his own writer on the set rewriting the scenes. I had some pretty good scenes with Newman, but I just didn't like acting opposite him. He didn't like me, he didn't like Barbara Rush, he tried to get her fired, he tried to get Vince Sherman fired . . . he was just lousy to work with. The one person he got along with was Robert Vaughn, who played a longtime friend, falsely accused of murder. Newman and Vaughn spent so many *hours* ad-libbing a scene in a hospital that Vince Sherman was going crazy. It was like they were doing an improv actors' company scene. But Paul Newman has remained a big star and Robert Vaughn was nominated for an Academy Award for *The Young Philadelphians* so, who knows, maybe Newman was right. Newman hated *Young Philadelphians,* but it's one picture of his that constantly reruns on television. Recently I ran into Vince Sherman, the wonderful director, at a Ray Courts autograph show at the Beverly Garland Hotel, and we reminisced about what a pain in the ass Paul Newman was on that film.

Vince remained one of my favorite directors, along with Phil Karlson. I worked three times for Phil, the last time in "The Scarface Mob," a two-hour *Desilu Playhouse*. It ended up as *The Untouchables* television series, which was perhaps the highlight of my career.

18
The Experience
of a Lifetime

During the fantastic era of alcoholic madness known as Prohibition, lawless elements which previously had specialized in gambling, vice and shakedowns hit the greatest illegal jackpot of all by catering to the nation's thirst.

Alcoholic beverages were forbidden. Ergo: the people demanded them. It was a cotton-mouthed generation which ignored an irritating law by imbibing such commodities as bathtub gin and needled beer.

Mobsters were quick to capitalize on the demand. The result was that, in a battle for "business" during the "dry" years from 1922 through 1933, they fought among themselves in murderous gang wars, shot up public places with arrogant abandon and made a national institution of the "one-way ride."

Thus began the foreword to *The Untouchables*, the 1957 autobiography of Eliot Ness in which he described how he and the rest of his United States Department of Justice prohibition detail broke the stranglehold that Chicago gangster "Scarface" Al Capone and his mob had on the Windy City and the rest of the nation.

The son of Norwegian-born parents, Ness was 26 when he headed Chicago's Prohibition bureau with the express purpose of smashing the Capone empire. His nine-man team of law officers, incorruptible agents just like Ness, was known as the Untouchables and their exploits regularly made newspaper headlines—partly because reporters were invited on their raids of speakeasies and breweries. *The Untouchables* eventually secured enough evidence to send

"The Big Fellow" himself, Al Capone, as he appeared in 1931 following an arrest. This broad-daylight appearance of Chicago's Public Enemy #1 caught a furor: Crowds gathered about the Federal Building as mounted policemen tried to keep order.

Capone to prison for federal income tax evasion.

The 1920s and '30s were the heyday of modern-day outlaws like Capone, John Dillinger, Ma Barker, Legs Diamond, Pretty Boy Floyd, Bonnie and Clyde and so many others, and in some ways there was a certain glamour about these men and women who lived by their guns. I was around at the time, a young teenager still living in New York, but I don't really remember reading about them in the newspapers; at the time, I loved baseball and had formed my own team ("The 13 Club") and was busy with activities like that. Also, we had gangsters closer to home than Chicago: My own Uncle Benny, the husband of my mother's sister Nancy, was one-half of the Perry Brothers* that ran Harlem, which at that time was largely Italian. They were small-time, picking up numbers and taking bets and loan sharking. Uncle Benny was my godfather at confirmation and his present to me was my first bicycle. My memory of him is that he was always flashing money and that he dressed sharp—I can still picture his beautiful navy blue coat with velvet collars and his hats, which were just like the hats we later wore on *The Untouchables*. Uncle Benny took me to

*Gangsters always seemed to Americanize their names. Uncle Benny's real name was Ben Peruso, but he and his brother Tony became the Perry Brothers when they ran Harlem.

my first baseball game at Yankee Stadium, which was a big thrill for me because I loved, and *still* love, baseball. That day at the ballpark I saw Babe Ruth and Lou Gehrig play. I'll never forget that on that day, Gehrig hit two home runs and Babe Ruth made a sensational shoestring catch, rolling over about three times and throwing the ball to home plate for an out. I sat right behind third base with Uncle Benny and five or six of his cronies, and they would bet on every pitch. "I'll betcha two to one this is a strike," "I betcha two to one this is a ball"—every pitch, they bet money!

I was at an age when knowing that Uncle Benny was on the wrong side of the law never really bothered me that much, to tell the truth. He was always good to *me*—every time I saw him, he'd give me a wristwatch or three or four bucks or *some*thing. And always with a smile. Years later, when I came back to New York to do personal appearances with **House of Wax**, Uncle Benny was still operating strong and he had the local alderman and others in his pocket. When I first arrived in New York to do **House of Wax** p.a.s at the Paramount Theater, Uncle Benny threw a big party for me one night at some pizza joint in Harlem, with the alderman and some other big wheels. There must have been 200 people there and Uncle Benny paid for the whole party. I was the Hollywood movie actor of the family and he loved showing me off.

One night after I did my thing at the Paramount Theater, I went back to the Warwick Hotel where I was staying. By now it was about 11:30 and I had been doing interviews all day long and then the Paramount Theater appearance, and I was pretty tired. It must have been about midnight when I was awakened by the ringing of the phone. I picked up the receiver and said hello, and I heard, "Horace! It's Uncle Benny." (He always called me by my real name, Horace.)

"Oh . . . hi, Uncle Benny," I said, half-asleep.

He said, "I'm in the lobby. I've got the alderman and his wife and a few other people with me, and we're coming up."

"Uncle Benny, I had a rough day . . . I've been doing interviews all day and I'm in bed . . . I'm in pajamas and I'm sleepin' . . ."

"What the hell's the *matter* with you?" he barked. "Did you forget about the party I gave you the other night?"

Surrendering weakly, I said, "Come on *up*, Uncle Benny!"

* * * * * * *

Back to Eliot Ness and his book *The Untouchables*: In 1959, Desi Arnaz decided that his company Desilu Productions would adapt it as a two-parter for the CBS anthology series *Westinghouse Desilu Playhouse*.

The first choice for the role of Ness, Van Heflin, turned it down. (Movie actors at that time scorned doing television. They looked down on TV, thinking it was way beneath them.) Another Van, Johnson, accepted the offer, but, because of a stage commitment, he too passed on the assignment. Next, they approached Robert Stack. Bob thought the idea was "old-hat, downbeat, a sure loser" and also decided to decline. But his agent, Bill Shiffrin, was insistent and, following what Bob later called "a violent argument," Bob finally consented. When Bob went to costuming, he was met by a Rumanian tailor who presented him with 1930s suits cut for Van Johnson and thought that Bob *was* Van Johnson.

Some of the others in the cast of the two-parter were Keenan Wynn and Bill Williams as two of Ness' Untouchables, Pat Crowley as Ness' fiancée and Neville Brand (with scar makeup, cigar and thick accent) as the ruthless and sadistic "Scarface" Al, scourge of Chicago. I had a supporting part, but on the wrong side of the law: Tony Liguri, a Capone henchman who ran the Montmartre Hotel where "Big Al" lived. Director Phil Karlson was from Chicago himself— he was born there, and was probably *still* living there during the Capone Era. Phil had already directed me in *Hell's Island* and *The Brothers Rico*, and I think he cast me in that *Desilu Playhouse* because he liked me. Phil was kind of a casual, almost mousy guy, quiet and unassuming—but a real good director. Phil liked me and I liked Phil.

When he starred in "The Scarface Mob," Robert Stack was just back from Europe where he had played the title role in a big historical picture, *John Paul Jones*. This was my first time working with Bob but actually the second time I met him. The first time, I was still a college student. Ruth Burch, a casting director, had seen me in a lot of plays at Loyola and was always giving me these oddball jobs—for example, she once sent me out to Adolphe Menjou's house to act out a scene with Menjou for Henri Gheon, the great French playwright. Another time Ruth called me and said that Irene McEvoy, a young socialite who had inherited a lot of money, was scheduled to make a screen test at Paramount and she needed somebody to help her prepare. "It's a love scene," Ruth told me, "and she's willing to pay you if you'll rehearse with her and do the test." I said okay. We rehearsed the scene at Irene's apartment and we rehearsed it in the living room of Marie's mother's house in Culver City—in 1947, at the beginning of our marriage, that's where Marie and I were living. One day I was rehearsing at Irene's apartment when her boyfriend came up and it turned out to be Robert Stack, who was already a motion picture star at the time. He didn't seem to mind at all finding me doing a love scene with his girlfriend and it was quite nice getting to meet him.

The "Scarface Mob" two-parter, written by Paul Monash and produced by Quinn Martin, turned out to be the most expensive show ever made for television—and a smash ratings hit for CBS. Over at ABC, which was then a fledgling network, executive Ollie Treyz saw it and knew right away they wanted to do it as a weekly TV series. And Desi Arnaz was willing to produce it. But when Ollie said he wanted Robert Stack to star, Desi had to admit, "I don't have him under contract for a series. I just had him under contract for the one show."

Suddenly Bob was being courted to star in a TV series of *The Untouchables*. Remember that he hadn't wanted to do "The Scarface Mob" on *Desilu Playhouse* in the first place, and he had even less interest in doing it as a series. So Bill Shiffrin, Bob's agent and a brilliant guy, knew that he had Desilu and ABC by the balls.

There was a meeting at Bob's house involving Bob and his agent Bill Shiffrin, Desi Arnaz of Desilu Productions and Ollie Treyz. In exchange for Bob's signature on the contract, Bill Shiffrin got the *world* for Bob. Bob was promised $10,000 an episode, which was unheard-of in those days, the highest salary on television. Bob also got *producer* approval, *director* approval, *actor* approval, *script* approval—*every*thing. Desi had no cards, he had to give Bill Shiffrin everything he wanted, because Bill had the royal flush—he had Robert Stack! Bob also asked for a three-year contract at a time when all contracts were for five years. (The studios would make their TV stars sign five-year contracts, because then if his show was a hit, the star couldn't ask for a bigger salary for at least five years.)

Well, Bob *got* his three-year contract, and after three successful years of *The Untouchables* he was in the driver's seat *again*—they had to give Bob a million dollars in Desilu stock to get him to sign for a fourth and fifth year. But Bob deserved it. He was a good actor and a wonderful individual.

The Untouchables premiered on ABC-TV Thursday night, October 15, 1959, with an episode titled "The Empty Chair" which picked up right where "The Scarface Mob" left off. Beginning with scenes from the finale of "Scarface Mob" (a convicted Capone leaving court for prison), the story of the premiere episode finds Capone's enforcer Frank Nitti (Bruce Gordon), mob bookkeeper Jake "Greasy Thumb" Guzik (Nehemiah Persoff) and other mobsters competing to sit in the throne recently vacated by the

king of Chicago hoodlums—Capone's "empty chair." Barbara Nichols, who was in *The Scarface Mob* as Brandy La France, a State Street stripper, reprised her role, helping Ness and his men (Jerry Paris, Nicholas Georgiade, Abel Fernandez, Steve London, Chuck Hicks) in their ongoing efforts to break the back of the Organization. Like "Scarface Mob," this premiere episode, and all the rest of the *Untouchables* shows, was narrated by Walter Winchell, the newspaper columnist-radio commentator who in his day knew many gang leaders personally and

Bob with Richard Conte on the set of one of the episodes of the later Untouchables series.

often startled his readers-listeners with inside news. (Occasionally threatened with gangland violence, Winchell would travel with his own set of bodyguards.)

The show, of course, quickly drifted away from the historical record, pitting Ness and his federal squad against Ma Barker (Claire Trevor), Dutch Schultz (Lawrence Dobkin), Vincent "Mad Dog" Coll (Clu Gulager) and the rest of that era's rogues gallery. I would watch *The Untouchables* when I could and I thought it was very good, but never dreamed that I'd ever end up being *in* it the way I did. I thought the show was really gripping, very honest—there was an impressive ring of reality to it all. Charles Straumer's stark black-and-white photography was magnificent, especially the night-for-night stuff that he did, and all the regulars and the guest stars were brilliant—they had such terrific guest stars every week. The Walter Winchell narration gave it an even greater feeling of authenticity.

Bob with several of the old cars used on the show.

For the first 13 episodes, they used Jerry Paris as Ness' number two guy, Martin Flaherty. Jerry, who was more of a comedic actor than a dramatic or action guy, later became a well-known television comedy director—*The Dick Van Dyke Show* (on which he was also a regular), *Here's Lucy, The Mary Tyler Moore Show, Happy Days*, series like that. But Bob, who had cast approval, came to feel that the chemistry was not right between him and Jerry. Jerry was let go after 13 episodes (narrator Winchell told the audience that Paris' character had been promoted out of the Untouchables) and a young actor named Anthony George came aboard as the new second banana, Cam Allison. I never got the story on what happened with Tony George, but I've got the impression that he was a guy who saw *The Untouchables* as a chance to make his move. He was a little too rambunctious and stepped on Bob's toes a few times, trying to make his mark. So in the last episode of the first season, "The Frank Nitti Story," Cam was killed off and Tony George left the show. (Bob's "actor approval.") Tony went on to do the TV series *Checkmate*, a crime drama, but he didn't have much of a career after that.

Right around that same period, I myself was having a bit of a tough time. That happens with actors. You'll be real busy, and then all of a sudden you'll go three, four months without working. That's the life of an actor. When you're under contract, being an actor is *fabulous*. But when you're a freelancer and you're out of work, it's *terrible*. (Even Bob Stack said that to me once—he said, "It's a great business when you're working. It's *hell* when you're not"—and *he* was a guy who never had to worry about money!) After being idle for a while, two or three months, I read in one of the trades, *Variety* or *The Hollywood Reporter*, that Gordon Douglas, was directing a Western with Clint Walker. I had done *I Was a Communist for the FBI* and *Mara Maru* and several other pictures with Gordon at Warner Brothers and considered him a friend, and so I did something that I rarely did: I called him up and told him my situation and asked, "Is there anything in the film that I could play?"

Gordon said, "To be honest with you, Paul, for an actor in your category, there's nothing in this film."

I repeated, "There's nothing at *all*?" I was desperate.

He said, "Well, there's an Indian you *could* play, but . . . we don't have any budget for it to afford you."

"Well, what'll it pay?" I asked.

Gordon told me to call Hoyt Bowers, head of casting at Warners at that time, and say that he (Gordon) would like me to play the Indian. I called Hoyt and told him, "Gordon says he can use me as an Indian in the film. What'll it pay?" Hoyt said it would pay 600 a week, and that the part would run six weeks. My heart sank a little. My regular salary at that time was $1000. An actor has to at least maintain his weekly salary. If he takes a lower-paying job, when the *next* job comes up, those casting people will know how much he made on the low-paying film and offer him that much, and all of a sudden you're going *backwards*.

I asked Hoyt, "Do you think you can get it up to a thousand? Or even 750?," and he offered to call and ask Steve Trilling, Jack Warner's right-hand man. Steve liked me—he'd used me in *The Young Philadelphians* and a lot of other pictures and he knew my work. But when Hoyt phoned me at home the next morning, he told me, "Steve said this whole picture has got a low budget, and we just can't do more than 600. But you can have the part if you want it."

Marie was in the room with me. I said, "Hold on a second, Hoyt," and I turned to Marie and I asked, "They can give me 600 a week for six weeks—$3600. What should I do?"

Marie knew the fix we were in as well as I did, but she said, "Forget it. Turn it down." She had more strength than *I* did. (It was the Sicilian in her, I guess!) I got back on the phone with Hoyt and I said, "I'm gonna pass on it," and Hoyt said that I had done the right thing; going backwards would not have been a good step in my career. Nevertheless, it was depressing, the fact that I'd had to turn it down. 3600 bucks would have paid a lot of bills.

Then, lo and behold, just the same way that I got *House of Wax* just when I was so despondent over losing out on *The Eddie Cantor Story*, Wilt Melnick called and said, "Jerry Thorpe of *The Untouchables* would like to see you in his office this afternoon. He wants to offer you the second lead in the show." I went over to the Selznick lot where *Gone With the Wind* was shot and where *The Untouchables* was now shooting and I met with Jerry, who I knew already (he directed me in an episode of *December Bride* with Spring Byington). Jerry was *The Untouchables'* new executive producer—Bob had replaced Quinn Martin. (Bob's "producer approval"!) Jerry said, "I know you're a capable and well-adjusted

Out of work and with eight kids, I was offered the second lead in one of TV's hottest series.

actor. Would you mind playing second fiddle to Bob Stack on *The Untouchables?*" I knew of course that *The Untouchables* was a big smash hit on ABC—the first hit ABC ever had—and Bob Stack had already gotten an Emmy Award for Eliot Ness. I said, "Hell *no* I wouldn't mind. I'd *love* to play it!"

Now that I had agreed that I would take the part if the financial arrangements could be worked out, I just had to wait for them to make an offer to Wilt. While I waited, luckily, I got work in an episode of Nick Adams' Western series *The Rebel*. One day Wilt phoned the set and said, "For *The Untouchables*, they're offering you seven out of 13 episodes at 750 a week." ("Seven out of 13" means that I would be guaranteed seven out of the next 13 episodes that were shot.) I said, "Wilt, I'll call you back," and then I spoke to Nick about it: "Nick, what do you think? Should I accept it?" He said, "*Definitely*. Take it. The show is a big hit, and 7 out of 13 will become 13 out of 13."

I talked to Marie and she also agreed, and so I accepted.

I was about to embark on the experience of a lifetime.

19
THE GOOD GUYS ...

Before I continue the story of *The Untouchables*, I should mention that by the time (1960), Gina, our "Caboose," had been born and now, with eight kids, our Wilbur Avenue house was getting painfully small even though I had added on a bedroom and a bathroom. As Marie and I began looking for another house, I put the old house up for sale for $20,000 (we had bought it for $10,750). A married couple, the Coopers, came to look at it, and seemed to like it. I said, "This has been a very happy house for us, but unfortunately, with eight kids, it's a little small." The man looked surprised and said, "Well, we have *nine* kids." I quickly countered with, "Well, you could always enclose the patio and add another bedroom!" They agreed to buy the house for $20,000, and I think they're *still* living in it. That house today is probably worth $500,000.

Meanwhile, we looked and looked for a new house. Joe Roberto, a builder in our parish, wanted me to buy his house on Wells Drive in Tarzana. It was a beautiful house on an acre of land, with an abundance of trees—orange, grapefruit, lemon, avocado, walnut, plum and peach. It was only two bedrooms and three baths, but he insisted, "I'll add three bedrooms and two more baths!" He sold me. With five bedrooms and five baths, I knew it would be more than comfortable for a family of ten. We bought the house just before I became a regular on *The Untouchables*. Some of the people who lived nearby were Natalie Wood and Robert Wagner, John Huston, Dean Jones and Bob Crane. My next door neighbor was a terrific guy named Charles Van Enger, the famous cinematographer for director Ernst Lubitsch; among his credits were the original *Phantom of the Opera* with Lon Chaney and *Abbott and Costello Meet Frankenstein*. Toward the end of the time that my family and I resided there, Jamie Foxx and Chuck Norris lived just a block away.

Our first horse, Tommy.

In addition to the three new bedrooms and two new baths, I added a big swimming pool, a basketball court and a bocci court. An old barn on the property was perfect for the four horses we eventually acquired.

The first horse we bought was Tommy, an old rodeo horse—I guess he was about 15 when we got him. He became like a pet, and all the kids just loved him. A.C. Curcio, a friend of mine with a ranch out in the Palmdale area, had a couple of horses (Big Red and a beautiful gray Arabian horse named Tammy) that nobody was riding, and one day he asked me if I would like to have them. I said, "Yeah, sure!" After that I got yet another horse, Buddy, so now we were up to four. Danny McLaughlin, the son of a neighbor, was a good horseman who taught all my kids how to ride.

In front of our house was a dirt road, and about a quarter-mile away was the start of the trails where we'd go riding. The kids and I would ride up in the hills and make 8mm Western movies. Some of the kids would be heroes, Charlie and others the villains, and I would direct. Sometimes I would put my little daughter Gina behind me on a horse and take her to school on horseback; Philip would also sometimes be brought to school this way. Needless to say, they were the envy of the whole kindergarten and first grade at the Wilbur Avenue School! I would even go to the bank on horseback, back in the days when Tarzana was small.

Mike holds the rein as Philip, Marie, Gina and I pose for another shot.

Back then, once you were on those trails, you couldn't see any homes at all, just beautiful, rolling, grassy hills with deer and coyotes and rabbits. One day when I was out with Gemma, we rode into an area where we hadn't been for two or three months, and as we came up over a knoll, we saw that on what *had* been beautiful hills were now 50 houses in the process of being built. We both stopped and looked with amazement—we were shocked! And so help me God, as we sat on our horses looking at all these frame homes going up, Gemma, who was only nine or ten, looked to me and said, "White man take Indian hunting grounds!" I'll never forget that.

One nice day after about two weeks of rain, my brother Charlie, C.P. and I got on horses and took a ride up Reseda Blvd. I was riding Tammy. As we got close to a riverbed, I suddenly noticed that the ground was getting softer. I dismounted and got the saddle off of her and held her reins, but she panicked because her feet were sinking deeper into the mud. Finally she pulled her head back and snapped away from me, and galloped off. Soon she was in the river, which after two weeks of rain was all mud with just a little bit of water on top—and she sank up to her neck. Only her head was sticking up out of the water.

Charlie and I went down to see if we could get her out, and when we realized we couldn't do it ourselves, I sent C.P., who was maybe 12 at the time, to get help. The next thing I knew, a couple of fire trucks pulled up and six or eight Los Angeles city firemen came out. And then cowboy-stuntmen like Joe Yrigoyen and "Red" Morgan started arriving on the scene. My kids had told *other* kids, and *they* told their parents, and word of what was going on had spread like wildfire throughout the neighborhood. As we continued to struggle to get Tammy out of the river, a CBS camera crew appeared on the scene! It took the firemen more than two hours to finally rescue her. A picture of me and the firemen struggling to free Tammy, distributed by the Associated Press, ran in papers all over the world.

* * * * * *

I think it was in early July when I started working on *The Untouchables*. The Sunday before my first day on the job, I announced a Rams game and, after it was over, Phil Carey, my friend Lou Enterante and I stopped at a Sunset Boulevard bar called The Losers. Inside, Lou and Phil began flirting with the beautiful young hatcheck girl. I didn't get involved. When we left later that night, Phil went for the car as Lou and I stood waiting on the sidewalk. But a car, waiting for the Sunset Boulevard traffic to ease up so that it could leave the parking lot, was blocking Phil's way. In the front seat of this car was a guy behind the wheel, the hatcheck girl in the middle and another guy in the passenger seat. And Lou, who was bombed and slurring his words, yelled out, "Come on, what are you waiting for, get going! What the hell are you, chicken shit??"

The car door opened and the driver started to climb out. He was a football player—a *giant*—and he had evidently seen Lou and Phil flirting with his girl! Getting out of the car, he hit Lou a shot, and Lou landed out in the street—a passing car screeched around him, just missing his head by inches! As he was continuing to beat the tar out of Lou and I was trying to get him to stop, the passenger seat guy jumped out of the car. His leg was in a cast but he was *another* giant, and he headed for Phil. This was at a time when karate was just coming into fashion, and so Phil put up his hands karate-style and said, "Take it easy, fella, take it easy!" Well, it worked: When Phil put up his hands, this guy stopped. Lou was still being pounded, so I said to the leg-cast guy, "Please, please, pull your friend off my buddy before he *kills* him!" Finally the leg-cast guy calmed him down and stopped his buddy from beating up Lou. I got into several fights because of Lou—he had a short temper—and *this* one ended with Lou a bloody mess: a big black eye, a cut on his nose and a split lip. I said to myself, "Son of a bitch, that could have been *me*, and tomorrow I'm supposed to start shooting *The Untouchables!*"

Fortunately it *was* Lou and not me and the next day I reported to the set of *The Untouchables* for my first day on the series. Robert Stack had cast approval on the series but evidently he knew of me and knew my work, because I was cast in the second male lead without first having to get together with Bob; I had my meeting with executive producer Jerry Thorpe and that was *it*. The first episode of the second season to be shot was "A Seat on the Fence" with a cast that included Frank Silvera and John McIntire. One day on the set in my first week of my working on the show, Bob Stack invited me and Marie up to his house for dinner.

Bob and his beautiful actress-wife Rosemarie Bowe had recently finished building a home on property his mother had owned in Bel-Air; by this time, Bob owned it. Put up between an existing swimming pool and tennis court, their dream house made the cover of *Architectural Digest*. (Rosemarie and I, of course, remembered each other from *The Adventures of Hajji Baba*—after all, we'd had a love scene together!) One thing they had at that house that I'd never seen before was an underground garage. You'd drive up the driveway and pull into this garage where there was room for about six cars—Bob loved cars.

We had dinner, just the four of us, and at one point Bob asked me if I'd ever seen the movie *Written on the Wind* (1956), in which he had starred with Rock Hudson. I had not, but I knew that Bob had been nominated for a Best Supporting Actor Academy Award for his performance in it. Bob said he'd like me to see it, so he put Marie and me in the den where he had his beautiful gun collection, his trophies and a projector setup. He got us comfortable and turned on the projector and left us there to watch the movie. *Written on the Wind* was a melodrama with Bob as an oil tycoon's playboy son, marrying secretary Lauren Bacall and looking forward to parenthood, then turning to the bottle when he learns he is impotent.

I was quite impressed with his performance. I also got the idea that Bob wanted me to see the movie because he wanted to *show* me that he was a good actor. And he *was*—he was *very* good in *Written on the Wind*. I realized during my years of working with Bob on *The Untouchables* that his approach to acting reminded me of Errol Flynn, with whom I had worked in *Mara Maru*. Like Errol, Bob didn't appear to be *doing* a lot when you were on the soundstage doing a scene with him, but later when you saw it on film, you realized that he was right on the money with his performance. As I mentioned, Bob was Oscar-nominated for *Written on the Wind*, but Anthony Quinn got the award that year for *Lust for Life*; Bob was very hurt that he didn't win, because he did a beautiful job. (Dorothy Malone, who played Bob's nymphomaniac sister in the movie, was nominated for Best Supporting Actress, and she *did* get the award.)

Bob didn't have much of a reputation as an actor until *Written on the Wind* and *The Untouchables* came along. Working with him on the show, I grew to really admire his work—I thought that he was terrific as Eliot Ness. Everybody thought it was an easy part, and in a way it *was*, but he was just so *right* for it. And as a person, I really loved Bob right from the start. I was kind of a guy from the wrong side of the tracks and he was a society guy, but we had lunch together every day and got along just great.

Bob's father, whom I never met, had been the head of one of the largest advertising agencies in the country, and one of his claims to fame was originating the slogan for Schlitz Beer, "Schiltz—the beer that made Milwaukee famous." I guess that's where the father made all his money. I don't know if Bob's mother was wealthy before she married Bob's dad; I *do* know that she not only had quite a social background but that she owned the property that Ciro's and the Mocambo and several other big places in the Sunset Boulevard area were on. In other words, Bob's parents were loaded. They divorced when he was one-year-old, and about two years later the mother took Bob with her to live in Paris. Bob began speaking French when he was three and didn't learn to speak English until he was six.*

Returning to the U.S., young Bob Stack's life was one of private schools, polo, fast cars, faster boats and the skeet fields; when he was 17, he broke the world's record at the National Skeet Shooting Championships. Turning to acting, he made his movie debut in 1939's *First Love*, in one famous scene giving star Deanna Durbin her first screen kiss.

As Untouchable Lee Hobson.

Now, two decades later, Bob was the star of one of the biggest shows on TV and, to my delight, my friend. In addition to the occasional get-togethers at his house, he invited Marie and me out on several social events. For instance, one weekend he took us to the automobile races out in Ontario. That was the sort of thing that he and Rosemarie enjoyed doing and he thought that Marie and I would enjoy it too, and the four of us had a nice day. On another occasion, we went to Chasen's for dinner. Chasen's was *the* restaurant at the time, a classy

---

*I don't recall Bob's mother ever coming on the *Untouchables* set, but she had a house right above Bob's in Bel-Air and I met her there at her house once or twice. Bob was devoted to his mother, and took very good care of her when she got older. A good man, Bob.

place, and so I ordered what I thought was appropriate, veal picotta or something. And to my surprise, he and Rosemarie ordered *hamburgers*. What I didn't realize was that, while Chasen's *was* a tony sort of place, it was also very famous for its hamburgers with raw Bermuda onions.

Bob and I got to be very friendly, and, of course, I also got to know the other Untouchables, Nick Georgiade (Rico) and Abel Fernandez (Youngfellow). They'd been on the show a year already—in fact, like me, they were both also in the original "Scarface Mob," Abel as an Untouchable and Nick as a heavy in a brewery scene. I knew my place on *The Untouchables*, I was in second position to Bob, and I thought I should make sure that *all* of us knew where we stood. By that time, I had done a lot of movies and I was higher up on the ladder than *they* were; *The Untouchables* was about the first good thing that Nick and Abel had ever done. So on my second day on the show I sat down with them at lunch at the studio commissary and I told them, "Look, Robert Stack's the star of this show, *he's* numero uno . . . I'm number two . . . and you guys are number three and four, any way you want to figure it. Don't step on my toes and I'll help you every way I can. If anything goes

"Don't step on my toes and I'll help you every way I can," I told Nick and Abel when I came onto *The Untouchables*.

wrong, if you need my help, I'll go to bat for you. We can run a smooth team here." They said they understood, and I think they could tell that I meant what I said. And, believe me, I did later have to go to bat for Nick, and for Abel *several* times. More on that later.

It all goes back to what I wrote in an earlier chapter: You have to give the star his due. I learned that when I did *Operation Pacific*, when they took scenes away from me and gave them to John Wayne. I felt bad losing out on them, but I knew that if John Wayne wanted to do those scenes, then he *would* do those scenes—because he was the star, and the star's gotta get his due! I was very loyal to Robert Stack, our star on *The Untouchables*, I was good to him and he was good to me. You young actors reading this: You *have* to give stars their due. If they've been in this business for 25 years and you're just a newcomer, don't challenge them. *Learn* from them. If they're generous to you, you be loyal to them. Don't step on their toes. I sensed that Tony George had done just that, and upset the cast harmony.

An example of my giving Bob his due on *The Untouchables*: For one episode, a new director named Stu Rosenberg came in. In one scene, the Untouchables' car would pull up to a speakeasy that we were going to raid; Bob would be driving, I'd be next to him in the passenger seat and Nick and Abel were going to be in the back. Stu gave us his direction: "All right, Paul, you jump out of the car and kick the door in and come in the restaurant. Bob, you're right behind him, then Nick and Abel right after that." Bob didn't say a word, but I saw his expression change and, of course, I knew right away what he was thinking. So before we shot the scene, I got Stu off to one side and I said, "Stu, let Bob go in the door first." Stu asked why.

I said, "Because he's the *star*, Stu. Let him come in that door first. *Then* me, then Abel and Nick. Don't let *me* go in first." He said, "But you're the first one out of the car, you naturally would be the first—" I said, "I don't give a damn about how it's done in *real life*. This is movies! Let *him* come in *first!*" Stu asked, "Are you sure?," and I said, "I'm positive." So Stu went up to Bob and said, "Bob, we're gonna have a little change here: You come in the door *first* . . ." And I could see Bob's whole expression change *back* again—and I'm sure Stu noticed, too, because Stu caught on right away! Stu was a funny guy who developed into a *hell* of a director, one of our best—he later directed *Cool Hand Luke* and a few other good pictures.

Coming in the door behind Bob and me on this and countless other raids were Nick Georgiade and Abel Fernandez. Strangely enough, both Nick and Abel were ex-boxers. Nick was an amateur boxer when he was a student at Syracuse University and later in the Army, when he was in Germany. And Abel was perhaps the only

Abel Fernandez was Mexican but his Untouchables character William Youngfellow was described as a full-blooded Cherokee and a former All-American football player.

Mexican *heavyweight* boxer. He was a professional and the California State champion. Abel got into the business after a left hook caught him in the Adam's apple and ended his career. His first film was *Second Chance*, a 1953 film with Robert Mitchum in which he played a boxer. He didn't have too much acting training but he was very athletic and moved like a cat.

Nick was discovered by Lucille Ball while doing a play in Hollywood, *A View from the Bridge*. She put him under a studio contract and I think—I *know*—that Nick was making very little money when he was assigned to *The Untouchables*, much less than Abel.

For *The Untouchables* we shot some interiors at the Paramount Desilu lot but most of it at Culver City Desilu. At Paramount we had an indoor Chicago Street set (used in case of rain) and at Culver City we had Eliot Ness' office and other sets. Then we had "40 Acres," the back lot in Culver City, where we had the outdoor Chicago Street set, the els, farmhouse, gas station and whatever other exterior sets we needed. The Culver City back lot was where we'd wreck cars and then rebuild 'em to use again. We had a fellow named Ed Chamey who was in charge of all the cars, which were an integral part of the show. For scenes where cars would be on fire, the special effects men would put some kind of gelatin on them and then set it off. On TV it would look like the whole car was destroyed, but actually only the gelatin would burn. After the take, the effects guys would immediately put out the fire and repaint the car and we'd use it again in the next episode! They were all actual vintage cars. Most of them were rented from car clubs and places like that, but the studio also owned a few outright—for example, Eliot Ness' car and two or three doubles. The old cars got more fan mail than the actors. This is true! Ed Chamey got *so* much mail from people asking about the Duesenberg and the Packard and all the rest!

Nick Georgiade as Untouchable Rico.

One thing I'll never forget about *The Untouchables* was that we worked *long* hours—12, 14 hours a day. They shot each episode in six days and it was an hour show with a lot of scenes and lots of action. So it was a long schedule. And most episodes featured a number of scenes that were shot night-for-night, rather than shooting during the daytime with a filter to make it *look* like night. It looks better when you shoot night-for-night, but of course that *also* meant that none of us ever got to see our wives! We'd get home at three or four in the morning and go to bed and sleep until 12 and then go back to work at two, so we couldn't have dinner with our wives. So once or twice a week Marie and Rosemarie would make dinner and bring it in and we'd all get together in Bob's dressing room—Bob had a nice one right behind the Desilu soundstage where we did most of our shooting, and the four of us would have candlelight dinners there. My kids came to the set of *The Untouchables* many times too. I have a couple of pictures of the kids, all eight of 'em, standing on the running board of an old car, with Bob and Marie and me in the shot too.

Another visitor to the set was Desi Arnaz, but he didn't come too often. He had a dressing room on the lot and, when we shot night-for-night, Desi might show up at two o'clock in the morning—always with a few drinks in him and feeling good. He would stop by the set and say *hello, how ya doin', boys?*, and then head off to his dressing room, where I had a feeling he mighta had a bimbo stashed! I don't know that for a fact, but I surmise that might be the case. He was very friendly and never interfered with the shooting. After the first year, he gave Bob a 300SL Mercedes convertible as a token of his esteem, for the great job Bob had done. Bob loved driving that car and he loved to take me for rides in it. He would goose it going up Beverly Glen and the vibration would go right through me and make my balls tingle!

Someone who doesn't get enough credit for *The Untouchables* was Charles Straumer, a real solid cinematographer and one of the reasons the show was as effective as it was. *The Untouchables* was black and white, and what Straumer and his camera operators could do with the shadows and the depth and the angles really seemed to capture the stark feeling of the era. In addition to being an excellent photographer, Straumer was also a nice, sweet man.

In charge of the special effects for the show was A.D. Flowers, a brilliant guy who could rig some great stuff. I remember Steve Cochran did a couple of *Untouchables*, and Steve always wanted spectacular death scenes. There was one scene where he walked through a door onto a warehouse set and we cut loose on him with machine-gun fire. Steve had an aluminum plate under his shirt, and on the plate were several "squibs," little explosives. When we fired at him, all these explosives burst right through the shirt, vest and jacket. It was kind of dangerous, but Steve loved doing that. In another show, he devised his own death scene: He was in a barn climbing a ladder up to the loft where a girl was hiding, and she shot him. To get the effect of him being shot, a blood ball was fired (not by the girl, of course, but by our special effects guy A. D. Flowers with a rifle-type gun) and it hit him right square in his forehead and burst.

Among the guns on the show were actual tommyguns. The property master or the special effects guys would pick them up at the Culver City police station in the morning and then check them

A classic group shot from *The Untouchables*.

back in at night. And there was always a guard on the guns. Of course, we also had fake tommyguns, guns that didn't actually work, but *these* were real tommyguns that fired full loads, blanks. They were quite impressive! The handguns on ***The Untouchables***, .38s, were real too.

Victor Paul, the stunt coordinator, was a wonderful guy. Victor was very knowledgeable about camera angles, and he could make a stunt look even more impressive than it really was, simply by the angle the camera caught it at. But as far as doing anything really dangerous, Victor was a little squeamish! In one episode, "Silent Partner," an actor named Allyn Joslyn was playing a gangster who shot at Bob and me from a warehouse catwalk; I fired back and Joslyn reacted as though he'd been shot. Now it was Victor's job to fall maybe 30 feet from the catwalk. Today the stuntmen use air bags to break their falls, but in those days, they put a mattress on top of about 20 cardboard boxes, big ones, two feet by two feet. They'd come flat and everybody would help making 'em into boxes and then cut the corners off. (You cut the corners off so that, when the body hits, the air rushes out of the boxes and they collapse and it cushions the guy's fall.) Poor Victor was scared to death.

When you do a fall like that, you fall forward and then, as you're going down, you tuck your head *in*, which causes your body to flip over and you land on your back. Well, I can still picture what happened that day: Victor was up on that catwalk with Allyn Joslyn's hat and overcoat on and then he went over the rail—and he forgot to tuck. He went right down like a torpedo and went into those boxes head first. We pulled him out of there and fortunately he was okay, but the way that hat was now crushed over his head, he looked like a drowned rat!

I began on ***The Untouchables*** in the summer of 1960 and got to know Bob, Nick and Abel and all the behind-the-scenes people as I worked with them—but, of course, throughout those early months, the first season episodes were still running on TV. Finally, on the night of October 13, 1960, the second season of ***The Untouchables*** began. Following the pre-credits sequence, the show's narrator announced, "Tonight's episode, 'The Rusty Heller Story.' Starring Robert Stack as Eliot Ness. Co-starring Elizabeth Montgomery . . . Harold J. Stone . . . David White. And introducing Paul Picerni as Untouchable Lee Hobson."

20
... AND THE BAD GUYS

Written by Leonard Kantor, "The Rusty Heller Story" was one of the all-time great **Untouchables** shows and Elizabeth Montgomery was wonderful as Rusty Heller, a beautiful but deadly Southern spitfire. The episode was set during the trial of Al Capone, another story of mobsters competing to seize the throne of the Federal Prison-bound gangster. Rusty Heller plays all sides: Flirting with a Capone bookkeeper (Norman Fell) in order to learn the location of the Capone empire's financial records; romancing a rival gangster (Harold J. Stone) should *he* become Chicago's next crime lord; and also cozying up to Eliot Ness, for whom she actually *does* carry a torch. "Rusty Heller" was directed by Walter Grauman, one of our better directors—he must have directed 30 or 40 of the 118 episodes that were made.

Elizabeth, who won an Emmy as Rusty Heller, was perhaps the most fun of any actress I've ever worked with in my life. The daughter of MGM star Robert Montgomery, she was like one of the boys—but she certainly was *not* "one of the boys," she was *all*-girl, a gorgeous young lady and a delight to be around. (She later gained fame in her TV series **Bewitched**.) There were very effective and unusual (for **The Untouchables**) scenes in which she flirted with Bob Stack, continually complimenting him on his blue eyes. Bob did have blue eyes, incidentally, so the cinematographer Charles Straumer used to shine a little "pinkie light" on them, making them look black on the black-and-white TV screen. That helped give Bob the strong, fierce appearance which was a big part of the character's appeal. Between takes, off-camera, Bob was like a little boy having a good time, always smiling and laughing and joking and being a lot of fun, but when the cameras were rolling and he became Eliot Ness, he rarely smiled. We had a saying on the set, "Don't smile, Bob—it makes you look *weak!*" When you look at *The Untouchables*, you'll have a tough time finding a scene where he smiles.

With Barbara Stanwyck in an Untouchables.

Elizabeth wasn't the only actress to play a tough character on *The Untouchables*, we had a number of them over the years—Barbara Nichols, Bob's *Written on the Wind* co-star Dorothy Malone, Ruth Roman, Patricia Neal, Joan Blondell, Barbara Stanwyck, Viveca Lindfors. We also had some of the best bad guys in the business. The actor who worked the show the most was Bruce Gordon, playing Frank "The Enforcer" Nitti, who in Al Capone's absence runs the Chicago underworld from a conference room at the Club Montmartre. Bruce had already been in "The Scarface Mob" where I was in a great scene with him: Al Capone (Neville Brand), Nitti (Bruce Gordon) and I, among others, give hit man Frank DeKova the *bacce de morte* (the kiss of death)—the Sicilian gesture where a Mafia soldier is kissed on the mouth before being sent out as executioner. There was another actor in the scene, too, a guy named Ric Roman, and he cooked up a joke to play on Bruce and Frank DeKova. He told Bruce, "Look, when you come to the kiss of death, watch out, because Frank DeKova is gay." And then, unbeknownst to Bruce, Ric went to Frank DeKova and did the same thing: "Look, when you come to the kiss of death, watch out, because Bruce Gordon is gay!"

When director Phil Karlson called "Action!" and it came time for Bruce to give Frank the kiss of death, Bruce had great trepidation. But, being the great actor that he is, he did it with such authority, planting the kiss flush on Frank's mouth. DeKova reacted the way he should have, in a scene of great realism. It was a moment of pure drama. Phil said "Cut!," and the whole set erupted in laughter. The two actors were dumbfounded, then suddenly realized that it was a big joke. To this day, I kid Bruce by telling him he looked like he really enjoyed it!

Bruce was newly arrived in Hollywood from New York, where he had just done the Broadway play *The Lark*, the story of Joan of Arc, with Julie Harris and Christopher Plummer. Bruce is a wonderful actor and he did a marvelous job as Frank Nitti. Today he lives in Santa Fe, New Mexico, and he and I regularly attend Ray Courts' autograph shows in L.A. and Chicago. It gives us a chance to get together several times a year.

Unfortunately, because of the way most of the *Untouchables* episodes of the show were written, we actors playing the Untouchables didn't get to work that much with Bruce or any of the other heavies. Occasionally Bob and I might have a scene with a bad guy, but for the most part the guys playing gangsters did *their* scenes with each other and the Untouchables did *our* scenes with each other. The good guys and the bad guys each "did their own thing," and we usu-ally didn't come together 'til the shootout at the end!

At a recent autograph show in (where else?) Chicago with *Untouchables* semi-regular Bruce Gordon, who played Capone's "Enforcer," Frank Nitti.

I want to devote the rest of this chapter to some of the sensational actors we had on *The Untouchables* playing the various heavies. If you think about it, the bad guys were the real backbone of the show. Robert Stack as Eliot Ness was in every episode and he was "officially" the star of *The Untouchables* but each week's guest star, "The Villain of the Week," whether it be Lee Marvin or Peter Falk or Telly Savalas or who*ever* it was, was really the central focus of each episode.

One of my first episodes, "The Purple Gang," starred Steve Cochran, who, of course, I knew well when we were at Warners. Wherever he went, Steve still always had two teenage girls with him—and never the same two girls. They'd be 16 or 17 years old, Norwegian or Swedish or Swiss. One of the girls was there to serve him tea on the set, the other to serve him drinks . . . and I guess they both would service him in his dressing room! Steve still had his German Shepherd Tchaikovsky with him when he did *The Untouchables*, or maybe the original Tchaikovsky had died and this was *another* Tchaikovsky. (The dog was named Tchaikovsky because he could play the piano: Steve had trained him to play certain notes with his paws.)

Steve died about five years later, under very lurid circumstances: During a trip to Mexico, he hired three local girls, 21, 19 and 14 years old, as his crew for a boat trip. Off the coast of Oaxaca, they ran into a hurricane, and Steve had to stay at the helm for two days and nights battling the storm. Then, as I heard it, he was stricken with appendicitis and passed out. The boat was not located until more than two weeks after it sailed, by which time Steve had died. And the girls, who knew nothing about sailing, were in a state of hysteria at being adrift with his decomposing body.

Joseph Wiseman was the bad guy twice in one season: First he played the title role in "The Tommy Karpeles Story," and then he came back later that same season and played a different character in another episode, "The Antidote." In the latter there was a scene where Wiseman was supposed to pick up an ax and chop away at the side of a beer vat until he made a hole and all the beer came gushing out. There was also a long glass tube running up the side of the vat that indicated how much beer was in it. Wiseman accidentally hit the tube with the ax and broke it, and the top part

My old pal from Warners, Steve Cochran, made a few *Untouchables* appearances.

of the tube slid down and caught him in the calf of his left leg. As a result of that accident, I believe that he walked with a limp for quite a long time.

Another "casualty" of an action scene was Norma Crane, a wonderful New York actress that Jerry Thorpe brought out to Hollywood for "The Lily Dallas Story." In that episode, Norma was married to a gangster (played by Larry Parks) but she was even more ruthless than he was, and in one scene she had to reach for a tommygun and open up on some guy. Well, it turned out that Norma was deathly afraid of guns and she dreaded having to do it. Right from the start, she was complaining to the director Don Medford, "Please, change that scene. I can't stand guns, I can't stand firing guns. I'm so worried about that scene . . ."

"Don't worry about it," Don reassured her. "When we come to that, *you'll* be able to do it." Our special effects guy, A. D. Flowers, had her hold a dummy tommygun and then the real tommygun, and finally she got up the courage to do the scene in which she was supposed to pull the trigger and spray a whole room with it. There were no rehearsals, of course—Don said *action* and she fired the tommygun. And when she finished the shot, she *screamed* in horror and she dropped to the floor. She was hysterically weeping and we couldn't stop her—she just went bananas! Don actually had to slap her in the face to bring her out of it. It took about two hours before she recovered from that scene.

Another actress who got hysterical was Cloris Leachman—but it was a different kind of hysterical! On an episode that Paul Wendkos was directing, "Man in the Middle," Cloris and the actor in the scene (I don't remember who it was) got on a laughing jag—in take after take, they'd break up with laughter. At first the director was laughing too, but after about 20 takes he knew that the shooting was falling behind and he finally got pissed off at her and he said, "Now you *stop* it, damn it. We're running out of time here and we've got to get this shot!" But she broke up again in the scene, and the director walked off the set and out of the soundstage! It was

When an *Untouchables* director called "Action!," that's usually what he got!

several hours before he came back, so everybody realized how serious he was. Cloris was a very sexy girl when she was young (and still today!) and she was a lot of fun and I loved working with her.

We had a little trouble once with Lee Marvin, who did several *Untouchables*. There was one day when he didn't show up for work and we found out he was arrested for drunken driving and we had to go get him out of jail! One star who had a real drinking problem was Wendell Corey, who was in "Power Play." Wendell's wife was with him constantly on the set, I think to see to it that he didn't hit the bottle. As it turned out, Wendell did not fall off the wagon; in fact, he did quite a good job.

In addition to veterans like these, a lot of up-and-coming young actors got some early exposure on *The Untouchables*. Victor Buono never really became a big name but he was certainly a big *man*—an oversized, blubbery six-foot-four, an imposing, robust actor in the Sydney Greenstreet-Laird Cregar mold. Buono was 23 years old and making a name for himself doing plays at the Globe Theater in San Diego, playing men of 50 and 60, when he started getting offered TV roles; he made his debut at Warners on an episode of *77 Sunset Strip* and then about a year later he came onto *The Untouchables* and played the title role in the episode "Mr. Moon." As a direct result of *The Untouchables*, Victor got a big career break: Bette Davis saw Buono on our show, either in "Mr. Moon" or the other episode he did, "The Gang War," and asked for him on *What Ever Happened to Baby Jane?*, the movie she was making with Joan Crawford. Playing a mama's boy in *Baby Jane*, Victor got Oscar and Golden Globe Award nominations.

Frank Gorshin had a wonderful part in one episode ("The Pea") as a busboy in a speakeasy who ends up taking over the joint. Frank entertained us constantly with his terrific impressions—he did all the gangsters for us, Jimmy Cagney and Eddie G. Robinson and so on, and we just loved them.

But bigger names than Victor Buono and Frank Gorshin came out of *The Untouchables*: Some of the future movie and TV stars who also cut their teeth on our show, mostly playing heavies, include Ed Asner (several), Robert Redford ("The Snowball"), Mike Connors ("The Eddie O'Gara Story"), James Coburn ("The Jamaica Ginger Story"), James Caan ("A Fist of Five")—the list goes on and on.

A guest star in one of the last episodes, "Blues for a Gone Goose," was Robert Duvall. In one scene Duvall was playing a piano and a wonderful actor named Marc Lawrence came in to kill him. (Marc was an actor who played gangsters for his entire career because he had a great pockmarked face for those roles.) Marc grabbed Duvall and got him to the floor and began choking him. Well, it was Duvall's misfortune that Marc was a real Method actor, and Marc began *really* choking Duvall! The poor guy couldn't get his breath and he started going crazy and kicking and trying to get loose! The director Sherman Marks got what he needed and yelled *cut*, and Duvall jumped up and started swinging at Marc! "You son of a bitch, you were really chokin' me! What the hell are you, *crazy*?!" Marc was trying to calm Duvall down—"Take it easy, kid, take it easy!"—but Duvall was furious, and he finally *did* get a good shot in on Marc.

Another actor who got carried away in a fight scene was George Kennedy. Although it was still very early in his career, in the episode "The King of Champagne" George was playing a major role as a deaf-mute. George was so conscientious about his work; he even went to a school and learned sign language in preparation. There was one scene where George was supposed to clench his fists together and bring them down on top of Bob Stack's head. Unfortunately for Bob, George was both a *very* big guy and a newish actor who didn't know how to fake a blow: George hit Bob on top of his head so hard, he knocked Bob out cold! George, of course, went on to become a very good actor and received an Academy Award playing a convict on a Southern chain gang in **Cool Hand Luke** with Paul Newman.

Charles Bronson was on **The Untouchables** a few times; I had first worked with him, of course, on **House of Wax**, back when he was still calling himself Charles Buchinsky. On the sets he was very quiet, almost somber. Between his looks and the way he kept to himself, I think some people did think he was still just a dumb polack from the Pennsylvania coal mines. But Charlie was actually a very bright fellow, and a sweetheart of a guy. We became friends over the years—I liked Charlie a lot.

We once had Peter Falk as a guest on the show, and in one scene some guy pulled a .45 on him. In the script, Falk's line was, "You

Chow-time on the set. Director John Peyser can be seen between me and Bob.

think I'm afraid of that gun?," but in the take he unexpectedly adlibbed, "You think I'm afraid of that cannon?"—I thought it was a great adlib. He did a lot of adlibbing like that; he was a very creative actor, and it was so impressive. Whenever Peter had a scene, we all used to stop whatever we were doing and watch him work. We did the same thing with the wonderful Luther Adler, who might have been in as many as four or five *Untouchables* and was always brilliant.

Like Marc Lawrence, Eduardo Ciannelli had just the perfect face for gangster roles. Ciannelli's career went way back and I thought he was a great actor. Much younger, but also having the right look for menacing parts, was my Tarzana neighbor (he lived only a block away from me) Henry Silva, who was in a couple of *Untouchables*. Nehemiah Persoff did quite a few shows as Jake "Greasy Thumb" Guzik. He was the kind of actor who got very loud—he would shout and scream—but very dramatic and very good. A wonderful actor and a nice guy.

One day I was in the dressing room with Bob Stack, just sitting around between takes, when Jerry Thorpe came in and started talking about a guy he'd seen on TV the night before playing Lucky Luciano on a TV show called *The Witness*, a live courtroom anthology series out of New York. "He was absolutely sensational as

Luciano," Jerry said. "It's a guy named Telly Savalas. I'm bringing him out here as soon as I can to do a guest shot on *The Untouchables*." That was how I met Telly, and we went on to become very close friends. Doing *The Witness* and then *The Untouchables* were big steps in Telly's acting career.

The story of how Telly broke into acting is an interesting one. In New York in the 1950s, he began working for the *Voice of America* radio program, along with doing a lot of other jobs in radio. (He received a Peabody Award for his radio work.) At that same time there was on TV this series *The Witness* where actors playing true-life gangsters (Capone, Dillinger, Dutch Schultz, etc.) were brought before a committee and interrogated, similar to a Congressional hearing. (The committee members were not actors; they were real New York attorneys.) The casting director of *The Witness* was a

Telly Savalas became a lifelong friend. Here we are on the sidelines at a Rams football game.

woman who knew that Telly's *Voice of America* duties included hiring actors to play Germans, Russians and so on, so when she needed an actor with an authentic German accent to play a small part on *The Witness*, she called Telly. When he recommended a German actor, she asked Telly to arrange for the guy to be in her office at ten o'clock the next morning.

At around 8:30 A.M. the next day, Telly found out that the actor was under the weather and wouldn't be able to make the interview—so he decided to go and try out for the part on *The Witness* himself. He went in at ten posing as an actual German actor and he met with the *Witness* people. He got the part! Telly spoke with the German accent for the entire day of shooting—since it was a live show, it was just a one-day shoot—and everything went well. At the end of the shoot there was a little cast party and David Susskind, the producer of the series, was there. Finally, after speaking with the German accent all day long, Telly suddenly began talking with his normal (New York) accent, and everybody was amazed. They'd been completed fooled, and they all got a big laugh out of it.

Several weeks later, an actor who was rehearsing to play the part of Lucky Luciano on *The Witness* just went dry. It was just one day before they had to do the show, and suddenly this guy fell apart. Susskind remembered Telly and what a great job he did fooling them with the German accent, and so he called and offered him the part. Susskind gave him a book about Luciano's life and told him to read it that night. "Then, tomorrow," Susskind told Telly, "get on the witness stand, and the lawyers will ask you questions. You just answer them however you feel Luciano would have answered them." Telly didn't need to learn any lines, he just had to speak his mind, and so he gave a tremendous performance. Well, Jerry Thorpe saw it and thought Telly was absolutely brilliant, and so we had him on *The Untouchables* three times. Pretty soon Telly was in the movie *Birdman of Alcatraz* with Burt Lancaster, who had also seen Telly on *The Witness* and was so impressed that he cast him. Telly got a Best Supporting Actor Oscar nomination for *Birdman*, which helped him to become a movie star. Then the CBS series *Kojak* made him a major TV star. By that time Telly and I were the closest of friends, and I was his dialogue director on *Kojak* in its final year. I'll tell you much more about Telly in a future chapter.

I'll close this chapter on great bad guys with a story about the day I brought my *own* "bad guy" to the set. Actually, calling Emmett Rocco a bad guy could not be further from the truth. He was a sweet, saintly guy whom I had met and gotten friendly with because he was in my parish; in fact, his daughter was a nun. But to look at Rocco, you would shiver, because he had a villainous appearance. Five-foot-ten and built like a bull, Emmett was an ex-heavyweight fighter from Ellwood City, Pennsylvania, who still had the *look* of a fighter, with the big nose and smashed-in face. He now delivered sides of beef which he would carry around on his back. I loved Emmett and I used to take him to the Rams games with me a lot. One day I got a crazy idea.

Emmett had a bit of ham in him; he liked to act, so I brought him onto the **Untouchables** set when we were doing "The Tommy Karpeles Story" with Joseph Wiseman. Our second assistant director was a guy named Bud Grace, an heir to the Grace family (the Grace Lines shipping family). Bud was a very sweet, genteel kind of individual, but also naive—he'd believe anything you'd tell him. Bud noticed Emmett standing around on the set and didn't recognize him, so he went up to Emmett and he asked, "Sir, what are you doing here? Do you have a pass?" And Emmett, already a very imposing figure without even opening his mouth, said in his deepest, most threatening voice, as I had rehearsed him, "I'm Tommy Karpeles. You're doing my life story here, and nobody got my permission!" The way he said it, Emmett scared the *shit* out of Bud! Emmett went on, "I want a copy of that script and I want to read it *right now!*" Well, Bud instantly became like Don Knotts: "Yes, sir!," "You sit right here, sir!," "I'll get the script for you right away, sir!" Then Bud ran and told Bob and the director, Stu Rosenberg. Of course, everybody was in on the gag except Bud.

Bud gave Emmett the script to read and Emmett sat on the set and went through it. Finally he said to Bud, "This is my life story, you son of a bitch! Get the fucking producer down here right now! I want to be compensated for this or you're gonna stop shooting!" Well, by now Bud was frantic, "Yes sir, yes sir!"—Bud was completely "sold" that this was Tommy Karpeles, a notorious gangster. Emmett was told that the situation would be checked into, and he left, but Bud was still all worked-up: "Oh my God—do

My good pal Emmett Rocco did all the cooking at my wedding to Marie.

you think he'll look for me on the way home? Should I get a gun? What should I *do*??" At that point, of course, we let him off the hook and told him that "Tommy Karpeles" was actually just a friend of mine. But we really had him going!

Emmett, who was the godfather of my son Philip, died very young, 54; delivering that meat was too much for him, I guess. His grave is very close to the graves of my mother-in-law and father-in-law in the San Fernando Mission Cemetery, and I put a flower on Emmett's grave and say a prayer for him every time I go out there. And I always think of the great acting job he did as Tommy Karpeles.

21
FRIENDSHIP & LOYALTY

Sometimes you work in a play or a TV episode or a movie and you become very close to your fellow actors. You have a lot of fun during the run of the show, and you become fast friends. Some, sadly, you never see again, which has happened to me *so* many times—for instance, with Errol Flynn. With some, you cross paths again years and years later. And others become lifelong friends.

One day during the run of **The Untouchables** I went fishing off of Santa Cruz Island with two of my lifelong friends from Warner Brothers days, Joe Breen, the writer and technical adviser on **Breakthrough**, and Nick Cravat, Burt Lancaster's circus partner and later his co-star in **The Flame and the Arrow** and **The Crimson Pirate**. We left Port Hueneme in Joe's boat and we were soon surrounded by 50 sharks off of Annacappa Island. Nick leaned over the side of the boat and started slapping the sharks on their dorsal fins as they swam by. I cried out, "Nick, don't do that!"—it was making me sick with worry. "You might fall in, you dumb fuck, don't *do* that!"

Joe asked, "You wanna catch one?," and I said, "Yeah, let's!" So Joe rigged the fishing line with a special steel leader—you can't use regular leader because they'll chew it right off. And sure enough, we caught this big blue shark. Joe was going to cut it loose, but I had a brainstorm: "As a joke, why don't we put it in Phil Carey's swimming pool?" They all laughed, and they thought it was a pretty good idea. We got it back to Port Hueneme, measured and weighed it (11 feet long, 280 pounds) and then squeezed it into the trunk of my Chevy convertible. But on the way to Phil's house, Nick asked Joe, "Is blue shark good to eat?," and Joe, a little surprised, said, "Good to *eat?*

When you go to a restaurant and you order swordfish, what you are really getting is blue shark!" (That's true: Back then, you'd never find "shark" on any restaurant menu, but nine times out of ten when you ordered swordfish, blue shark was what you got.)

Nick said, "Well in *that* case, fuck putting it in Phil's pool! Let's cut it up and put it in our freezers." We went to my house and got it onto my back patio, and Joe went to work on it. Joe was brilliant at doing that sort of thing. Once on his father's estate in Hidden Valley, Joe and I once shot a deer and, right in his father's barn, he gutted it, skinned it and cut it up into chops in about 20 minutes.

After Joe cut the shark into steaks, we packaged it. Nick got some, Joe got some and I got some; the only thing left of this big blue shark was the head with the mouth open and all the teeth showing. I decided I'd bring it to the studio the next day so that some of my friends on the set could see the shark we caught. It so happened that, the next day on *The Untouchables*, we were scheduled to shoot a scene where Bob Stack and I go to a morgue and he lifts the sheet that's covering a "corpse" (actually a dummy, of course) and says, "That's *him* all right" and throws the sheet back. So, between me and the prop man Al Greene and our director Paul Wendkos, we decided to put the shark's head on the gurney along with the dummy and cover it with the sheet. Everybody was in on it except for Bob.

When it came time to rehearse the scene, Wendkos said, "Bob, there's no need to rehearse, let's just shoot it. You and Paul, you just come in, you lift the sheet, you deliver your line, you throw the sheet back and then walk out. All right . . . *action!*" Bob and I walked onto the morgue set, Bob lifted the sheet, he looked down and there was the shark head. And, son of a gun, without batting an eye Bob said, "That's *him* all right"—he delivered the line perfectly—and flipped the sheet over. We were all expecting him to break up, and he didn't. The joke was on *us*! That is the way Bob was—he was *so* concentrated on his work. But after Wendkos said *cut*, Bob said, "Oh, you son of bitches . . . !" and started laughing along with the rest of us.

Bob was such a professional that nothing ever bothered him. He would go through every scene and do it methodically and beautifully. Eliot Ness was a foolproof part—the audience automatically loved the character. Nevertheless, Bob made it his own. The way Errol Flynn became Robin Hood, Bob became Eliot Ness. He was a multimillionaire at the time and on many occasions I asked myself, "Why the hell does this guy work so hard?" But acting was his profession, he *wanted* to do it, and he did it.

Probably the funniest thing that happened on *The Untouchables* was an incident that I once talked about on Johnny Carson's *Tonight Show*—and after I told the story, a lot of comedians, including Danny Thomas, turned it into a joke in their nightclub acts. But it was a true story. I was sitting in one of the portable dressing rooms on the set one day with Bob, as I often did, and I was helping him with his lines. Our assistant director at the time was Bob Daley, who went on to become a producer for Clint Eastwood on *Dirty Harry* and *Play Misty for Me* and probably a dozen others. Daley came into the dressing room and said, "I just got the weirdest phone call . . . ," and, of course, Bob Stack and I wanted to hear all about it. Daley said that an Italian woman had called and the conversation went something like this: She asked, with a heavy Italian accent, "Izza theez *The Untouchables* company?" and Daley said, "Yes ma'am, it is."

Posing inside one of the show's vintage cars.

She said, "My name izza Mrs. Ponticello, and I amma the secretary of the Italian-American Federation. I got a leetle complaint to make about your show *The Untouchables*. All of the time onna your show *The Untouchables*, you show Italian people azza bad people, shoot-a, fight-a, kill-a. Italian people, we not like that. We like to eat, we like to sing, we like to dance. We don't like violence. If you don't stop showing Italian people bad people onna your show, somebody gonna throw a bomb inna your studio!"

There were funny moments during shooting too, a lot of 'em involving Nick Georgiade. If you've seen the show, you can picture a scene (we did it in just about every episode) where all the Untouchables walk into their office in the Federal Building, hang up their hats and get to work. Bob always came in first, put his hat on the rack; I came in after him, put my hat on the rack; Abel put his hat on the rack, and then Nick. Well, one day as we were doing the first take, right in the middle of it, Nick's hat fell off the rack, and so we had to do it again. Well, *every time*, for six, seven takes, Nick would put his hat on the rack and the hat would fall. Paul Wendkos, the director, got the giggles behind the scenes, and pretty soon he had to put a handkerchief in his mouth so that he wouldn't laugh. Nick was trying so hard but Wendkos couldn't stop laughing, and finally Wendkos said, "Nick. When you come in, leave your hat *on*!"

One night on the back lot we were shooting a scene where the Untouchables arrive in their old car at this warehouse. The director, I think it was Stu Rosenberg, said, "Drive with the lights off and pull up to the warehouse and then get out of the car, walk up the ramp and look in the window." Nick was driving. It was very dark and very quiet, we pulled up to the warehouse with the lights off and we started to get out—and as Nick got out of the car, the car headlights went on. Stu said, "Nick! Don't put the lights on when you get out of the car!," and Nick said, "I didn't touch nothin'!" We drove up again—we got out—and the lights went on again. We did it three times before finally somebody, I think it was Ed Chamey, the guy in charge of all the old cars, realized that on the center of the steering wheel were two little silver handles for the lights, and every time Nick grabbed the wheel as he got out, he was inadvertently hitting that handle and turning on the lights.

In addition to playing Bob's sidekick, I would also work as his dialogue coach. He was a quick study but still, with Ness playing a substantial role in every story, it was a task for him to learn all that dialogue.

We had so many crazy things happen with those old cars. Another time on the back lot, Nick was driving our car and we pulled up to a motel that was on a bit of an incline; the four of us were supposed to jump out and go into the motel. Well, we climbed out and walked up onto the porch when all of a sudden the director started yelling, "Cut! Cut!!" We looked back and the car was rolling backwards down the hill toward some of the crew, and everybody was running to get out of the way. Nick had forgotten to put on the brake! The car ran over five or six director's chairs and some lights and other equipment before finally it came to a stop. I remember several near-misses like that, but, fortunately, we had no bad accidents.

On the more serious side, there were several occasions when Abel Fernandez came close to getting fired because of his drinking, and I would go to bat for Abel and get Bob *not* to fire him. Abel was always there, but much of the time he had a hangover. They had Steve London (playing the Untouchables' wiretap expert Jack Rossman) in reserve in case of a no-show, which never happened. Just a few drops of some Murine for some bloodshot eyes, and Abel would be ready.

(Steve, incidentally, wasn't one of the "regular" Untouchables although he did appear in a number of episodes every season. Steve was tall and good-looking, a nice, very quiet guy who never got in anybody's way. I heard that Steve eventually became a lawyer and that he now lives in Pasadena. I haven't seen him in 30 or 40 years.)

Then there was one time when Nick decided he was going to ask for a raise because he knew that Abel was making more than he was. Nick figured that he was doing the same work as Abel and he wanted the same money that Abel was getting. (Nick was making less than Abel because Lucy had signed Nick to a studio contract starting at 150 a week. At this time, he was only up to about 250, and Abel was making 750 a show.) Well, Nick did ask for more money, and Desilu wouldn't give it to him. Nick made up his mind that he was going to hold out, and if they didn't give him the money he was going to quit. At that point in the show's run, it *wasn't* fair that Abel was making more. Nick deserved the raise, so I didn't blame him for what he was doing.

One night after work I went up to Bob Stack's house and, as we sat at his bar over a couple of Scotches, I pleaded the case for Nick. "Bob," I said, "Nick's asking for the same amount of money that Abel's getting. They won't give it to him, and they wanna drop him."

Bob said, "Paul, I can't get involved in that. That's not my department. That's Jerry Thorpe's department, that's the financial department. I can't—"

I said, "Bob. If we lose Nick, we're gonna get somebody *else* in there. And who knows if we're still gonna have the smooth group that we have now. It's to your advantage, and the show's advantage, if we keep Nick. Nick is on time, he does his work well, he's well established. If we bring another guy in, how do we know it won't upset the apple cart?" I managed to convince him—Bob must have thought back to Jerry Paris and Tony George, his two sidekicks prior to my coming onto the show. And Nick got his raise.

Then there was a situation that arose between Bob and me. As I mentioned in an earlier chapter, when Desilu was initially "courting" Bob, trying to get him to star on **The Untouchables**, one of the conditions laid down by Bob and his agent Bill Shiffrin was that he wanted a three-year contract, not the five-year contract that was customary for TV series stars in those days. (If a series turned out to be popular, producers didn't want their stars to be able to hit them up for a big, astronomical raise for at least five years.) Well, when those three years were up, *The Untouchables* was still big and strong, and so Desilu wanted an additional year or two from Bob. But, of course, Bob and Shiffrin were holding out—they had a strong position for a substantial raise.

After Bob and Shiffrin and Desi Arnaz and the other studio boys had been negotiating back and forth about this for a while, along came a script called "Silent Partner" that featured me *big*. In terms of screen time and being the center of attention, my character Lee Hobson was about equal to Bob's Eliot Ness in this episode—Lee saves Eliot's life during a gunfight, Lee has a tense confrontation scene with Eliot, Lee is kidnapped by gangsters and has to be rescued—it was "my" episode. And don't think that Bob didn't *notice* this! It seemed like the studio was trying to show that the series could work with*out* him. And, all of a sudden, I became aware that Bob was now cool to me. He and I used to have lunch every day at a restaurant called Tracton's, right near the studio. Once in a while we'd eat with the other guys at the studio commissary,

When Bob started giving me the cold shoulder, it was especially mystifying and distressing since the two of us, and our wives, had even done some socializing and made some public appearances together, like at Hollywood Race Track (pictured).

but for the most part it was just me and Bob at Tracton's, or wherever, because we did a lot of work together. But suddenly he was ducking me at lunchtime. I couldn't understand it.

The next thing that happened was, while we were shooting "Silent Partner," a guy came onto the set to interview Bob. In the past, Bob *always* would say to the interviewer, "I want you to meet my co-star Paul Picerni . . . ," and he would include me in on the interview. Well, this time a magazine writer came on the set . . . and Bob shut me out. Completely.

Once these things started happening, I'd come home from the studio at night and I wouldn't be able to sleep—I was sick over what was going on. Bob was so *cold* to me; it was just terrible. It was like when a sweetheart just cuts you off! This went on for three or four days, and I even told Marie about it. Then I put two and two together and I realized, "Bob thinks the studio is grooming me to step into his place and take over the show if he doesn't sign. He thinks they're gonna groom me to push him out, or at least groom me and then 'threaten' him with me so that he signs his contract."

A couple of days later, we were shooting at night on 40 Acres, the back lot at Desilu Culver. It was a cold night and we had our little dressing rooms out there, and it must have been about one o'clock in the morning when I knocked on Bob's door intending to talk to him about the situation. When he opened the door, I said, "Bob, can I talk to you for a second?," and he said, yeah, come on in. Still with that cold attitude.

Bob was sitting there, holding a newspaper or a magazine, as I stood and said my piece. It was hard for me to say the words, because I was filled with emotion. "Bob, I want you to know something. I'm loyal to *you*." I said a second time: "I'm loyal to you. If you don't do the show next year, *I don't do the show*. You understand? If you decide not to sign that extension on your contract, I won't do the show without you. If you're in, I'm in. I'm loyal to you. That's all I want you to know."

Bob looked surprised, and very pleased. I could tell he realized that I meant it. He said, "Thank you, Paul" . . . he stood up . . . he shook my hand . . . and I left. And that was that. We finished that night's work. And from that day on, it was smooth sailing again. Bob eventually signed for two more years; Desilu gave him

After Bob and I patched things up, we remained friends until the end of his life. Here's a 1987 shot of Bob with Marie and me.

$1,000,000 in Desilu stock as a signing bonus.

As wonderful an experience as doing *The Untouchables* was, you kept in mind that Bob Stack had producer approval, director approval, actor approval—an almost unprecedented amount of "say" for the star of a TV series. And a lot of people were fired because of that. Bob would tell Bill Shiffrin that he didn't like *this* one or he didn't like *that* one, and Bill would be the hatchet man. The very first year, Jerry Paris was let go after about 13 episodes, and Tony George was let go after the next 13, and the executive producer Quinn Martin also was fired. I don't know the story behind Quinn's disappearance, he was "before my time" on the show—all I knew was that, after the first year, Quinn was gone.* Almost every year we would change producers, sometimes for the better and sometimes *not*. Bob in his quiet way was capable of doing these things because he knew what was right for the show, and he knew what he wanted. The only one that he had to answer to was Desi.

*Quinn Martin almost immediately went on to do a series called *The New Breed*, about an elite squad of L.A. cops on the trail of criminals that the regular cops can't nail using traditional police procedure. In other words, it was *The Untouchables* again, just with modern-day cops. He stole the idea!

One *Untouchables* director who did quite a few episodes and then was not invited back was Johnny Peyser. He was a good director—not one of our best, but good—and a nice, likable guy. Johnny directed a two-parter called "The Big Train," set right after the conviction of Al Capone (Neville Brand, in his only appearance on the *Untouchables* series itself). Frank Nitti and the rest of the Capone mob learn that "Big Al" is going to be moved from the Federal Penitentiary in Atlanta to the new escape-proof island prison Alcatraz on a special train, and they lay out a plan to intercept the train and spring him at a stop at a hick town in the west. The Untouchables find out about the scheme and are in the town waiting for them. We were shooting on a Western town set on 40 Acres, and part of the scene called for Bob Stack and me and seven or eight police officers to come up the street firing our guns at the train station where the gangsters are holed up. Well, Johnny Peyser, rushed for time, realized that it would take forever to shoot a gunfight in which the lawmen come up the street, in shots showing one or two or three of them at a time, sneaking around corners, ducking in and out of alleys and alcoves, and running from pillar to post as we shoot at the train station. So, to save time and film, he came up with the idea of having Bob lead us, eight or ten abreast, up this Western street toward the train station with blazing guns. When Bob found out Johnny intended to do it this way, he actually asked him, "W-w-what are you doing?" Johnny said, "Well, if you overpower the gangsters in the train station with all this gunfire, they won't have a chance to put their heads up, they'll stay down. You all just march up the street and capture the train station." That's the way he shot it, this big group of us looking like the Rockettes kick line, firing our guns while boldly parading up the street.

Well, a day or two later, after Jerry Thorpe our executive producer saw in the rushes this gun battle footage of us coming up the street ten abreast, he came into Bob's dressing room where Bob and I were running lines and all he said was, "Jesus, I haven't seen *that* done since the Revolutionary War!" That footage is still in the episode because it would have taken too much time and money to reshoot the scene, but Jerry didn't care for it—and so that was the last episode that Johnny Peyser directed.

* * * * * * *

One day just before the beginning of my second year on the show, I got a call from my mother, who was still living in Corona, Queens, the rough Italian neighborhood where I grew up. She was still raising my younger sister Marilyn and my brother Charlie. Charlie hadn't finished high school and now he was knocking around from job to job, including construction work on skyscrapers—he was able to walk the planks 30 stories up. Charlie was also working for Joey Narro, the Mafia boss of Corona, picking up numbers and picking up bets. Worried about him, my mother called me and said, "Paul, you've got to get your brother out of New York. He's traveling with the wrong crowd. Get him to California if you can, because if he stays *here* he's going to end up in jail."

I figured that the only way I could get him out here was to arrange for him to become my stand-in on *The Untouchables*. A stand-in is the guy who stands on the set in place of an actor while the cameraman and grips and electricians work together to get the right camera angles and the right light on him. Meanwhile, the actor can be in his dressing room brushing up on his lines, or just relaxing. (It takes quite a while to light a shot; in the old days it used to take 45 minutes, especially with a cameraman like Charles Straumer, who was very meticulous.) Then when the company is ready to shoot, the actor can simply step in and do the scene.

I had a wonderful stand-in, an oldtimer named Bill Scully who had been standing in for me for many years. Bill was very popular in the business and I knew he'd find another job right away and that he'd be all right, so one day I told him, "I like you, Bill, but I'm thinking of bringing my brother out here from New York," and I explained about my mother calling and what the situation was. Bill said, "I understand, Paul. Don't worry about me, I'll be okay. You go ahead and give your brother a break, bring him out."

When Charlie came out to the Coast, I got him a Screen Extras Guild card. Getting someone their first Extras Guild card was always a hassle, but I happened to know Eddie Rio, the fellow who ran the Guild. I went down to see him, told him I wanted my brother to be my stand-in and we had no problems. Charlie started working as my stand-in.

On the first day, as I was driving Charlie to work, I said, "Now here's what you have to remember: You have to be at work on time. Stay near the camera as much as you can. Don't go drifting around the set or get into card games in the corner like the other extras do, *stay near the camera.* That's where you'll learn the business. Try to talk to members of the crew, 15 minutes a day, this guy and that guy, so you'll get to know the different departments, and you'll get to know the people. They can help you, and you can learn." Well, that's exactly what he did.

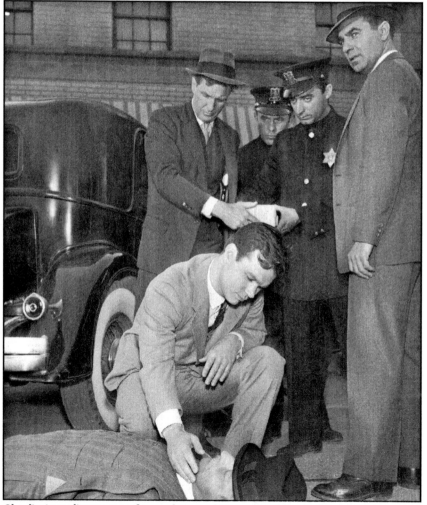

Charlie in policeman uniform, doing a bit on an *Untouchables* episode with me and Darryl Hickman (kneeling).

Small, non-speaking roles paid extra money; I remember the first time Charlie had one on *The Untouchables*, playing a hoodlum that Bob Stack and I chased down an alley. Charlie was supposed to run down the alley ahead of us, climb a ten-foot chain link fence (with barbed wire at the top), jump down on the other side and get away. Well, Charlie was quite the athletic young kid, and when we did the shot, he went flying down the alley, bounded over that ten-foot fence in two or three leaps, jumped down and he was *gone*. He ran and climbed so fast and made it look so easy that, after the shot, Bob looked at me in amazement and said, "How the hell did he do that?" I said, "I'll *tell* you how, Bob: He did that for real in New York, running from the cops!"

Charlie learned a lot from Victor Paul (real name: Phil Romano), our stunt coordinator on the show. From Vic, Charlie learned to drive the old cars and do car chases, fights, high falls and so on. Charlie was basically my stand-in and stunt double, but I didn't have that many stunts to do. The first time he did anything for me, he had to run and fall. I don't remember if he was supposedly ducking some bullets or *what* the story behind it was, but Charlie did that running fall for me and that was his first stunt doubling an actor.

I'll never forget Charlie's first *big* stunt: He was going to get shot by the Untouchables and fall about 40 feet, off the top of a wooden staircase that led up to a warehouse loft. (I don't remember what actor he was doubling—it might have been Richard Conte.) High falls are kinda tricky if you don't know what you're doing, and Charlie had never done one before, but he was ballsy and ready to go. Charlie Horvath, an experienced stuntman with whom I had worked many times, happened to be on the set, and Horvath told Charlie how to do it. As Charlie went up the stairs, I was down below, behind the camera, watching, and saying my prayers that he didn't get hurt. Well, he landed on his back on the mattresses and boxes exactly the way Horvath told him to do it, and he was fine. Horvath went over to him and said, "Charlie, I couldn't have done it better myself. You were great." That was Charlie's "baptism of fire" and his first big checks. Stunts came under S.A.G. and paid the same rate as an actor.

Charlie and Victor Paul became very close through the years: Vic hired Charlie a lot in the early days and then, as the years went on and my brother became very big in the business, *he* began hiring *Vic* every chance he got. (Vic is today 75 or 76 and is well-to-do and occasionally—not too often, but occasionally—he *still* works as a stuntman!)

One thing that helped Charlie in his career was that he had the mentality of a kid from the streets of Corona. In New York, if somebody promised you something, that was *it*—they had given you their word. But here in Hollywood, it was a little bit different. We had a first assistant director named Teddy Schilz, a nice little guy. Teddy grew up in California, kind of a rich kid, and he was fascinated by Charlie, who came from the streets of New York. Teddy had grown up a sissy kid, and here was this *tough* kid. One day he promised Charlie that he would give him a silent bit as a taxi driver. (A silent bit made more money than a straight stand-in or an extra.) All day long he told Charlie, "Don't worry, you're going to do the bit." Charlie waited and waited, and when it came time to do the shot, Teddy gave the bit to another guy, some friend of his. It was as if Teddy was testing Charlie's strength—assistant directors love to have extras kiss up to them. I wasn't aware of what had happened.

After Bob Stack and I finished shooting for the day, we walked together out to the parking lot to go to our cars; at that time, I had a beautiful car that I had bought from Bob, a great Mark 7 Jaguar sedan that looked like a little Rolls-Royce. And all of a sudden I saw Charlie, holding Teddy Schilz by the throat and banging him up against the side of my Jaguar! Charlie was yelling at him, "You son of a bitch! You told me I was going to do that bit, you mother-fucker! You cocksucker!" He was banging the shit out of little Teddy until Bob and I came over and broke it up. But that was Charlie. Teddy hadn't kept his word, he used someone else as the taxi driver, so to Charlie he "broke the code"—the code of the streets that Charlie knew from his days back in New York.

That's the thing that kinda carried Charlie all through the business: He didn't take crap from *any*body, including the stars. From that day on, Teddy Schilz respected Charlie and he never, never fooled around with Charlie again. If Teddy said something to Charlie, he would always keep his word. As a matter of fact,

Charlie as a sailor set ablaze during the Japanese attack on Pearl Harbor in the 1970 movie *Tora! Tora! Tora!*

Teddy—later the head of production at Universal—became one of Charlie's big boosters.

The Untouchables was the beginning of Charlie Picerni's career. I must say I'm very proud of what he's accomplished through the years. He went on to become a top stunt coordinator on big features like ***Die Hard*** and ***Lethal Weapon***, and directed over 40 television episodes. Pretty good for a kid from Corona, New York, who never finished high school. I was loyal to my kid brother, and he's been loyal to me. More on Charlie in the coming chapters.

I made a lot of loyal, lifetime friends on *The Untouchables* and other shows—people like Phil Carey, Tony Caruso, Mike Connors, Burt Lancaster, Jimmy Darren, Frank Gorshin, and, of course, Abel Fernandez, Nick Georgiade and Robert Stack. And one guy who became my very best friend of all time, Telly Savalas.

22
ON THE ROAD WITH
THE UNTOUCHABLES

During a trip back East to New York to visit my mother, I made a guest appearance on *The Tonight Show With Johnny Carson*, then a New York-based talk show. Also on the show that night was Oleg Cassini, the famous dress designer. This was in the early 1960s when John F. Kennedy was president, and I knew that Oleg designed the dresses of the First Lady, Jackie Kennedy. I asked him about this during a commercial break, and he said, "Would you do me a favor, Paul? Ask me that question when we go back on the air." I told him I would.

The break ended and Johnny and Oleg again began talking back and forth; I waited until I found just the right opening and I interjected, "Oleg, don't you design the dresses for our First Lady?" And the son of a bitch laughed in a scornful way and said (with his accent), "Oh, Paul—everybody knows *that*!" He asked me to do him a favor and then he made me look like a jerk on national television!

My pal Harry Guardino and Gloria Talbott share a scene with Bob in the *Untouchables* episode "The Contract."

That was one of the memorable things that happened as I was making promotional appearances for *The Untouchables*. An earlier trip to New York was one of *the* most memorable. The Schick Razor Company, one of the sponsors of the show, brought me to New York, along with Nick and Abel, just to visit the Schick factory in Connecticut and have lunch. (No Bob Stack, though—Bob never went on any of those things.) Well, Abel partied all night the night before, so *he* didn't make it, but that morning around ten o'clock a limousine picked Nick and me up in front of the Park Sheraton Hotel where we were staying and took us to Connecticut. If I'm remembering right, the Schick guy who invited us there was their head of publicity and promotion, and I got the impression that the *big* guy, the chairman of the Schick board, wasn't that happy about him spending all that money to bring us East to do something for Schick that wasn't really going to pay them *back* that much. We were there more or less just to meet the workers, the office people and so on—Schick picked up the whole tab for our trip, and I never quite knew what was in it for them. They even gave Nick and me boxes and boxes of Schick razors!

The next day, back in Manhattan, Nick, Abel and I were supposed to pose for publicity photos in front of the Sheraton—we had phony tommyguns, an old car and our Untouchables wardrobe including gun holsters and fedoras. As we posed for pictures, a number of passersby gathered to watch. All of a sudden a police car pulled up with a couple of cops in it and one of them, a sergeant, started calling out to us: "Hey, hey! What are you guys doin'?"

"We're taking some still pictures," I told him.

"*You* can't do that," he said. "You gotta get a permit."

I said, "You don't have to have a permit to take *still* pictures! Every tourist takes still pictures in New York. We're not makin' a movie, we're the Untouchables and we're just takin' stills."

"Nah, nah, nah," the sergeant said. "You gotta go downtown and get a permit. You're stopping traffic with all these fans."

Being a New Yorker, I knew what he was getting at. I said, "Sergeant . . . c'mere," and I took him aside and I told him, "Listen. If you come up to my suite, I'll give you a whole box of Schick razors. Would *that* help?" And, of course, he said, "Shit, yeah!" So I brought him up to the suite and gave him about 20 razors, and he said, "You can take all the pictures you want!"

As long as we were in New York, ABC wanted us to meet Ollie Treyz, the head of the network. The three of us visited him in his office at ABC. The only thing I remember about that meeting was that a shoeshine boy came in to shine Ollie's shoes, and while he was there Ollie said, "Can I buy you fellows a shine?"

The highlight of the trip was when the Untouchables raided Toots Shor's. For those of you too young to remember, Toots Shor's was a very well-known restaurant; it was "*the* place" at the time. All the Broadway stars would hang out there, big celebrities like Sinatra, the baseball players from Joe DiMaggio on down, and all the "Damon Runyon characters" of Broadway. I don't remember now who came up with the idea, whether it was ABC publicity or the great New York newspaper columnist Earl Wilson, or if all of them put their heads together, but that was the plan, to raid Toots Shor's. I got an old Eliot Ness-type car and my brother-in-law Tony Tamburro (my sister Eleanor's husband) to drive it.

We set out from the Sheraton, up near Central Park. Inside the car was Earl Wilson, with Tony driving, and on the running boards were Nick and Abel and me, shooting at people with our fake sub-machine-guns as we went down Broadway! (I doubt if we could get away with that in New York City today!) When the car pulled up in front of Toots Shor's, the sidewalk was teeming with fans as the three Untouchables kicked in the doors and "raided" the place. Toots was in on it, of course, and he came at us, calling us sons of bitches and kicking and throwing punches at us, as though he actually *was* a speakeasy owner trying to fight off the cops! He really got into the act! So did the restaurant patrons, scurrying for the exits with their "molls"—everybody had a good time with it. There were photographers there taking pictures, and, of course, Earl Wilson wrote up a big story for the papers, **THE UNTOUCHABLES RAID TOOTS SHOR**. It was a lot of fun.

That same night, Toots took my family out to dinner—me, my mother, my sister Marilyn and my brother Charlie, who was also in New York at the time. He brought us to Danny's Hideaway, another popular New York restaurant, he showed us the town, he was great to us—but he talked the whole time, you couldn't stop him. He talked like a machine gun, constantly, constantly, constantly, to the point where nobody else said anything. Finally at one o'clock in the morning we ended up at Lindy's Restaurant, where they had the greatest cheesecake in the world, and from the time we met Toots to the time we were at Lindy's, he hadn't once stopped talking. At one point Charlie and I went downstairs to the restroom and we were standing side by side doing our business, and Charlie said, "You know . . . if there was a painting of an ear on a wall, that guy could talk for six more hours!" I'll always remember that line!

One other unforgettable line came out of that trip. In the lobby of the Sheraton Hotel there was a 70-year-old Italian shoeshine boy named Dominick. As I was getting a shine one day, I thought back to the incident where the woman from the Italian-American Federation called the *Untouchables* set and said if we weren't careful, somebody might throw a bomb in our studio. I asked, "Dominick, how do you feel about the Italians being portrayed as gangsters on *The Untouchables* on television?"

He paused for a moment, and then he looked up at me from his position and he said, "I wanna tell-a you one t'ing, my friend: If it wasn't-a for Marconi, there ain't gonna *be* no television!" Which was his way of saying that there are good and bad in all peoples, including bad Italians and good Italians. A lot of popes were Italian, and so was Marconi, da Vinci, Michelangelo and so on—so for every bad Italian, there are maybe a thousand good ones. So I'll also always remember that great line of Dominick's. And here's another memorable comment about our show: A priest once said to me, "*The Untouchables* is like a morality play. The bad guys were very bad and the good guys were very good—they were untouchable. And the good guys always won."

* * * * * * *

While I was doing *The Untouchables*, a local automobile dealer offered Bob Stack a new Pontiac for free. Bob turned him down. "If I accepted, I'd be indebted to him," Bob told me later. "I'd be called upon to do him some favor or to make an appearance at his dealership or something like that. I'd rather not." Bob was right—but I didn't follow his advice! I accepted a new Chevrolet from Terry York, a Chevrolet dealership in Encino, each year for five years. They *did* call upon me to pose for pictures and they used my name in advertisements, but I didn't mind.

* * * * * * *

Being the co-star of a hot TV series like *The Untouchables* also opened the door for other fun opportunities. Because I was well known for being on the show, I was asked to be the honorary mayor of Tarzana, and I accepted. I would also emcee the occasional Chamber of Commerce banquet, but mainly my job was to cut ribbons at grand openings—stores opening or banks opening or whatever. I opened up a lot of stores that are still in operation in Tarzana today, and I also cut the ribbon on the new post office. But that was so long ago, they've since built *another* new post office!

Every year the Los Angeles Dodgers have a special baseball game, "Hollywood Star Night," where movie stars compete against sportswriters, or against the television sportscasters, or something like that. Back in 1962 or '63, the Untouchables were asked to be the umpires at this game. Bob Stack wouldn't do it, naturally; the poor guy had so much work, he didn't want to work on Sunday. So they invited Edward G. Robinson to be the head of the Untouchables umpire crew, and he accepted.

Well, it wasn't quite that casual: Eddie G. being the professional that he was, he insisted that we go to his house to sit down together and figure out what we were going to do. Nick, Abel and I, and one

The Untouchables, the ballplayers and umpire Edward G. Robinson (in hat).

of the Dodgers publicity guys, went to Eddie G.'s house in Beverly Hills and talked about it and rehearsed it. Which I thought was terrific, because it showed what a real pro Eddie G. was. He came up with certain things that we could do that might get a laugh. They were all sight gags—for instance, we decided we'd have one of the ballplayers start arguing with us umpires about a call, and then we'd pull out a tommygun and "shoot" the guy! Three or four days later, when the day of the game arrived, Edward G. Robinson and the Untouchables made our entrance into the Coliseum in a vintage car. We three Untouchables rode in standing on the running boards of the car and, when the car stopped, over the public address system came, "Ladies and gentlemen, the Untouchables and the head umpire, Eddie G. Robinson!" We opened the car door and he stepped out, and we took "center stage" and started doing all the comedy bits we'd planned out. That's a nice memory I have of Eddie G.

* * * * * * *

I had the good fortune of later working with Edward G. Robinson in one of his last pictures, the 1970 TV-movie *The Old Man Who Cried Wolf.* Eddie G. played the title role, the witness to a murder who keeps trying to tell people, including his own son, but nobody believes him—they think he's crying wolf. But, of course, *the bad guy* believes him, and now is trying to kill him! Also in the movie were Marty Balsam, Ruth Roman and Ed Asner, who got his start on *The Untouchables*, and it was directed by my close friend Walter Grauman, also from *The Untouchables*. I played a police detective and, in the scene I had with Eddie, he came into my office and I interrogated him. Between takes, Eddie got me off to one side and said, "Paul, my hearing is shot, I can't hear a damn thing. So when you finish your line, just close your mouth. I'll watch your lips and when you stop, I'll know it's my cue to start." And that's what we did.

A funny side story: When Eddie initially read the script, he saw that there was a lot of physical stuff for him to do—climb stairs and a fire escape, run down a street and so on. Eddie, who had to be almost 80 at the time, told his agent Max, "There's quite a bit of action in this. Ask Wally Grauman if they can extend the shooting schedule from 14 days to 16 days, so that I can have a little breather in between scenes and recover from all this exertion. I want to make sure I can get *through* this thing!" Max went to Wally, who happened to be the director *and* producer, and explained the situation and requested an extension on the shooting schedule. Wally talked to the production company and they said, "Okay, we'll do that to accommodate Mr. Robinson," and Wally got back to Max with the good news. Now Max went back to Eddie and told him it was now a 16-day schedule instead of 14, and Eddie said, "Oh, that's wonderful. Wonderful, wonderful, wonderful. Thank you so much . . ."

Then he paused and thought for a moment, and said, "Listen, Max . . . now that it's 16 days, don't you think we should renegotiate and get more money?" That's *so* typical of actors!

* * * * * * *

One of the most memorable offshoots of **The Untouchables** was doing a nightclub act based on the show. **The Untouchables** was very popular in Mexico, and one day after we had finished shooting the third year and we actors were on hiatus, I got a call from a fellow named Marvin Fisher, a personal manager who had taken Mike Connors down to Mexico City the year before as a nightclub act. Mike sang and danced and did some comedy, and he'd had great success with that. Now Marvin was calling to ask me if I'd be interested in doing an **Untouchables** nightclub act in Mexico City with the other guys. I said, "Well, Bob Stack won't go . . ."

Studying the script for the stage show.

Marvin said, "No, I didn't think Bob would. But you and Nick and Abel . . . you could make some money down there. *The Untouchables* is so big in Mexico City." He told me he could get us $6,000 a week, which sounded pretty good, and then he said, "If you can put a little act together, we'll make a deal. You'll appear in Mexico City for two weeks and then, if the show's successful, we'll go on to Puerto Rico and Latin America for a few weeks."

I got the okay from Nick and Abel—they were all for it—so now I was free to start working on the act. I had a friend named Johnny Bradford, who was producing *The Judy Garland Show* at the time; he offered to help me put it together, and his choreographer Danny Daniels said he would stage it. Alan Copeland, a fine musician, began doing all the arrangements for the band and the songs, some of them parodies of songs in *West Side Story*. Tony Romano, who was Bob Hope's guitar player and made the tours with Hope all over the world for the troops, agreed to become our band director and go to Mexico with us to do the show.

We rehearsed right here in Tarzana; a friend of mine had a restaurant with a back room where there was a piano. We put the whole act together in just two weeks, with me writing most of the comedy stuff. Before you knew it we were singing, we were dancing, we were doing comedy routines. And very soon after that, we were all in Mexico City—me, Nick, Abel, Tony Romano and also my

Our opening night in Mexico City: Band director Tony Romano, me, Evangelina Elizondo, Nick, Abel and my brother Charlie.

brother Charlie, whom I brought along to do the opening sequence, which was a big fight scene.

In Mexico our impresaria was a movie star named Evangelina Elizondo. I didn't know this at the time but I soon discovered that she played around a lot with her leading men. One night her husband had caught her with her young leading man, an actor who was very popular in Mexico—and the husband shot and killed him! So by the time we met her, her husband was in jail and her leading man was dead, and she wasn't too popular with the Mexican people because they loved that leading man and they blamed *her* for it. Evangelina booked us at the Teatro Iris, a giant opera house in Mexico City that could hold maybe 5,000 people. We were supposed to do a seven o'clock show there, and then later in the evening we would have another show to do at the Los Globus nightclub.

Nick was the comic of the act, and there was a spot in the show where he had to have a mustache, stuck onto his upper lip with collodion. Kiva Hoffman, our makeup man on *The Untouchables*, had given us a makeup kit with everything we'd need—the collodion, a mustache and so on. Opening night at the Teatro Iris, just before we were ready to go on, I was backstage when I heard a scream from the makeup room. What had happened was, Abel (who was always red-eyed because of all the Scotch he drank) saw a little Murine bottle and decided to put a few drops in his eyes, to reduce the redness. Well, what he did was put *collodion* in his eye—stupid Kiva had put collodion in a Murine bottle! God, was it painful for Abel! And this was about 20 minutes before we were supposed to go on, opening night! We thought it was the end of our act. The makeup girl used water to rinse it out and rinse it out. The curtain was delayed for about 20 minutes, but finally Abel could go on.

Picture in your mind, on the big stage of the Teatro Iris, a Chicago street set; on it are old cars and at least 30 or 40 extras, dancers and other people walking back and forth making it look like a busy street. You hear a car chase off-scene, the sound of a police siren and the screeching of brakes. The extras on stage run about like they're in a panic. Finally there's the sound of a big crash.

In Mexico, the poor people would go to a place like the Teatro Iris, which was government-run and the admission was maybe five pesos, and the society people and their beautiful women would go to plush, expensive nightclubs like the Los Globus. This picture is of Evangelina and me during a Teatro Iris show.

At that point, three stuntmen run out on stage—my brother Charlie and two Mexican stuntmen, all playing gangsters. They come on firing their guns (blanks, of course) back into the wings, at whoever is chasing them. Then the announcer says, "Los Intocables!," which means "The Untouchables" in Spanish, and onto the stage come Nick, Abel and me in our Untouchables outfits, shooting at the gangsters. The gangsters run off the stage and into the audience, and the Untouchables go after them. All of us are firing our guns and the audience is going crazy. Then we all come back up on stage and we have a big fight. I knock out one gangster and Abel knocks out another, and the only one left is Charlie. Well, Charlie knocks Abel out, then he knocks *me* out, and now he's standing on the stage looking groggy and exhausted. Nick walks up to him like a gay guy and just taps him on the cheek, and Charlie collapses. There was a big laugh from the audience there, with some of the people shouting out, "Ole! Maricone!" That was our opening, the way we made our entrance.

At another point in the show, I said (in Spanish), "I'm Paul Picerni. I'm Italian. And Italians like to sing," and I sang. Nick said, "I'm Nick Georgiade and I'm Greek, and *we* like to dance," and he did a little Greek dance. Abel said, "I'm Abel Fernandez and I'm Mexican," and again the audience went crazy. Then he said, "We like to make love," and that was where Evangelina jumped into his arms. This routine was part of in the act in both places, the Teatro Iris and the Los Globus. So was our opening number, a parody on the song "Together." Alan Copeland wrote a lot of great lyrics like (to the tune of *West Side Story*'s "She's So Pretty"):

Abel with Evangelina.

Hey Frank Nitti,
It's a pity,
That the city is after your hiiiiide.
Mr. Nitti, don't you know you're gonna end up fried?

As I mentioned earlier, most of the songs were from *West Side Story*, including a takeoff on "Maria" which was titled "Mafia." That was our show. At seven o'clock we would do it at the Teatro Iris for the general run of the Mexican population, and then at ten we did it at the nightclub for some very well-dressed, high-class Mexican people. At the nightclub, in addition to the full band, we had about 20 beautiful showgirls. I built the act around Nick playing the buffoon and getting all the laughs. Nick was the comedian, I was the straight man and Abel was the Mexican interpreter. It was a big production with comedy, music, action and, of course, the theme music from *The Untouchables.*

I should also mention that after opening night, Tony Romano suggested that one of my songs, "What Kind of Fool Am I?," be taken out of the act. I was crushed, but he was right. I never could hit the high notes like a Sammy Davis could!

Fighting with Charlie on stage.

The reviews were in the papers the next day and a few of them made us sound like a big fraud. One headline read "Intocables, No: Infumables!," which means "*The Untouchables* With No Fire"—the critic felt cheated and very upset that Robert Stack wasn't with us. I expected that would happen, so I quickly wrote "a telegram from Bob Stack" explaining why he wasn't part of the act and I cast a Mexican comic to come on stage to read it. What it said, in effect, was, "Dear people of Mexico, I'm so sorry I couldn't make it but I had another commitment. However, I want you to know that ever since I did *Bullfighter and the Lady* in Mexico, I have always had a place in my heart for the Mexican people"—that kind of b.s. Well, audiences cheered when they heard it, and they were placated!

We stayed at the Maria Isabel Hotel, right on the famous Paseo De La Reforma. The Maria Isabel was fairly new at the time, and we were on the twelfth floor—I had a suite which I shared with Charlie, and Abel and Nick were in rooms across the hall. We'd have our meetings in the living room of the suite, discussing possible changes and so on. One day while Nick, Abel and I were in the living room preparing for the show that night, Charlie went into the bedroom, out the window and onto the 12-inch ledge, and he walked along this ledge until he was outside the living room window. Then he started knocking on the window and calling out, "Paulie! Nick! Abel!" Well, I have acrophobia, and so does Nick— he's worse than I am. We saw Charlie standing on this ledge outside the window, 12 stories up, and we both turned green. I cried out, "Charlie, get off that ledge, you son of a bitch! Get off that ledge!" I almost passed out; it was a very scary moment. Abel didn't mind, Abel was laughing, but I was shaken by it, and Nick got violently sick and threw up, he was so upset.*

To get around, we had a limousine and a little black Mexican driver who looked like Sammy Davis, Jr. He was very proud that he was chauffeuring the Untouchables. One night we were in the limo after leaving the Los Globus and a Mercedes pulled up next to us at a stoplight. In the Mercedes were two well-dressed Mexican couples who had been at the Los Globus. Our chauffeur looked over at them and then pointed to us in the backseat and said very proudly, "Los Intocables!" ("*The Untouchables!*"). And the Mexican driver of the Mercedes reached over, opened the glove compartment of his car, took out a .45, pointed it at our chauffeur and repeated, "Los Intocables!" The little guy stepped on the gas and we took off!

Our rooms at the Maria Isabel Hotel were, of course, paid for by our impresaria Evangelina, but we had to pay for our incidentals like laundry and telephone calls and booze. At this time, Abel was drinking Scotch, which was about $32 a bottle. After the first week, we got our first hotel bills. I looked at mine and said, "Hey, $47, that's not too bad," and Nick said, "Mine is $32," and Abel said, "Jesus, my bill is only $480. Boy, what a good time I had for that kind of money!" He was drinking a bottle of Scotch a day, maybe two! One night, Abel came off stage and very excitedly said, "Were we *great*, were we *terrific* tonight!" And I looked at him and I growled, "You son of a bitch! If you drink before the show tomorrow night, *you're goin' home!*" He was so happy and loose that he

---

*Charlie did that to me again a few years later in San Francisco. Our friend Victor Paul was working in the movie *The Boston Strangler* up there and Charlie and I decided to spend a couple of days with him and go to a couple nice restaurants and clubs. Our hotel room was on the twenty-second floor and Charlie walked out on that ledge the same way. Oh my God, it just makes my heart palpitate. I don't think it's funny but *he* thinks it's hilarious!

As the Intocables, we wore our real Untouchables hats, but the guns were toys.

thought he was great on stage—when you're drunk, you think you're doing everything right. But he wasn't, he was half-bombed and slobbering his words! After that, he waited until after the show to start drinking.

Evangelina Elizondo was 38 or 40 years old, gorgeous—and anxious to play around. Evangelina didn't go on the make for Abel (she considered herself a high-class Mexican and Abel a low-class one) but she did go on the make for me, and, of course, I turned her down. She finally took up with Nick Georgiade—who, once he was shacked up with her, started making demands involving the show. I had set up the whole act and I was like the leader, and he began challenging my position. So we got into a real beef. Abel was with me all the way, he just loved me, but Nick was trying to throw his weight around: "Let's change this," "Let's change that . . . " He was getting so many laughs in the show that he'd started thinking he was the star.

There was more friction when Evangelina booked the three of us into a movie called *La Edad de la Violencia* that happened to be in production while we were down there. It was a gangster movie, and she was clever enough to get us in it, *playing* gangsters—it would only be one day's work, and the offer was $6,000 for the day's work, 2,000 apiece. When I look back on that situation now, 2,000 apiece seems fair, but at the time I thought, "No, no, no, no. I'm a well-established movie actor, and my *Untouchables* salary is a lot better than Nick and Abel's. I should get more than Abel and Nick." I felt that I should get 3,000 and they should get 1,500 apiece, or something like that. I wouldn't budge, I told Evangelina that was the way it had to be, and eventually I did get the biggest chunk—I ended up with 2,500, Nick with 2,000 and Abel, who was the peacemaker, the one who didn't want to cause trouble, with 1,500. Abel didn't give a shit about money; all he wanted was his bottle of Scotch!

The three of us picked up a few extra dollars making an appearance in the Mexican-made *La Edad de la Violencia*.

But the battle over the movie salary was another point that caused us to get rid of Nick. When we finished our two-week engagement in Mexico City, we were supposed to move on to Puerto Rico. However, I told our manager, Marvin Fisher, that I wasn't going to do it anymore with Nick and Evangelina; that was *it*. But now, as long as we were in Mexico anyway, I suggested to Abel, Charlie and Marvin, "Let's all go to Acapulco and have a little vacation."

A chauffeur named Jose took us in his big Buick Road Master the 250 miles to Acapulco and we checked into the Las Brisas Hotel, a beautiful place where each two-story cottage had its own swimming pool. As soon as we got there, Charlie dove off the second story into the pool—and then Abel did the same thing! Abel was a frustrated stuntman!

One night while we were driving around Acapulco, I noticed a nightclub right on the water called the Bumbum Club (pronounced *boom boom*). It wasn't as elaborate as the Los Globus but it was a nice place, and there were live shows there. I suggested to Marvin, "Why don't you try and book us in this club? Maybe we can pick up some money down here," and he said, "Good idea!" Marvin went to the club and, sure enough, the owner was *very* interested. I can still picture his face—he looked like Oscar Homolka, a real tough guy, so let's call him Oscar. Marvin and Oscar made a deal: $500 a night plus a percentage of the house over a certain amount of money.

With Nick now gone, I decided to give his part to Charlie—and I thought he played it even better than Nick did! We hired a couple of stuntmen, we rehearsed a couple of days with Charlie now in the act, we rehearsed the girls that we needed, we opened at the Bumbum Club and the place was *packed*. It looked as though everybody in Acapulco came! Marvin went to Oscar at the end of the evening and asked, "What about our percentage?" He said, "Awww, we didn't quite make the guarantee . . . " Well, for the whole week that we appeared, the place was jammed every night—the people down there loved **The Untouchables**—but, according to Oscar, we never *did* make the guarantee! He was always able to get away with telling us that, even though (after opening night) Marvin *sat next to the cash register* every night to keep tabs on things. So we never made any extra money over and above our salaries, but we had a lot of fun.

Marie flew down to join us, we all met her at the airport, and we had a great time—we were treated *royally* in Acapulco. We went to see the cliff divers and we were wined and dined, and everything was first-class. We also enjoyed going to Roquetta Island. At that time, the only way to get there was by boat, and there was no pier. The boat would hit the shore and you'd jump over the side onto the beach. Well, Marie fell off the boat into the water! On Roquetta Island they have the borracio burros (drunken donkeys) that drink beer; you put the beer bottle in the sand and a burro picks it up out of the sand and drinks. Every time I go to Acapulco, I go to Roquetta Island because they have the borracio burros and they have great huachinango, which is red snapper smothered in garlic and grilled—*so* good!

There was also a big water ski show in Acapulco—about 100 girls on skis and big motor launches pulling them around the Bay in all kinds of formations. The owner of the water ski show loved *The Untouchables* and one day he insisted on taking us out on a speedboat. He took us all over Acapulco Bay water skiing, and it was a lot of fun. I had a 16mm movie camera with me, and at one point I said to Charlie and Abel, "Why don't you guys come by the pier in the speedboat? I'll be on the pier and I'll take movies of you going by." Aboard the boat there was a driver, his assistant, Charlie and Abel. As it came past the pier going about 40 MPH, Charlie decided to do a flip off the side. And Abel, the frustrated stuntman, of course, then had to do it too—but when *he* hit the water, he was knocked unconscious! When you jump in the water at that speed, you have to know how to hit, or it's like landing on cement. Fortunately, the driver's assistant was there to dive in the water and grab Abel and save him. I got that on movie film, Abel hitting the water like a rock.

On Roquetta Island in Acapulco: Marvin Fisher, me, Abel, Charlie and our chauffeur.

After about two weeks in Acapulco, we got back in the Buick Road Master with our driver Jose and started back through the mountains toward Mexico City. The car was really loaded down— me and Marie, Charlie, Abel, Marvin Fisher and Jose the driver. And in the trunk and the backseat was all our luggage plus all our props, the guns, the costumes and so on. There must have been a number of recent rockslides in those mountains because there were lots of rocks in the road, and, sure enough, in the cold middle of the night, 11 or 12 o'clock, we were going down this pitch black mountain road and we hit a boulder the size of a basketball, or bigger. It put a hole in the oil pan of the car, and as we continued on, all the oil leaked out. Abel got under the car and found the hole, and he tried to plug it: He sharpened a little piece of wood to a point with my Boy Scout knife, wrapped a rag around it and hammered it into the hole. (I guess he thought it was a canoe!) Jose had a couple of extra quart cans of oil, which he then put in, and that took us a *little* further, but it still leaked out. So there we were in the middle of the mountains late at night, dark and cold, with no oil, no way to continue on. Somebody had told us that in those mountains there were a lot of bandidos—Indian bandits who would sometimes stop cars and rob them. So it was scary.

We waited and waited, and finally a car came along from the other direction and the driver agreed to give Marie, Jose and me a lift back to a village that we passed maybe a half-hour earlier, to get a five-gallon can of oil that we could put in the Buick. After the three of us left, it was just Abel, Charlie and Marvin in the Buick. Marvin was a sweetheart of a guy, but kinda timid, so, of course, he was frightened. *Really* frightened. Charlie having a sense of humor, he took advantage of that. He looked out the window and pretended to spot a bandido out in the darkness: "Abel . . . did you see that guy behind the rock?"

Abel: "Where? Where?"

"Over there—see him? See him??" Charlie whispered. "He just ducked down!"

Abel was in on the gag, and pretty soon they were *both* doing it: "There he goes!," "Look! There's another one over there!" Marvin was scared shitless, he was panicky: "Oh my God, what are we gonna do? What are we gonna do??"

Charlie said, "Listen, in the trunk we've got the guns from the nightclub act. Abel, you sneak out your door, I'll sneak out mine. We'll get the guns and we'll load 'em with the blanks and we'll scare the shit out of 'em!"

"No, no!" Marvin cried out. "Don't antagonize 'em! Don't antagonize 'em!"

Charlie snarled, "Fuck you, we're gonna *do* it." With that, Abel and Charlie sneaked around the back of the car in the pitch black, opened the trunk and got out the guns—those were the days when you could transport guns back and forth without too many problems. They then loaded the guns up with the blanks. These blanks were full loads, the kind of blanks that go off like an explosion.

Charlie and Abel got back in the car and Abel said, "All right, Charlie, you take the one on the right side and I'll take the one on the left side. We jump out of the car on the count of three and we'll let 'em have it!"

"No, no, please, please, don't antagonize 'em!" Marvin babbled. "There may be 20 of 'em, you don't know *how* many are out there!"

Charlie and Abel paid no attention to him—Abel counted, "One . . . two . . . *three!*" and they jumped out of the car—*pow, pow, pow, pow, pow, pow!* Well, Marvin started to cry, and *peed his pants*—they literally scared the piss out of him!

Marie, Jose and I eventually came back with the five-gallon jug of oil and we got going again. In the next village I paid Jose off (and even gave him some extra money to get the car fixed) and we hired another car to take us the rest of the way to Mexico City. We checked back into the Maria Isabel Hotel and had to wait a few more days to get our visas cleared with the Mexican theatrical union (our appearance at the Bumbum Club had somehow violated our contract with Evangelina). Finally, Marie, Abel, Charlie and I left Mexico. Nick stayed with Evangelina—and Marvin, the poor guy, couldn't leave the country because he'd entered by car, and then sold the car. And that's against Mexican law!

Marvin did finally make it home. Abel gave up drinking Cutty Sark. I never did see Evangelina again. And Nick and I eventually forgot our differences and we've been close friends all through the years.

23
END OF THE ROAD WITH
THE UNTOUCHABLES

The last producer we had on *The Untouchables* was a real ass.

Lennie Freeman was a guy who thought he knew it all. I remembered Lennie from when he was an actor, before he became a TV producer. He produced some *Route 66* shows, and now he was our executive producer on *The Untouchables*. Bob Stack and his agent Bill Shiffrin brought Lennie in, I believe because Lennie gave them a b.s. story that he was going to do more episodes that centered on Eliot Ness. That wasn't right for the show. On *The Untouchables*, each episode's new bad guys were the "stars" and the Untouchables were the characters who were just *there* week after week. The audience did love us, but you can't do stories about Eliot Ness every week because after a while they just don't pay off.

The first episode Lennie produced was a race track story. Reading the script, I noticed that my character Lee Hobson wasn't the second lead in the story; he was now simply "in the pack" of other Untouchables. The first day of shooting we were at Hollywood Park Race Track and Lennie came out with us. I saw him outside my trailer, so I went up to him and I said, "You know, Lennie, my part in this episode is . . . *terrible*. For two years of the show now, Bob's had a lot of scenes with me; I've been the second lead. But *this* show, I'm not number two, I'm not even three. I'm *four*."

Lennie's comeback was, "You don't want to do the show?"

Now I was even *more* annoyed. "It's not that I don't wanna do the show," I said. "But I don't think it's right that you're kinda pushing me back."

He said, "Well, if you don't want to do the show this week, you don't have to. I can cut you out." He was showing his strength.

The conversation ended like that, so I went to Bob and I told him what I felt: "Lennie Freeman is new on the show, Bob, and he doesn't know our relationship and what's transpired before . . ." Well, Bob took care of it; either Bob or Bill Shiffrin let Lennie know "Paul is the Number Two guy" and that was the way it had to be. Lennie Freeman was a lousy actor who never "made it," and he was an even worse producer.

Up 'til now I've been writing mostly about the guys I met in the course of doing **The Untouchables** but there were also a number of notable women. One was Mrs. Eliot Ness, who visited the set one day. Ness was dead by then—in fact, he died even before the publication of his book on which the show was based. But Mrs. Ness, Betty, came to the set with their son, who I think was in his early teens. I wish I recalled more about that day, but I just remember meeting her and the boy. I met them only briefly, and never saw them again.

An episode called "Man Killer" provided a nice reunion with Ruth Roman, the leading lady in **Mara Maru** with Errol Flynn a decade before. In the interim between that movie and **The Untouchables**, she and her young son were aboard the Italian luxury liner the **Andrea Doria** when it went down in history (and in the Atlantic!) after colliding with another liner in the fog off Nantucket. Ruth's three-year-old son was lowered into a lifeboat, but when Ruth was halfway down the rope ladder, that lifeboat pulled away and she was separated from her child! They were later reunited but, needless to say, it was a very stressful experience for both of them! One day on the **Untouchables** set, Ruth told me the whole story. I always liked Ruth, and so it was good to work with her again.

Ida Lupino was a wonderful actress, a movie and TV director (one of the few in Hollywood) and the wife of actor Howard Duff. She directed a couple of **Untouchables** episodes, and we all thought she was marvelous. We called her "Mother"—that's what she liked to be called! At that point I'd already had the fun of meeting her and acting opposite her on an episode of **Four Star Playhouse** where she played a woman of 90 and then, in flashbacks, minus all the old-age makeup, the same character as a young woman, living in the Old West and falling in love with a cowboy. In the flashbacks, I was the cowboy, a character named Latigo Randy. It was a nice part and I even had a love scene with Ida where I had to kiss her. I got a little overzealous with my kiss—you might say it was like a French kiss!—and she pulled back and scolded me, "Paul. Howard wouldn't *like* that!"*

Abel, Nick and Bob showed up on the occasion of my 50th wedding anniversary.

One of the *Untouchables* episodes Ida directed had Lee Marvin as a guest star. In those days, Lee would occasionally not show up for work because he'd be on a bender, but on *this* show, I think because of Ida, he was on his best behavior. In the final scene, the Untouchables trapped Lee in a sewer under the city and he was like a cornered rat—a broken, frightened man. It was very dramatic. After Lee had rehearsed it, he was sitting next to me on the sound-stage; I shouldn't have done it, but I put my two cents in. "Lee," I said, "don't you think that maybe in this particular scene, your character would break down and cry?" He looked at me strangely and he said, "If *you* were playing the part, you might cry. If I play the part, I don't cry!" From that day on, I rarely put my two cents where another actor had his own ideas!

*On a *Bonanza* I had to kiss the gorgeous Patricia Medina. I kissed her like I kissed Ida—I got a little rambunctious again. This time I got slapped. But it was worth it.

Years later I was doing a **Starsky and Hutch** and the guy who played Starsky, Paul Michael Glaser, was in the same position I was in on **The Untouchables** that day I butted in with Lee Marvin: Glaser at that point had been starring in the show for two or three years and he thought he knew it all. I had a scene in an office where I was spooked by a voodoo doll and got hysterical. Glaser, David Soul (Hutch) and a wonderful black actor named Roscoe Lee Browne were also in the scene. Well, Glaser started telling the director what to do, telling the co-stars what to do, and he tried to tell *me* what to do: "Come on, you're not *doing* enough, you've gotta do *more!*" I got very upset but I didn't say anything. In between takes, I went into an adjacent room and I asked Roscoe Lee Browne, "Am I playing this scene right or is Glaser correct, is there something wrong?" Browne said, "You're playing it *exactly* right. Don't listen to that asshole. You play it the way you were playing it." So you young actors, try and remember those two incidents, and don't ever try to tell another actor how to play a scene. There are so many ways an actor can approach a scene, each actor has a different way of doing it, so don't try to impose yourself on another actor. That's a lesson I learned from experience.

The cake made for me on my 83rd birthday.

I still feel bad about what happened one time when I brought a guest onto the **Untouchables** set. Back in my Warner Brothers days, I did screen tests opposite a lot of actresses, and I never forgot one beautiful brunette, a total unknown who couldn't have been more than 21, who was up for the lead in **Force of Arms** (eventually played by Nancy Olson). I never got to play a real good love scene in a film, but in this screen test of hers we did a terrific love scene, me playing the Bill Holden part. The girl in that test was Frances Zucco, the daughter of George Zucco, the famous monster movie guy from the old Mummy series. Well, several years later she called me, I think to see if I could get a part for her father in an episode of **The Untouchables**. I'm Italian, I thought *he* was Italian (the name Zucco is Italian), so I invited him to the set. I always enjoyed helping out-of-work actors. I didn't specify that I was going to get George a job, or that I was going to be able to entertain him or anything; I just said, "Come by the set and I'll introduce you to Bob Stack and to some of the other people, and maybe something will happen." I was doing it as a favor to Frances.

George arrived around 11:30 or 12. For a man his age, he looked pretty strong, and I thought he was in good shape. I introduced him to Bob and to the director, and to whoever else was on the set. He sat down in a director's chair and I spent as much time with him as I could. But when it came time for lunch, I guess I wasn't even *thinking* about Zucco at that moment, because when Bob said, "Let's go to lunch," I jumped into Bob's car with him and we took off for Tracton's—leaving George Zucco behind on the set! About an hour later we came back and there he was—and *was he angry*! He was steaming! "How *dare* you do this to me! You invite me here and then you leave me stranded, you don't even invite me to lunch!" I began to stammer out an apology—what I did was terrible, and I felt *so* bad about it. Of *course* I would have invited him to lunch, but the fact that he was there slipped my mind. It's been more than 40 years since that happened and I'm still embarrassed about it!

But for every "bad" memory like that, I remember a dozen great experiences, like the New Year's Eve when Desi invited us all out to his ranch. By this time, Desi and Lucy had split, and he had married a woman named Hirsch, the widow of a wealthy man who had owned a big stable of thoroughbreds. Nick and Marie and I attended, and it was a nice party. Lucy at the time was doing a show on Broadway, a big musical called **Wildcat**. During this New Year's Eve party the phone rang, and Desi picked it up in the big living room where we were all gathered. He shouted, "Be quiet, everybody! Be quiet! It's Lucy!" She was calling from New York to wish Desi, and *every*one there, a Happy New Year. As they talked, the tears came to Desi's eyes, and the conversation ended with Desi saying, "And I love you *too*, Lucy." We couldn't hear Lucy's half of the dialogue, of course, but from Desi's reaction we could tell there were still feelings between them. It was a nice moment.

* * * * * * *

A number of factors led up to the cancellation of **The Untouchables** at the end of its fourth year. For one thing, other studios came out with shows very similar to ours, trying to cut into our pie. There was **Target: The Corruptors** with Stephen McNally as an investigative reporter taking on the men behind the rackets; **The Roaring Twenties** with Rex Reason, the same kind of stories, set in New York City in the Prohibition Era; **Cain's Hundred** with Mark Richman as an ex-gangland lawyer now working on the right side of the law to smash organized crime; and a show I mentioned earlier, producer Quinn Martin's **The New Breed** with Leslie Nielsen and John Beradino, which was **The Untouchables** with modern-day cops. All these other shows didn't help the life of **The Untouchables**. Then, too, there was Lennie Freeman deciding to do stories spotlighting Eliot Ness, which wasn't what **Untouchables** fans wanted—I think that also killed off interest.

With Abel and Nick at a Hollywood autograph show.

But those weren't the real reasons that the show went off. The truth is that Desilu at one time had six or seven big shows (including *The Lucy Show* with Lucille Ball and *The Untouchables*) and they were shooting at three studios: on the old RKO lot, at Desilu Culver City, which was the old Selznick lot, and at Desilu Cahuenga. Well, by 1963 they had lost several shows and they just weren't getting enough income to pay for the three studios that they were maintaining. And believe it or not, *The Untouchables*, although it was a hit, was losing money every week. I'm a little hazy now on the figures, but if I'm remembering right the show was costing Desilu about $65,000 an episode to make, and ABC was paying them $65,000 for each episode. So Desilu didn't make any profit on it—Desilu was counting on making their money after the show went off the air and the reruns started running in syndication. Sometimes an episode would go over budget, it would cost Desilu (say) 75,000 but they were still only getting 65,000 from ABC, so they were *losing* money on the show even though it was popular! The only way they could make a profit was to release the show in reruns. But Desilu had a contract with ABC that stipulated that they (Desilu) couldn't syndicate the reruns until after the series went off the air—ABC didn't want the show competing with itself (the first-run *Untouchables* episodes on ABC competing with *Untouchables* reruns). So in order to recoup their money, Desilu had to stop shooting *The Untouchables* after four years and release it in reruns so they could get back on their feet.

It was a shame the show came to an end, because I think we could have gone for another two or three years. Fortunately for Desilu, it did become a big hit in syndication. The reruns played all over the world, and it was especially popular in France, Germany, Latin America and Japan. I don't think it ever played in Italy, though!

One day a few years later, maybe 1965, I tried to drive onto the Desilu lot and the cop at the gate stopped me. He asked me who I was and if I had a pass, and I told him I was Paul Picerni from *The Untouchables*. He was a new guard, he didn't know me from Adam and he wouldn't let me through the gate. Here I had been one of the stars of *The Untouchables*, one of Desilu's top series, and now I couldn't even get on the lot! Upset, I got on the phone and called

Gary Morton, now the husband of Lucille Ball, a hell of a guy who was now running the studio for her. "I hate to bother you," I told Gary, "but I want to talk to you about something and the guard won't let me through the gate." Gary spoke to the guard and I was allowed onto the lot, and I went to Gary's office and laid my cards on the table. "Gary, since the show ended, I haven't worked too much. I know I have a lot of residuals coming from *The Untouchables* and I was wondering if you'd be interested in buying me out at a discount."

"To tell you the truth, Paul, we sold *The Untouchables* to Paramount, so I'd have to call their lawyer." He did while I waited, but the answer came back no. Well, eventually it was a good thing for me that they didn't buy me out, because I ended up collecting probably five times the amount of money I would have been willing to settle for that day. In the 1970s, because of the success of the Godfather series and other gangster movies, the *Untouchables* reruns again came back to TV in a big way.

Six or eight years after that, I was playing golf with Bob Stack at a Los Angeles Police golf tournament at Rancho Park. Bob told me that Paramount wants to do *The Untouchables* again, and I said, "Well, why don't we *do* it, Bob?"

Bob said, "They want to do a feature," and again I said, "Let's *do* it!"

"Nah, we're too old," Bob shrugged.

"Shit, we're *not* too old, *we* can still do it," I insisted, but Bob didn't think we could, and I could tell that his mind was made up. Well, several years later, Bob did do an *Untouchables* feature—but he didn't use any of the old gang! It was a 1991 TV movie called *The Return of Eliot Ness* which, I have to say, was really lousy.

And now I'll tell the *real* behind-the-scenes story of how I got hired for *The Untouchables*, a story I didn't know myself for the first several *months* that I worked on the series. All during the 1959-60 season of the show, when Bob Stack was partnered with Jerry Paris and then Tony George, there were throughout the country Italian people up in arms about the depiction of Italians on *The Untouchables*. Pall Mall cigarettes was one of the show's sponsor, and so the Italian-run longshoreman's union in New York wouldn't load Pall Mall cigarettes onto ships to be shipped overseas. In fact,

Pall Mall cigarettes were "mysteriously" being left on docks all over America! Frank Sinatra hated the show, and Cardinal Spellman sided with Sinatra. Even J. Edgar Hoover hated *The Untouchables*. And the Mafia didn't like it either.

Johnny Roselli, whom I had first met in Monterey during the making of *Breakthrough*, was a representative of the Mafia. He was actually associated with Al Capone in the old days, and at this point (1960) he was running much of Las Vegas, mainly the Tropicana Hotel.

My old friend from Warner Brothers, Joe Breen, Jr., was very close to Johnny, and Joe was the one who told me this story after I'd been on *The Untouchables* for a while: Following the end of the first season, Johnny and Frank Sinatra had a meeting with Desi Arnaz at the Wilshire Hotel on Wilshire Boulevard in Beverly Hills, and Johnny and Frank told Desi that they didn't like the fact that all the gangsters on *The Untouchables* had Italian names. "Call 'em Smith, Jones, Pulaski, anything else you want, but cut down on the Italian names for the gangsters," Desi was told. And Johnny added, "And, by the way, why don't you have an Italian actor play one of the good guys?"

Desi answered, "I *do*. I have a character named Rico Rossi. He's Italian."

"Yeah," Johnny said, "but he's being played by a Greek. How 'bout getting an actor like Paul Picerni?"—Johnny still remembered me from our meeting on *Breakthrough*, where he told me, "Don't ever change your name." Johnny was a good-looking guy, he spoke very quietly, he was a real gentleman . . . but you knew what was underneath that attractive surface appearance, and you knew that if you crossed him, you were in trouble. So when Johnny said, "How 'bout Paul Picerni?," that was *it*—that was when Paul Picerni, Italian actor, was called in to play the second lead on *The Untouchables*.

* * * * * *

Most of the time, when you finish a show, you never see the people again. But I remained good friends with Bob Stack, Abel Fernandez and Nick Georgiade. Through the years we played golf together and saw each other on many other occasions. I see Nick every time I go to Las Vegas, and we're on the phone quite often.

Nick, me, Bob and Abel at Gemma's 2001 wedding.

He lives with his daughter Anastasia in Vegas, where he's done very well in real estate. Abel and his lovely wife Josey live in Whittier, California, surrounded by their beautiful family. Abel and I have been together at several recent autograph shows. Bob, Abel and Nick all showed up for my daughter Gemma's wedding at the Casa Italiana in October 2001.

As you know, we lost Bob in November of 2003. The way I found out was that a *Los Angeles Times* writer phoned my house to ask for a quote from me that he could use in the obituary he was writing for Bob; he assumed that I'd already heard the terrible news, but I had not. Even though I felt a great loss, I was able to give him a quote which did appear in the following day's paper:

BOB INHABITED THAT ROLE. IT WAS FLAWLESS. HE *WAS* ELIOT NESS AND WE JUST FOLLOWED HIS LEAD. MY THREE YEARS WITH ROBERT STACK ON *THE UNTOUCHABLES* WAS THE HIGH POINT OF MY ENTIRE CAREER.

24
DON'T GET TYPED, AND
DON'T GET SICK

Actors are supposed to become the characters they play. Robert Stack became Eliot Ness; Peter Falk became Columbo; Boris Karloff became Frankenstein's Monster; Bela Lugosi was *always* Dracula.

But some stars worked differently. They developed the characters to fit themselves. Every character John Wayne played was John Wayne. Gable was always Gable. Cagney was always Cagney. Monroe was always Monroe. And so on.

It's easy for an actor, after a long run in a television series, to be typecast. Some actors are cut out to be *actors*—each part they play is a different character. And some actors are cut out to be movie stars. Burt Lancaster tried so hard to become the characters he played. The Birdman of Alcatraz, Elmer Gantry, the Marine sergeant in *From Here to Eternity*, the Italian truck driver in *The Rose Tattoo*—Burt did his best to make them real people. But he was cut out to be a movie star. His personality was so strong that he couldn't camouflage it. He was always Burt Lancaster. He was a true movie star.

It works to your benefit either way. Your strong personality can make you a star, because it overpowers the characters you play. Or the repetition of one character can overpower your personality and make you a star. Jason Alexander will always be George Costanza and Michael Richards will always be Cosmo Kramer. Not that there's anything *wrong* with that!

Following a lengthy run as a character on a hit TV series, an actor will usually find that his career hits a stone wall when the show leaves the air. You get so established as your TV character that people can think of you only in that role. You'll be "typed." After *The Untouchables*, everybody in town thought of Bob Stack as Eliot Ness and he didn't work much for three years, until he finally got a new series, *The Name of the Game*. Well, I went through the same kind of dry spell. That's the point at which you have to start scrounging around and calling on your friends. Billy D'Angelo, the line producer of *Batman*, used me on a couple of episodes as one of the henchmen of Catwoman (Julie Newmar). It wasn't much of a role, but it was a two-parter, two weeks work, and so I did it for the money. Then Bob Crane put me in a *Hogan's Heroes*. And so on.

One of my neighbors was Johnny Stephens, a casting director who at the time was casting Fred MacMurray's TV series *My Three Sons*. My daughter Gina, who was eight or nine at the time, liked to play with Johnny's kids. Having been preceded in the Picerni lineup by four boys, Gina was very athletic: She played baseball and football with her four older brothers; she was the best swimmer and horseback rider; she was an outstanding athlete. In short, she was a real tomboy. One day Johnny called me and said, "Paul, the guest-star part in our next *My Three Sons* episode is a part that Gina would fit perfectly—*if she can act*. May I send you the script?"

Daughter Gina played Mike, a tomboy and neighborhood terror, in an episode of *My Three Sons*. Belatedly, I was given the role of her dad!

I didn't know if Gina could act or not; she *had* never acted, outside of some 8mm home movies that I made! But when I got the script, I saw that the part *would* be ideal for Gina: The character was a little tomboy who plays baseball. Gina read a few lines with me, and she was pretty darn good. So I took her in to read for Johnny and the director, Freddie de Cordova, later the producer of the Johnny Carson **Tonight Show**. Freddie agreed that she could do it.

The next day, Johnny called me and said, "There's a one-day part for Gina's father in the script. Would you mind playing it?" Of course, I agreed immediately. And so there I was, supporting my youngest daughter—and she was getting paid more money and would have better billing! It was a lot of fun. Gina was great in the show, and we made a perfect father-and-daughter team. Gina went on to do an episode of **The Flying Nun** show and a few other series; later on, she did stunts for Charlie on **Starsky and Hutch** and other shows. To this day, she still gets residuals from **Starsky and Hutch** and the movie

Another acting role for Gina, in an episode of **The Flying Nun** with baseball Hall of Famer Don Drysdale.

Private Benjamin, in which she played a "stunt part" as a member of Goldie Hawn's platoon. She also did a lot of the stunts for Goldie in that movie. But she's a lot happier today being a design carpenter and living in San Francisco.

A side note on **My Three Sons**: Fred MacMurray had an ideal set-up on that series. He didn't want to work the whole year 'round on the show, so he made a deal with the producers that he would come in and do all of his scenes for 26 shows (a year's worth of episodes) in a period of three months. To simplify things, Fred's character was often said to be away on business trips. That way, Fred could appear in some episodes sitting in a hotel room talking to members of his family on the telephone. The producers had to make a special arrangement with the Screen Actors Guild to enable them to accommodate Fred's schedule. It was an unusual deal, and I don't know if any other actor has ever had one like it.

Would you recognize us from *The Untouchables*? That's me and Bruce "Frank Nitti" Gordon in an episode of Lucille Ball's TV show.

By this point, 1964 or '65, I was open to any job where I could make a few bucks. One day I got a call from Spanky McFarland, who as a youngster played the leader of the kids in the old "Our Gang" shorts. Now he was an adult, of course, and he was doing publicity for some redneck who was running for the job of chief of the sheriff's department in Seattle, Washington. Spanky said, "We're gonna have a big rally for my friend at the ballpark and I've got Georgie Jessel coming to make an appearance. Would you and Nick Georgiade come up here and appear along with Georgie? If you do a five- or ten-minute routine, I'll give you and Nick airfare and hotel and 300 bucks apiece." I said I'd talk to Nick and get back to him.

Nick was agreeable, and so a few days later, he and I were on a plane to Seattle along with Georgie Jessel, a great comic from the old days and a good friend of George Burns and Eddie Cantor and all those veterans. On the plane, Nick, Georgie and I worked out a cockamamie routine where Georgie was Eliot Ness and Nick and I were his sidekicks.

In Seattle we met Spanky, who was then probably in his mid-thirties. He was a big man—over six feet tall and about 300 pounds. I remembered what a cute little kid he was, so it was weird to see that he had turned into this king-sized guy who reminded me of a carnival character, a con man. The fellow that Spanky was working for, the candidate for sheriff, was a real crook—and I got the feeling Spanky was just as bad!

On the night of the rally at the baseball stadium, there was a big crowd. It was getting to be time for us to go on, but we still hadn't seen our money. For Georgie, this set off alarm bells—he'd been around a long time and was a sharp guy, and he knew what to do in those situations. In one of the big stadium men's rooms, with Nick and me there, Georgie told Spanky that we weren't going on 'til we got our money. (Nick and I were supposed to get 300 apiece and Georgie 500.) Spanky assured us, "You'll get your money, you'll get your money . . . ," trying to get us to go out on the field and do our routine, but I agreed with Georgie and backed him up: "No, no, no, Spanky. We're not goin' on until we get the money." We were at an impasse, the clock was ticking and the crowd was waiting. Finally, Spanky's friend, the guy who was running for sheriff, joined us there in the men's room and whipped out a wad of hundred-dollar bills and paid us all off. Now, of course, we went out and we did the routine.

After the rally, Spanky told Nick and me, "I want you to come to my apartment; we're having a little party. Georgie's coming too." Nick and I went back to our hotel to clean up and get ready, and sure enough Spanky sent a car to pick us up. By the time we got to the apartment, Georgie was gone; Spanky had fixed him up with a hooker, and now Spanky was planning to fix Nick and me up with girls. We didn't want any part of *that*, but we had a few drinks with Spanky and the sheriff nominee and some girl. All of a sudden, the door burst open and this gangster-type guy, a real hoodlum, barged in. He looked at the group of us and then he went after the girl and started whacking the hell out of her! Evidently he was her boyfriend, and after slapping her around, he grabbed her and pulled her out of the place. I couldn't believe that adorable little Spanky from Our Gang grew up to be a big fat con man who was pulling shit like this!

As far as my acting career went, things remained slow. My buddy Phil Carey was also having a hard time getting work. One night Phil, his wife Maureen, Marie and I went for dinner to the Tail of the Cock restaurant on Ventura Boulevard and we talked about what we could do to revitalize our careers. Phil suggested we invest in a trip to New York and see if we could get some work there. There were still a few live shows shooting in New York, and my friend Harry Guardino was doing a TV newspaper drama called *The Reporter*. In fact, my brother Charlie was *already* working on *The Reporter*: I'd suggested to Harry that Charlie would be a good double for him. I'd also talked about it to the show's producer, Keefe Brasselle, my old buddy from Warner Brothers days. Keefe then hired Charlie to come to New York and work as stunt coordinator.

In New York, Phil and I shared a small suite at the St. Moritz Hotel and we saw Harry and Charlie, but unfortunately nothing was right for us in *The Reporter* (the whole series only lasted 13 episodes anyway). The whole trip was a waste. But I did run into Soupy Sales in a deli across from NBC; he was subbing for Johnny Carson on *The Tonight Show* for a week, and he asked me to be a guest. So all that came out of our New York trip was another appearance on *The Tonight Show*!

But when I came back from New York, a strange thing happened: Someone from ABC called Wilt Melnick because he had seen me on *The Tonight Show*, and this fellow asked Wilt if I'd be interested in doing a daytime series—a soap opera. Soaps were frowned upon in those days, the way movie actors looked down on doing TV in the beginning. They were the bottom of the ladder for an established actor. But I needed work, and this was work. Believe it or not, I was being offered the starring part, and the job would pay more than I was making on *The Untouchables*!

With Peggy McCay, who played my wife on the ABC soap opera The Young Marrieds.

Thus, Dr. Dan Garrett was "born" on ABC's new soap *The Young Marrieds*. The cast consisted of only six main characters: Dr. Garrett and his wife, played by the wonderful actress Peggy McCay; their neighbors, a couple played by Mike Mikler and Lee Meriwether (Miss America 1954); and a second young couple, playing newlyweds.

The Young Marrieds was shot live every day, five days a week. We would start rehearsing every morning at nine A.M., block the show and break for lunch. At one o'clock, we would have a technical rehearsal with the camera crew. At two, we would have a full dress rehearsal. At three, we would shoot the show. It went out live, so if you made a mistake, they didn't stop. At 3:30, when the show ended, you would take off your wardrobe and wash your face and they'd hand you the script for the *next* day's script. At four you'd sit around a table with the other actors and have a run-through of the next day's script and make a few minor changes. At six, you'd go home and learn all your dialogue for tomorrow. First it was Marie cueing me on my lines at home every night, but eventually she got tired of it. Then I went through all the kids. (C.P. lasted the longest!) And somewhere in there, you also had to get some *sleep!* We went through this routine every day, five days a week. Believe me, it was tough.

Lee Meriwether had been pressured to do the show and had agreed. She was also rehearsing a play with Carroll O'Connor at this same time. But when the play people found out she had signed up for **The Young Marrieds** they told her, "You can't *do* a soap opera. You're signed to do our play. Get yourself out of it." So Lee gave her notice the very first day when she showed up for rehearsal! After just two weeks, she left the show.

On the Monday after her last episode, an actress who was as beautiful as a Miss America, Susan Brown, replaced her in the role of Mike Mikler's wife. Believe it or not, none of the crew noticed that it was no longer Lee in the role. Nor did the audience. No one could tell the difference! I said to myself, "Oh, boy . . . an actor can be replaced on *this* show very easily!"

As I mentioned earlier, there were only six regulars on **The Young Marrieds**. Today's soaps have *30* regulars, and so none of them has to learn a large number of lines. But *we* did. If you forgot your lines, you could always look at the teleprompter, an off-camera screen on which your dialogue is displayed—it rolls by as you speak, controlled by a technician. The only trouble with teleprompters is that, if you're making eye contact with another actor in the scene and you forget your lines, now your eyes have to shift to the teleprompter. The audience sees your eyes going back and forth and they start wondering what's going on. In an earlier chapter I described how on **Dragnet** Jack Webb would tell his actors, "Don't look at me, just look at the teleprompter and read your lines." On Raymond Burr's show **Perry Mason**, Ray never looked at the other actors, he used the teleprompter *all* the time, because he had oodles of dialogue.

I didn't know how to use teleprompters. Having been in plays and motion pictures, I had to memorize all my lines and look directly at the other actor or actress when I delivered them. So I never did use the teleprompters, I learned 15 or 20 pages every night.

One weekend I was planning to go on a deer hunting trip to Mammoth Lake with my brother Charlie, Harry Guardino and my buddies Lou Enterante and Vic Romito. (Vic was a stand-in and extra from waaay back—he worked on the silent **Ben-Hur**.) The plan was to drive there on Friday night and come back Sunday night. Before I left, Marie asked, "Paul, what about learning your dialogue for Monday?" I said, "Well, I'll look it over. And if worst comes to worst, I can always use the teleprompters."

We went hunting and we didn't get any deer, but we had a lot of laughs with Harry, Vic, Lou and my brother along. And Monday morning I went in to work on **The Young Marrieds** not knowing one word of dialogue—I hadn't even *looked* at the script and I was tired from walking the mountains. Then, disaster: I got on the set and tried to use the teleprompters, and realized that I didn't know how to do it. It was stressful, it was embarrassing, my eyes were going back and forth from the other actors to the teleprompter—that day on **The Young Marrieds** set was one of the worst days of my life as an actor. Any aspiring actors who are reading this: You have *got* to be prepared, you have *got* to do your homework, and you have *got* to know what you're doing.

One young actor came onto **The Young Marrieds** and played a minor role in several episodes. We had lunch a few days and I liked him very much—I thought he was very bright and clever. Being the "older actor," I handed out some free advice one day, telling him, "Chuck, you should think about producing and directing. You have a great mind and you seem to have a good talent as a writer. But as far as being an actor . . . I think you oughta forget about it. Just think about directing and producing and writing." Do you know who the actor turned out to be? Charles Grodin. I never *dreamed* that he would become as big as he did in films! In the course of my career I've told two young actors to give it up, Charles Bronson and Charles Grodin!

After two years of the grind of **The Young Marrieds** (about 250 episodes), I was exhausted. But the show was successful; in fact, it was getting ratings higher than its stablemate **General Hospital**, a soap opera with my pal Johnny Beradino starring as Dr. Hardy.

NBC had a hit late-night show (*The Tonight Show*) and ABC wanted to have one too, so they hired Joey Bishop to do a talk show. But for this to happen, they needed a soundstage with an audience area. The *Young Marrieds* soundstage at ABC, at Prospect and Talmadge in Hollywood, had an audience area. Believe it or not, ABC dropped *The Young Marrieds* because they needed our soundstage for Joey Bishop; we were replaced in that 3-3:30 time slot by *The Nurses*, a soap out of New York where they had a soundstage available. But before ABC could get our soundstage ready and converted for the Bishop show, time ran out; the Bishop show was shot instead at the old El Capitan Theater in Hollywood. We'd been cancelled to make room for Joey Bishop, and then it wasn't shot on our soundstage after all! And after all *that*, the Bishop show flopped! It was gone in a short time.

After *The Young Marrieds* was cancelled, I was out of work again. Not only was I out of work, but I was physically exhausted. The stress of learning all those lines day in and day out for two years had taken its toll. I went to see my physician, Dr. Saliba, who gave me a complete physical and then sent me to the Sansum Clinic in Santa Barbara for two weeks of tests. It was determined that I had developed diabetes.

For the first time in my life, I felt defeated, really down. I had never been sick before, so I didn't understand what was happening. No longer would I be able to go on location. I had to watch what I ate. I couldn't drink wine or alcohol. I had to exercise regularly. I had to avoid sugar. I couldn't have a *donut*. I might black out from *low* blood sugar. I might go into a coma from *high* blood sugar. I was a mess. "My life is over. My career is ended." I thought I could never act again. That was my mental state.

With all of that, I was out of work, and I had eight kids to support, all of them still in private schools. Nick Cravat and I were still very close; he was Uncle Nick to my kids, and he and I would run at Crespi High School track in the morning several days a week. When Burt Lancaster wasn't busy, he would run with us. At this time, Burt was preparing to make *The Scalphunters*, a fairly low-budget Levy-Gardner-Laven Western for United Artists release. Burt told me I could play one of the Scalphunters; it wasn't going to be much of a part, but the job would run for six weeks in

Philip, Mike, Gina and my nephew Charlie (holding picture) get a chance to meet TV's _Batman_, Adam West.

Durango, Mexico.

Could I do it? Would I be able to go on location with my condition and be able to perform? These were the thoughts that went through my head.

25
THE SCALPHUNTERS

D r. Saliba assured me I would be physically capable of doing *The Scalphunters*; I just had to take Diabanese pills before each meal and watch what I ate. I wasn't so sure. I knew *one* thing, though: I wouldn't have to worry about exercise. I'd be getting plenty of *that* riding horses and scalping Indians in the film!

In *The Scalphunters*, Burt Lancaster starred as a trapper who teams with an escaped slave (Ossie Davis) to recover his annual yield of furs, stolen by Telly Savalas' ruthless Scalphunter gang. Shelley Winters played Telly's cigar-smoking mistress and I was one of Telly's Scalphunters, along with Dabney Coleman, Dan Vadis, several stunt-men and, of course, Nick Cravat. (Nick got his screen name "Cravat" from an old Western he had seen; an Oscar winner called *Cimarron* with Richard Dix as "Yancey Cravat." In fact, Nick's character name in *The Scalphunters* was Yancy!) The director was Sydney Pollack and *Scalphunters* was one of his first pictures; Burt had "discovered" him when he (Sydney) was a dialogue director.

Nick and I flew down together to Mazatlán, taking two crates of equipment (pistols and rifles) with us. We were picked up at the airport by a studio driver and taken to Durango, where we met up with Telly. Durango was a small, sleepy town with a large Mexican federal prison. Nick and I and the rest of the "lowbrow actors" had rooms at a motel (right next door to the prison!), Telly had a suite at the Posada Duran and Burt Lancaster and Jackie Bone, the hairdresser with whom he was living, had a rented house. I knew I'd be getting my required exercise just by doing the action scenes in the movie, but I was happy to also learn that there was a nine-hole golf course where I could play on my days off.

I had heard that, early in Shelley Winters' career, around the time of *A Double Life*, she and Burt had a romance. But now this was 20 years later and Shelley was quite matronly, a little overweight—not nearly as gorgeous as she was when she was young. Nevertheless, the first thing she did was make a move on Burt. But Burt didn't pay any attention. Then she made a move on Telly, who was playing her lover in the movie but had no intention of doing so in real life! Then she made a move on *me*, and I didn't take the bait. Finally she ended up with another one of the Scalphunters, Dan Vadis, an actor who had done muscleman and gladiator-type movies in Europe. After just a short time, Shelley and Dan were going at it pretty good.

One night we were getting ready to shoot a big outdoor scene featuring all the Scalphunters and six or eight girls playing Mexican hookers. The shot was to start on a goat on a spit over an open fire, and Dan was going to slice a piece of meat off the goat and sample it. Then the camera, on a big crane, would pull back and show the whole scene of the Scalphunters and all the women having a great time singing, dancing and making merry. As we were getting ready to rehearse, the prop man said to Dan, "Don't slice the meat off the goat in the rehearsals, or by the time we get to the take the goat will look lousy. Wait for the take." And Dan's reaction was to tell the prop man, "Ahhh, fuck you!" (Dan was always smoking pot or doing some kind of drugs, so he was always half out of it.) This was a big shot that we were preparing to do and a lot of rehearsal was required, and Dan kept slicing meat off the goat. Finally the prop man got a-hold of Sydney, our director, on the side and he said, "Mr. Pollack, would you tell Mr. Vadis not to cut the goat in the rehearsals? Tell him to wait for the take. Otherwise, half the goat'll be gone!" So Sydney, up on the camera boom with the camera operator, politely called out, "Oh, Dan, Dan! Don't cut the meat in the rehearsal, wait for the take." And Dan said, "Fuck you!"—this time to Sydney Pollack the director!

Sydney said, "*What?*" and again Dan said, in front of the whole company, "Go *fuck* yourself!" And at that point, Sydney said, "Get off the set. You're fired!" Then Sydney said to the first assistant, "Send him home. Get him *out* of here." As Dan left, Sydney told me that I would be taking Dan's place in the shot, cutting the sliver

That's me as one of the Scalphunters. We shot the picture in Mexico.

of meat off the goat.

We were shooting close to a river and Dan wandered away, down toward its banks. Shelley went down there after him and they chatted and then she came back up to the set and went into a tirade: "You can't do that! You can't fire Dan! If you fire *him*, you fire *me* too!"— she screamed and yelled at Sydney for firing Dan. But Sydney was serious, and he had no intention of bringing Dan back. At that point, Burt stepped in and tried to pacify Shelley—Burt was one of the producers of the picture along with Levy, Gardner and Laven, and he knew they needed Shelley. He didn't give a shit about Dan, he could get another Scalphunter, but Shelley he needed! (Dan still had something left to do in the picture, a fight scene with Burt, but they could have replaced Dan easily, any one of the stunt guys could have done the fight.) Shelley continued to make a scene, there was crying and sobbing, and eventually Burt said, "You make Dan come back here and apologize to Sydney in front of the whole company, and we'll take him back." And Dan, half-stoned, wouldn't do it! It must have been an hour before they got the situation resolved. Dan finally agreed to apologize, and we got on with the shot.

The day after Shelley put her job on the line by fighting for her lover, she returned to Hollywood because she was up for a Golden Globe for her performance in *Alfie* with Michael Caine.* With the producers' blessings she attended the awards banquet (she didn't win) and came back two days later. In the meantime, Dan Vadis took up with one of the Mexican hookers and forgot all about Shelley! That was Dan for you! When Shelley came back and found out about this, she was ready to kill him right in front of everybody! They had a big fight and she called him a son of a bitch. And then *she* took up with Armando Silvestre, the Mexican actor who played the Indian chief in the show. That was Shelley for you!

Shelley would always be sweet as pie until she was well established in a film, and then she would become a pain in the ass and very demanding. One day when we were sitting on the set, one of the producers, Jules Levy, came by. Spotting him, Shelley started to cry. With tears running down her cheeks, she said, "I don't understand it, Jules. Burt has his own makeup man, why don't I have *my* own makeup man? Why can't I get Bill Phillips down here? *You* know he's my makeup man. I want my own makeup man!"

"Shelley, we can't *afford* it," Jules said. "We've got two makeup men down here already, and we can't afford a third."

"Well, I want my own makeup man," Shelley insisted, continuing to cry. Jules finally said, "All right, all right, I'll fly Bill Phillips down. He'll be here tomorrow," and he walked away. As soon as he was out of earshot, the "tearful" Shelley instantly became the laughing Shelley and said, "Boy, I got him, didn't I, fellas? Pretty good performance, right?"

Once she did 35 takes in a scene with Telly. Telly had to take a frying pan out of the fire, walk a few steps, throw away whatever

---

*Talking to me about *Alfie* one day, Shelley said, "You know, I didn't get any salary for that picture. What they did was give me a new Rolls-Royce for playing the part." That gave me an idea that I later used for Telly several times, and I'll tell you about that later.

was in the pan and then walk back to the fire. She inevitably would get to a certain point in the scene and then say, "Oh, I would like to do it again." If it had been me in the scene with her, I would have wanted to punch her. But Telly went on and on and did it 35 times and had tremendous patience.

The thing that made this trip to Mexico so sensational for me was being with Telly. We'd worked together before, of course, on *The Untouchables*, but it was in Durango on *The Scalphunters* that we bonded and became such good friends that we saw each other constantly, day in and day out on the set, at dinner and at night. Something about Telly just registered with me. He was from New York and I'm from New York, but it was more than that, there was something about him. He was so bright and so clever. He was also a con man, but lovable and entertaining. And such a marvelous storyteller. Over the years, stories of his that I heard for the first time in Durango I heard 30 *more* times, as he'd relate them to other people, but he told them so well that I enjoyed them every time.

Durango was about 200 miles due east of the beautiful beach city of Mazatlán. In 1967, the Mazatlán Hotel was the best of the few hotels on the sandy beaches of Olas Altas Bay. One weekend we drove there in Telly's big Lincoln Town Car—me, Telly, Nick Cravat and Telly's go-fer, David Gross. We had a terrific time—there's great jumbo shrimp in Mazatlán!—and on Monday morning we headed back to Durango, where we had to be at work at ten o'clock.

When we got to the top of the mountain that separates Mazatlán from Durango, we ran out of gas. Telly always seemed to tempt fate: We started down the mountain with a dead engine, coasting, no power steering and no power brakes. Whenever I got into a dangerous situation with Telly driving, he would say either, "Don't worry, you're in your mother's arms!" or "I'm one of the top three drivers in the world." It was really precarious going down the mountain. Screeching around corners, the big Lincoln was straining to stay on the road. I did something I did numerous times when driving with Telly: I made an act of contrition and put my future in the hands of the Lord!

At last we reached the bottom of the mountain and rolled to a stop. In the middle of nowhere. It was about 9:15. No way would we get to work on time.

But with Telly's luck, the first vehicle that came along was a tow truck. It must have been Telly's guardian angel driving it! The driver sold us a can of gas and we were on our way. We got to work with ten minutes to spare!

Telly was making $5,000 a week on *The Scalphunters* and getting $1500 a week per diem. But you'd think he was making a million. It was impossible to pick up a check when Telly was around. One night the Jaffe brothers (the heads of United Artists) and Levy, Gardner and Laven, the producers, came down to Durango and we all went out to dinner—Burt, Shelley, Ossie Davis, Telly, Nick, me, Sydney Pollack—14 of us. When the check came, *Telly* picked it up. I couldn't figure him out. With all that brass there, someone else should have taken it; Telly wasn't that big at the time. But I later learned from Telly that Omar Sharif had told him, "When you throw bread out to the ocean, it breaks up into small pieces and comes back to you on each wave a thousandfold." It's true. The more Telly spent, the more he made. (I've learned to do that too—I *love* to pick up checks. I'm old enough now to know that you can't take it with you. I've seen friends of mine die and leave millions, and then watched their children fight over it. So don't be afraid to pick up a check. The money will come back to you double and then some.)

While on that *Scalphunters* location, I taught Telly how to play bridge because I knew that Burt liked bridge. Then, in order to have a fourth for bridge, Burt flew down Solly Biano, the Warner Brothers talent guy who had discovered Burt at the Pantages Theater and discovered *me* at the Las Palmas Theater. Every night the four of us would sit on the Posada Duran patio and play bridge. We'd be out there 'til three or four in the morning, and if we didn't have to work the next day we'd be at it 'til five or six, when the sun came up. We'd play for pesos, and every night Telly and I would owe them a bundle of pesos! Solly was an excellent player and so was Burt, and they were always partners; Telly and I were outclassed. But Burt loved beating us, he didn't give a damn. Every night Telly and I would owe Burt and Solly three, four hundred pesos, which didn't amount to a *lot* of money—one peso was about a dime.

In another moment, my Scalphunter character will be shot off that rock by
Burt Lancaster.

This one night when we were playing, it must be two o'clock in the morning and Telly was sitting across from me (dozing), Burt was on my left and Solly on my right. Burt got a terrific hand and he bid "two no trump," which means that he had like 22, 24 points in his hand. (There's only 40 points in the whole deck.) When your partner bids two of anything, that's what's called a demand bid and you can't pass, you *must* name some suit. So Solly gave him a bid because he *had* to. Burt was tingling with excitement. But after it went around a few more times, I was able to tell that things weren't going well for Burt and Solly. I had 14 points in my hand, so when Burt got up to a slam bid, I said, "Double," which means whatever points we got in this hand would be doubled. With 14 points in my hand, I knew he *couldn't* make a slam bid. Burt looked at me and defiantly he said, "*Re*-double!" Well, when Solly put down the dummy and he didn't have a single point, Burt almost shit. He slammed the table hard enough that Telly came out of his doze, and then Burt and Solly started going back and forth at each other: "Solly, why the hell did you bid?," "Well, you gave me a demand bid!," "You shouldn't have bid with a hand like that!," "You gave me a demand bid, I *had* to bid!" Loud and excited, they started having a big argument—I was just barely holding in my laughter! Telly was now wide awake from all the yelling.

Finally they finished arguing, but Burt was still furious, and also determined to play the hand out. To make a long story short, not only did we set them, but we set them six down, doubled and re-doubled, and it amounted to about 3,000 points at a peso a point! I slapped the table and exuberantly I yelled out, "We *got* 'em, Telly, we *got* 'em! Finally, we beat the bastards!" I reached out across the table to shake Telly's hand—and Burt, furious, slapped me in the face!

"You're a *loser*," he growled at me. "You're a *born loser*. You've been a loser all your fucking *life!*"

I grabbed his hand and through gritted teeth I said, "Don't you do that, Burt! What the hell's the matter with you? Are you fuckin' *crazy?*"

Telly looked at me and he started shaking his head like "no, no, no," trying to get across to me, "Don't go any further. Don't challenge him." But I was ready to challenge him—I didn't give a shit about Burt Lancaster or the movie or anything, because he had slapped me. It didn't really hurt, it was just two fingers across the cheek, but the mere fact that he slapped me made me furious. But I took Telly's unspoken advice, "Don't take it any further." I threw his hand down, I stared at him, I got up from the table and I walked out.

I later went up to Telly's room and we talked about what had happened, rehashed it all, before I went to my motel and went to bed. The next day was Sunday and at about 10 or 11 o'clock Telly called me and said, "Listen, Burt just called me. He asked if I wanted to play golf today. I said, yeah, I'd love to. And then Burt said, 'Oh, bring Paul along too.'"

Inviting me to golf, that was Burt's way of apologizing. And I accepted the invitation (and Burt's unspoken apology) and I played golf with them. It was Telly and me against Burt and Jackie, his girlfriend. And inevitably they beat us at golf too!

An aside: Burt once said to me, "Why don't you get a group of your friends and we'll have a bridge game at your house?" Marie invited about ten of our bridge friends over, along with Burt and his girlfriend Jackie Bone. We set up four four-player tables in the living room and had a big spread of cold cuts, drinks and other goodies on the dining room table. The evening was going great, Burt was having a good time, and all the other people were enjoying being in the same room playing bridge with the great Burt Lancaster. Suddenly all the "good vibes" stopped with a thundering roar: I was at a table with Burt and Marie and a delightful lady—I emphasize *lady*—named Mrs. Wainwright, Burt's partner, when in the process of bidding four spades, Burt let out with a resounding fart. Everybody at the four tables looked up and all talk ended. They all looked in our direction, astounded. Burt continued as if nothing had happened; "Your bid, Paul," he said quietly. I was dumbstruck. He was so concentrated on his bridge hand that I don't think he knew what he did! Either that, or he didn't care; maybe to him, it was merely a natural function of the body. It was this power of concentration that made him a great star.

* * * * * * *

About six weeks into the shooting of **The Scalphunters**, we were coming up on the day when they were going to film a scene of me being shot and killed by Burt, my last scene in the picture. After that, I was scheduled to go home. (The picture was going to go on shooting another four weeks.) One day I said to Burt, "I've got to talk to you," and he said, "Okay, let's take a walk." As we strolled through the woods, I told him I thought it'd be much more effective if he shot and killed Dabney Coleman instead of me. I told him that, story-wise, I had a good reason for that, but actually I just wanted to get another four weeks work. I was having a lot of fun with Telly, he and Burt and I were playing golf on our days off—I didn't want to be killed off and sent home. I wanted them to kill off Dabney Coleman and send *him* home! Anyway, I told Burt my bogus "story reason" why my character should continue to live and Dabney's should die, and as we walked through the woods, Burt thought about it and thought about it. Finally said, "You know something? You might be right. Let me discuss it with Sydney." Well, he did speak to Sydney, but what I didn't know was that Dabney was Sydney's tennis teacher! To make a long story short, Burt came back to me and said, "Sorry, Paul, Sydney didn't go for it," so I ended up getting killed and going home. It was a phony "story reason" and Sydney saw right through it. But Burt didn't dismiss it, he actually thought about it. Burt was good to me.

I've already mentioned that Burt and Nick Cravat and I would run the quarter-mile track at Crespi High School in Tarzana; afterwards we'd have breakfast at a coffee shop. One morning at the track, when Nick wasn't there, when it was just Burt and me, I said to him after the run, "Instead of going to the coffee shop, come to my house. Marie will fix us some eggs." He said okay and came to the house and he sat at our table and Marie made us a nice bacon-and-eggs breakfast. My daughter Nicci, who was 18 or 19 and a freshman at Pierce College, came walking into the kitchen in her pajamas, and who's sitting in her kitchen but Burt Lancaster. I introduced them and Burt asked her how she was, and asked about college. She said, "I'm majoring in Communications Arts and it's a big rough day for me today because it is finals." Burt chatted and chatted with her, because he loved young people—and also because I think he was a frustrated teacher! Being asked about her school and her classes by Burt Lancaster really made Nicci's day.

Nick Cravat and I remained friends for many years. Here he is in my kitchen with my daughter Nicci and my sister Paula.

That night when the family was sitting in the dining room having dinner, the phone rang. Gina got up and answered it, and then she called out, "It's Burt Lancaster." I got up, thinking it was for me, and Gina said, "It's not for you, Daddy. It's for Nicci."

Nicci, rather surprised, went to the phone, and from the dining room I could hear her half of the conversation: "Yes, Mr. Lancaster . . . It went well, Mr. Lancaster . . ."—they talked for about five minutes. Burt just wanted to know how the final test went! But that's the kind of guy Burt was, very interested in young people.

26
MY TRAVELS
WITH TELLY

The weeks I spent in Durango on **The Scalphunters** were the beginning of my long, close friendship with Telly Savalas. When I finished shooting, Marie met me at the Mazatlán Hotel and we had a second honeymoon. We spent an additional few days in Puerto Vallarta and a quick trip by boat to Yelapa Bay. We had so much fun and romance. We were like Burton and Taylor when he shot **The Night of the Iguana**! I took a picture of Marie in Yelapa Bay and it's my favorite. I've now got it in a frame on top of the TV in my den, and every time I look at it, I remember, and my temperature rises!

When Telly got back home, his agent, Jack Gilardi, rushed him into a Metro picture called **Sol Madrid**, a cops-and-Mafia thriller with David McCallum. On one day's notice, Telly had to replace Orson Welles, who was sick. As a result, Gilardi was able to jump Telly's salary up to $20,000 a week for two weeks. Telly asked me to meet him at MGM to help him learn the dialogue in a hurry. Pages and pages and pages of dialogue! Telly, fortunately, was a quick study, and he did it.

Telly, his wife Lynn and the three girls, Christina, Penelope and Candace, lived in a house in Woodland Hills a few miles from mine. (Christina was Telly's daughter by his first wife, Katherine.) After Telly's hectic two weeks at MGM, we were both out of work again. Telly would come by my house every morning about 10:30 and I'd hear the distinctive sound of the Spanish bus horn on his big Lincoln. I'd go out and meet him in the driveway and we'd make the rounds together—hit a few studios just to be seen and to remind people that we were available. Usually we'd end up having lunch at Schwab's Drugstore, a hangout for out-of-work actors, writers, directors, etc. Telly said to me one day, "Whenever I have out-of-town visitors, I drive by your house and I tell them, 'This is where Paul Picerni lives. That guy on *The Untouchables.*'" He knew how to make a guy feel good—especially one who was battling the fears of a disabling malady.

When I got back from Mexico, Dr. Saliba took me off the Diabanese pills and put me on shots of insulin. He said it would be more effective. (He was right, and I've been on insulin ever since.) It was Telly who helped me get over my depression about my condition.

When Telly was in the Army, he spent a whole year at a hospital in Washington, D.C. recovering from injuries suffered during the War. I know Telly had wires in his leg, and we've all seen the shriveled-up forefinger of his right hand. Although I questioned him many times, he never told me how it happened, he would always sidestep it. I've since asked his brother Gus, and still never got the true story. Telly would always say, "Oh, I'll tell ya about it someday." He never did. That was the mystery of Telly. He never gave you it all; he kept you wanting more. That's part of what made him a great actor.

Next, Telly was signed to do a picture in Madrid for Columbia, a low-budget Western called *Land Raiders*. George Maharis was going to play the hero and Telly would be playing his brother, a villainous town boss who hates Indians so much he puts a bounty on Indian scalps. Calling me from London, Telly asked if I wanted to go to Madrid and play his sidekick in it. I said, ". . . *Yes!!*" Not so much that it was a good career move, but because I knew we'd have a great time. The cast also included Arlene Dahl and a young newcomer, 19-year-old Janet Landgard. All the other actors lived in London or Madrid.

I joined Telly and his family at their London flat a few days before Telly and I were to report to Madrid. Their flat was just a few blocks from Hyde Park and walking distance to the Colony Club. It wasn't long before Telly and I were at the Colony Club playing baccarat. The casinos in England were very different from the ones in Vegas. English casinos were small . . . quiet . . . sedate . . . everyone well-dressed. It was almost like being in a church!

Telly's mother Christina was "Miss Greece" at the 1939 World's Fair. Some of her religious paintings have been displayed in museums around the world.

When you play baccarat, you get two cards and the dealer gets two cards. Tens and picture cards were zero points, aces through nines counted for one point through nine points. The two cards that add up closest to nine wins. For example, a king and a three add up to three. A four and a five add up to nine. And so on.

Telly loved to double-up, so after he won three hands in a row his bet was up to £400. At the time, a pound was worth $2.80, so that bet was sizable. (*My* bets never exceeded £10.) I said to Telly, "Win this next hand and I'm going to give you a Tarzan call"— something I'd been doing since I was 12 watching the old Johnny Weissmuller movies. Sure enough, he won, and I let out with a Tarzan call that would cause a thousand elephants to stampede. It bounced off the walls. There was a sudden quiet from all the

English patrons—a look of amazement. And then a burst of laughter filled the entire casino. Well, that night I did six more Tarzan calls, to the delight of all the reserved English at the Colony Club. Telly won "a chunk" and I won too.*

Soon Telly, his little white Mercedes convertible and I were sailing on a ferry from Southampton, across the Channel to France; from our debarkation point in France, we would drive to Spain. During our long ride through Western France, we made a 2:00 A.M. stop for coffee at a small café. There were three or four Frenchmen in the place. When they spotted *me*, they began shouting, "*Le Incoragible*! Oh, monsieur! Eliot Ness! Al Capone!"—they went bananas! It had been several years since I had done **The Untouchables**, but it was very current in France, and apparently very *big* to these three Frenchmen. It was gratifying to be recognized so far away from home; it made me feel so good. That was one of the few times that people made a fuss over me and ignored Telly! (Telly's shaved head usually made him a standout everywhere we went. In Spain they called him "El Delon"—The Bald Head.)

Finally Telly and I arrived at the Castellana Hilton in Madrid, where we shared a big, beautiful two-bedroom suite. We drove to the **Land Raiders** location together every day. The Western sets were ones that Sergio Leone had used for some of his Spaghetti Westerns with Clint Eastwood. I loved the Spanish horses, which were so regal-looking with their curved necks.

Madrid had some fabulous restaurants, and each night we tried a new one. Soon we bonded with some of the other cast members and our dinner parties grew. Janet Landgard, her mother and the delightful English actor Guy Rolfe joined us every night, and our conversations were very stimulating. Needless to say, Telly held his own in these discussions. Telly had attended NYU for several years before producing radio shows for ABC and Voice of America in the '50s. His mother Christina was a very wise woman and an accomplished artist whose work is on display in many museums. She was also Miss Greece during the 1939 New York World's Fair.

---

*Incidentally, an American producer named "Cubby" Broccoli and his wife were in attendance that night. Some months later, I had lunch with Telly and "Cubby" in London when "Cubby" signed Telly to do the James Bond movie *On Her Majesty's Secret Service*.

Telly was well-read, he was smart, and pro-Greek. In fact, he was pro-Greek to a fault! With Telly, anything that was Greek was the ultimate. When we were on Rhodes on the set of *Escape to Athena*, we were having a discussion about great sculpture. He said there was no one to compare to the Greek sculptor Appollonius. I asked, "What about the Italian sculptor Michelangelo?"

Telly responded flatly, "No comparison!"

I said, "Let's settle it. We'll ask David Niven," who was sitting nearby, reading a book.

"Okay. He's a man of great knowledge," Telly said.

We approached him and I said, "Mr. Niven, how would you compare Michelangelo to Appollonius?" There was a pause, and then David said, "Who is Appollonius?"

George Maharis and I play a game where you try to knock your opponent off-balance, as Telly referees, on the *Land Raiders* set.

I said, "*Thank you*, sir!" And as we walked away, Telly grumbled, "He's not as smart as I *thought* he was!"

Telly was something else. One day on *Land Raiders* we came back from location to the hotel still in our Western wardrobe, dusty and dirty. We stopped in a little men's shop off the lobby, and Telly started looking at some sports shirts. He said to the young Spanish salesman, no more than 19, "Do you have these in extra large?" The kid said, "Yes, sir, Mr. Savalas. What color would you like?" Telly said, "You know what? We need to go upstairs and clean up. Bring some of these shirts up to my suite in an hour and I'll pick one out."

An hour later, there was the kid with an armful of shirts, 14 of them. He spread them out on the rug, all different colors. "Which color do you want, Mr. Savalas?"

Telly said, "I want *all* of them."

The kid's mouth fell open. "*All* of them?"

Telly repeated, "Yes, all of them." The kid, flabbergasted, again asked, "All *14* of them, Mr. Savalas?," and Telly said, this time very firmly, "*Yes. All* of them." Telly signed the ticket and the kid, who of course had just made a sizable commission, left. I'm sure he did a dance going down the hall to the elevator! I said, "Telly . . . why did you do that? Are you nuts? You got a *closet* full of shirts, what the hell are you gonna do with all these new ones? You'll never *wear* them!"

Telly said, "I know that. But did you see the look on that kid's face when I said, 'All of them'?" That's what made Telly so great. He bought the shirts just to make that Spanish boy happy, to give him something to remember.

He did this with so many people. There was a secretary in Jack Gilardi's office who was sweet and efficient, but had such lousy teeth. Telly, in his own gentle way, convinced her to get her teeth fixed and he would pay for it. *She* did, and *he* did. She married Don Rickles! I think back on incidents like that and I realize that perhaps even *I* have no idea how many lives Telly touched.

Once when we were shooting an episode of his TV series **Kojak** on Skid Row in Los Angeles, we had to walk from the brightly lit set through a dark alley to get to our motor home. Suddenly there was a filthy black bum approaching Telly—it was really frightening. Mike, our security officer, shouted, "Hey there! Move on, *move on!*" Telly said, calmly, "Hold it, Mike, hold it," and then, indicating the bum, said, "This is a friend of mine. This is my *friend.*"

Telly put his arm around the bum and asked him what his name was. The bum said, "Jimbo, Telly."

Telly said, "Jimbo, would you like some coffee? Come with me." He led Jimbo to the crafts table and said, "Take whatever you want, Jimbo." Our still photographer Pete was nearby, and Telly called him over, instructing him, "Get a shot of me with my pal Jimbo here." As Pete got ready to take the shot, Telly again put his arm around Jimbo—Jimbo with the biggest smile in the world. After the flash, Telly said, "Jimbo, come back tomorrow night and Pete will give you that picture." Jimbo said, "*Thank* you, Telly. God bless ya, Telly. God *love* ya, Telly." It made me want to cry. Telly made everybody feel that he was their best friend.

Another thing about Telly was his uncanny way with women. I often wondered why Sophia Loren married Carlo Ponti; he was a producer, yes, but he was short and he was bald. What did he have to attract the most beautiful woman in the world? Well, he must have had what Telly had. Telly was no Robert Taylor but, wow, could he sweet-talk the ladies! The way Telly entertained women, his stories, his humor, his mystery, his charm were astonishing. One night during **Land Raiders** we were having dinner in Madrid with two TWA stewardesses, and the words he was saying to one of the girls were sheer poetry. The pretty young thing was taking it all in. Suddenly he was Cyrano de Bergerac in Prince Charming's body. We all listened intently, especially the girl Telly was concentrating on. She was mesmerized, starry-eyed, on the verge of fainting. (Or of having an orgasm!) I leaned over to the other girl and whispered, "Whatever he's saying to *her* goes for me too!" The girls laughed. The mood was dispelled. Telly looked at me, shook his head and mumbled, "You dumb *fuck*!"

One beautiful young English girl in **Land Raiders**, I can't remember her name, had a very small role as part of the wagon train moving westward. The wagon train is attacked by Indians and in one short scene she is dragged from a wagon by some Indians and her blouse is partially ripped off, baring her breasts. Very apprehensive about doing the scene, she asked Telly's advice. He said, "Come to my suite tomorrow and we'll work on it."

On Sunday, she showed up for her "acting lesson." We sat in the living room; she and Telly on the couch and me close by in an armchair. He told me to not move from my chair no matter what, and then he directed his attention to the girl: "To be a successful actor, you must have no inhibitions. You must have complete *freedom* to do what must be done to deliver a sincere performance." The words poured from his mouth with sincerity, like he was an experienced professor. He now was Stanislavski with a young student. She listened intently to every word. He continued, "You must be oblivious to everything that might cause you any concern. Free. Totally free. Now, take off your blouse."

Without flinching, she did what he said. Telly again began speaking. No longer Stanislavski, he was now Svengali and she was his slave! She did whatever he said. She was totally relaxed, and before long she was stark naked except for her high-heeled shoes. I was amazed. Telly said, "Now I want you to walk over to that bowl of fruit on the table and get an orange and give it to Paul." I almost couldn't control myself! This beautiful young naked girl walked over to the table, picked out an orange and started to give it to me.

Suddenly there was a knock at the door. The spell was broken, but there was no panic. The girl picked up all her clothes and went into the bedroom. I can't remember today who was at the door— the maid, the assistant director or Adolf Hitler! All I can remember is the transformation of a frightened 19-year-old girl *into a young actress.* The following day she did the scene to perfection, then went back to London. We never saw her again.

Our group went out to dinner on the night before we were scheduled to shoot a big climactic barroom scene. I reminded Telly, "We better cut the evening short and go back to the hotel and work on the scene." He refused. We were having too much fun for him to worry about work.

The next morning Telly and I were driving to work, Telly at the wheel and me trying to cue him. It was no use; it was too much— about six pages of dialogue. He could never learn it in time. We got to the set and there were all the townspeople whom Telly was supposed to address as the Apaches prepared to attack. Finally everyone was assembled, maybe 50 people counting the crew, cast and all the extras, and now Telly, our star, was called in. The director Jerry Juran started to give Telly his position for his big speech. Telly said very casually, "What scene is this, Jerry?"

Jerry said, "The big scene where you address the townspeople."

Telly reacted with faked surprise. "*What??* Nobody told me we were going to do this today!"

Jerry looked shocked. "Didn't you get a call sheet yesterday?" With great sincerity, Telly lied that he had not.

Suddenly there was a discussion between the first, second and third assistant directors. Fortunately for Telly, not one of them could remember giving Telly a call sheet (even though one of them certainly *had*)! Jerry profusely apologized to Telly, and then said, "Telly, if you don't mind, let's try and do the scene anyway. We'll break it up, shoot it in small cuts. We *gotta* do it." Telly bravely agreed, "Oh, okay, Jerry, sure . . ."—now he was doing them a *favor*! This was Telly the Con Man!

Telly's father, a baker who delivered bread and pastries, was the one from whom Telly inherited "the con." Telly often said that his father became a millionaire three times and lost his fortune each time. Telly was the same way. Money-wise he was constantly up and down, and you could never tell if he was broke or if he had 5,000 in cash in his pocket.

The *most* unusual thing that happened on **Land Raiders** took place the day Telly and I were out in the countryside with a second unit, shooting some horseback shots and chase footage, while Jerry Juran was elsewhere, directing a scene involving a Portuguese actor. Charlie Schneer, the producer of the picture, came out to see me and Telly, and he was very upset: "My God, we're having a hell of a time with this Portuguese actor. He's terrible. *Terrible*! He looks great as a Mexican bandit but he can't remember his *name*, he just can't *do* it." Then Charlie dropped the bombshell: "Paul, I want you to replace him."

I said, "What? . . . No, no, no, it's impossible." I refused because I "felt" for this poor actor—it would end his career, his ego would be shattered. (Telly once said to me, "Never tamper with a person's ego. It's his most prized possession.") Charlie said, "We're going to have to replace him anyhow, Paul. I *know* you're capable of doing the Mexican dialect. You could save us a lot of money and time. A whole day of shooting will be lost if we have to stop shooting and bring another actor in from London."

"But how can we get away with me playing two parts in the same movie?"

"We'll *disguise* you," Charlie replied. "We'll give you a scar, a mustache, we'll change your hair, give you Mexican makeup. We can *do* it, Paul. Please, please, you've got to pull me out of this jam!"

Finally Telly convinced me to do it and promised that he'd help me—*he* would help *me* learn the dialogue for a change! But I stipulated that the other actor had to be gone by the time I came

Heavily made-up, I stepped in and replaced a Portuguese actor in _Land Raiders_—in addition to playing my _own_ role in the picture!

to the set, because I didn't want to see his pain. During the hour I spent in the makeup chair being transformed into a Mexican bandit-friend of George Maharis, Telly helped me memorize the dialogue for this long scene. By the time the makeup was completed, I had learned enough to get the scene underway. And by the end of that day, I had for the fourth time successfully replaced another actor. But never before had I played two characters in the same film! I received credit as Paul Picerni for one part and as H.P. Picerni for the other.

I should mention that Telly also acted as my agent for the part: He told Charlie I should be paid $1,000 for the day's work. In cash. _Cash._ Telly _loved_ cash! Charlie quickly agreed. _Too_ quickly. We should have asked for more! That night Telly, his family and I had dinner at our hotel with Amadeo Curcio, a Tarzana neighbor of mine; he had stopped by to see me on his way home from the Venice Film Festival. Amadeo flew home the next day and gave Marie the $1,000. _Cash!_

At one point, Telly told me that his wife Lynn and the three girls were en route to Bilbao, in Northern Spain, by ferry. Telly wanted to get to the pier early so that, when his little girls came off the ferry and down the ramp, he would already be there waiting and waving up to them. The night before their arrival, Telly and I and Telly's Spanish limo driver spent the night in St. Moritz in the south of France, near the border of Spain, in a hotel that was totally empty because this was a time when American tourists were boycotting France—we three were the only ones in the whole hotel! Well, the night clerk forgot to give us our eight A.M. wake-up call, and when we woke, we had only 30 minutes to get to Bilbao, which was 30 or 40 miles away. Telly drove like crazy—he and I were in his Mercedes (with the top down) and the limo driver was right behind us. I don't know how the hell the limo driver kept up with us because we were flying! As we drove through Bilbao, a city the size of Chicago, we hit traffic, but that didn't stop Telly. At one point a cop in the middle of the street tried to stop us but Telly went right by him. As he did, the cop spun like a top. I think we might have hit his arm! At another point, Telly drove up on the sidewalk to bypass stalled traffic—people were scrambling out of the way! He was so determined to *be* there when his family came off the ship, he did all these crazy things.

It was like magic: The very moment we got to the pier and pulled to a stop, Lynn and the girls started coming down the ramp from the ship and spotted us. It must have looked to them like we'd been sitting there waiting for an hour! Telly was like that: He put his family first and he wanted to make sure that they knew that they were important to him.

We had so much fun with the kids at the pool at a Madrid swim club. Telly was the Big Bad Bwana Devil, Penelope was Jane, Candace was Cheetah (Candace would make the cute "ooh-ooh-ooh" monkey sounds) and I was Tarzan. Telly would "kidnap" little Jane and Cheetah, and I would let out a Tarzan yell and dive into the pool and come to their rescue. (My Tarzan call, already the talk of London, also became known all over Madrid!) Telly and I would do one of our fake fights where he'd "punch" me and I'd go down and then I'd bounce back up and "punch" *him*. Actually, most of the time I took all the beating, because he didn't know how to "take it"!

Soon it all came to an end and we were all back in London. There we had lunch at the Dorchester with Herman Cohen, the producer of an upcoming picture called **Crooks and Coronets**. Herman wanted Telly for the starring role opposite Warren Oates but they came to an impasse in their negotiations: Herman wanted to give Telly the same deal he had on **Land Raiders**, which was I think $100,000, and Telly wanted more. Neither one of them would budge. Remembering what Shelley Winters told me about **Alfie**, I excused myself to go to the men's room, and then secretly signaled Telly to join me. In the men's room I told him, "Do what Shelley did—ask for a Rolls-Royce." He did, and that's what he got—a hundred-grand plus a Silver Shadow Rolls-Royce.

I was supposed to be in **Crooks and Coronets** too, as an American gangster. But England's agreement with the Screen Actors Guild was that only three American stars would be allowed in an English production. They said I didn't have a big-enough name, so Cesar Romero played what would have been my part.

Telly, his family and I sailed home to America on the final voyage of the U.S.S. **United States**. (Telly hated to fly—he only flew when he absolutely had to. He lost a role in **Taras Bulba** because he would have had to fly to South America to do it, and at that time he wouldn't fly at all.) While we were making the voyage, there was a bridge tournament. Telly and Christina were partners, and I drew a partner from the group. Somehow Telly and Christina won the tournament. Knowing Telly, I had a feeling he padded his score. He cheated at golf too!

When we got to New York, Telly went on **The Tonight Show With Johnny Carson**. As prearranged, Johnny at one point said, "I understand you won the bridge tournament on the ship." Telly responded, "Yes, I did." Johnny's next question was, "Who taught you how to play bridge, Telly?," and he answered, "Omar Sharif."

In the green room backstage after the show, I said to Telly, "You *bastard*. Why didn't you tell him the truth? *I* taught you how to play bridge." Telly answered, "Omar Sharif is a bigger name."

I had to laugh. That was Telly!

27
LOCATION—ALL-
EXPENSES-PAID VACATION!

When I shot **Breakthrough** in 1950 on the beautiful peninsula of Monterey Bay, California, one of the older guys in the Warners crew told me, "You'll never be on a better location." He was almost right. During my long career, I've been on locations in many parts of the world, and every one of them was like an all-expenses-paid vacation. Writing about **The Scalphunters** and **Land Raiders** in the previous chapters has made me think about it, and I realize that I've never been on a location that I didn't enjoy.

When you shoot on location, your airfare is paid for, first class, as per Screen Actors Guild provisions; your hotel room is paid for; plus you receive per diem for your meals. Per diem varies according to the prices for meals in the city you're in. They average out the costs of breakfast, lunch and dinner in that city, and pay you accordingly. If, for example, breakfast in that city runs about $10, lunch $15 and dinner $20, then they will pay you $45 per day. Per diem in Durango, Mexico, might be $20 a day while per diem in Tokyo might be as much as $100 per day. They're usually very fair about paying you.

If you are a major star, the per diem is negotiable. They will give the star anywhere from $1500 per week to $20,000 per week, but the star will have to pay for his/her own hotel and all meals. Sometimes the star will rent a house on the location and hire a staff (a cook, a maid and so on). Usually the company will supply a limo and driver.

In addition to Durango, Mexico (**The Scalphunters**) and Madrid, Spain (**Land Raiders**), some of the other places where I've shot movies and TV movies are Monterey, Sacramento, San Diego and

San Francisco, California; Louisville, Kentucky; Yakima, Washington; Mexico City and Durango, Mexico; New York City; Madrid, Spain; Rhodes, Greece; Umag and Zagreb, Yugoslavia; and Puerto Rico.

I even shot some television shows on location: *Boots and Saddles* (Kanab, Utah), *Rawhide* (Tucumcari, New Mexico), *26 Men* (Tucson, Arizona), *Hellinger's Law* (Dallas), a *Lucy* special, *Kojak* and *Vega$* (Las Vegas) and—one very memorable location— two weeks in Hawaii on *Starsky and Hutch*. I even shot on location for several commercials: Webber Barbecue (Fort Lauderdale, Florida, and Chicago), Bacardi Rum (Puerto Rico and Hawaii), a coffee commercial (Tokyo), and so on.

The film *Che*, about the revolutionary Che Guevara, was set in Cuba but shot in Puerto Rico, where I spent about a week. Omar Sharif was Che Guevara and Jack Palance played Fidel Castro; I had a small part as a jailed ex-Communist and had a scene or two with Omar. The director was Richard Fleischer. This was another "money part," something I did for the paycheck and the chance to go to the location, not for the part itself. My brother Charlie was also on the movie as one of Castro's men—Charlie and 10 or 15 other stunt guys made up Castro's platoon.

The first night we were there, Omar took the entire company to a fancy restaurant for dinner—the whole thing was on him. Omar was like Telly Savalas: When you were in his presence, nobody else could pick up a check. After dinner when we came out of the restaurant, there were all these local Puerto Rican union guys with banners, yelling and screaming; 20th Century-Fox was having trouble with some union down there. They directed their anger at Omar because he was the star of the picture and, to them, he represented the company. All the stuntmen surrounded Omar for protection and got him into his limousine before the union guys could create any problems.

Later that night I was walking back to the hotel with three of the stunt guys, Charlie, Victor Paul and Teddy Grossman. As we cut through an alley, we passed a lot of barrels full of waste paper, and across the top of a couple of them was a mannequin. It was a naked, brown-skinned female mannequin with a beautiful body, but no head, and the legs were cut off at the knees. Teddy, who had a tremendous sense of humor, said, "Let's take this beautiful body back to the hotel, we'll have some fun with it."

There was another stuntman at the hotel named Phil Adams, an Italian kid (real name: Granucci) who was a real character. We decided to play a joke on him. We put this mannequin in Teddy's bed, put the pillow where the head would have been and brought the sheets up partway, so all you could see was this brown torso with the gorgeous breasts. Then Teddy went down the hall and knocked on Phil's door: "Phil! Phil! We got a girl! You gotta see this! Charlie's with her now." Phil got all excited and pretty soon he came down the hall with a towel wrapped around himself—no shoes, no nothing, just the towel. We opened the door and whispered to him, "Be very quiet." Entering the dimly lit room, Phil approached the bed and saw Charlie nestled next to the "girl." Phil saw the beautiful exposed breasts and whispered, "God Almighty, she's gorgeous . . . !" At that point, Charlie pulled back the sheets and lifted up the pillow. No legs, no head. "*Oh my God!*" Phil screamed out, almost hysterical!

Another fun memory of that Puerto Rico trip was playing football on the beach, the actors vs. the stuntmen. There were about six stunt guys, and on the actors' side were me, Omar Sharif, Robert Loggia, Woody Strode and a couple others. The thing that amazed me was how gutsy Omar was. He didn't know anything about football and these stuntmen were tackling us and everything, and Omar was ballsy as hell. We didn't beat them, but we gave them a hell of a game.

According to Charlie, Omar wasn't quite as ballsy one night after production moved to the 20th Century-Fox back lot. I had finished in the picture by then but Charlie was still working in it. Director Richard Fleischer and Omar had started going off to Palm Springs every weekend and working on the script. Suddenly Che Guevara, Omar's character, had all the juicy dialogue and good scenes, and there wasn't much left for Jack Palance's Castro. They were shooting on the Fox back lot around a campfire when Palance finally blew his top. He started ranting about Omar and Fleischer pulling this shit behind his back, and he was very upset about it. Palance bellowed, "You and your fucking pretty boy leading man are rewriting the fucking script!" Omar just kinda cowered. He butted heads with six stuntmen on the beach in Puerto Rico, but Jack Palance scared the hell out of him!

At another "low point" in my career, another movie and another chance to go on location presented itself. One day in 1968, a fellow nicknamed Grenade (I can't remember his real name) called up and said he was about to do a picture in Mexico City and he wanted me to play the lead—the first and only time I was offered the lead in a picture. He sent me the script, and it was a murder story—almost a horror movie—called *The Fearmakers*. Dolores Del Rio, a movie star from the '30s and '40s, was the leading lady but it was going to be made on a low budget, less than a million. Grenade said that a lot of Mormons were investing in it.

I read the script and saw that the role he was offering me was a good one—the male star lead. I would be the manager of an opera star (Del Rio) who secretly has a henchman terrorizing her in order to get her money. I invited Grenade to the house to talk about it. (Bob Stack once told me, "Always invite people to your house to negotiate. It gives you an advantage." He always did that, and his house would intimidate people. It worked for me, too.) Grenade assured me again that Dolores Del Rio would be playing the opera star. I asked, "But how are you going to pay me?

Vintage glamour shot of my *Fearmakers* leading lady Katy Jurado. She slept with all her leading men but me.

You've only got a small budget, and I have to get a certain amount of salary." He asked me how much I wanted, and I said I'd like to get at least $5,000 a week for the six weeks I'd be in Mexico City, a hotel room, a driver and per diem.

Grenade said, "Okay, we'll give you 5,000 a week, but we can't give it to you up front."

"Then how can I *do* it?" I asked him. "I've got a family to support." "I'll tell you what we'll do: We'll give you 1500 a week and we'll defer 3500 a week. As soon as we sell the picture, we'll pay you the balance that we owe you, $21,000." I thought about it, and since I wasn't doing anything at the time, I agreed. I went out to the Hollywood men's store Sy Devore's and bought a fabulous wardrobe for the movie, five or six new outfits.

They went down to Mexico and lined up the sets, the studio space and the locations. But in the meantime, Dolores Del Rio backed out—I was told that, all of a sudden, she didn't want to do it anymore. To replace her, they signed Katy Jurado, the Mexican actress who had played Gary Cooper's ex-girlfriend in the classic Western *High Noon* (and received a Golden Globe for her performance); she was later Oscar-nominated for the Western *Broken Lance*. Katy, instead of Dolores Del Rio, was okay with me. Our line producer was Lyman Dayton, a fellow whose father-in-law, a Mormon dentist, was putting up the bulk of the money for the picture. Lyman had no experience whatsoever.

The apartment building where I stayed was right on the Reforma, the main street of Mexico City. The director Tony Carras and I shared the three-story penthouse, which had a living room, kitchen, maid's quarters and three bedrooms upstairs. Tony was basically a film editor, but he'd directed a couple things before.

At Churubusco Studios (where Nick Georgiade, Abel Fernandez and I cameoed in *La Edad de la Violencia* a few years earlier), I met the rest of the *Fearmakers* cast, all Mexican actors. Katy Jurado was very nice, as was Carlos East, who would be playing my sidekick and doing all my dirty work. We soon started shooting.

Every night I'd call home and talk to Marie, and ask her if she'd gotten a check yet. Every night the answer was no. On the Friday after the first week I said to Lyman Dayton, "I've got a little news for you. Unless my wife gets a check by Sunday night, I don't report for work Monday morning."

"Paul, we're having a little trouble," he said, and he started explaining to me that he had to pay for the sets, pay for *this*, pay for that . . .

I said, "I don't care. If my wife doesn't get a check by Sunday night, the first payment of 1500, I don't show up for work Monday morning." I talked to Marie the next day (Saturday)—no check. I talked to her Sunday morning—no check. But finally Sunday night she called to tell me that somebody showed up at the house and gave her a check for $1500, so I went to work on Monday morning. Every weekend we went through the same routine.

With Katy and Anthony Carras.

Katy Jurado was a lovely girl and we had dinner a few times. Evidently she had had affairs with all her leading men, including Marlon Brando*, and didn't intend this picture to be an exception. Of course, I had no intention of having an affair with Katy. One morning in makeup, the Mexican makeup lady said, "Don't you

---

*Katy herself told me about that. She stayed with Marlon, then went home to her husband Ernie Borgnine. "Where the hell you been all night?" he demanded, and she said, "Marlon called and said he needed a shoulder to cry on, so I went up and spent some time with him." But Ernie knew they were shacking up, so he kicked her in the leg and broke it!

like Katy? Why won't you go to bed with her?" I said, "Because I'm a married man." The makeup lady said, "Katy's very disappointed. All of her leading men make love to her, and you don't make love to her." Needless to say, Katy had put the makeup lady up to saying these things to me. I said, "Listen—I *like* her, but I'm not that kind of person."

And *Katy* wasn't the kind of person to give up easily. About three weeks into the picture, she came to the apartment and made a special Mexican dinner for me and Tony Carras. She was really trying hard to get me in the sack, but nothing was happening. The 1968 Olympics were then being held in Mexico City and she knew I had eight kids, so she gave me eight beautiful commemorative Olympic coins, one for each of them. They were solid silver, and must have cost $10-15 each. I appreciated it but, again, nothing happened.

About four weeks into the film, I finished early one day and I was leaving the set in my chauffeured limo when a girl waved us down. It was the Puerto Rican actress who was playing the maid in the picture—a very sexy-looking gal. "Mr. Picerni, are you going into town? Do you mind if I get a ride with you?" I didn't mind at all, and told her to get into the car. Unbeknownst to me, Katy saw this, and she went into a tirade—I mean, a real "Lupe Velez tirade"! She screamed at Lyman Dayton, at Tony Carras, at our Mexican producer—she screamed at *everybody*. Then she got into her car and took off for home (Cuernavaca, a town about 50 miles from Mexico City). As far as she was concerned, she was finished in the picture, she was not coming back to work anymore!

Monday came around and she didn't show up for work, Tuesday she didn't come to work. Tony Carras sat me down in the suite Tuesday night and said, "Paul, you've got to do me a favor. You've got to go to bed with Katy Jurado."

I said, "No way, Tony! I can't do that."

"You've got to, in order to save the picture! We're stymied; we can't do a thing without her. Either you go to bed with her, or we can't finish the picture."

"I'm sorry, then you can't finish the picture," I told him. I realized that they were in a bad spot, but I wasn't going to compromise myself by going to bed with Katy Jurado just to save the ***The***

Fearmakers! Eventually they somehow ironed it out and Katy came back. She had a puss on her for the next two weeks—and at one point I had a love scene with her! She was hot as a pistol, and she wasn't acting. But I *was*. We got through that okay.

Marie came down to visit, and stayed about a week. While she was there, Katy was great; she even became friendly with Marie. (I didn't tell Marie anything about the situation.) My henchman in the movie, Carlos East, was a good-looking young blonde actor; you would never think he was a Mexican, but he was. He was a funny guy. In those days, everyone was smoking marijuana. Not *me*, but Carlos did, and so did his girlfriend. After Marie arrived, one day she and I were going to have lunch with Carlos and his girlfriend. We were in one of these tiny cars, maybe a Fiat, Carlos and his girl in the front and Marie and me in the back, and Carlos and the girl started smoking their marijuana. I knew what they were smoking but Marie, who is very naive and didn't know anything about marijuana, said, "Gee, what kind of cigarettes are you smoking? They smell weird!"

Carlos said, "These are Mexican cigarettes. They *all* smell like that," and then he and his girlfriend rolled up the windows. They kept smoking their "cigarettes" and the car filled up with smoke, and Marie and I got stoned from second-hand smoke! Boy, did we make love that day!

Eventually we finished the picture. I got my 1500 a week for the six weeks, but I didn't get the rest of my money. To this day I still haven't collected the balance, even though the picture has had limited release. But there was a kind of compensation in that beautiful location—I love Mexico City, I think it's really a great spot. I've had a good time every time I've been there. I've lost count of how many times I've made that trip; it got to the point where I could speak Spanish, and I began doing interviews on Mexican TV.

When I came home from doing **The Fearmakers**, I again began doing the usual on Sundays, announcing the halftime shows at the Rams games at the Los Angeles Coliseum. One day when the Rams were playing the Baltimore Colts, I was standing in front of the bandstand going over the show with Johnny Boudreaux, the bandleader, when Burt Lancaster and his friend Carroll Rosenbloom, then the owner of the Colts and later the owner of the Rams, came walking down the tunnel that led from the dressing rooms to the field.* Burt spotted me and, after we exchanged hellos, he asked, "What have you been up to?" I told him I was up for a part in *his* new film, producer Ross Hunter's *Airport.* "Oh, good, good, good," he said. "What part?" I said, "The part of Dr. Campagno."

On the plane mock-up as the doctor in *Airport*.

Burt thought about it for a long moment and then he said, "You'd be very good in that part. I'll put a word in with Ross Hunter. Call me tomorrow and remind me." The next day, which was Monday, I called his office at Goldwyn Studios and he said, "I've already talked to Ross, and—you got the part. He just wants you to come in and say hello to George Seaton, the director, as a courtesy." That was easy. Most times, parts don't come easy, but

*Rosenbloom was, I believe, somehow involved with the Mafia. Years later, when he lived in Florida, his daily routine was to swim a mile or two in the ocean off Fort Lauderdale. Then one day his body was found after he had drowned. The talk was that he was assassinated by the Mafia—that a couple of Mafia scuba divers grabbed him by his ankles, pulled him down and held him. That way, there would be no marks on the body.

sometimes they come *very* easy! I *was* right for the part, and, of course, Burt's recommendation had cinched it.

Airport was the story of an in-flight jetliner damaged by a bomber's explosive device and struggling to reach the nearest landing spot. I worked for six weeks on the film on the Universal soundstage where they had built the interior of the big plane. Also appearing in those scenes were Dean Martin, Barry Nelson, Helen Hayes, Van Heflin and (of course) Burt's old buddy Nick Cravat. When we were working on the airplane set, Burt wasn't; his character, the general manager of the airport, never left the ground. Because we would never work the same days, Burt told me and Nick that we could use his dressing room on the lot. So for six weeks, we had Burt's big, beautiful bungalow. It had a large sitting room, kitchen, bedroom and a large bath with a shower. When the Universal tour trams would come by, I would hear the tour guide's voice on the p.a.: "And this is Burt Lancaster's bungalow!" Sometimes I would go to the window and wave to the people on the tram through the curtains. They wouldn't be sure if I was Burt or not, but it made them scream with delight. I gave 'em a big thrill!

My first scene on the plane was with Jacqueline Bisset, who was playing a stewardess. Van Heflin (playing the bomber) had set off his bomb, blowing a hole in the plane, and Jackie's stewardess character was badly hurt in the blast. As the doctor, I was examining her as she lay on her back on the floor of the plane. The director George Seaton said, "Okay, Paul, let's see what you're going to do." I knelt down besides her, opened her blouse and put my stethoscope on her left breast—as I'm sure you'll recall, she was really quite well-endowed. Jacqueline, whom I hadn't even met yet, opened her eyes and looked up at me with an expression of surprise and she asked, "Are you a real doctor?"

George responded, "Yeah. He got all his training at Warner Brothers!"

One day just before the lunch break, George gave the entire cast and crew and extras a lecture as we all sat in our seats on the big plane set: "I don't want anyone drinking at lunch. That means *every*one—including the lead players! People have been coming back from lunch late, sometimes unprepared to work, causing too many delays. If anyone comes back from lunch and I detect any alcohol, that person will be *dismissed*!" His speech was a lot longer than that, and he stressed every word. When we broke for lunch, I happened to be walking out of the soundstage door with Van Heflin and I heard him mumble, "I'll be a son of a *bitch* if anyone is gonna take away my martinis at lunchtime! I'll quit the fucking *business* before that happens!" And he was serious!

Dean Martin had a beautiful trailer on the set. Right next to the trailer was a big net into which he would hit golf balls between takes. Sometimes Dean would have lunch in his trailer with the leading lady, Jacqueline Bisset. One day I walked by and the whole trailer was shaking with a rapidly increasing beat. I think our leading man was having dessert.

Around that time, Telly left for Umag, Yugoslavia, to appear in the World War II film **Kelly's Heroes**, an unusual picture about a group of G.I.s who capture a town and discover about 4,000 bricks of gold bullion in the town's bank vault. After he was in Yugoslavia for a few weeks, Telly called me and said, "Almost everything has been cast, but why don't you and my brother George come over, *on me*, and maybe you'll end up with something in the film?" Marie wasn't thrilled with the idea, but I went along with it. George and I picked up the airplane tickets at Telly's business manager's office and we were on our way. **Kelly's Heroes** starred Clint Eastwood and also featured Carroll O'Connor, Harry Dean Stanton, Don Rickles, Gavin MacLeod and an actor fairly new to the business, Donald Sutherland.

When I arrived in Umag, I was surprised to find Telly romantically involved with Sally Adams, a young actress he met on the James Bond movie **On Her Majesty's Secret Service**. Sally's young daughter was also with her, a seven-year-old, Nicollette Sheridan—lately of **Knots Landing** and **Desperate Housewives**. I had a long talk with Telly, telling him he was living dangerously—I said that if he continued this romance, he was going down a path where he could lose Lynn and his kids. He said, "*No chance.*" One day while Telly was on the set shooting, I had breakfast in the hotel coffee shop with Sally. Between her beauty and her soft British accent, I could see why Telly was smitten. We talked about the weather and whatnot, and then she said, "Paul . . . ," with her lovely soft British accent, "don't you think Telly and I would make a beautiful

Nicholas, Telly's son by Sally Adams, and Sally's daughter Nicollette Sheridan.

baby together?"

"Wow," I thought. "This girl spells trouble!"

That night I told Telly about our conversation and said, "You better watch your step. This girl is gonna get herself pregnant, and you're gonna louse up your marriage and your career and everything." He said, "It'll never happen," but I could tell he was hopelessly in love with this 25-year-old beauty.

We were staying at a nice hotel in Umag, right on the water. George Savalas was my roommate, and although he was a fuck-up, he was brilliant when it came to certain things. He frequently entertained and educated me with lectures on astronomy, astrology and Greek mythology. We would lie in our beds at night, missing our wives, Marie and Robin, and George would talk and teach. He was very knowledgeable, like a college professor. As smart as Telly was, *George* was smarter in some areas. He lacked Telly's charisma and charm, but his ego was larger than Telly's! Naturally he didn't have Telly's talent—not too many people did. George was a handsome guy but he weighed about 280 pounds.

I had my tape recorder with me and after dinner I would sometimes pass the time in the lobby by doing "man on the street"-type interviews with the other actors. (I used the name "Michael Dwan" in these sessions; "This is Michael Dwan coming to you from Umag, and I'm here with So-and-So, and, tell me, sir, how do you feel about . . . ?") Carroll O'Connor and Don Rickles were frequent guests of "Michael," and, of course, Telly and George and all the others. I remember doing an interview with Carroll where *he* took on the character of a prejudiced white Irishman. When I look back, it was the birth of Archie Bunker, the main character in his hit TV series *All in the Family*. I wish I still had that damn tape!

Rickles kept us all entertained by jokingly giving us updates on the impending court case Telly would be involved in once his wife filed for divorce. It was all in fun but eventually it became fact! Because Telly once said that someday he would make a record album and do a nightclub act, *a la* Sinatra, Don also kidded Telly about his future music album "A Touch of Telly." Which, strangely enough, *also* became fact!

With Telly, left, and George Savalas, right, on *Kelly's Heroes*.

There was an actor on the show named Richard Davalos, who liked to smoke pot. (It seemed like a *lot* of the guys in that cast were pot smokers, and also the director, Brian Hutton.) In every shot he was in, Davalos would sharpen his bayonet—that was his gimmick. Soon the thing was razor-sharp. One day, someone on the crew was sick, and Telly insisted that the doctor on the set take that person into town, to the local clinic, for treatment. While the doctor was gone, they started shooting a shot of the men in the patrol climbing over a stone wall. Telly was followed over the wall by Davalos—who accidentally stumbled and slashed Telly's arm with the bayonet! A six-inch gash in Telly's forearm was bleeding profusely, and there was no doctor around. The assistant director wrapped a towel around Telly's arm and rushed him the 25 miles into town. Sixteen stitches were required to close up the wound, but Telly was back at work that afternoon.

After dinner one night, Telly and I and George and Sally were walking around the piazza in nearby Trieste, Italy. It was very cold. When we saw a men's store open, Telly walked in and bought the only coat they had that fit him. It was green—an ugly green. He paid $100 for it and he wore it out of the store. As George and I walked behind Telly and Sally, I noticed that the price tag was hanging out of this ugly coat behind Telly's neck. I said, "Hold up, Telly. Let me get this tag off."

He said, "No, no, no. No, leave it there."

"Why?" I asked. "Are you gonna return it?"

"No," he said, "It makes it *distinctive* with the tag hanging out." That's another one of the many things that made Telly different!

Shooting of **Kelly's Heroes** continued and they were getting close to the end of the picture, and now it didn't look good about George and me getting parts. Then suddenly they had a problem with the actor playing the transportation sergeant, and they turned to George. George had very little acting experience, but was physically right for the part. I helped him with the lines, and he was good in it—he was very funny, he was believable, and he came over great. But nothing for *me* yet. We were in Yugoslavia now for two months; I was suffering, thinking about Marie and the kids at home with no money coming in. At one point, Telly loaned me $1000 and I sent it home.

One weekend we drove to Rome, the four of us—me, Telly, Sally and George. (By this time, Nicollette was back in London with her father or grandmother.) In a store there, Telly was fitted by Rossini, a famous Italian tailor, for some new suits. Then at the Cavalieri Hilton Hotel, also in Rome, we played bridge to pass some time, Telly and Sally against me and George. We played for money— pretty good stakes, in fact. After George and I won two rubbers in a row, Telly said, "You'll never win again. If you win in the next rubber, I'll buy a tailor-made suit for *each* of you. By Rossini." Well, the next day, George and I were fitted, and the following week, when we went back to Rome to pick up Telly's suits, ours were ready too. The whole time we were in Yugoslavia, I don't think we ever lost a rubber.

With plenty of time on my hands, I read the **Kelly's Heroes** script several times, and I never liked the ending. So one day I wrote a new ending. I showed it to Gabriel Katzka, the producer, and he liked it. Brian Hutton, the director, liked it. Clint liked it. They decided to shoot it, and they said they were giving *me* the part of a character I had created, an M.P. sergeant at a checkpoint who in the new ending would stop a truck driven by Clint. "What are you carrying under the tarp in the back of the truck there, sergeant?" the sergeant would ask, and Clint would respond, "Four thousand bricks of solid gold bullion"—which was the truth. The sergeant would snarl, "Don't be a *wiseass*, soldier! Move on! C'mon, get *outta* here, move out!" and then wave him through. And that was the way the picture would end. The producer Gabe Katzka said he would give me $500 for the day's work—it was better than nothing.

I reported for work . . . and it started to rain. It rained for *ten straight days*. I was paid $500 a day for the part for *ten days*. By the time we finished, I got a check for $5,000. God is good!

The funny thing is, they didn't use my ending when the picture came out! I think they went back to the original one.

One night about a week before shooting was to wrap, we were all sitting in the lobby when word came through that the bank set was on fire. The company still had scenes to do on that set. A lot of us went out to the set and tried to fight the fire, but it burned to the ground. The rebuilding of that set delayed the finish of the picture by about two weeks. The rumor was that the Yugoslavian crew had

Challenging Clint Eastwood in the *Kelly's Heroes* finale, which I wrote. Ultimately it was not used in the picture.

burned it so that they could prolong the picture and get a few extra weeks work.

When the picture ended, Telly and Sally drove the little Mercedes convertible over the Alps back to London. George and I flew to London, arriving there before Telly and Sally, of course, and stayed at Telly's flat until they arrived. A few days after Telly and Sally's arrival, George flew home. But Telly insisted I stay a little longer and then fly with him and Sally to New York. He never told me why. He never gave away all the information—that was his way.

In New York, we checked into the Garden City Hotel on Long Island, where Telly grew up. Christina, Telly's mom, and Leo, his stepdad, still lived there, along with his brother Teddy and his sister Catherine and their families. While Sally hid out at the hotel, Telly and I visited with Christina and Leo and some of the other family members. About a week later, Telly and I got in our rented station wagon and headed for the pier in Newark. Finally I found out what he was up to: He'd had the little Mercedes shipped over by boat, and now we were picking it up at the Newark docks.

We headed back to New York, Telly in the Mercedes and me in the station wagon. As we came up on the Holland Tunnel, the traffic was bumper to bumper, and by the time we got to the mouth of the Tunnel, the cars in all the lanes were stopped. Telly was in front of me in the Mercedes and so, feeling mischievous, I gently bumped him from behind. He leaned out the window and yelled back, "You do that again, buddy, and you'll be in a lotta lotta fuckin' trouble!"

Telly and I are welcomed back to the U.S. by the mayor of Garden City.

I yelled back, in a sissy voice, "Oh, I'm so scared to *death*, you big man!"—and I bumped him again. He yelled back a second time, and I taunted him and bumped him again and again. Finally he jumped out of the convertible and I jumped out of the station wagon. The people in the other cars on all sides were aghast—needless to say, they didn't know that we knew each other and that this was all in fun. Telly and I yelled and screamed at each other, then we went into one of our fake fights. He hit me a shot in the jaw and I went sprawling over the hood of the wagon. I faked trying to fight back as he hit me again and again and again. On my back on the hood, holding my face, I acted groggy, like I was almost unconscious. Telly yelled a few more expletives and he got back in his car just as the traffic started to move.

A couple from the car to my left got me to my feet. "Are you all right? Are you all right? *We* recognized that bully!" the man said as they helped me back into my car. I assured them that I could drive, and I was off into the Tunnel.

At the time, Rona Barrett, the gossip columnist, had a TV show where she spotlighted Hollywood celebrities. One of her top news flashes that night was, "Actor Telly Savalas seen beating up a motorist at the mouth of the Holland Tunnel! Telly seems to be playing his bad guy parts in real life!"

(Telly and I would get into "arguments" and "fights" like that all over the world. The last time we did it was in a nightclub in Spain; the next thing I knew, I was unconscious. The owner of the nightclub didn't know that Telly and I were friends, and he, of course, assumed that I was just some troublemaker. And so, along with my next gin and tonic I got a Mickey Finn! So Telly and I stopped doing that after a while!)

Soon Sally was on her way back to London—and, unbeknownst to us, she was carrying Telly's next "beautiful baby." (Over the coming several months, Telly kept going back and forth to London to see her, telling his wife every time, "I've got to go over there for looping.") Meanwhile, Telly and I were on our way to California in the Mercedes convertible. With Telly behind the wheel, the car was going up to 120 miles an hour. Telly repeated his usual catchphrases ("You're in your mother's arms" and "I'm one of the top three drivers in the world"), but what I was saying in my head was "The Act of Contrition":

OH MY GOD I AM HEARTILY SORRY FOR HAVING OFFENDED THEE AND I DETEST ALL MY SINS BECAUSE I DREAD THE LOSS OF HEAVEN AND THE PAINS OF HELL, BUT MOST OF ALL BECAUSE THEY OFFEND *THEE*, OH LORD, WHO ARE ALL GOOD AND DESERVING OF ALL MY LOVE. I FIRMLY RESOLVE WITH THE HELP OF THY GRACE TO DO PENANCE AND TO AMEND MY LIFE, AMEN!

On the Pennsylvania Turnpike just out of Pittsburgh, Telly was going over a hundred miles an hour when we were stopped by two state troopers. We pulled off to the side and they asked him for a driver's license and the ownership papers. Telly opened the trunk and handed them a bunch of papers—all in German (Telly bought the car in Munich). The troopers were befuddled by Telly's quick line of gab. It was like two o'clock in the morning, and they insisted we follow them to the courthouse in a little town nearby. Soon we were in front of a judge—actually, a justice of the peace—who started with a long lecture on the dangers of speeding and then asked to see Telly's driver's license. Telly said, "I gave it to the troopers at the side of the road on the Turnpike." Well, the troopers had evidently lost it there.

The judge continued with his long lecture, during the course of which I heard him say something about a $100 fine. Telly evidently missed that, and he started to counterattack: "Your honor, when I get out to California, I'm gonna go on the Johnny Carson show and I'm gonna expose this little racket you have going here in this township!" The judge began to bristle. I stood up and said, "Your honor! May I speak to Mr. Savalas for a second?"

I took Telly out in the corridor and I said, "Telly, why don't we cut this thing short and just pay the fucking hundred-dollar fine?"

Telly looked surprised. "What? A hundred-dollar fine? You heard him say that?" I was right, Telly *had* missed hearing that. Telly said, "Well, fuck *yeah*, let's pay it and *go*!" We went back in and paid the fine, and Telly asked for his papers back. They gave him the papers for the car, but the troopers still couldn't find his driver's license. One said, "We must have dropped it where we stopped you. We'll go back there and help you find it."

The cops got in their car and Telly and I got in the Mercedes, and we followed them back to the spot on the turnpike. The cops pulled over, got out and started to look around. As *we* came down the turnpike on-ramp toward where the cops were searching with their flashlights, Telly suddenly floored the gas pedal and we sped off, leaving them in the dust! I said, "What the hell are you doing?"

He said, "I never gave them a driver's license. I don't even *have* one!" By that time, we were in the next county!

A few days later, again with Telly driving, we ran into a cloudburst. The convertible top was down and it was raining buckets, but strangely enough we weren't getting wet. It turns out that we were going so fast, the airflow over our heads at that speed was acting as a shield! We did finally stop under an overpass and put the top up.

We went from Chicago to Las Vegas nonstop except for two quick gas/coffee/pee-pee stops. Las Vegas! Caesar's Palace! Blackjack! Baccarat! We were back in action! R.F. and B.—room, food and beverage on the house! The perks of being a star! We had it all. For Telly, of course, this was after **The Dirty Dozen** and **Birdman of Alcatraz**, and I still was recognized as one of the

Untouchables. But Telly was *still* on the rise. You can't imagine the perks once Telly reached his peak as the star of TV's **Kojak**. Enjoy it while you can, because it doesn't last forever. Nothing does!

Speaking of a career being "still on the rise," that certainly described my brother Charlie at that time. In the early '70s, he was offered the job of stunt coordinator on three series simultaneously: **Kojak, Starsky and Hutch** and **Matt Helm**. I, of course, recommended **Kojak**, because I liked the idea of the three of us (Telly and Charlie and me) working together, but he chose **Starsky and Hutch** because that series featured a lot of stuntwork involving cars, and Charlie was an expert at car work. That proved to be a wise decision: **Starsky and Hutch** went on for five years and Charlie eventually started his directing career on that show.

If I were sharing a foxhole during a war, my first choice for a buddy would be Audie Murphy. My *second* choice would be Charlie. He could act so fast in an emergency, and save a life. Once on a Don Knotts-Tim Conway movie being shot on location in North Carolina, a stuntman had to drive a car into a river. He did—but when the car went under, the stuntman couldn't get out. The seat belt had jammed. Charlie quickly had a tow truck back up to the river's edge, grabbed the tow truck chain, dove into the water and wrapped the chain around the axle of the submerged car. Then the tow truck pulled the car out of the river, saving the guy's life. Then there was the time Charlie and I were in Hawaii, when I was a guest star on a **Starsky and Hutch** called "Playboy Island." We were getting ready for a night shot on the beach, and the set was surrounded by oil lamps on poles. Charlie and I were sitting there in a couple of director's chairs while the crew was putting the finishing touches on lighting the set. Doug, a crew member with long hair and a full beard, was walking past one of the oil lamps when his tool belt caught on to one of the lamp poles. The oil pot dropped on his head and he went up in flames. As Doug started running toward the water, I yelled out, "Charlie! Look!" But practically before I could get both those words out, Charlie had tackled Doug, pulled Doug's own jacket over his head and extinguished the flames. Again, he saved a guy's life. To this day, every time Charlie walks on a set where Doug is working, Doug embraces Charlie for a long time. I've seen it happen myself.

28
ALL ABOUT TELLY—
EVERYBODY'S BEST FRIEND

In 1973, Telly did a two-hour special for CBS called *The Marcus-Nelson Murders*. It was a fact-based story of a New York cop (Telly, in an Emmy-nominated performance) trying to prove that a 19-year-old black kid is not guilty of the murder of two young white girls. Telly didn't use the name of the real-life detective he was playing; he invented his own character name: He suggested the first name Theo, which was his uncle's name, and also came up with what he thought was a catchy (and Greek-sounding) *last* name, Kojak. When *The Marcus-Nelson Murders* turned out to be a smash hit in the ratings, CBS wanted to do it as a series. This was the birth of *Kojak*. Like Robert Stack was *made* for the role of Eliot Ness, Telly was made for the role of Theo Kojak. Audiences loved

Telly with his daughter Penelope.

him as the street-smart 13th Precinct (Manhattan) detective who would bend rules until he cracked a case.

Just prior to the start of *Kojak*, Telly and his wife Lynn split. Telly had finally told Lynn about Sally and her baby outright, and he asked for a divorce. He sold their home (the former Paul Newman house on Whittier Drive in Beverly Hills) and bought a Beverly Hills condo for Lynn and the three girls, Christina, Candace and Penelope. For Sally, Nicollette and Sally's adorable new infant son, Nicholas Savalas (Telly's baby), Telly bought a house on Copa de Oro in Bel-Air. The owner was Frank Sinatra; he'd bought it for *his* new wife Mia Farrow, but their marriage ended even before they could move in.

The new Sheraton Hotel, adjacent to Universal Studios, became Telly's permanent residence for the rest of his life. They gave him a free suite and eventually a free two-bedroom apartment there. Telly became a fixture in the hotel lobby bar and, just by hanging out there, Telly helped fill up the hotel with tourists from all over the world. To vacationers from Japan and Europe and many other countries, to be able to see Telly Savalas walking across the lobby of their hotel was a big thing! The Sheraton even opened a sports bar in the hotel and named it Telly's.

When *Kojak* began airing in October 1973, it had only three regular characters: Kojak, a young cop played by Kevin Dobson and Telly's boss, the older inspector, played by Dan Frazer. There was nothing in it for me. Telly put his brother George and his friend Vince Conti as extra cops in the squad room. They were not much more than background extras. With Telly's help, George developed his character Stavros into a very nice supporting role during the five-year run of the series.

Telly and Sally never married, and once *Kojak* was underway, Telly spent more and more time at the hotel so he could be close to work. He could roll out of bed at the Sheraton, drive down the hill and be at the studio in two minutes. About this time, Lee Marvin was being sued for palimony by a woman he had once lived with; I have a feeling that Telly's lawyer advised him *not* to spend *too* much time at Copa de Oro, to spend more time at the hotel . . . just in case.

Telly, looking like he's had one too many, and Marie at Caesar's Palace.

Marie and I spent many nights at the house on Copa de Oro playing bridge with Telly and Sally. It was me and Telly against the two girls. One night they bid a slam and were on their way to making it. We got down to the last three cards and Telly said, "Hold it, hold it, everybody. How many cards do you have?" We each had three. Telly said, "I only have *two*. Misdeal!" Sure enough, there was a card on the floor not far from Telly's right foot. We all knew that Telly had cheated but, of course, we couldn't prove it. Sally was *furious*. Later that same night, Telly and I bid a grand slam. (These hands come along once in a lifetime.) Telly was playing the hand. When we got down to the last two cards, Sally said, "Hold it, hold it, everybody! You all have two cards, I only have one. *Misdeal!*"

One night when we were playing bridge (it must have been about three in the morning), the phone rang. It was Telly's brother, Constantine, calling from Athens. I could see by Telly's response that something was seriously wrong. Teddy, Telly's younger brother, was visiting Athens with his wife, their daughters and their 12-year-old son. The young boy overnight came down with a strange malady and suddenly died. Telly was in shock. The next day when we were at work at Universal on **Kojak**, I expected Telly to call his mother in New York and tell her the sad news. He couldn't do it. A whole day went by . . . and another. On the third day I said, "Telly, you *must* call your mom," and finally he said, "Okay. Keep everyone out of the trailer."

As he went into his trailer, I stood outside the door and stopped people from entering. Suddenly George appeared. I stopped him too, saying, "George, Telly's calling Mama. He wants to be alone." George barged in on him anyway. When Telly said, "Leave me alone a minute, George," George flew into a rage: "Who the hell do you think you are? It's *my* nephew and *my* mother too, you egotistical bastard!" He yelled and screamed. Telly said, calmly, "Well, then, why don't *you* call Mama and give her the bad news?" George stormed out of the trailer. Telly made the call and from outside I could see through the window that his back was moving convulsively, and I could hear the sobs. It was a difficult moment for my dear friend.

The next day, Telly asked me to go to New York with him for the funeral. He and George weren't talking. I acted as the go-between. The three of us flew back to New York together. It was a sad time.

While Telly was doing *Kojak*, I kept busy with a lot of television shows: *Emergency, Gunsmoke, Adam-12, The F.B.I., Banacek, The Night Stalker, Police Story, McCoy, The Incredible Hulk, Barnaby Jones* and so on. Of course there were a couple of guest shots on *Kojak*. I always enjoyed playing romantic leads, so I really enjoyed playing that kind of a part in an episode of *Alice.* Linda Lavin was a lovely leading lady and it was great to work with her. I guess she enjoyed it too, because at the end of the show she gave me a beautiful note along with a gift.

I also did the series *O'Hara, U.S. Treasury* with David Janssen. David, playing the title role, would go to (say) Denver and pick up a sidekick there and tackle his assignment. The next week he would go to (say) Salt Lake City and pick up a sidekick *there*—in other words, each week he had a different sidekick. I guess that approach wasn't working. One day I stopped in at Ptomaine Tommy's, a famous hamburger joint near Vermont Avenue in Los Angeles, and I ran into Jack Webb and Ray Heindorf, who had been music director at Warner Brothers when I was there. We chatted for a few moments, and the next thing I knew, Webb called me in to play David Janssen's permanent partner on *O'Hara.* No longer would he have a new partner in every city; I was going to be the new, Lee

Hobson-like sidekick. I only got to do about four or five episodes, because trouble arose. Jack Webb and David Janssen owned the show, and they were using Universal Studios to make it. Universal had a habit of padding the charges. For instance: One day when we were out near a little lake on the back lot, an antiquated machine in the middle of the lake was making a *chug chug chug chug* noise. David asked the assistant director, "What the hell is *that?*," and the guy said, "That's the heater. It's warming up the lake." David asked, "For *what?*," and the a.d. replied, "For when you and Paul have to go in the lake and pull out the body."

David asked, "How much is Universal charging us for that?" When the a.d. told him it was $900 an hour, David said, "Get it the hell outta here!" But that's the kind of thing Universal was doing to them, so that there wasn't much profit for David Janssen and Jack Webb's company. After the first year, I guess David and Jack said, "Shit, they're killing us," and so they stopped shooting the show. Otherwise, I would have had a series for another couple of years.

David was quite a drinker. One morning on *O'Hara, U.S. Treasury*, when we were working on location on a street in Hollywood, I went into David's trailer-dressing room and he asked me if I wanted "a little screwdriver." I said, "Well, I don't drink, usually, during the day, David . . ." The truth was that I didn't drink that much at all. But he insisted, "Aw, come on, have a screwdriver." So he gave me a screwdriver, which is orange juice and vodka; I drank the one, he had a *couple*. Then we got into a car to do a scene. Well, David did *his* dialogue fine—but *I* was starting to mumble! I must have sounded like Errol Flynn in *Mara Maru*! So I didn't do any of *that* anymore! David drank pretty good. We usually wrapped shooting about four o'clock every day, because that was when *he* would start to slur his words.

* * * * * * *

While Telly was living in London, he and an English writer put together a screenplay called *Mati*, a strange story about a psychiatrist in an insane asylum who has a run-in with the Devil in the form of a beautiful woman. Telly was obsessed with making this into a film, and I spent hours with him working on the script. In order to *make* it, he first had to raise at least a million dollars. After a few false starts, finally he got the money from a man named Arthur Sarkissian, a haberdasher he had met in London (Sarkissian in turn got the money from his uncle, a rich Iranian). We enlisted Howard W. Koch at Paramount to produce the picture. A million-dollar budget was rather slim for a feature, even though Telly agreed that he would take no salary for starring and directing.

I was the dialogue director and Telly the director on *Mati*.

During a summer hiatus from shooting *Kojak*, we had the opportunity to shoot *Mati* at Paramount. I was hired as dialogue director but I was Telly's right-hand man all through the picture. With a skimpy budget, the sets provided by Howard Koch were pretty bad, and the cast was worse. Everything was low-budget—*really* low-budget. It was worse than Monogram! Telly cast mostly newcomers in the lead roles. Priscilla Barnes, a gorgeous girl with little or no experience, was cast as the Devil. She later went on to have some success as a regular on *Three's Company*. Cast in another prominent role was Debbie Fuerer, another beauty, but she had no experience at all. But with Telly directing, they both gave good performances. The girl who played Telly's wife, Diana Muldaur, was magnificent. *Mati* was shot at Paramount and at locales close by.

Telly, of course, was brilliant as Dr. Mati but nothing could overcome the overall poor quality in all phases of the low-budget production. The film lacked an ending; no matter how hard we tried, we couldn't solve the problem. Howard couldn't get a release for the film. The Iranian investor, of course, wanted to get his money back, and he decided that the trouble was the leading lady (Priscilla). Believe me, *that* wasn't the trouble, but he decided to get a new leading lady, Laura Johnson, and reshoot all of Priscilla's scenes with her. All of this was done without Telly's participation, incidentally; by this time, he was back to shooting *Kojak*. Replacing Priscilla, of course, didn't help. To the best of my knowledge, *Mati* was never released theatrically. Eventually it came out on video cassette titled **Beyond Reason** but the Iranian never recouped a penny of his million-dollar-plus investment.

One day during the filming of *Mati*, Howard Koch had called Telly and said, "Do you want to go partners with me on a racehorse?" (Howard had already asked Walter Matthau and been turned down.) Telly asked, "How much?," and Howard said, "3,000 apiece." I went out to Hollywood Park at five o'clock the next morning with Telly and Howard to watch a workout with trainer Mel Stute. The horse worked out at 1:02 flat for five furlongs—not the greatest of times. 59 flat would be great. But they bought the horse anyway, because it was so cheap (just $6,000) and because the horse had such a great bloodline: It was a two-year-old gelding out of Bold Commander, a son of the great sire Bold Ruler. They named the horse "Telly's Pop." The name came about because during the run of *Kojak*, Telly was trying to quit smoking by sucking on lollipops instead of lighting up. He even sucked on lollipops on camera in the show, which became one of Kojak's trademarks.

Everything Telly touched at this time was a winner, and Telly's Pop was no different. He broke his maiden with his first race. His second race was a small ($25,000) stakes race. Out of "our group," Marie and I were the only ones there—Telly and Howard were both working and had to miss the race—and Telly's Pop won again. Next it won a $100,000 two-year-old stakes race at Hollywood Park. At the end of horse races, the winning horse's owners and their friends usually go down onto the track to take a picture with the horse.

With each race that Telly's Pop won, the crowd in the picture grew and grew until there were scores of people in the photo, which is very unusual. Customarily the people in the photo are just the owner, the jockey and the trainer.

Telly's Pop working out at Hollywood Park Race Track in 1975.

Next we went to Del Mar for *another* $100,000 race. Telly's Pop, with Mexican jockey Francisco Mena riding him, won again. Telly flew his mom, Leo and Leo's old buddy Mike out for the next race at Golden Gate in San Francisco—another $100,000 race for two-year-olds. Leo and his old buddy were $2 bettors back in New York at Aqueduct on the Island, and now here they were sitting in the Derby Club watching the big race with the owner! They were in Heaven! Telly's Pop won again. In 1975, Telly's Pop won $355,000, not to mention all the side bets we all cleaned up on. The crowds in the winners' circles must have been in the hundreds by then!

Now the world-famous Kentucky Derby was coming up at Churchill Downs and Telly's Pop was the prohibitive pre-race favorite. Suddenly, disaster struck. Telly's Pop got hurt in a pre-dawn workout and had to be euthanized. It was over. But, boy, was it fun while it lasted.

Telly with another of his many horses. None of them came close to Telly's Pop.

Telly wanted me to be with him on the final year of *Kojak* so I signed on as his dialogue director. It was a happy time for both of us. We worked hard all week and on Friday nights we would drive to Vegas. (We loved Vegas; at one point, Telly even talked Matt Rapp and Jim McAdams, the producers of *Kojak*, into shooting an episode there so we could be close to the tables!) Many times, instead of driving, we would fly by private jet with Sally and Marie. We would dine at the Palace Court and see the shows. This was a time when all the hotels had big-name performers like Dean Martin, Frank Sinatra, Sammy Davis, Jr., Don Rickles and so on, and we saw them all. Oh, what fun! Telly had carte blanche in as many hotels as he wanted in Las Vegas. At Caesar's Palace he'd have the Frank Sinatra suite with its five bedrooms and the grand piano in the living room. We would sometimes have suites in three or four different Las Vegas hotels at the same time. And everything was comped—complimentary R.F. and B. (room, food and beverage). My credit line was about $5,000 and Telly's was $50,000, so we could get markers up to that amount. We lost more times than we won—they knew what they were doing!

One night we all went to the Riviera to see Liza Minnelli. I had never experienced a performance like the one she gave that night. She was absolutely brilliant. When it was over, the audience stood up and gave her an ovation. Telly, standing next to me applauding, said over the roar of the crowd, "Liza Minnelli is proof that God exists . . . !" What a review, huh?

Part of the reason that Telly loved Las Vegas was because it was a 24-hour town—and Telly suffered from insomnia. Telly would get in bed and watch television until he would be practically paralyzed with sleepiness, and yet he often still would not fall asleep. Here and there he might catch a few winks of sleep during the night, but never enough.

Nick Georgiade, Telly and I in Vegas.

Dean Martin had at the time a TV series where each week a celebrity was "roasted," and Telly was scheduled to be the next "roastee." Telly, Sally, Marie and I flew to Las Vegas in a private jet for the big show at the MGM Grand Hotel. These jet rides were so much fun. Telly would get a few drinks in him and then get on his knees and sing songs to Sally, and Marie and I would get the biggest kick out of that. The night before the event, the four of us went to see Don Rickles perform at the Riviera Hotel. Rickles had us holding our sides with laughter. He kidded Telly about some of the things that happened during the making of *Kelly's Heroes* and so on, and then he introduced a new number in his act where he sang and danced "I'm a Good Guy" while flitting across the stage *a la* Gene Kelly. Watching Don Rickles try to dance like Kelly was *hilarious*, and we were practically rolling in the aisles.

The four of us came back to the MGM Grand at the side entrance and got out of the limo feeling pretty good. Marie decided to do an impression of Don's "I'm a Good Guy" and she danced down the highly polished marble walk to the door. We all laughed until suddenly she took a Brodie! We took her to the hospital (we were laughing all the way!) with a badly sprained ankle. For the rest of the weekend, I had to push her around in a wheelchair. But she was there at ringside the next night to watch a host of great stars—Bob Hope, Danny Thomas, Lucille Ball and all the rest—roast Telly.

At the Dunes in Vegas with Telly and his youngest brother Teddy.

When Paul Anka finally got his wish and did a *Kojak*, he hosted a cast party after the show was finished. I think he was paid $2500 and he spent the whole thing on the party! Telly and I once flew on Paul's jet to Washington, D.C. to do an AIDS benefit with Elizabeth Taylor hosting. At the hotel in Washington, I asked Telly what he was going to do when he got on stage the next day. He said, "I don't know. Can you write something?" I went to my room and I stayed up until four in the morning writing dialogue for a whole routine for Telly and Bob Hope, five or ten minutes of material. I was laughing to myself and thinking it was terrific. The next morning I showed it to Telly, and he liked it too. When the limo picked us up to take us to the theater, there was Bob Hope. We got in and before either of us could say a word, Hope said, "Telly, I'll bring you on stage and you say such-and-such, and then *I'll* say such-and-such . . . ," etc., etc. In two minutes, Hope gave Telly the whole routine, probably one he had done a million times before. Telly didn't even dare bring out what I had written, and I never opened my mouth. The old pro had it all done, and it was well-tested and foolproof. Elizabeth introduced Telly and Bob to the audience and their fame made them an instant hit.

We flew on to New York with Paul Anka after the show. Paul wasn't going back to the Coast, so Telly asked Paul if he could stop in Minnesota on the flight back with the jet. Paul said, "Whatever you want." (By that time, Telly had a new girlfriend, a beautiful 19-year-old named Julie Hovland in Duluth.) Paul Anka's jet took us to Duluth and we visited with Julie and her mother Gloria. We came back home and a few days later Telly got a bill for the side trip to Duluth from Paul Anka's pilot for $800!

Telly and Julie Hovland.

Telly was set to direct the next *Kojak*. The lead guest star would be playing a police chief from another precinct, and there were some other good parts in it. Since a lot of the Vegas headliners were always kissing up to Telly hoping to get a guest shot on *Kojak*, I said to him, "Why don't we cast the show with all big names? For example, let's get Johnny Carson to do the police chief. And Sammy Davis would be great for the stool pigeon in the poolroom." Telly liked the idea, so we got in touch with Johnny and sent him a script. He called back and said that he was flattered, but he didn't think he could do it. As hard as we tried, we couldn't talk him into it. We finally got Danny Thomas to play the part.

One night when we went to Caesar's Palace, Sammy Davis, Jr., was appearing in the big room. I said to Telly, "Let's call Sammy about doing the stoolie." He said, "*You* handle it." I called, got a-hold of Sammy's man and told him I wanted to talk to Sammy about doing a *Kojak*. In ten minutes he called back and said, "Sammy says come backstage an hour before the show tonight." I went back with the script, and Sammy's man ushered me into the big star dressing room, the same one that Sinatra used. Sammy greeted me in a long satin robe—to his ankles!—and we sat at the bar in the dressing room and talked. I told him that Telly would be directing and that, although the stoolie had only two scenes, they were good ones and they were both with Telly. I promised him that we would shoot the scenes to suit his schedule and so forth. He said, "If Telly wants me to do the part, he's got me."

"Naturally, we couldn't afford your salary," I added. The top of the show, the most they would pay for a guest star, was only 2500.

Sammy said, "Whatever. No problem." I left him the script and we shook hands and left.

When Telly and I got back to Universal on Monday, we got together with *Kojak* producer Jim McAdams and told him we had lined up Sammy Davis to play the stoolie. Right away Jim said, "Oh, no!"

I said, "Why? What's wrong?"

He said, "We cut that character out of the script!"

I told Telly, "You better call Sammy." He said, "*You* call him." I said, "I think he deserves a call from *you*, Telly." Poor Sammy. He never heard from either one of us.

In Yugoslavia on *Kelly's Heroes*, Telly told me someday he would record an album and do a nightclub act. I laughed at his audacity. Now it was time for him to prove me wrong. Telly's agent, Jack Gilardi, told Telly that the Sahara Hotel wanted him to do two weeks at their hotel in Tahoe and two weeks at their hotel in Vegas.

And they were offering to pay big money, too, I think 40 grand a week. When Telly accepted, Gilardi went into action: He hired a musical director and a dance director and before you knew it we were in a rehearsal hall preparing for the Tahoe opening. Soon Telly was dancing and singing *a la* Dean Martin or Frank Sinatra—and doing a pretty good job of it! One number would involve George: Telly planned to bring George out on stage and they would do a Greek dance surrounded by a troupe of Greek dancers *a la* Zorba the Greek. As George rehearsed, I saw that, despite his weight, he was very graceful.

Just a week before the opening, Gilardi told George that he would be getting $5000 a week and that he (George) and his family would be staying at the hotel. But George knew that Telly and Sally were staying at a big five-, six-bedroom house on the lake—a house provided by the hotel. So George balked. He wanted more money, and he also wanted to be provided with a house for himself, his wife Robin and their kids while they were there. As I mentioned earlier, George's ego was bigger than Telly's. I tried to talk to George—I explained that he was being paid out of Telly's money, not by the hotel, and told him to be reasonable. I even said, "Telly's the star, not *you!*" But he wouldn't listen and, sad to say, Telly eventually had to dismiss him.

Telly's older brother Constantine, who was in Athens at the time, had just retired from the State Department. Only a week before the Tahoe opening, Telly flew Constantine over and he stepped into George's spot. Constantine had a great singing voice—a solid, professional voice. As a youngster, he competed on *The Major Bowes Amateur Hour* and went right down to the wire before losing to Steve Lawrence in the finals.

Telly and son Nicholas.

Jack Gilardi, Marie and I went up to Tahoe and stayed at the big house on the lake with Telly and Sally. The opening went well. After the two weeks, Telly opened at the Sahara in Las Vegas. One night, Frank Sinatra and comedian Pat Henry came to the show and sat at a table down front center. It was customary for the entertainer to introduce any celebrities in the audience, so, of course, Telly introduced Frank. In my life, I've never heard a performer give *any* celebrity an introduction like the one Telly gave Frank that night. It was absolutely brilliant. I wish I had a recording of it.

After the show, Telly, Vince Conti and I walked across the street to the Stardust with Frank Sinatra and Pat Henry. We had some drinks in the lounge and suddenly Frank told Pat, "Get up and *do* something!" Pat got up on stage and did 20 minutes of his act. When Frank spoke, everyone jumped!

After five years of **Kojak**, Telly was very tired, but Universal wanted him to do another series right away. Telly wasn't interested, but Jim McAdams went ahead regardless and put together a pilot called **Hellinger's Law** with Telly as a criminal lawyer. We went to Houston to shoot it; I played a part and was Telly's dialogue director. The director, Leo Penn, gave his son Sean Penn a small part as a pot smoker. I worked briefly with the kid, and he was quite impressive.

One of the first movies Telly did after the end of **Kojak** was **Beyond the Poseiden Adventure**, the 1979 sequel to the smash-hit Irwin Allen disaster film **The Poseidon Adventure**. I was also in that, playing a fairly nice part, with Irwin Allen now directing; much of it was shot on Catalina Island, off of L.A. We had fun with Sally Field, Peter Boyle, Jack Warden, Shirley Jones, Mark Harmon, Slim Pickens and especially Michael Caine, one of the best storytellers I've ever met. Jack Warden wasn't far behind.

That same year, we went to Greece to do **Escape to Athena**, an all-star film about WWII P.O.W.s preparing to break out—and simultaneously planning a big art heist! Ten weeks on the island of Rhodes was the ultimate. **Escape to Athena** had a great cast: Roger Moore, Claudia Cardinale, David Niven, Elliott Gould, Stefanie Powers and, of course, me and Telly. In addition to playing a Greek partisan, I also doubled as Claudia's dialogue director because George Cosmatos, the director, wanted me to help her with her English. She really didn't need much help—her English was better than George's!

In 1978, when we did *Escape to Athena*, Telly was at the height of his popularity because of *Kojak*. And, of course, the Greeks also loved him simply because he *was* Greek. Cast and crew all stayed at the same hotel, *not* the best one on the island; the best was the Rhodos Palace. When I learned that the Rhodos Palace was practically empty, I went to its general manager and I asked him if he'd like to have Mr. Savalas stay at his hotel. He said, "But of *course*."

"What could you do for us?" I asked.

The answer came quickly: "You name it." He was so thrilled!

I said, "The best suite for Mr. Savalas . . . a suite for me . . . and three extra rooms for Mr. Savalas' brother, his two daughters, and one extra room. Plus all of our meals. All free."

Without hesitation the manager said, "All free . . . you *got* it." That's part of the reason Telly liked to have me around: I could always come up with stuff like that!

A short time after we moved into the Palace Hotel, it was sold out. All the tourists from Germany and elsewhere wanted to be in the same hotel as Kojak. Now we could use all our per diem and hotel money for gambling, which we did at the big state-run casino. Marie and my youngest daughter Gina came over after a few weeks and stayed until the end of the shoot. It was Heaven. The days we didn't work, we played golf. Every night after dinner, we were in the casino playing blackjack. Marie and Gina were really lucky in the casino. I think the Greek dealers liked Gina—she was just 21 and gorgeous. From the money they won in the

In Rhodes with Telly.

casino, Marie bought a beautiful mink coat tailor-made for her, and Gina was loaded down with gifts.

There was one golf course on the island, state-owned—and, believe it or not, the state offered to give it to Telly! He turned it down on the advice of some rich Greek that we met. There were too many strings attached. I was the one who introduced him to that Greek, and that fellow eventually agreed to buy Telly a three-, four-hundred-thousand-dollar condo in London if he (Telly) would do some benefits on the island of Cypress for him. He was such a con man, that Telly.

In the meantime, Telly and I piled up the markers. On the last day, we asked the casino manager what we owed. I owed a little over $6,000 and Telly owed around $12,000. We couldn't leave the country until these markers were paid—they held our passports. That day, we played golf; after the last round, we were supposed to go to the casino and pay up. Telly and I had played golf for the whole ten weeks, and each day I kept track of how much he owed me or I owed him. By the last day, Telly owed me $800. He offered to pay me but I said, "Look, use the money to get our markers down at the casino tonight."

We went to the casino and Telly took a whole blackjack table. He put a $100 chip on each of the seven spots on the table—he was playing $700 in one hand—and won them all when the dealer busted. He doubled-up and won again. And so on and so on. Inside of 20 minutes, he said, "Take my marker down." He had enough money to pay off his $12,000 marker, with some left over! I said, "Telly, what about *my* marker?"

He said, "*You* do it yourself."

I said, "But you're a better player, Telly. Keep going, keep going!"

"No, no, no," Telly said. "I want you to do it your*self*." So I took over. I was a little nervous, but he insisted. Our luck held up, and before you knew it, I was able to take my marker down. We left Rhodes with a lot of wonderful memories. As for the movie we'd gone there to make—*Escape to Athena* opened and closed in one week!

In addition to all of the movies, I worked with Telly on his commercials. He was national spokesman for the Ford Motor Company and Bacardi Rum. We even went to Japan to do some

With San Diego Chargers owner Alex Spanos, Barbara and George Bush, and Telly.

coffee commercials. As you can see, Telly and I did a lot of traveling! Many of our trips were for celebrity golf tournaments. We were even invited to a golf tournament in South Africa. What a great trip that was. Marie came along, and so did Telly's girlfriend, Julie. (They later married and had two beautiful children.) We spent time in Johannesburg, Capetown, Bophuthatswana, and again finished up the trip in Telly's London flat. We also went to several tournaments in Sun Valley, Idaho. They were like all-expenses-paid vacations. The perks of being an actor!

I was off to Yugoslavia again in 1987 for the TV movie *The Dirty Dozen: The Deadly Mission*, again with Telly. It was the only time I ever had a serious argument on the set with another actor, Bo Svenson. On location one *very* cold night I was in the back of an Army truck with 50 women and children who were extras in the movie, waiting for Svenson to arrive so that we could do the scene. For 30 minutes the women and those poor kids shivered in that below-freezing truck. After a while, I complained to the director, and when Svenson finally arrived I chewed him out in front of the whole company, calling him a prima donna. "I was in makeup!" he alibied. I screamed, "This is *a war movie*! Who the hell is going to see your makeup?" I didn't care that he was six-four; I came close to punching him out. Finally the producer calmed me down.

Around 1990, Telly had a triple bypass. He was a dexiocardiac, which means that his heart was on the right side. A day after the operation, the doctor said they would have to go back and do it over, which he did. When they wanted to do the operation a *third* time, Telly refused.

About this time, I'd begun spending a lot of time with my brother Charlie because of a tragedy he was living through. I still stopped by the Sheraton Hotel, *with* Charlie, to see Telly at least once a week. What a dear man he was. He loved his kids—he was a great father. As busy as he was, he always found time to go to Buckley School to see Penelope or Candace in school productions. I would go with him to watch track meets or tennis matches that Candace was in. He continued to do that sort of thing even after his health began to fail. And how he loved his mother, that great woman, Christina Savalas. When her husband Leo died, Telly brought her out to California and gave her a suite at the Sheraton and put a car and driver at her disposal. She was a fixture in the hotel restaurant, where she gave good advice to the young waitresses and everyone else who worked there. She was beloved by family and friends and the entire hotel staff. Telly used to buy her a hundred Scratch Off tickets at a time, and she enjoyed sitting and scraping them. Once she told me that when Telly was about four years old back in New York, each time a family problem arose she would seek his counsel and he would give it—and it was always right. As I mentioned, his third wife, Julie Hovland, gave Telly two beautiful children, Ariana and Christian. I'm sure someday we will hear from Christian. What a bright boy! At the age of six, he could sing the entire score from Andrew Lloyd Webber's **The Phantom of the Opera**. And his daughter Ariana, a teenage beauty, is now studying to be an actress.

In January 1994, I was living in Rome with Marie and my grandson Bryan. Knowing that Telly had now deteriorated quite a bit (he was in fact bedridden), one day I called him at the Sheraton and said, "Telly, I'm coming home to see you."

"No, no, no, I'm okay," he insisted.

I said, "Telly, I have an audience with Pope John tomorrow, and I'll ask him to say a mass for you."

Telly said, "You don't have to do that." There was a pause, and

Telly, Christian, Julie and Ariana.

then he said, "... Maybe you *better*." So I did. They said a mass for Telly at the Vatican.

A week later, his brother Gus called and told me that Telly had passed away. It was a heartbreaking thing for all of us. I've had many friends in my lifetime, but none to compare with Telly. What fun we had. Isn't that what it's all about?

29
CLOSING THE FILE ON JOHNNY ROSELLI

In earlier chapters, I've mentioned my first meeting with Johnny Roselli on *Breakthrough* and revealed that, years after our initial encounter, it was Johnny who helped get me the part on *The Untouchables*. Now let me tell you the end of Johnny Roselli.

In the mid-1970s, not long after the Marlon Brando movie *The Godfather* became a big hit, I got together with Dick Wesson and worked on a nightclub act. My whole life, I wanted to be a straight man doing a nightclub act; I wanted to be Dean Martin to Jerry Lewis. In the '40s, Dick had a nightclub act with his brother Gene (Gene was the straight man and Dick was the comic), and now Dick and I were planning to pair up. One of our comedy routines was a Godfather bit where the Godfather (Dick, with cotton in his mouth) finds out that his *consigliere* (me) has absconded with some of the Mafia's money. Here is the script, which I recently rediscovered amidst some old scripts and papers; it was part of the act which Dick and I rehearsed and played in different clubs around town:

GODFATHER

(Music: *Godfather* theme)

DICK: Mmmmmmm. (*sound a la* Godfather) Paulo—
            Paulo!

PAUL: Don Giovanni—you wanted to see me?

With Dick Wesson, with whom I put together a nightclub act.

DICK: Yes, Paulo—consilieri—yes. Paulo, you remember Salvatore Cuciliano?

PAUL: Sally Cucu—sure.

DICK: You know, I gave him the *bacha da morte.*

PAUL: The kiss of death? So that's what happened. I thought it was an accident when he went off that cliff in your Cadillac.

DICK: It was an accident. It was supposed to be *his* Cadillac.

PAUL: So you gave him the kiss of death.

DICK: Right on the mouth. He was as ugly as a Boston bulldog.

PAUL: A *facha de brute*. Big moustache—smoked those stinky little black cigars.

DICK: Had grease and tobacco juice all over his mouth.

PAUL: And you had to kiss him right on the lips.

DICK: Atsa dumb. Why not give the kiss of death on the nose, the cheek, the back of the head, the belly button—any place but on the lips.

PAUL: 'At's the custom, Don Giovanni—gotta be right on the mouth.

DICK: Yuck! I had to gargle for two weeks afterward.

PAUL: You know that Sally Cucu murdered maybe 30 guys.

DICK: At least. He was dangerous—a lunatic. We had to get rid of him. He was capable of slitting his own mother's throat.

PAUL: But you gave him a wonderful funeral—28 cars.

DICK: Well, why not? He was a nice guy. Paulo, how long you been consilieri to the family?

PAUL: 28 years, my don, I have the honor you call me concilieri.

DICK: All that time—something's been bothering me.

PAUL: What's that?

DICK: What means consilieri?

PAUL: It means I look after the legal business of the family.

DICK: Oh—'ats what you been doin'.

PAUL: Also, I make the financial investments for the family.

DICK: Which brings me to the business at hand. We found out you been blowin' a fortune of the family's money in Vegas—gamblin', drinkin' and chasin' broads.

PAUL: That's a lie. Ask my wife.

DICK: She's the one who ratted on you.

PAUL: Oh boy. I'm in trouble?

DICK: You're in trouble. 20 members of the family took a vote. 19 guys give you this. (*thumb down*)

PAUL: And the other guy?

DICK: He gave you this. (*Italian gesture*)

PAUL: Oh boy!

DICK: Now it's my duty to give you the kiss of death. The *bacha de morte.* Tomorrow at four o'clock you gonna be at the bottom of the ocean sleepin' next to a halibut.

PAUL: No, Don, please—I beg you. (*kneels*)

DICK: Stop that! Don't be a coward! Get up off your knees and pucker up!

PAUL: (*rises*) All right. I will be worthy of the family tradition.

DICK: That's better. Now pucker up—damn it! (*Paul closes his eyes*) Why are you closing your eyes?

PAUL: I always close my eyes when I kiss.

DICK: What the hell do you think we're doing here— playing spin the bottle? Now open your eyes and pucker up!

PAUL: One moment, Don. (*uses breath spray*)

DICK: Now what the hell are you doin'?

PAUL: I don't want you to say I got bad break like Sally Cucu.

DICK: You dumbbell. You ready now?

PAUL: All set.

(*Paul puckers—they kiss. Play this to the hilt after many delays, adlibs. They finally kiss.*)

PAUL: Jackpot! Oh boy! Arrividerci!

DICK: Well, at least that wasn't as bad as Sally Cucu. In fact, it wasn't bad at all. What are you doin' 'til four o'clock tomorrow?

(*Musical tag:* Tarantella)

Around this time, my friend Joe Breen phoned and said that Johnny Roselli, who at the time was living with his sister in Florida, was coming to the Sansom Clinic in Santa Barbara for his annual physical, and that he wanted to see us. So Joe, Dick Wesson and I drove up to Santa Barbara and we played golf with Johnny. At one point, Johnny drew our attention to the foursome behind us and said, "You see those guys? All the fuckin' FBI. Every place I go, they follow me."

We went out to dinner that night, and Johnny again told us he was being constantly harassed and hounded by Federal agents. I don't know who brought it up, it might have been Joe, but all of a sudden Dick and I were talking about our nightclub act, and Joe (who had seen it) looked at me and said, "Why don't you do that *Godfather* routine for Johnny?"

Part of the true-life Scarface Mob: Al Capone with Johnny Roselli, right.

I said, "Naaah, we can't do that for Johnny!," but Johnny insisted: "Come on, do it, do it!" So Dick and I did the whole Godfather routine, right to the end—"Tomorrow, at four o'clock, you gonna be at the bottom of the ocean, with the fish!" Johnny roared with laughter.

Several weeks later, in the bay off of Miami, Florida, an oil barrel floated to the surface. Some fisherman who had seen it pop out of the water towed it in . . . opened it up . . . and inside they found Johnny Roselli. Just like in our routine! He'd been dead long enough that his body had started to decompose, and the released gases caused the barrel to rise to the top. To this day, we don't know who killed him. There was a rumor that the CIA had once asked Johnny and another gangster, Sam Giancana, to kill Fidel Castro, and they refused—and that the government decided to bump off Johnny and Giancana before they talked. I have no idea who did it, only that Giancana was shot and killed in the basement of his Oak Park, Illinois, home in 1975 and that, the following year, the remains of Johnny Roselli were found in the waters of Dumfoundling Bay.

30
LIFE GOES ON

The phone rang.

It was very early on the morning of December 14, 1990. Marie and I had just returned from a cruise to Acapulco the night before. Who could be calling us at this hour?

It was a police officer. "Get over to your brother's house as soon as possible. His wife has been killed in an automobile accident." Sandy dead? I couldn't believe what I was hearing.

I rushed to Charlie's house in Hidden Hills, about eight miles from mine in Tarzana. I was met at the door by two officers. "Where's my brother?" I asked.

"He's out back in the garage," one answered.

My sister Paula, Charlie, Aunt Nancy, me, Marie and Sandy, Charlie's wife, tragically killed in a 1990 car crash.

I walked into the garage to find Charlie sitting at a workbench holding a handgun up to his temple. I took the gun away from him and he collapsed in my arms. "Why did you leave him alone?" I yelled at the two policemen. The cops and I subsequently gathered up all the guns in the house and locked them in the trunk of my car.

Charlie had met Sandy Bobrowitz during the filming of *Kojak* at Universal. Sandy was then in college; she and another college girl, her friend Kathy, sneaked off a studio tour tram and wandered onto the soundstage where *Kojak* was shooting. They were full of excitement about meeting the star of the series—and they also got to meet the show's stunt coordinator, Charles Picerni. It didn't end there. Sandy, a journalism major at Pierce College, seized the opportunity to arrange for an interview with Telly Savalas for her school paper. This meant she would be coming back on the lot, this time with a legitimate pass. It also meant she would see Charlie again. She was only 19, very pretty, very athletic. She didn't know at the time that Charlie was married and had two sons. He was also twice her age.

The inevitable happened: a divorce for Charlie and, eventually, his marriage to Sandy.

After their wedding, Charlie's career really took off. In 1988 he was the stunt coordinator on producer Joel Silver's action blockbuster *Die Hard*, and every other picture Joel did for the next several years. Sandy graduated from college and law school and became a lawyer for Twentieth Century Insurance Co. They bought a beautiful home in Hidden Hills, remodeled it, added a pool and stables for their horses and raised German short hair bird dogs. They did everything together, even going to Rome on location for *Hudson Hawk*, which Charlie stunt-coordinated. They rode their horses, played tennis, hunted, and went fishing on their boat. Charlie was making *biiiig* money with Joel Silver with hit after hit, and his life with Sandy was like a love story out of a novel. She was advancing up the ladder in her law career and Charlie was now directing second units and coordinating some of Warner Brothers' biggest hits.

Fifteen years went by—fifteen happy years—until that fateful night. Her company was having a Christmas party at the Bel-Air Country Club. She asked Charlie to come but he said, "No, you go alone. It's *your* office friends." When the dinner party was over, she

Charlie and I during the shooting of an episode of TV's *Seven Days.*

got in her Nissan 300ZX sports car and headed home. As she turned onto Sunset Boulevard, heading west toward the 405 Freeway, one of her co-workers, another lawyer, turned onto Sunset in his DeLorean. They were feeling good, and a little race ensued. Sandy was a good driver, and she took off and passed the DeLorean easily. She accelerated up the hill but then hit the turn a little too fast, and collided head-on with a van coming the opposite way. She and the two young girls in the van all died instantly.

Could Charlie ever recover from this devastating tragedy? My sisters, Eleanor and Paula, and I consoled him. His many friends from Stunts Unlimited were by his side constantly. So were his sons, Charles, Jr., and Steve, both budding stuntmen. His good friend Frank Orsatti stayed at his house for weeks. Charlie was never alone. He was scheduled to start as stunt coordinator on *Ricochet* with Denzel Washington and John Lithgow; I thought the best thing for him would be getting back to work. He couldn't think of it. He was a basket case. No way could he function.

We had a meeting with Joel Silver, who was most sympathetic. He needed Charlie. He originally wanted Charlie to *direct Ricochet*, but Charlie said he would wait for a better script. I told Charlie I would pick him up and drive him to work every day. I would go to all the production meetings with him, and I'd stay with him every step of the way until he recovered. Finally he agreed to give it a try.

At the production meetings, I would take notes on what had to be done, what stunts were needed, what doubles we required. Charlie was often there in body only . . . his mind was elsewhere. He was suffering every minute of the day. On occasion he would flare up and go berserk. It happened once when we were on the freeway: He was behind the wheel, and he began screaming and driving erratically. I yelled at him and forced him to pull over to the side of the road. Until the car stopped, I thought we were both going to die. By an amazing coincidence, my son C.P., just one of the hundreds of cars driving by, saw us and stopped. He got in our car and talked to Charlie and was able to quiet him down. From then on, I drove.

After attending four or five *Ricochet* production meetings with Charlie, the line producer Jim Herbert took me aside one day and said, "Paul, we want to put you on salary for the run of the picture." "No, no," I said. "I'm doing this for my brother, until he recovers." But Jim insisted that I accept a contract as Charlie's assistant stunt coordinator. So I was with Charlie every day, helping him—hiring stuntmen, working out the big fight scene on the L.A. Watts Towers between Denzel and John Lithgow and so on.

After about six weeks on *Ricochet* (and with two weeks to go), we began having production meetings with director Tony Scott on Joel Silver's next picture, *The Last Boy Scout*. We kept Charlie so busy, overlapping meetings on *Boy Scout* while finishing up with *Ricochet*! The *Boy Scout* cast included Bruce Willis, Damon Wayans and a beginner named Halle Berry, for whom Charlie designed a great death scene (she is sprayed by gunfire and dies on the hood of a car). After *Boy Scout*, we did *Lethal Weapon* with Mel Gibson and Danny Glover. Charlie was getting better but still suffering. I stayed with him for *True Romance* with Patricia Arquette, Christian Slater and James *The Sopranos* Gandolfini. Again Tony Scott directed, from a script by Quentin Tarantino. Here again Charlie created a memorable fight scene, this time between Arquette and Gandolfini. By the time we did *Father Hood*, with Patrick Swayze, he was almost fully recovered. I also worked with him a short time on a Sylvester Stallone movie set in the future, *Demolition Man*. By this time, three years had passed and he had met a wonderful girl named Nancy Young who helped bring him all the way back. They were married a few years later.

During the filming of these pictures, I earned my keep by doing some stunt driving and other minor stunts. To this day I think Tony Scott, the director, thinks I'm an old stuntman! He probably never saw *The Untouchables* or *House of Wax.*

Charlie with wife Nancy.

Jumping back for just a moment to the beginning of this story: One night several days after Sandy's funeral, all the stunt guys that Charlie had hired through the years were at Charlie's house, and then we all went to a Calabasas restaurant called the Sagebrush Cantina. There on a patio, seated at a long table, were maybe ten stuntmen, including Charlie of course, and their wives. I was there with Marie and also my nephew Steve, who was married to a wonderful girl named Katina, a real New York kind of gal. As Virginia, a tall, pretty waitress, was taking our orders, I got a crazy idea. I do a gag where I turn my back to an audience and have someone pretend to slap me in the face, and I can make it look very real by the way I jerk my head back. It's very effective. I took Virginia aside and said, "Listen, the guys at that table are stuntmen. They do fight scenes in movies and they think they're hot stuff. I'm gonna rehearse a little fight scene with *you*, and here's what we'll do . . . " I showed her how to throw the slap, how to hit me, and then I said, "When you bring me my beer, I'll stand up and I'll say, 'I didn't order this kind of beer,' and we'll get into an argument and I'll raise my voice, and when I put up my hand, you pretend to slap me and I'll go down."

Virginia said, "I better talk to the manager about this," and soon I was talking to him, a big young guy . . . who happened to want to be a stuntman! After I told him what I wanted to do, he said, "Yeah, that's okay. I'll stand by and watch it."

I sat back down and a few minutes later she came over with the beer and we went into our routine: "I didn't order this beer!," "That *is* what you ordered!" and so on, both of us gradually raising our voices. I stood up, she slapped me, I went down to my knees beside the table and she turned and headed back into the restaurant. Well, my little niece Katina jumped out of her chair and bellowed, "You don't hit my uncle like that, you *bitch*!"—and she ran and leapt on Virginia's back and knocked her to the floor! I hurried over and grabbed Katina and broke it up. The whole time, Charlie was half-laughing, "I *told* you not to do that, *you dumb fuck*!"

On January 29, 2005, at the age of 82, I left for Miami, Florida, to start work on another picture with Charlie, a comedy called *Retirement* with Peter Falk, Rip Torn, George Segal and Ossie Davis. It was the first production of Charlie's newly formed company, Corner Stone Pictures.

Mike Pietrzak, a brilliant young man of 25, Jon Warner, a talented 29-year-old writer, and Charlie were the three partners who put together the company. During the development of the *Retirement* screenplay, I helped them by writing several scenes. One was a scene in which I would act opposite the picture's leading lady, Nancy Young—Charlie's lovely and very capable actress-wife.

Charlie wanted me to be with him for the entire shoot, so he gave me the title of "Creative Supervisor." I think I am the first and only

"Creative Supervisor" in the history of Hollywood! The real reason he wanted me along is so that he would have someone to yell at! For every ten suggestions I made, he might use one. The others got a "No, you dumb fuck!" ("You dumb fuck!" is what Telly Savalas used to call me when we'd argue, and Charlie picked that up from him!) But I did manage to get a few "Thank you, Pauls" along the way.

With one of my favorite fans and most wonderful friends, John Gloske, on the Seven Days set.

Despite the many problems we were confronted with, Charlie did a magnificent job. He is *so* creative. The scenes in the script just came to life when he staged them.

Charlie handled the actors with great patience. He gave them free rein, and it helped to bring out the best in them. There *was* some friction between Peter and Rip in the early going, but they produced great comedy together. It seems that through the history of Hollywood, most great comedy teams have had friction, from Abbott & Costello to Martin & Lewis. Peter and Rip were funny, but both of them were constantly trying to get the *last* laugh, so to speak. Despite their hassling, Peter came to me several times and said things like, "Rip was really funny in that scene with the girl at the strip joint . . . " And Rip would say, "Peter's a pain in the ass. But he's good!" I was reminded of the old Hollywood story about John Wayne coming to his director John Ford and saying, "That Ward Bond is a shit." And Ford responding, "Yeah . . . but he's *our* shit!"

Although Peter and Rip hardly talked off-camera, I think they respected each other's ability. They are two "eccentric," talented actors.

George Segal's character was patterned after my uncle, Dominick (Ace) Leone. George was easy to work with, and did an excellent job. As for Ossie Davis, I had already worked with him in *The Scalphunters*, the Burt Lancaster Western we shot in Durango, Mexico, in 1967. It was I who had suggested Ossie for the part of Marvin Jeffries in *Retirement*, and Charlie went along with his casting immediately. In December of '04, a few weeks before the start of shooting, Charlie and I watched on TV as Ossie and his lovely wife Ruby Dee were honored at the Kennedy Center with Life Achievement Awards.

Possibly the last photo of Ossie Davis. He died the night it was taken.

It was good to see Ossie again in Miami, and we reminisced about our days in Durango with Burt, Telly Savalas and Shelley Winters. On the third day of filming in South Beach in Miami, we shot a scene in which Peter Falk and Ossie stepped off a party bus as hundreds of bikini-clad beauties skated by. Peter's line was, "What *is* this place?," and Ossie responded, "It must be Heaven!" This was his last line on film.

Early the next morning, Charlie and I were in a chauffeured car on our way to work with my grandson Bryan, who was working as a stand-in in the picture. Charlie's cell phone rang. He answered; I heard him say something softly; and then he hung up. Then he turned to me and said, "Ossie is dead."

At the Park Shore Hotel on Miami Beach, where we were staying, Ossie had fallen in his room early that morning. He was able to phone his wife Ruby in New York, and she in turn called the hotel desk to tell them what had happened. The desk clerk and Ossie's grandson, Muhammad Jihad, opened Ossie's door and found him unconscious on the floor. By the time the medics arrived, the dear man was dead.

Ossie's two daughters, Nora and LaVerne, arrived the next day and, in the garden at the hotel, we held a memorial service with our entire company on hand. One of his daughters told me that she remembered meeting me in Durango during *The Scalphunters* when she was only ten years old. Then they left to escort his body to New York City for the funeral. Ossie was 87. What a fine man he was. What a great life he had. The night of the day he died, before curtains rose at 8:00, Broadway theaters dimmed their lights in his honor.

During the credits at the end of *Retirement*, Charlie planned to dedicate the film to Ossie and to show his final scene on film and his line, "It must be Heaven!"

The problem now confronting Charlie was the need to replace Ossie. Such names as Danny Glover, Harry Belafonte and Sidney Poitier were mentioned, but Charlie decided to go with Billy Cobbs as Ossie's replacement. (During the early prep work on *Retirement*, Billy had auditioned for the part of Marvin, but we had gone with Ossie instead.) Billy did a fine job, fitting right in with the other old guys.

We shot two weeks in Miami, two weeks in New Orleans and finished up with three fun-filled weeks in Las Vegas. What made it all the more enjoyable for me was the number of Picernis in the company. Besides me and Charlie, my son P.V. was the property master, and Charlie's two sons, Steven and Chuck, handled most of the stunt driving. (Steven also did the second unit directing.) My grandson Bryan Picerni worked for the full seven weeks as the number one stand-in for the stars. My sister Paula made a brief appearance dancing with George Segal in New Orleans, and Steven's wife Katina did some stunt driving in the desert outside of Las Vegas. All in all, we fought, we laughed and we loved.

We had a couple of setbacks just as we were about to leave Miami for New Orleans, where we were planning to shoot several sequences with Coolio, the rap star. Charlie had made advance arrangements to shoot at an actual Louisiana mansion and on an outdoor concert stage. At practically the last moment, we discovered that the mansion and the concert stage were no longer available to us. Charlie had to quickly improvise and find a mansion in Miami that looked like Louisiana, and also a concert stage. Miraculously, he did find the sets, and with the help of his great cinematographer Tom Priestley he made them work. In fact, I think he even improved on what we would have had in New Orleans.

My wife Marie seemed to enjoy the fact that Bryan and I would be away for so long: While we were gone, she remodeled Bryan's bathroom, she remodeled *our* bathroom, and she filled one wall of our den with "Paul Picerni memorabilia"! Between projects, she came to visit us three times on location. When she visited the first time, I was a little jealous because our grandson Bryan got the biggest hug!

Besides the four top stars in this film, there are others who stand out, including Chris Diamantopoulos, who played the role of Nancy's French suitor. Also memorable in this film are two talented guys who may steal the picture, Taylor Negron and Mario Cantone, who play two hilarious gay guys who, after a series of madcap robberies, go off a cliff in a stolen car *a la* Thelma & Louise. They survive. Look for them for sure in the sequel!

Making a good movie requires a lot of talented behind-the-scenes people. Besides the obvious ones (director, cinematographer, sound, etc.), "the guys in the trenches"—the grips, the electricians, the drivers, the prop men, the caterers, etc.—are also integral. When visitors come on a set and see 100 people who look like they're just standing around, they comment, "What a *waste!*" They don't understand. Each one of those crew people has a job, and they're right there when it's their turn to come up to bat. During Charlie's long association with Joel Silver, he came to know many talented

Marie and I on one of the many cruises we've taken—this one to Alaska.

people like "Tookie," our script girl; Tom Cooney, our sound man; grips, electricians and other crew members. They all liked Charlie, and enjoyed working with him. His many years of experience, from stand-in to director, have made him many friends, and people like him and respect his talent. I was *so proud* of him. His ego is big . . . but egos *must* be big to succeed. Let's not call it "ego," but . . . self-confidence. He started as my stand-in on *The Untouchables* in 1961 and today, after directing about 70 television episodes, he's a full-blown feature film director.

Now my grandson Bryan has started out by working as a stand-in on *Retirement*. And so . . . life goes on!

INDEX

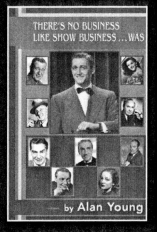
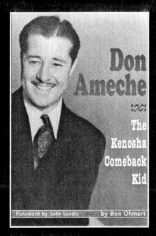